Spring Roo 1.1 Cookbook

Over 60 recipes to help you speed up the development of your Java web applications using the Spring Roo development tool

Ashish Sarin

PUBLISHING

BIRMINGHAM - MUMBAI

Spring Roo 1.1 Cookbook

First published: September 2011

Production Reference: 1190911

Published by Packt Publishing Ltd.
Livery Place
35 Livery Street
Birmingham B3 2PB, UK

ISBN 978-1-84951-458-3

www.packtpub.com

Cover Image by Sergey Suchok (sevlad.main@gmail.com)

Credits

Author
Ashish Sarin

Reviewers
Tobias Lütticke

John Joseph Ryan III

Acquisition Editor
Usha Iyer

Development Editors
Neha Mallik

Reshma Sundaresan

Technical Editors
Vanjeet D'souza

Mehreen Shaikh

Project Coordinator
Joel Goveya

Proofreaders
Aaron Nash

Lisa Brady

Linda Morris

Indexer
Hemangini Bari

Production Coordinators
Nilesh R. Mohite

Alwin Roy

Cover Work
Nilesh R. Mohite

About the Author

Ashish Sarin has more than 11 years of experience architecting and developing applications using Java EE technologies. He is a Sun Certified Enterprise Architect for Java EE Platform. He has authored many articles on portlets and rich Internet applications using Liferay, DWR, JSF, and Spring Portlet MVC.

Ashish is also the author of *Portlets in Action* (http://manning.com/sarin/) by *Manning Publications*.

Writing Spring Roo 1.1 Cookbook has been a very satisfying experience because of the multitude of technologies it covers.

I would like to thank Tobias Lütticke for providing excellent feedback during the review of the book. It helped a great deal with improving the technical content and presentation of the book.

This book owes a great deal to John J. Ryan III for doing an outstanding job of ensuring that each and every recipe is well tested and well presented to readers. As the book's content moved from Spring Roo 1.1.1 to 1.1.3, John made sure that we don't miss out on any relevant recipes and technical details. It has given me a lot of confidence that recipes covered in this book will work as described.

Special thanks to Vanjeet D'souza and Mehreen Shaikh for doing an excellent job of ensuring that the book meets Packt's standards.

Thanks to Neha Mallik for doing an outstanding job at improving the structure and presentation of the book. Thanks to Usha Iyer as well for giving me the opportunity to write for Packt.

About the Reviewers

Tobias Lütticke has more than 11 years of experience in the software field. As a consultant and software architect, he has shaped various mission-critical applications for German blue chip companies and his current employer. His background also includes project management and teaching of software development best practices. Early in his career Tobias developed a passion for Open Source and agile development methodologies that still drives his work. He is fortunate to have been involved in the successful delivery of two major Roo-based projects; one of them is a public-facing geographic information system almost entirely built with Open Source components.

Tobias is a certified Scrum Master, Project Management Professional (PMP), and he holds a Computer Science degree from Karlsruhe Institute of Technology, Excellence University, Germany.

Currently, he works as a Senior Application Solution Architect for a New Zealand government entity, where he architects enterprise applications and leads development teams to see his solutions through to fruition.

Tobias enjoys writing and shares his experience in the software development space through articles he publishes in various magazines as well as through his book on OpenSSH.

John J. Ryan III is the founder and Director of Systems Engineering for Princigration ™ LLC. He specializes in portal web development and system integration of Java based technologies. He has extensive experience in data-centric systems across a wide array of technology stacks and implementation languages. John has a BS in Computer Science and Engineering from the University of Texas at Arlington and an MS in Systems Engineering from Southern Methodist University.

John says, "Don't measure a person's skill by what they can recite. Measure their ability to pick up a new skill or define a new problem. Life and business is about solving new problems, not reciting technical verse."

In addition to the technical review of this publication, John has participated in several Spring and Portal based book reviews and considers himself an expert in only one area, quickly becoming effective in any domain.

I would like to thank my wife, Nancie for her support. I would also like to thank my dad, Joe for teaching me the value of hard work and my mom, Ann for showing me the power of a positive attitude. Finally, I would like to thank Yahshua for all the goodness in my life and on the earth.

www.PacktPub.com

Support files, eBooks, discount offers and more

You might want to visit www.PacktPub.com for support files and downloads related to your book.

Did you know that Packt offers eBook versions of every book published, with PDF and ePub files available? You can upgrade to the eBook version at www.PacktPub.com and as a print book customer, you are entitled to a discount on the eBook copy. Get in touch with us at service@packtpub.com for more details.

At www.PacktPub.com, you can also read a collection of free technical articles, sign up for a range of free newsletters and receive exclusive discounts and offers on Packt books and eBooks.

http://PacktLib.PacktPub.com

Do you need instant solutions to your IT questions? PacktLib is Packt's online digital book library. Here, you can access, read and search across Packt's entire library of books.

Why Subscribe?

- ▸ Fully searchable across every book published by Packt
- ▸ Copy and paste, print and bookmark content
- ▸ On demand and accessible via web browser

Free Access for Packt account holders

If you have an account with Packt at www.PacktPub.com, you can use this to access PacktLib today and view nine entirely free books. Simply use your login credentials for immediate access.

Table of Contents

Preface

Spring Roo is an easy-to-use productivity tool for rapidly developing Java enterprise applications using well-recognized frameworks such as Spring, Hibernate, AspectJ, Spring Web Flow, Spring Security, GWT, and so on. Spring Roo takes care of creating Maven-enabled projects, enterprise application architecture based on your choice of technologies, unit and / or integration tests based on your choice of testing framework, and so on. The bottom line is that if you're using Spring, then you should consider using Spring Roo for increased productivity.

Spring Roo 1.1 Cookbook brings together a collection of recipes that demonstrate how the Spring Roo developer tool simplifies rapidly developing enterprise applications using standard technologies and / or frameworks such as JPA, GWT, Spring, Flex, Spring Web Flow, Spring Security, and so on. It introduces readers to developing enterprise applications for the real world using Spring Roo tool. The book starts off with basic recipes to make readers comfortable with using Spring Roo tool. As the book progresses, readers are introduced to more sophisticated features supported by Spring Roo in the context of a Flight Booking application. In a step-by-step by fashion, each recipe shows how a particular activity is performed, what Spring Roo does when a command is executed, and why it is important in the context of the application being developed.

Initially, you make a quick start using Spring Roo through some simple recipes. Then you learn how Spring Roo simplifies creating the persistence layer of an enterprise application using JPA. You are introduced to the various Roo commands to create JPA entities, create relationships between JPA entities, create integration tests using Spring TestContext framework, and so on. Following this, the book shows you how Spring Roo simplifies creating the web layer of an enterprise application using Spring Web MVC, Spring Web Flow, and how to create Selenium tests for controller objects.

Subsequently, we focus on using Spring-BlazeDS, GWT, JSON, and so on. Spring Roo commands that are used to incorporate e-mail and / or messaging features into an enterprise application are demonstrated next. Finally, we wrap it up with some miscellaneous recipes that show how to extend Spring Roo via add-ons, incorporate security, create cloud-ready applications, remove Spring Roo from your enterprise application, and so on.

A fast-paced guide that helps you effectively use Spring Roo for developing enterprise applications.

What this book covers

Chapter 1, Getting Started with Spring Roo, covers simple recipes to introduce readers to the Spring Roo tool. You will learn how to use some of the basic features of Spring Roo that makes it an easy-to-use productivity tool.

Chapter 2, Persisting Objects Using JPA, covers Spring Roo commands for setting up a JPA provider, creating JPA entities, and creating unit and integration tests.

Chapter 3, Advanced JPA Support in Spring Roo, focuses on Spring Roo commands for adding dynamic finder methods to JPA entities, creating relationship between entities, and creating JPA entities using database reverse engineering support in Spring Roo.

Chapter 4, Web Application Development with Spring Web MVC, covers Spring Web MVC support in Spring Roo. The recipes in this chapter show how to scaffold a Spring Web MVC application from JPA entities, internationalize the web application, and add different themes to it.

Chapter 5, Web Application Development with GWT, Flex, and Spring Web Flow, shows how Spring Roo can be used to scaffold GWT and Flex applications from JPA entities. This chapter also shows how Spring Roo let's you quickly get started with developing applications using Spring Web Flow.

Chapter 6, Emailing, Messaging, Spring Security, Solr, and GAE, covers a multitude of topics related to adding emailing support, messaging using JavaMail API, incorporating application security using Spring Security, adding search capability using Solr search server, and developing applications for Google App Engine (GAE).

Chapter 7, Developing Add-ons and Removing Roo from Projects, wraps up the book with some advanced topics such as how to create Spring Roo add-ons, install an add-on, remove Roo from your project using push-in refactoring, adding Roo support to an existing project using pull-up refactoring, and upgrading to a newer version of Spring Roo.

What you need for this book

- ▸ Spring Roo 1.1.3 or 1.1.4 or 1.1.5
- ▸ Eclipse Helios IDE (or later) or STS
- ▸ Maven 3.x
- ▸ Java SE 6 or later
- ▸ MySQL database
- ▸ Google Plugin for Eclipse IDE

- ► Solr server
- ► GnuPG
- ► H2 database

Who this book is for

Spring Roo 1.1 Cookbook is for developers new to the Spring Roo tool but with experience in developing applications using Spring framework, AspectJ, JPA, GWT, and technologies/ frameworks supported by Spring Roo. If you are new to the Spring framework, then it is recommended to refer to a text covering Spring, before reading this Cookbook.

Conventions

In this book, you will find a number of styles of text that distinguish between different kinds of information. Here are some examples of these styles, and an explanation of their meaning:

Code words in text are shown as follows:

The `perform eclipse` and `perform command` commands are processed by Maven add-on of Spring Roo.

A block of code is set as follows:

```
<filter>
    <filter-name>HttpMethodFilter</filter-name>
    <filter-class>org.springframework.web.filter.
        HiddenHttpMethodFilter
    </filter-class>
</filter>
```

When we wish to draw your attention to a particular part of a code block, the relevant lines or items are set in bold shown as follows:

```
<mvc:annotation-driven
    conversion-service ="myConversionService" />

<bean id="myConversionService" class= "..format.
FactoryConversionServiceFactoryBean">
    <property name="converters">
        <list>
            <bean class="com.flight.myCustomConverter"/>
        </list>
    </property>
</bean>
```

Any command-line input or output is written as follows:

```
roo> logging setup --level DEBUG --package ROOT
Updated SRC_MAIN_RESOURCES\log4j.properties
```

New terms and **important words** are shown in bold. Words that you see on the screen, in menus, or dialog boxes for example, appear in the text like this: "Create a new Flight Description by selecting the **Create new Flight Description** option from the menu and entering values for **Origin**, **Destination**, and **Price fields**".

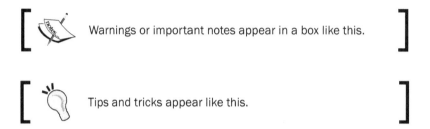

Warnings or important notes appear in a box like this.

Tips and tricks appear like this.

Reader feedback

Feedback from our readers is always welcome. Let us know what you think about this book— what you liked or may have disliked. Reader feedback is important for us to develop titles that you really get the most out of.

To send us general feedback, simply send an e-mail to feedback@packtpub.com, and mention the book title via the subject of your message.

If there is a book that you need and would like to see us publish, please send us a note in the **SUGGEST A TITLE** form on www.packtpub.com or e-mail to suggest@packtpub.com.

If there is a topic that you have expertise in and you are interested in either writing or contributing to a book, see our author guide on www.packtpub.com/authors.

Customer support

Now that you are the proud owner of a Packt book, we have a number of things to help you to get the most from your purchase.

Downloading the example code

You can download the example code files for all Packt books you have purchased from your account at http://www.PacktPub.com. If you purchased this book elsewhere, you can visit http://www.PacktPub.com/support and register to have the files e-mailed directly to you.

Errata

Although we have taken every care to ensure the accuracy of our content, mistakes do happen. If you find a mistake in one of our books—maybe a mistake in the text or the code—we would be grateful if you would report this to us. By doing so, you can save other readers from frustration and help us improve subsequent versions of this book. If you find any errata, please report them by visiting http://www.packtpub.com/support, selecting your book, clicking on the **errata submission form** link, and entering the details of your errata. Once your errata are verified, your submission will be accepted and the errata will be uploaded on our website, or added to any list of existing errata, under the Errata section of that title. Any existing errata can be viewed by selecting your title from http://www.packtpub.com/support.

Piracy

Piracy of copyright material on the Internet is an ongoing problem across all media. At Packt, we take the protection of our copyright and licenses very seriously. If you come across any illegal copies of our works, in any form, on the Internet, please provide us with the location address or website name immediately so that we can pursue a remedy.

Please contact us at copyright@packtpub.com with a link to the suspected pirated material.

We appreciate your help in protecting our authors, and our ability to bring you valuable content.

Questions

You can contact us at questions@packtpub.com if you are having a problem with any aspect of the book, and we will do our best to address it.

1
Getting Started with Spring Roo

In this chapter, we will cover the following topics:

- ▶ Setting up Roo
- ▶ Getting help and hints from Roo
- ▶ Creating a Roo project
- ▶ Importing a Roo project into Eclipse or IntelliJ IDEA IDE
- ▶ Configuring logging
- ▶ Viewing properties defined in a properties file
- ▶ Managing properties defined in a properties file
- ▶ Creating a Java class
- ▶ Adding attributes to a Java class
- ▶ Creating a Java interface
- ▶ Referring to a type from the Roo shell
- ▶ Creating application artifacts from Roo script

Introduction

Java provides an excellent platform for enterprise application development but has often been weighed down by productivity issues. For instance, if you want to develop a web application, then you need to learn a web framework, create JSPs or views, implement service layer, integrate services with a persistence framework, implement persistence logic, create configuration files for different application layers, write unit and integration tests, write build scripts, and so on. Phew! It seems like a lot of work to even create a simple web application that uses a standard set of Java frameworks. This is the reason why many organizations moved to platforms, which offer quick-start to developing simple or medium complexity applications. With the arrival of open source frameworks like Spring and Hibernate, Java platform received a big boost in terms of developer productivity and simplicity; it was still off the mark when it came to productivity levels compared to platforms like Ruby on Rails, until Spring Roo arrived.

Spring Roo is the next generation rapid application development tool for Java programming language. It is an open source tool, which comes under the umbrella of SpringSource (`http://www.springsource.org/`) projects. Applications developed using Spring Roo make use of the Spring programming model, which already has a proven track record of delivering portable, testable, and maintainable enterprise applications.

Spring Roo is an easy-to-use tool for rapidly developing Java enterprise applications using well-recognized frameworks such as Spring, Hibernate, AspectJ, Spring Web Flow, Spring Security, GWT, Flex, and so on. Spring Roo takes care of creating project structure for your enterprise application, adding support to use Maven for building and deploying the application, creating application architecture based on your choice of technologies, creating unit and integration tests based on your choice of testing framework, and so on. Spring Roo provides an interactive, intuitive, text-based interface through which you enter the details of your application in a step-by-step fashion to create a working application in minutes.

 When using Spring Roo, it's up to the enterprise application developer to choose the technology or framework to use in developing the application. For instance, you can choose Hibernate or OpenJPA for persistence and Spring Web Flow or GWT for the web layer.

So, what do you need to learn to develop applications using Spring Roo? As we will see shortly, you need to learn hardly anything to develop enterprise applications using Spring Roo. Spring Roo's key goal has been to utilize existing knowledge of enterprise developers and automate most of the tasks that a developer had to perform in a typical enterprise application development project. This results in increased developer productivity with nearly no learning curve. Isn't it exciting that you can rapidly develop Java enterprise applications using standard Java technologies without learning anything new?

Before we jump into using Spring Roo tool, let's have a look at the key benefits of using Spring Roo:

- *Improved enterprise developer's productivity*: Spring Roo improves enterprise developer's productivity by auto-generating code based on instructions provided by developer or inferred from the code already generated by Spring Roo.

- *Productivity improvement throughout project lifecycle*: Spring Roo not only gets you quickly started with the project but it also gives you productivity improvements over the lifetime of the project.

- *No extra layers of abstraction*: Spring Roo doesn't attempt to hide implementation details from enterprise developers, making it easy for developers to understand the code and modify it as per their need.

- *No runtime dependency*: If you develop applications using Spring Roo, at runtime your application code is *only* dependent on frameworks that you used for developing the application, nothing more, nothing less.

- *No vendor lock-in*: At any time you decide to move away from using Spring Roo, you can use Eclipse IDE or STS (Spring Tool Suite—SourceSource's Eclipse flavor) to remove Spring Roo specific details from your application.

The following figures shows what you can do with Spring Roo and the benefits that you get:

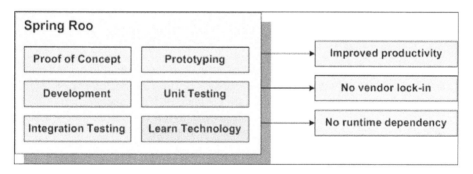

The given figure shows that you can also use Spring Roo for creating proof of concepts, for creating prototypes, and for learning new technologies. With Spring Roo you can quickly create a working application in minutes, which makes it an ideal candidate for developing prototypes and creating proof of concepts. A developer can use Spring Roo to create a simple application using the technology that (s)he wants to learn and play around with it or go through the Roo-generated source code to quickly learn about the technology.

In this chapter, we will look at recipes that will help you get started with using Spring Roo for developing your enterprise application. The recipes in this chapter focus on demonstrating how you set up Roo, create a Roo project, create some of the project artifacts, get help and hints on various Roo commands from the Roo shell, and import Roo project in your favorite IDE. This chapter will set the stage for more advanced recipes that we will see in the later chapters of this book.

Setting up Roo

The first thing that you need to do to get started with using Spring Roo is to set up the Roo tool on your laptop or desktop.

In this recipe, we will look at how you can install Spring Roo and verify that it's ready to use.

What do I need to learn to effectively use Spring Roo?

If you are an experienced Java enterprise developer, then you hardly need to learn anything new to use Spring Roo. If you know how AspectJ ITDs (Inter-type Declarations) work, then it will be helpful to understand what Spring Roo does behind the scenes. As you go through the various recipes in this book, you will find enough details on how Spring Roo makes use of AspectJ ITDs.

Getting ready

As you are going to install Spring Roo, you first need to download Spring Roo ZIP archive from the official home page of Spring Roo (`http://www.springsource.org/roo/start`). Also, ensure that you have the following software installed on your machine:

▶ Java SE 6 or later (`http://java.sun.com/javase/downloads/index.jsp`).

▶ Apache Maven 3.x or later (`http://maven.apache.org/download.html`). Examples in this book make use of Apache Maven 3.0.2

How to do it...

To install Spring Roo, all you need to do is to follow the given steps:

1. Unzip the downloaded Spring Roo ZIP archive into a directory. Once you have unzipped Spring Roo ZIP file, you will see the directory structure (excluding the `cache` directory) as shown in the following screenshot:

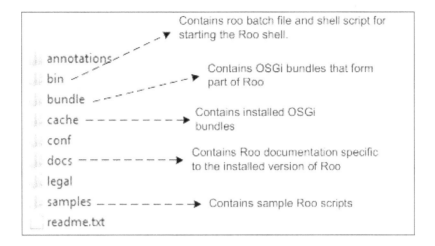

2. Set the JAVA_HOME environment variable to point to the Java SE installation directory.

3. Set the ROO_HOME environment variable to point to the Roo installation directory.

4. If you are using Windows, add the ROO_HOME/bin directory to the PATH environment variable. If you are using Linux or Mac OS X, then create a symbolic link to the ROO_HOME/bin/roo.sh shell script.

5. Roo installation isn't complete unless you verify it. So, create a ch01-recipe sub-directory in the C:\roo-cookbbook directory, open command prompt, and go to the ch01-recipe directory. Now, execute the roo.bat batch file, as shown in the following commands:

Downloading the example code

You can download the example code files for all Packt books you have purchased from your account at http://www.PacktPub.com. If you purchased this book elsewhere, you can visit http://www.PacktPub.com/support and register to have the files e-mailed directly to you.

```
C:\>cd roo-cookbbook
C:\roo-cookbbook>cd ch01-recipe
C:\roo-cookbbook\ch01-recipe>roo


    ____  ____  ____
   / __ \/ __ \/ __ \
  / /_/ / / / / / / /
 / _, _/ /_/ / /_/ /
/_/ |_|\____/\____/      1.1.1.RELEASE [rev 156ccd6]
```

```
Welcome to Spring Roo. For assistance press TAB or type "hint"
then hit ENTER.

..

roo>
```

6. If you see the output as shown, it means you have successfully installed Spring Roo. You will notice that when you execute `roo.bat` or `roo.sh`, the command prompt changes to `roo>`. You are now ready to play with Spring Roo.

How it works...

Spring Roo is built on top of Apache Felix (`http://felix.apache.org/site/index.html`) OSGi container, which promotes modularity and dynamic assembly of applications. The `bundle` directory contains OSGi bundles that form part of Spring Roo release. These bundles provide core services required by Roo and add-ons that support code generation. When you first start Spring Roo by executing Roo batch file or shell script, then these bundles are installed and copied into the `cache` directory of your Spring Roo installation.

There's more...

Spring Roo comes with certain core services and base add-ons that are part of Spring Roo distribution. Core services like the Roo shell, file system monitor, bootstrap, and so on, provide the necessary infrastructure for the add-ons to perform their intended responsibility. Add-ons are at the heart of Spring Roo and they provide the code generation functionality. For instance, the e-mail add-on adds e-mail support and the JPA (Java Persistence API) add-on helps with setting up a JPA provider, creating JPA entities, their relationships, and so on.

As Roo add-ons are OSGi compliant, you can additionally create a custom add-on or download a third-party add-on and install it as part of your Spring Roo installation to extend Roo's functionality.

Using Spring Roo with Eclipse/STS

As Roo is a command-line driven tool, you may want to integrate it with a feature rich IDE like Eclipse or STS to simplify application development. If you are using STS, you don't need to worry about integrating Roo with it because support for Roo is built into STS. If you want to integrate Roo with Eclipse, you can install STS components in Eclipse, in the same way as you install any other Eclipse plugin.

If you are using any other IDE or you don't want to integrate your Eclipse IDE with Spring Roo, you can run Spring Roo in the background and use your favorite IDE to develop your enterprise application. As you make modifications to your enterprise application using your IDE, Spring Roo will work in the background to manage the enterprise application.

The following screenshot shows Spring Roo was started from inside Eclipse IDE. It shows that the **roo>** prompt is now displayed adjacent to a text box where you can enter your Roo commands:

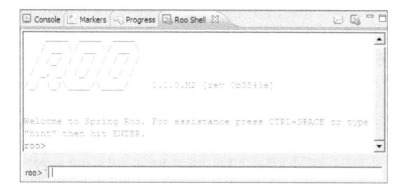

If you compare the output shown in the given screenshot with the output that you saw earlier when you started the Roo shell from command prompt, you will notice that they are not the same. Really? Yes, in the case of Eclipse or STS, to use auto-completion (as suggested in the welcome text) feature of Roo commands, you need to use *CTRL + SPACE* instead of *TAB*.

See also

▶   The next recipe, titled *Getting help and hints from Roo*, shows how Spring Roo provides context-sensitive hints on using the Roo shell and how to access help at any given time.

Getting help and hints from Roo

One of the key features of the Spring Roo shell is that it provides context-sensitive hints to the developers. The hints feature of Spring Roo provides step-by-step guidance on developing a working enterprise application in minutes. For instance, if you haven't created a Roo project in the directory from which you are running the Roo shell, issuing the `hint` command tells you how to go about creating a Roo project. If Roo finds that the directory from which the Roo shell is executing contains a Roo project but a JPA persistence provider is not set up yet, it suggests you set up a persistence provider (such as OpenJPA and Hibernate) for your project.

What is a Roo project?

A Roo project is nothing but a Java project whose source code consists of Java source files and `.aj` (AspectJ) files. If you decide to move away from Roo, you can easily do so because there is no runtime dependency of the generated code on any Roo libraries. Refer to the *Removing Roo-specific details from your project* recipe in *Chapter 7* to see how to use IDEs like Eclipse and STS to remove Roo.

The `help` command provides a list of commands that are supported by a particular version of Spring Roo, accompanied with a short description of the purpose of the command. The commands listed by the `help` command are the only commands that you can execute from the Roo shell.

It is important to note that you may not be able to execute some of the Roo commands listed by `help` command, if they are not applicable to your Roo project. For instance, if you haven't set up a JPA persistence provider for your enterprise application, the Roo shell doesn't allow you to execute commands for creating JPA entities.

Getting ready

To execute the commands defined in this recipe, first create an empty directory from which you will start your Roo shell. For instance, you can create a sub-directory named `ch01-recipe` inside the `cookbook-recipe` directory in the `C:` drive. Go to the `ch01-recipe` directory and execute `roo.bat` batch file to start the Roo shell.

How to do it...

To get help and hints from Roo follow the given steps:

1. To get help from Spring Roo, all you need to do is enter the `help` command in your Roo shell. But, we will do it a bit differently in our case. Instead of entering the complete command name, enter the letter h and press *TAB* (if you are using standalone Spring Roo installation) or *CTRL + SPACE* if you are using Spring Roo installed in Eclipse IDE or STS. You will get the following output from the Roo shell:

    ```
    roo> h
    help    hint
    roo> h
    ```

    As shown in the given code, the Roo shell provides the list of matching commands that it finds. In this case, it's `help` and `hint`. Now, enter he into the Roo shell and press *TAB* or *CTRL + SPACE*. You will notice that now the Roo shell automatically completes the command for you to reflect the matching `help` command.

    Once you enter the `help` command, you will get the list of commands supported by Spring Roo, shown as follows:

    ```
    roo> help
    .....
    * class - Creates a new Java class source file in any project path
    * interface - Creates a new Java interface source file in any
    project path
    * project - Creates a new project
    ```

```
* quit - Exits the shell
* version - Displays shell version
.....
```

As you can see, the `help` command provides a short description about all the commands supported by Spring Roo. For instance, it tells you that you can use the `quit` command to exit the Roo shell and the `version` command to know the version of Spring Roo that you are currently using.

2. Now that you know how `help` command is useful, let's try out the `hint` command, shown as follows:

```
roo> hint
Welcome to Roo! We hope you enjoy your stay!
Before you can use many features of Roo, you need to start a new
project.
To do this, type 'project' (without the quotes) and then hit TAB.
Enter a --topLevelPackage like 'com.mycompany.projectname' (no
quotes).
When you've finished completing your --topLevelPackage, press
ENTER.
Your new project will then be created in the current working
directory.
....
```

As you can see from the given output, Spring Roo shows the hint on how to go about creating a project using the `project` command. We will make use of the `hint` command in later recipes to discover how it is useful in creating a fully functional project.

How it works...

As mentioned earlier, Spring Roo consists of core services and add-ons. Add-ons are meant for generating code based on commands executed by the developer. While executing commands like `hint` and `help`, Roo is not generating any code. You can say that these commands are processed by the core services and not by any Spring Roo add-on.

There's more...

Spring Roo also provides with the option to pass arguments to Roo commands, which is covered in the following section. Also when you execute a command from the Roo shell, it is recorded in a Roo script file, which is explained in the *Log file for executed Roo commands* section.

Passing arguments to Roo commands

Like most Roo commands, the `help` and `hint` commands accept arguments. Arguments are additional parameters that are passed to a Roo command to customize command behaviour. For instance, the `help` command accepts a `command` argument and the `hint` command accepts a `topic` argument.

Earlier, we saw that the `help` command provides high-level details about commands supported by Spring Roo. The `command` argument is used to specify the name of the command for which detailed help information is needed, including information about required and optional arguments that can be passed to the Roo command. Similarly, the `topic` argument of `hint` command provides detailed information on a particular topic. The `command` and `hint` arguments are optional arguments; Roo shell doesn't force you to specify them.

In most cases Roo expects you to specify arguments in the following format:

```
--<argument-name> <argument-value>
```

To simplify using the `hint` and `help` commands, Roo lets you specify arguments without un-necessary frills. For instance, you can enter the `help project` command to get help information on the `project` command or you can enter the `hint jpa` command to get hints related to JPA.

The following output from the Roo shell shows the results from executing the `help project` and `hint jpa` commands:

```
roo> help project


Keyword:                    project
Description:                Creates a new project
 Keyword:                   ** default **
Keyword:                    topLevelPackage
    Help:                   The uppermost package name (this becomes the
<groupId> in Maven and also the '~' value when using Roo's shell)
Mandatory:           true
. . . . .


roo> hint jpa
Roo requires the installation of a JPA provider and associated database.


Type 'persistence setup' and then hit TAB three times.
. . . . .
```

As you can see from the given output, the `help` command gives the exact details about a command. For instance, the `help project` command suggests that the `project` command accepts a mandatory argument named `topLevelPackage`. The `hint jpa` command provides high-level details about the `jpa topic`.

So, the question arises, how do you find the topics on which hints are available? Well, you can find these topics from Roo by executing the `hint topics` command, shown as follows:

```
roo> hint topics

The following hints are available to help you use Roo:
general, start, jpa, entities, fields, relationships,
controllers, finders, eclipse, logging
Just type 'hint topic_name' (without quotes) to view a specific hint.
```

The given output suggests that Spring Roo provides hints on the following topics: `jpa`, `entities`, `fields`, `relationships`, and so on.

The `help` and `hint` commands are the most often used commands; it is recommended that you should use them as and when required while working with your Roo project.

Log file for executed Roo commands

Let's say that you created an enterprise application using Spring Roo consisting of Spring Web MVC and Hibernate frameworks. Additionally, you executed Roo commands to add e-mail and JMS message sending support to some of the classes that you created as part of your enterprise application. Now, let's say a similar project needs to be created in your organization, which makes use of Spring Web MVC, Hibernate frameworks, and requires e-mail and JMS message sending functionalities. You can either re-execute all the Roo commands (that you used in your earlier enterprise application) to create the new enterprise application, or you can simply execute the Roo script from the earlier enterprise application.

When you execute a command from the Roo shell, it is recorded in a Roo script file, named `log.roo`. You will notice that a `log.roo` script file is created in the `ch01-recipe` directory. The `log.roo` script contains the commands that you executed using the Roo shell and also the details of when you started the Roo shell or exited it. This feature of Spring Roo can be useful if you want to review the commands that you executed or if you want to execute the same set of commands using the `script` command of Spring Roo. In a moment you will see how to execute a Roo script file, in the *Creating application artifacts from Roo script* recipe of this chapter.

▸ The next recipe, *Creating a Roo project* shows how you can use the `help` command to discover the details of the `project` command, which is used for creating a Roo project.

Creating a Roo project

This is the first recipe in which you will see Spring Roo doing some real work to help you create a Java enterprise application. This recipe shows how to go about creating a Roo project using `project` command. The end result of following this recipe will be a project, which follows standard Maven directory structure. The project created in this recipe can be packaged as a JAR file because it doesn't have a web layer. In *Chapter 4, Web Application Development with Spring Web MVC* and *Chapter 5, Web Application Development with GWT, Flex, and Spring Web Flow* you will see how to create a web layer of an enterprise application using Spring Roo. The project that you will create in this recipe will act as a foundation for the rest of the recipes in this chapter.

Getting ready

The first thing that you need to do is to create an empty directory in which you are going to create your Roo project. Create a `ch01-recipe` sub-directory in the `C:\roo-cookbbook` directory, if you haven't created it yet. Start the Roo shell from the `ch01-recipe` directory by executing the Roo batch file or shell script, as shown here:

```
C:\roo-cookbook\ch01-recipe>roo
```

How to do it...

To create a Roo project, execute the `project` command from your Roo shell, shown as follows:

```
roo>project --topLevelPackage sample.roo.flightapp --java 6 --projectName
flight-app

Created C:\roo-cookbook\ch01-recipe\pom.xml
.....
Created SRC_MAIN_RESOURCES\META-INF\spring\applicationContext.xml
Created SRC_MAIN_RESOURCES\log4j.properties


sample.roo.flightapp roo>
```

Notice the change in the Roo prompt after the execution of the `project` command. The change in prompt indicates that you are now working with a project whose top-level package is `sample.roo.flightapp`. If you start the Roo shell from a directory, which already contains a Roo project, then the Roo prompt will not change.

How it works...

The following table describes the purpose of each of the arguments passed to the `project` command:

Argument	Purpose
`topLevelPackage`	This is a *Mandatory* argument, which identifies the base or root package of your project. You will refer to this package frequently in your Roo commands using the tilde symbol (~). The value of this argument becomes the value of the `<group-id>` element in maven's `pom.xml` file.
`java`	This is an optional argument, which specifies the version of Java (must be 5, 6, or 7) with which the source and compiled classes of the Roo project should be compatible with. If unspecified, the Java version is auto-detected by Spring Roo.
`projectName`	This is an optional argument, which specifies the name of the project. The value of this argument becomes the value of `<artifact-id>` and `<name>` elements in maven's `pom.xml` file. If unspecified, the last part of the package name specified as the value of `topLevelPackage` argument is used. For instance, if the `topLevelPackage` argument value is `sample.roo.flightapp`, and the `projectName` argument is not specified, the value of `projectName` argument is assumed to be `flightapp`.

Use TAB or CTRL + SPACE regularly for discovering mandatory and optional attributes, and their pre-defined values

As it's hard to remember all the mandatory and optional attributes of different Roo commands, it's recommended that you use *TAB* (if you are using standalone Roo) or *CTRL + SPACE* (if you are using Roo from within Eclipse or STS) to use the auto-completion feature of Roo. Roo not only provides auto-completion of Roo commands (as we saw in an earlier recipe), but it also displays the mandatory arguments of a command when you press *TAB* or *CTRL + SPACE*. If you want to know about the optional arguments of a command, simply enter -- followed by *TAB* or *CTRL + SPACE*. To restrict users from entering any arbitrary value, a command argument may accept only a particular value from a set of pre-defined values for that argument. The pre-defined values are defined by the add-on responsible for processing the command. If an argument accepts a value from a set of pre-defined values by Roo, it is displayed when you press *TAB* or *CTRL + SPACE*.

Spring Roo distribution comes with a **Maven add-on**, which is responsible for processing the `project` command. There are more Roo commands that are processed by the Maven add-on, which you will see later in this book.

The output of `project` command shows that it creates directories with name `SRC_MAIN_JAVA`, `SCR_MAIN_WEBAPP`, and so on. These are logical names given to standard directories created by the Maven add-on. The following table shows the directories to which each of these names map in the case of the `flight-app` project:

Path value	Project directory
SRC_MAIN_JAVA	Refers to the root of the Java source directory, which contains application's Java sources: ch01-recipe\src\main\java.
SRC_MAIN_RESOURCES	The root of the directory, which contains resources (Spring's application context XML, database properties file, `log4j` properties file, `persistence.xml` file, and so on) required by the Java enterprise application: ch01-recipe\src\main\resources.
SRC_TEST_JAVA	The root of the Java source directory, which contains unit and integration tests: ch01-recipe\src\test\java.
SRC_TEST_RESOURCES	The root of the directory, which contains resources required during unit and integration testing: ch01-recipe\src\test\resources.
SRC_MAIN_WEBAPP	The web application directory, which contains web pages, images, style sheets, and web application configuration: ch01-recipe\src\main\webapp.
ROOT	Refers to the root directory of the project, which is ch01-recipe in case of flight-app project.
SPRING_CONFIG_ROOT	Refers to the directory, which contains Spring's application context XML file. In the context of flight-app project this refers to ch01-recipe\src\main\resources\META-INF\spring.

As evident from the execution of the `project` command, not only did it create a maven-ized project, it also created Spring's `applicationContext.xml`, maven's `pom.xml` file, and a `log4j.properties` file. The following XML code shows the contents of the `applicationContext.xml` file, which contains some interesting details:

```
<beans ..>

  <context:property-placeholder
        location="classpath*:META-INF/spring/*.properties"/>

    <context:spring-configured/>

    <context:component-scan base-package="sample.roo.flightapp">
    <context:exclude-filter
                expression=".*_Roo_.*" type="regex"/>
```

```
    <context:exclude-filter expression=
        "org.springframework.stereotype.Controller"
        type="annotation"/>
    </context:component-scan>
</beans>
```

The important inferences that we can derive from the content of `applicationContext.xml` are:

- The definition of the `<property-placeholder>` element of Spring's `context` namespace indicates that you must put your properties files that contain configuration information for Spring beans, in the `META-INF/spring` directory so that they can be picked up by Spring's application context. In the next chapter, we will see how this is used by Roo-generated applications to read database properties from an external properties file.

- The `<spring-configured>` element of Spring's `context` namespace specifies that objects that are annotated with `@Configurable` annotation are configured using Spring, even if they are created outside of the Spring container. The objects created outside the Spring container include objects that are created programmatically using the `new` operator or by reflection. We will see example usage of `@Configurable` annotation in *Chapter 2, Persisting Objects Using JPA*.

- The `<component-scan>` element of Spring's `context` namespace specifies that Spring components (that is, components annotated with `@Service`, `@Repository` and `@Component` Spring annotations) found inside the `sample.roo.flightapp` package or its sub-packages are automatically registered with Spring's application context. Later in this chapter, we will use this feature to create a service class in the `flight-app` project, which is auto-registered with Spring's application context.

The other important artifact that was generated during the project creation is the `pom.xml` file that is used by maven. The following XML code shows how the argument values specified in the `project` command are used in creating the `pom.xml` file of the `flight-app` project:

```
<project >
    .....
    <groupId>sample.roo.flightapp</groupId>
    <artifactId>flight-app</artifactId>
    <packaging>jar</packaging>
    <version>0.1.0.BUILD-SNAPSHOT</version>
    <name>flight-app</name>
</project>
```

You may notice that the value of the `<packaging>` element is `jar` and not `war`. The reason for this lies with the fact that we haven't yet added a web layer to the `flight-app` application. We will see in *Chapter 4, Web Application Development with Spring Web MVC* and *Chapter 5, Web Application Development with GWT, Flex, and Spring Web Flow* how we go about creating a web application using Spring Roo.

The `pom.xml` additionally contains Maven plugins, which are available to Roo projects by default. The following table summarizes some of the important Maven plugins that are available to our newly created `flight-app` project:

Maven Plugin	Usage
IDEA plugin	You may use this plugin to convert the flight-app project into an IntelliJ IDEA project.
Eclipse plugin	You may use this plugin to convert the flight-app project into an Eclipse project.
AspectJ compiler plugin	This plugin weaves AspectJ aspects into your project classes. This plugin is used internally by Spring Roo. We will see the AspectJ compiler in action in Chapter 2.
Tomcat and Jetty plugins	You can use these plugins during development to run Tomcat or Jetty in embedded mode to test your web application.

There's more...

You won't always be starting a project from scratch, and you may find Spring Roo compelling enough (which you will, as we go through its various features) to use in your existing Spring-based Java projects. In such scenarios, you need to do the following:

1. Convert your existing Spring-based project into a standard Maven project as created by Spring Roo's `project` command.

2. Add the AspectJ compiler plugin to the `pom.xml` file of your project.

3. Move bean definitions in your existing project to the `applicationContext.xml` file in `META-INF/spring` directory.

4. Move the properties file used for configuring Spring beans to `META-INF/spring/` directory.

There are other things you will need to do to convert your existing projects into a Roo project, which we will discuss in relevant recipes.

See also

▶ The *Configuring logging* recipe discusses how to configure logging in Roo projects

▶ Refer to the *Creating a Java class* and *Create a Java interface* recipes to find out how you can use Spring Roo to create classes/interfaces in your application

Importing a Roo project into Eclipse or IntelliJ IDEA IDE

As explained in the *Setting up Roo* recipe, you can either use STS or Eclipse with STS components installed to work with Roo projects. Alternatively, you can create necessary project files to import the Roo project into Eclipse or IntelliJ IDEA IDE (for working directly with Java sources and configuration files) and run the Spring Roo shell separately in standalone mode to execute Roo commands.

In this recipe, we look at how you can import a Roo project into Eclipse or IntelliJ IDEA by executing commands provided by Spring Roo.

Getting ready

Start the Roo shell from the `C:\roo-cookbook\ch01-recipe` directory, which contains the `flight-app` Roo project.

How to do it...

To import the Roo project into Eclipse or IntelliJ IDEA follow the given steps:

1. To create Eclipse-specific project files, execute the `perform eclipse` command from the Roo shell, shown as follows:

   ```
   roo> perform eclipse
   ```

   Alternatively, you can use the `perform command` to execute the `eclipse:eclipse` Maven goal of the Maven Eclipse plugin, shown as follows:

   ```
   roo> perform command --mavenCommand eclipse:eclipse
   ```

2. To create IntelliJ IDEA specific project files, use the `perform command` to execute the `idea:idea` Maven goal of the Maven IDEA plugin, shown as follows:

   ```
   roo> perform command --mavenCommand idea:idea
   ```

How it works...

The `perform eclipse` and `perform command` commands are processed by the Maven add-on of Spring Roo. The `perform eclipse` command generates Eclipse IDE specific configuration files, such as `.project` and `.classpath` files. Behind the scenes, the `perform eclipse` command executes the `eclipse:eclipse` goal of the Maven eclipse plugin.

The `perform command` is used to execute a Maven command. It accepts a single *mandatory* argument, `mavenCommand`, which identifies the Maven goal to execute.

 Maven IDEA and Eclipse plugins are configured in the `pom.xml` file by Spring Roo at the project creation time; you don't need to add them to your Roo project to use the commands shown in this recipe.

There's more...

If you are using any IDE other than STS, then ensure that you install AJDT (AspectJ Development Tools), as it gives better development experience when working with projects that make use of AspectJ aspects. For instance, when you open a Java source file in Eclipse IDE (that has AJDT installed), the `Cross Reference` tab shows the various AspectJ declarations that apply to the selected Java source file, and you can select these declarations to open the corresponding AspectJ ITD files.

See also

 ▶ Refer to the *Setting up Roo* recipe to know how to use STS or Eclipse (with STS components) for developing with Spring Roo

 ▶ Refer to the *Removing Roo-specific details from your project* recipe in *Chapter 7, Developing Add-ons and Removing Roo from Projects* to see how you can convert your Roo project into a normal Java project

Configuring logging

In the *Creating a Roo project* recipe, you saw that when you create a new project, a `log4j.properties` file is automatically created with default logging configuration. In most real projects, you'd like to customize the default logging configuration. By default, the `log4j.properties` file configures root logger at `ERROR` level and logging is not enabled for the project.

In this recipe, we will look at the `logging setup` command to modify the logging configuration.

Getting ready

Start the Roo shell from the `C:\roo-cookbook\ch01-recipe` directory, which contains the `flight-app` Roo project.

How to do it...

Using the `logging setup` command you can specify the logging level and the package to which it applies, as shown in the following steps:

1. The following `logging setup` commands are used to change the logging level of rootLogger to `DEBUG` (which is `ERROR` by default) and enable `DEBUG` level logging for all classes in the `flight-app` application:

```
roo> logging setup --level DEBUG --package ROOT
Updated SRC_MAIN_RESOURCES\log4j.properties


roo> logging setup --level DEBUG --package PROJECT
Updated SRC_MAIN_RESOURCES\log4j.properties
```

As the output from the command execution suggests, some changes have been made by Roo to the `log4j.properties` file.

Keep an eye on the output of a command

When a Roo command is executed, it displays information about what files and directories have been created or which files have been updated. This can be helpful if you want to check the code that is generated on execution of a command.

2. To confirm that the changes have been made to the `log4j.properties`, you can either view it directly by opening the file or you can use the `properties list` command (explained in the next recipe).

How it works...

The `logging setup` command is processed by the **Logging add-on** of Spring Roo. The following table describes the arguments that the `logging setup` command accepts:

Argument	Purpose
`level`	This is a mandatory argument, which identifies the logging level. It can only take one of the pre-defined values, like `DEBUG`, `ERROR`, `INFO`, and so on.
`package`	This is an optional argument, which specifies the package to which the logging level applies. It can only take one of the pre-defined values, such as `PROJECT`, `ALL_SPRING`, `PERSISTENCE`, and so on.

There's more...

As of Spring Roo 1.1.3, using the `logging setup` command you can't specify a custom package name as the value of the `package` argument; therefore, you can set a custom package name either by using the `properties set` command (explained later in this chapter) or by directly editing the `log4j.properties` file.

See also

▸ The *Viewing properties defined in a properties file, Removing a property defined in a properties file*, and *Adding properties to a properties file* recipes show how you can manage properties files in your Roo project.

Viewing properties defined in a properties file

If your project contain properties files, you may want to view their content. For instance, when we created the `flight-app` Roo project earlier, a `log4j.properties` file containing logging configuration was also created. In this recipe, we will look at the `properties list` command to view the contents of the `log4j.properties` file.

Getting ready

Start the Roo shell from `C:\roo-cookbook\ch01-recipe` directory, which contains the `flight-app` Roo project.

How to do it...

To view the contents of a properties file, the `properties list` command requires a path to the properties file and its name. The following `properties list` command displays the contents of the `log4j.properties` file:

```
roo> properties list --name log4j.properties --path SRC_MAIN_RESOURCES

log4j.appender.R = org.apache.log4j.RollingFileAppender
log4j.appender.R.File = application.log
...
log4j.logger.sample.roo.flightapp = DEBUG
log4j.rootLogger = DEBUG, stdout
```

How it works...

The **Properties file add-on** is responsible for processing the `properties list` command. The following table describes the arguments it accepts:

Argument	Purpose
`path`	It is a mandatory argument that identifies a path to the properties file. It only accepts pre-defined values like `ROOT`, `SPRING_CONFIG_ROOT`, `SCR_MAIN_WEBAPP`, and so on.
`name`	It is a mandatory argument that specifies the name of the properties file whose content you want to view.

See also

> ▸ The next recipe, *Managing properties defined in a properties file*, shows how you can add, remove, and modify properties defined in properties files in your Roo project.

Managing properties defined in a properties file

In this recipe, we look at Roo commands, which you can use to add, remove, and modify properties defined in a properties file. We will use the `log4j.properties` file of the `flight-app` project to demonstrate the use of commands.

The following table shows the properties that we will add, modify, and remove from the `log4j.properties` file:

Property	Action
`log4j.appender.R.File = application.log`	**Modified** to `log4j.appender.R.File = flightapp.log`
`log4j.rootLogger = debug, stdout`	**Modified** to `log4j.rootLogger = ERROR`
`log4j.appender.stdout = org.apache.log4j.ConsoleAppender`	*Removed from* `log4j.properties`
`log4j.logger.sample.roo.flightapp.service = ERROR`	*Added to* `log4j.properties`

Getting ready

Start the Roo shell from the `C:\roo-cookbook\ch01-recipe` directory, which contains the `flight-app` Roo project.

How to do it...

To manage the properties defined in a properties file follow the given steps:

1. The `properties set` command is used to modify properties shown as follows:

    ```
    roo> properties set --name log4j.properties --path SRC_MAIN_
    RESOURCES --key log4j.appender.R.File --value flightapp.log

    .....

    roo> properties set --name log4j.properties --path SRC_MAIN_
    RESOURCES --key log4j.rootLogger --value ERROR
    ```

2. The `properties remove` command is used to remove properties, shown as follows:

    ```
    roo> properties remove --name log4j.properties --path SRC_MAIN_
    RESOURCES --key log4j.appender.stdout
    ```

3. The `properties set` can also be used to add a new property, shown as follows:

    ```
    roo> properties set --name log4j.properties --path SRC_MAIN_
    RESOURCES --key log4j.logger.sample.roo.flightapp.service --value
    DEBUG
    ```

How it works...

Like the `properties list` command, the `properties set` and `properties remove` commands are provided by **Properties file add-on**. The following table describes the arguments that both the `properties set` and `properties remove` commands accept:

Argument	Purpose
path	It is a mandatory argument that identifies a path to the properties file. Refer to the *Viewing properties defined in a properties file* and *Creating a Roo project* recipes for details on the values it can accept.
name	It is a mandatory argument that specifies the name of the properties file whose property you want to remove
key	It is a mandatory argument that specifies the key of the property that you want to remove from the properties file.

The `properties set` command accepts all the arguments that the `properties remove` command accepts. Additionally, it accepts a mandatory argument, `value`, which specifies a value of the property being set by the `properties set` command. If a matching property is found in the properties file, the existing property is updated with the new value. If no matching property is found, a new property is added to the properties file.

There's more...

You can also change the properties file using your favorite IDE. If you are creating a new Roo project which acts as a template for creating other projects, using properties commands to add, modify, and remove properties from a properties file can be valuable.

If you want to modify logging configuration, you should first consider using the `logging setup` command (explained earlier in the *Configuring logging* recipe). If you want to modify database properties, you should use database commands (explained in the *Managing database configuration properties* recipe in *Chapter 2, Persisting Objects Using JPA*).

See also

▶ The *Configuring logging* recipe explains how to configure logging using Spring Roo commands

▶ The *Managing database configuration properties* recipe explains how to configure database properties using Spring Roo commands

Creating a Java class

You can create Java classes in your Roo project, either by using the IDE of your choice or by using the `class` command. If you create a class using Roo, boilerplate code (which includes `toString`, and get and setter methods for attributes) is generated automatically and managed by Spring Roo, and is kept in a separate AspectJ ITD file.

Getting ready

Start the Roo shell from the `C:\roo-cookbook\ch01-recipe` directory, which contains the `flight-app` Roo project.

How to do it...

You can create a Java class using the `class` command, as shown here:

```
roo> class --class sample.roo.flightapp.service.FlightService
--rooAnnotations

Created SRC_MAIN_JAVA\sample\roo\flightapp\service

Created SRC_MAIN_JAVA\sample\roo\flightapp\service\FlightService.java

Created SRC_MAIN_JAVA\sample\roo\flightapp\service\FlightService_Roo_
Serializable.aj

~.service.FlightService roo>
```

When the `class` command is executed, notice that the Roo prompt changes to refer to the newly created Java class. In the next recipe, titled *Adding fields to a Java class*, we will see how the changed Roo prompt simplifies performing commands on the referred class. Also, notice that the service directory is automatically created by Spring Roo, if it doesn't exist.

 Some command arguments, like `rooAnnotations`, act as a flag for the command processor, and you don't need to specify their value. Simply specifying them as part of the command means that the value of the argument is true or yes.

How it works...

The `class` command accepts the arguments listed in the following table:

Argument	Purpose
class	It is a mandatory argument that identifies the fully-qualified name of the Java class that you want to create. You can either specify the fully-qualified class name using the tilde symbol `'~'` or you can use the *TAB* (or *CTRL + SPACE*) multiple times to let Spring Roo complete the package name for you.
	The `'~'` symbol refers to the top-level package of the Roo project. For instance, in `flight-app` project, it refers to `sample.roo.flightapp` package. You can use this symbol to specify the package (relative to top-level package) in which you want to create your Java class.
rooAnnotations	It is an optional argument that specifies the common Roo annotations, such as `@RooJavaBean`, `@RooToString`, and `@RooSerializable`, which are added to the generated Java class. If unspecified, these annotations are not added to the generated Java class.
path	It is an optional argument that specifies the path to the source directory in which the class is created. By default, the path is `SRC_MAIN_JAVA`.
extends	It is an optional argument that specifies the fully-qualified name of the class, which the Java class extends. You can use this argument to create a class which extends from a superclass.
abstract	It is an optional argument that indicates whether the class is an abstract or concrete class. You can use this argument to create an abstract class.
permitReserved Words	It is an optional argument that indicates whether Roo should allow creating a class whose name is a reserved word. By default, Roo doesn't allow creating Java classes whose name uses reserved words. For instance, by default you cannot create a class named `New`.

As evident from the list of arguments accepted by the `class` command, Spring Roo doesn't provide any argument to let you specify the interface(s) that the generated Java class implements. If you want your Java class to implement one or more interfaces, you need to manually modify your class definition.

As the output from `class` command suggests, apart from `FlightService.java`, Roo creates a `FlightService_Roo_Serializable.aj` file—an AspectJ ITD that makes the `FlightService` class implement `java.io.Serializable` interface.

The AspectJ ITDs generated by Roo have the following naming convention:

`<java-class-name>_Roo_<add-on-name>.aj`

Where `<java-class-name>` is the name of the Java class to which the AspectJ ITD applies.

`<add-on-name>` is the name of Spring Roo add-on responsible for managing the AspectJ ITD

The `*_Roo_*.aj` files are managed by Roo and you should not directly modify or delete them.

The following code shows how the `FlightService.java` file generates the `FlightService` class using the `class` command:

```
package sample.roo.flightapp.service;

import org.springframework.roo.addon.javabean.RooJavaBean;
import org.springframework.roo.addon.tostring.RooToString;
import org.springframework.roo.addon.serializable.RooSerializable;

@RooJavaBean
@RooToString
@RooSerializable
public class FlightService { }
```

In the given code, Roo annotations were added to the generated `FlightService` class because we specified the `rooAnnotations` argument in the `class` command.

To simplify debugging, developers commonly override the `toString` method of the `java.lang.Object` class to output a string containing the value of all the attributes of the class. With Spring Roo, you are relieved of this task because if your class is annotated with `@RooToString` annotation, Spring Roo takes care of creating and updating the `toString` method as you add, modify, or remove attributes from your Java class.

When you add an attribute to your `FlightService` class, Roo creates a `FlightService_Roo_ToString.aj`—an AspectJ ITD that adds the `toString` method to the `FlightService` class, and a `FlightService_Roo_JavaBean.aj`—an AspectJ ITD that adds getters and setters methods for the attributes defined in the `FlightService` class. The creation of these aspects is triggered by the presence of `@RooToString` and `@RooJavaBean` annotations in the `FlightService` class.

To see these two ITD files, add the following attribute to `FlightService` class:

```
private String origin;
```

If your Roo shell is running, as soon as you save the `FlightService` class, Roo will generate a `FlightService_Roo_ToString.aj` file and a `FlightService_Roo_JavaBean.aj` file in the same package as the `FlightService` class. If you observe the Roo shell, you will find that Roo reports that it has created a `FlightService_Roo_ToString.aj` and `FlightService_Roo_JavaBean.aj` files, as shown here:

Created SRC_MAIN_JAVA\sample\roo\flightapp\service

FlightService_Roo_ToString.aj

Created SRC_MAIN_JAVA\sample\roo\flightapp\service

FlightService_Roo_JavaBean.aj

The following code shows how `FlightService_Roo_ToString.aj` AspectJ ITD adds the `toString` method to the `FlightService` class:

```
package sample.roo.flightapp.service;

privileged aspect FlightService_Roo_ToString
{

    public String FlightService.toString()
    {
        StringBuilder sb = new StringBuilder();
        sb.append("Origin: ")
        .append(getOrigin());
        return sb.toString();
    }
}
```

The given code shows that `FlightService_Roo_ToString` is a `privileged` aspect, that is, it can access even **private** members of other aspects and classes. The declaration, `public String FlightSerivce.toString()`, adds a `public toString` method to the `FlightService` class that accepts no arguments and returns a `String`. Everything inside the curly-braces is the implementation of the `toString` method. Each declaration in an AspectJ ITD file identifies the target of that declaration. In the code, `FlightService` in the declaration means that the `FlightService` class is the target; therefore, it will add the `toString` method to the `FlightService` class. In the *Adding fields to a Java class* recipe, we will see how the `toString` method is automatically updated by Spring Roo when you add more attributes to the `FlightService` class.

The following figure summarizes how the `FlightService_Roo_ToString.aj` file in the previous listing declares adding the `toString` method to the `Flight` class:

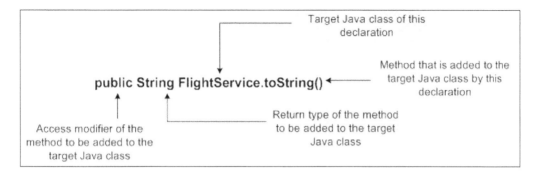

 In Spring Roo, AspectJ ITDs are responsible for adding fields, methods, and constructors to Java classes and to make them implement interfaces or extend from a superclass. Spring Roo is responsible for managing these ITDs and you should not directly modify or delete them.

The following code shows the `FlightService_Roo_JavaBean.aj` AspectJ ITD file:

```
privileged aspect FlightService_Roo_JavaBean
{

   public String FlightService.getOrigin()
    {
       return this.origin;
    }

   public void FlightService.setOrigin
    (String origin)
    {
       this.origin = origin;
    }
}
```

The given code shows that `FlightService_Roo_JavaBean.aj` is also a `privileged` aspect and it introduces two methods into the `FlightService` class: `getOrigin` and `setOrigin`, to get and set the value of the `origin` attribute.

The `FlightService_Roo_Serializable.aj` AspectJ ITD defines that the `FlightService` class implements the `java.io.Serializable` interface, as shown here:

```
package sample.roo.flightapp.service;

import java.io.Serializable;

privileged aspect FlightService_Roo_Serializable
{

    declare parents: FlightService implements Serializable;

    private static final long FlightService.serialVersionUID
      = 5059552858884348572L
}
```

In the given code, the `declare parents: FlightService implements Serializable` statement declares that the `FlightService` class implements the `java.io.Serializable` interface. The following figure summarizes what this declaration means:

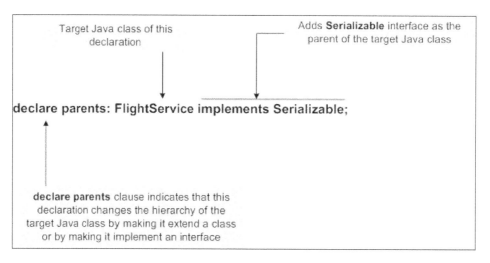

The statement `private static final long FlightService.serialVersionUID = 5059552858884348572L`, adds a `serialVersionUID` field (it's the field which you define if your class implements the `Serializable` interface) to the `FlightService` class that contains it.

There's more...

If you want Roo to manage the creation of the `toString` method and getter and setter methods for attributes of the class, it is recommended that you use the `rooAnnotations` argument in the `class` command.

 Roo annotations have source-level retention, which means that your application is not dependent on Roo annotations at runtime.

Moving existing Spring projects to use Spring Roo

If you are moving your existing Spring-based project to Roo, you can make out from this recipe that you should do the following:

1. Remove the `toString` method and add the `@RooToString` annotation to all your existing classes.

2. Remove the implementation of `Serializable` interfaces from classes and instead annotate the classes with the `@RooSerializable` annotation.

3. Remove getters and setters methods from your Java classes and instead annotate the classes with the `@RooJavaBean` annotation.

 Registering the service class with Spring's application context

Using Spring Roo you can't create a service class, which is automatically registered with Spring's application context; therefore, if you want your service class to be auto-registered, then annotate it with the `@Service` annotation. The service class will be registered with Spring's application context as long as it is inside the top-level directory (for more information refer to the `<component-scan>` element, described in the *Creating a Roo project* recipe).

@RooToString—customizing the name of the toString method

We saw that using the `@RooToString` annotation creates a method named `toString` in the corresponding AspectJ ITD file. You can use the `toStringMethod` attribute of the `@RooToString` annotation to specify a custom name for the `toString` method, as shown here:

```
@RooToString(toStringMethod = "myTostring")
public class MyCustomClass { private String myAttr; }
```

In the given code, the `toStringMethod` attribute specifies `myToString` as the name of the method to act as the `toString` method for the `MyCustomClass`. The ITD file corresponding to the `@RooToString` annotation: `MyCustomClass_Roo_ToString.aj` will now create a method similar to `toString` but with the name `myToString`, as shown here:

```
privileged aspect MyCustomClass_Roo_ToString
{
    public String MyCustomClass.mytostring ()
    {
        StringBuilder sb = new StringBuilder();
        sb.append("MyAttr: " ).append(getMyAttr());
        return sb.toString();
    }
}
```

@RooToString—excluding properties from the toString method

In some cases, you may want to restrict properties from being part of the auto-generated `toString` method. The `@RooToString` annotation provides an `excludeFields` attribute, which lets you specify an array of attributes that should be excluded from the auto-generated `toString` method, as shown here:

```
@RooToString(excludeFields={"someAttribute"})
public class MyCustomClass { .. }
```

In this code, the `@RooToString` annotation instructs that the `toString` method of the `MyCustomClass` class must not include the `someAttribute` property.

See also

▸ The *Adding attributes to a Java class* recipe explains how you can add attributes to a Java class using roo

▸ The *Creating a Java interface* recipe explains how you can create a Java interface from the Roo shell

Adding attributes to a Java class

You can add attributes to your Java classes in your Roo project, either from your IDE or by using the `field` commands of Spring Roo. There are advantages in adding attributes using Roo as opposed to using an IDE, which we will see in this recipe. The following table shows the name and type of attributes that we will add to a `Passenger` class in the package `sample.roo.flightapp.domain` of the `flight-app` project:

Field name	Type
firstName	java.lang.String
lastName	java.lang.String
age	java.lang.Integer
address	sample.roo.flightapp.domain.Address

Getting ready

Start the Roo shell from the `C:\roo-cookbook\ch01-recipe` directory, which contains the `flight-app` project.

How to do it...

Roo provides field commands, which you can use to add different types of fields in your Java class, shown as follows:

1. Create an `Address` class, which is an attribute type in the `Passenger` class, as shown here:

   ```
   roo> class --class ~.domain.Address --rooAnnotations
   ```

2. Create a `Passenger` class, to which we want to add attributes using the `field` commands, as shown here:

   ```
   sample.roo.flightapp.domain.Address roo> class --class ~.domain.
   Passenger --rooAnnotations
   ```

3. Add `firstName` and `lastName` attributes to the `Passenger` class using `field string` command, shown as follows:

   ```
   sample.roo.flightapp.domain.Passenger roo> field string
   --fieldName firstName

   Updated ..Passenger.java
   Created ..Passenger_Roo_JavaBean.aj
   Created ..Passenger_Roo_ToString.aj

   .. roo> field string --fieldName lastName

   Updated ..Passenger.java
   Updated ..Passenger_Roo_JavaBean.aj
   Updated ..Passenger_Roo_ToString.aj
   ```

4. Add an age attribute to the Passenger class, using the field number command, shown as follows:

```
.. roo> field number --fieldName age --type java.lang.Integer

Updated ..Passenger.java
Updated ..Passenger_Roo_JavaBean.aj
Updated ..Passenger_Roo_ToString.aj
```

5. Add an address attribute of type Address to the Passenger class, using the field other command, shown as follows:

```
.. roo> field other --fieldName address --type sample.roo.
flightapp.domain.Address

Updated ..Passenger.java
Updated ..Passenger_Roo_JavaBean.aj
Updated ..Passenger_Roo_ToString.aj
```

The given output for each of these commands shows that when an attribute is added to the Passenger class for the first time, the Passenger_Roo_JavaBean.aj and Passenger_Roo_ToString.aj files are created. You may notice that every time you add an attribute, the Passenger_Roo_JavaBean.aj and Passenger_Roo_ToString.aj AspectJ ITD files are also updated.

How it works...

Spring Roo provides multiple field commands for adding different types of attributes to the Java class. For instance, field string is for adding a String type field, field date is for adding a java.util.Date or java.util.Calendar type field, field other is for adding a field of custom Java type, and so on.

 Some of the field commands, like field set and field reference, apply only to JPA entities, and are therefore not applicable to every Java class that you create in your Roo project. Also, field commands accept certain arguments, which make sense only if the target Java class is a JPA entity. We will discuss JPA entity specific field commands in *Chapter 2*.

The field string, field other, and field number commands accept the name argument, which identifies the name of the attribute to be added to the Java class. The field other and field number also require the type of the attribute.

The following code shows Passenger_Roo_JavaBean.aj AspectJ ITD, which was modified by Spring Roo when we added fields to the Passenger class:

```
privileged aspect Passenger_Roo_JavaBean
{
    public String Passenger.getFirstName()
    {
        return this.firstName;
    }
    public void Passenger.setFirstName(String firstName)
    {
        this.firstName = firstName;
    }
    ...
}
```

The given code shows that `Passenger_Roo_JavaBean.aj` was updated by Spring Roo to introduce getter and setter methods for each of the fields added to `Passenger` class. This was possible because of the presence of `@RooJavaBean` annotation in the `Passenger` class.

The following code shows `Passenger_Roo_ToString.aj` AspectJ ITD, which was also modified by Spring Roo when fields were added to the `Passenger` class:

```
privileged aspect Passenger_Roo_ToString
{
    public String Passenger.toString()
    {
        StringBuilder sb = new StringBuilder();
        sb.append("FirstName:").append(getFirstName()).append(",");
        sb.append("LastName: ").append(getLastName()).append(", ");
        sb.append("Age: ").append(getAge()).append(", ");
        sb.append("Address: ").append(getAddress());
        return sb.toString();
    }
}
```

As the given code suggests, it introduces a `toString` method to the `Passenger` class, which returns a concatenated `String` containing the value of each of its attribute. This was possible because the `Passenger` class was annotated with the `@RooToString` annotation.

What if I add an attribute using IDE?

Spring Roo actively monitors changes to classes that are annotated with Roo annotations, and any change to classes triggers Spring Roo to update the corresponding AspectJ ITD files. So, it doesn't matter whether you add attributes to your Java class using Roo shell or an IDE.

The following figure shows how Spring Roo manages AspectJ ITD files:

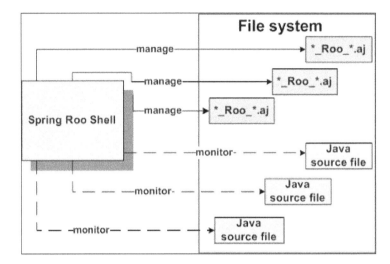

The given figure shows that when you start the Spring Roo shell from a directory, it actively monitors the Java classes in the file system that are annotated with Roo annotations (for example @RooToString, @RooJavaBean, and so on). When any of these Java classes are modified using an IDE or any other editor, Spring Roo checks if the AspectJ ITD files (which follow the naming convention *_Roo_*.aj, as explained earlier) corresponding to the Java classes are in sync with the Java classes. If they are not, it updates the AspectJ ITD files accordingly. Spring Roo makes use of add-ons to make modifications to the AspectJ ITD files.

There's more...

This recipe showed that if you want Roo to automatically generate a toString method and getter and setter methods for all the attributes, then annotate your class with @RooToString and @RooJavaBean annotations.

What if I add an attribute when Spring Roo is not running?

When you start Roo shell, it checks if AspectJ ITDs are in sync with the corresponding Java classes. If there are differences, then Roo updates the AspectJ ITD files to reflect the current state of the Java class. At this time Roo may even remove an ITD file if it finds that it is no longer required. For instance, if you remove all the attributes from Passenger class, then the corresponding Passenger_Roo_JavaBean.aj and Passenger_Roo_ToString.aj files are automatically removed by Roo.

Spring Roo doesn't provide commands to remove or modify an attribute. So, if you want to remove or modify an existing attribute of a Java class, you can do so using your IDE. Spring Roo will take care of removing or modifying the attribute in corresponding AspectJ ITD files.

@RooJavaBean—controlling the generation of getter and setter methods

We saw that using `@RooJavaBean` annotation introduces getter and setter methods for all the fields in a class. In some cases, you may want to control the generation of these getter and setter methods. `@RooJavaBean` allows you to do so using the `gettersByDefault` and `settersByDefault` attributes. These attributes specify whether getter and setter methods should be generated by default or not. The default value of these attributes is `true`, which means the `@RooJavaBean` annotation will create getter and setter methods in the corresponding `*_Roo_JavaBean.aj` ITD for all the fields defined in the class.

If you specify the value of both `gettersByDefault` and `settersByDefault` elements as false, then Spring Roo deletes the corresponding AspectJ ITD file.

See also

- The *Creating a Java interface* recipe shows how to create a Java interface using Spring Roo

- The *Adding fields to persistent entities* recipe of *Chapter 2, Persisting Objects Using JPA* shows the additional arguments that are available in `field` commands

Creating a Java interface

You can use Spring Roo's `interface` command or an IDE to create a Java interface. In this recipe, we will see how we can create an interface named `FlightServiceIntf`.

Getting ready

Start the Roo shell from the `C:\roo-cookbook\ch01-recipe` directory, which contains the `flight-app` Roo project.

How to do it...

Spring Roo provides the `interface` command to create a Java interface, as shown here:

```
roo> interface --class sample.roo.flightapp.service.FlightServiceIntf

Created SRC_MAIN_JAVA\sample\roo\flightapp\service\FlightServiceIntf.java

sample.roo.flightapp.service.FlightServiceIntf roo>
```

How it works...

The following table describes the arguments that the `interface` command accepts:

Argument	Purpose
class	It is a mandatory argument, which specifies the fully-qualified name of the Java interface.
path	It is an optional argument, which identifies the directory in which to create the interface, default being SCR_MAIN_JAVA.
permitReservedWords	It is an optional argument, which instructs Spring Roo to allow reserved words in the name of Java interface.

There's more...

Using Spring Roo you can't add `constants` or declare methods in your Java interface. To add constants or methods, you need to use your IDE. You may have noticed that the `rooAnnotations` argument is not available for the `interface` command; therefore, you can safely assume that Spring Roo doesn't generate any code corresponding to a Java interface when you make modifications to it.

See also

▶ The *Creating a Java class* recipe shows how to create a Java class using Spring Roo

Referring to a type from the Roo shell

In some scenarios, you may want to set the focus of your commands to a particular Java type. For instance, you may want the Roo shell to execute `field` commands on a particular Java type, so that you don't need to specify the `class` argument in your `field` commands.

Getting ready

Start the Roo shell from the `C:\roo-cookbook\ch01-recipe` directory, which contains the `flight-app` Roo project.

How to do it...

Spring Roo provides a `focus` command, which lets you change the target of your commands to a different Java type. The following sequence of steps shows how we can use the `focus` command to switch from one type to another:

1. Execute the following `focus` command to specify that you want to work with the `flight-app` project. This will change the Roo prompt to reflect the top-level package name of Roo project:

   ```
   roo> focus --class ~
   ```

2. Create `FlightDesc` class using the `class` command. Use ~ to denote that you are specifying the package name for the class with respect to the top-level package of the project. This will change the Roo prompt to refer to the `FlightDesc` type, shown as follows:

   ```
   sample.roo.Flightapp roo> class --class  ~.domain.FlightDesc
   --rooAnnotations


   Created SRC_MAIN_JAVA\sample\roo\flightapp\domain\FlightDesc.java
   ```

3. Create a `Flight` class using the `class` command. This will change the Roo prompt from `FlightDesc` type to refer to the newly created `Flight` type, as shown here:

   ```
   ~.domain.FlightDesc roo> class --class ~.domain.Flight
   --rooAnnotations


   Created SRC_MAIN_JAVA\sample\roo\flightapp\domain\Flight.java
   ```

4. Use a `focus` command to switch to the `FlightDesc` type. This will change the Roo prompt from referring to `Flight` type to `FlightDesc` type, as shown here:

   ```
   ~.domain.Flight roo> focus --class ~.domain.FlightDesc
   ```

5. Add `from_city` and `to_city` attributes to the `FlightDesc` class as shown here. As the currently referred type by Roo prompt is `FlightDesc`, you don't need to specify the `class` argument:

   ```
   ~.domain.FlightDesc roo> field string from_city
   ```
   ```
   ~.domain.FlightDesc roo> field string to_city
   ```

6. Without changing focus to the `Flight` class, add a `flight_Id` attribute to the `Flight` class by using the `field` command along with the `class` argument, as shown here. The `class` argument specifies that the target of the command is the `Flight` class and not the currently referred `FlightDesc` class:

```
~.domain.FlightDesc roo> field number --fieldName flight_Id --type
java.lang.Integer --class ~.domain.Flight
```

How it works...

The `class` argument of the `focus` command lets you specify the fully-qualified name of the Java type with which you want to work. The ~ symbol is used to indicate the top-level package of the Roo project that you specified during creation of the Roo project.

[The use of the ~ symbol simplifies providing the value of any argument that expects a fully-qualified name of a Java type in your Roo project.]

There's more...

The use of the `focus` command is mainly to simplify writing commands targeting a particular Java type. If you don't want to use the `focus` command in a situation, then you can always use the `class` argument of the command to specify the target Java type of the command.

See also

▶ The *Creating a Java class* recipe shows how to create a Java class using Spring Roo

▶ The *Adding attributes to a Java class* recipe shows how to add attributes to a Java class using Spring Roo

Creating application artifacts from Roo script

In some scenarios, you may want to generate complete enterprise application skeleton by feeding a set of Roo commands to Spring Roo from a text file. To address such scenarios Spring Roo provides the `script` command, which allows you to execute commands contained in a text file. The convention is to name the script file containing commands with a `.roo` extension.

Roo script is nothing but a text file containing Roo commands. The commands are executed in the order they appear in the text file.

In this recipe, we look at how we can execute the commands contained in a ch01.roo text file that accompanies this book. The ch01.roo file contains commands, which let's you create a fresh flight-app project.

Getting ready

If your Roo shell is still open, then exit it and remove all the files from the C:\roo-cookbook\ch01-recipe directory. Download the ch01.roo file from the book's website and copy it to C:\roo-cookbook\ch01-recipe. Start the Roo shell from the C:\roo-cookbook\ch01-recipe directory.

How to do it...

To create the application skeleton execute the script command, by specifying the file containing Roo commands, as shown here:

```
roo>script --file ch01.roo --lineNumbers
```

How it works...

The script command accepts the following arguments:

Argument	Purpose
file	It is a mandatory argument, which specifies the name of the file that contains Roo commands
lineNumbers	It is an optional argument that instructs the Roo shell to print the line numbers of the command being executed from the file

There's more...

One of the features that you will **not** find in Spring Roo is to revert the execution of a previous command. For instance, if you added a field using the `field` command and now you want to rollback the changes it made, then it is not possible. If you have mistakenly executed a Roo command, you can remove it from the `log.roo` file and re-execute the commands in `log.roo` using the `script` command.

If a Roo command fails for some reason, it is commented out in the `log.roo` file. So, you don't need to worry about removing commands that failed execution from your `log.roo` file.

See also

▸ The *Setting up Roo* recipe show how you can get started with Spring Roo.

2
Persisting Objects Using JPA

In this chapter, we will cover:

- ▶ Setting up a JPA provider for your project
- ▶ Viewing database configuration properties
- ▶ Managing database configuration properties
- ▶ Creating persistent entities
- ▶ Adding JSR 303 constraints to persistent fields
- ▶ Creating integration tests for persistent entities
- ▶ Creating new 'data on demand' for testing entities
- ▶ Creating mock tests for persistent entities
- ▶ Executing persistent entities tests
- ▶ Controlling auto-generated methods of persistent entities
- ▶ Creating applications that interact with multiple databases
- ▶ Packaging your Roo project

Introduction

Java Persistence API (**JPA**) provides a standard API for persisting Java objects to a relational database. The recipes in this chapter look at Roo commands that configure the data source and JPA provider (for example, Hibernate and OpenJPA), and Roo commands that create persistent entities of your enterprise application.

If you're using Spring *only* in the persistence layer, you'll see in this chapter how Roo can be used to quickly develop the persistence layer of your application. You'll notice that applications generated using Roo don't have a DAO (Data Access Object) layer because the domain entities generated by Roo are themselves rich in flavor, with finder and CRUD methods defined in the persistent entities. Also, Roo-generated applications don't have a service layer for abstracting business services (which in turn could access persistent entities). If you want to create a service layer for your enterprise application, it is left up to you to create services. You should create a service layer for your enterprise application if the business logic spans multiple persistent entities, if you want to put transactional boundaries in the service layer, or if you want the business logic to be contained in the service layer, and so on.

In *Chapter 4, Web Application Development with Spring Web MVC* and *Chapter 5, Web Application Development with GWT, Flex, and Spring Web Flow* we'll see that Spring Roo generates the web layer of the application, which directly interacts with the persistent entities—leaving behind service and data access layers.

Setting up a JPA provider for your project

In enterprise applications, data is persisted in one or more data stores. JPA provides a standard API for managing data in relational databases. In this task we'll look at the `persistence setup` command to configure a JPA persistence provider for a Roo project.

Getting ready

Create a sub-directory `ch02-recipes` inside the `C:\roo-cookbook` directory.

To set up a JPA provider, we first need to create a Roo project. To create a new Roo project, download `ch02.roo` file from the book's website and copy it to the `ch02-recipes` directory.

Open the command prompt and go to the `ch02-recipes` directory. Now, start the Roo shell and execute commands in `ch02.roo` script using the `script` command, as explained in the *Creating application artifacts from a Roo script* recipe of *Chapter 1*. Successful execution of the `ch02.roo` script creates a `flight-app` Eclipse project which you can import in your Eclipse IDE.

How to do it...

The following steps will demonstrate how to set up a JPA provider:

1. To set up Hibernate as the JPA provider for your application, execute the `persistence setup` command, as shown here:

   ```
   ... roo> persistence setup --provider HIBERNATE --database MYSQL
   --databaseName myFlightAppDB

   Updated SRC_MAIN_RESOURCES\META-INF\spring\applicationContext.xml
   ```

```
Created SRC_MAIN_RESOURCES\META-INF\persistence.xml

Created SRC_MAIN_RESOURCES\META-INF\spring\database.properties

Updated ROOT\pom.xml [Added dependencies mysql:mysql-connector-
java:5.1.13, org.
hibernate:hibernate-core:3.6.1.Final, ..]
```

2. Execute the `perform eclipse` Roo command, as shown here:

   ```
   ..roo> perform eclipse
   ```

3. Import the flight-app Roo project into your Eclipse IDE.

> It is recommended that whenever you find that a Roo command updates the `pom.xml` file, then executes `perform eclipse` (for Eclipse IDE) or perfom command `--mavenCommand idea:idea` (for IntelliJ IDEA), you should update the classpath settings of the project. This should be followed by refreshing your project in the IDE.

How it works...

The `persistence setup` command is processed by the **JPA add-on** of Spring Roo. The following table describes the arguments that the `persistence setup` command accepts:

Argument	Description
provider	This is a mandatory argument that specifies the JPA provider that you want to use for your enterprise application. This argument accepts a pre-defined value, like HIBERNATE, OPENJPA, and so on.
database	This is a mandatory argument that identifies the database product used by your enterprise application to persist application data. It accepts a pre-defined value, like MYSQL, DB2, and so on.
databaseName	Identifies the name of the database which your enterprise application interacts with. This argument is useful only if you're not using a JNDI-bound data source in your enterprise application.
hostName	Identifies the location of the remote database. Defaults to `localhost`.This argument is useful only if you're not using a JNDI-bound data source in your enterprise application.
jndiDataSource	Specifies the JNDI-bound data source that is used by the application.

Argument	Description
username	Identifies the username required for connecting to the data source.This argument is useful only if you're not using a JNDI-bound data source in your enterprise application.
password	Identifies the password required for connecting to the data source.This argument is useful only if you're not using a JNDI-bound data source in your enterprise application.
applicationId	Identifies the application identifier if you want to deploy the application on Google App Engine. We'll discuss this argument in detail in the *Deploying a GWT application on GAE* recipe in *Chapter 6*.
persistenceUnit	Specifies the name of the persistence unit to be used in the Roo-generated persistence.xml file. You must use this argument if your application interacts with multiple databases.
transactionManager	**[Supported since Spring Roo 1.1.5]** Name of the transaction manager corresponding to the persistence unit. You must use this argument if your application interacts with multiple databases.

As the output from the persistence setup command suggests, the following files in our flight-app Roo project are created or modified:

▶ persistence.xml: this is a *newly* created file which is used by a JPA provider to discover persistence provider information, which is Hibernate in the case of the flight-app project.

▶ database.properties: this is a *newly* created file which contains data source information, such as username, password, data source URL, and driver class.

▶ applicationContext.xml: this file was created when we created our Roo project. This file is now modified to include data source, transaction manager, and JPA EntityManagerFactory definitions. Later in this section, we'll see these definitions in detail.

▶ pom.xml: this file was created when we created our Roo project. It is now modified to include project dependencies on MySQL connector, Hibernate, Hibernate Validator, and so on. This shows that Roo adds dependencies to your project only when you add additional functionality to your enterprise application. For instance, if you are not using JPA, then JPA-related dependencies are not added to your project unless you execute the persistence setup command.

The following XML fragment shows the `persistence.xml` file created by Spring Roo:

```
<persistence ....>
 <persistence-unit name="persistenceUnit"
                   transaction-type="RESOURCE_LOCAL">
   <provider>org.hibernate.ejb.HibernatePersistence</provider>
   <properties>
     <property name="hibernate.dialect"
         value="org.hibernate.dialect.MySQL5InnoDBDialect"/>
     <property name="hibernate.hbm2ddl.auto" value="create"/>
     ...
   </properties>
 </persistence-unit>
</persistence>
```

The preceding listing shows that Roo creates a `persistence.xml` file based on the JPA provider and database information that you supplied to the `persistence setup` command. The `name` attribute of the `<persistence-unit>` element specifies the persistence unit name. If the `persistenceUnit` argument of `persistence setup` is not specified, then by default, Roo sets the `name` attribute value to `persistenceUnit`. The `create` value of the `hibernate.hbm2ddl.auto` property indicates that every time Hibernate `SessionFactory` is created, the database is re-created. You may want to change the value of `hibernate.hbm2ddl.auto` from `create` to `validate` or `update` or `create-drop`, depending upon how you want Hibernate to manage your database schema based on the mappings provided in JPA entities.

Also, if your enterprise application updates multiple data sources, then you should set the value of the `transaction-type` attribute of the `persistence-unit` element to `JTA'` (Java Transaction API), instead of `RESOURCE_LOCAL`.

The following code shows the elements that were added to the `applicationContext.xml` file when you executed the `persistence setup` command:

```
<bean class="org.apache.commons.dbcp.BasicDataSource"
   destroy-method="close" id="dataSource">
  <property name="driverClassName"
            value="${database.driverClassName}"/>
  <property name="url" value="${database.url}"/>
  <property name="username" value="${database.username}"/>
  <property name="password" value="${database.password}"/>
  ...
</bean>

<bean
  class="org.springframework.orm.jpa.JpaTransactionManager"
  id="transactionManager">
```

```
    <property name="entityManagerFactory"
              ref="entityManagerFactory"/>
    </bean>

    <tx:annotation-driven mode="aspectj"
        transaction-manager="transactionManager"/>

    <bean
        class="org.springframework.orm.jpa.
        LocalContainerEntityManagerFactoryBean"
        id="entityManagerFactory">
      <property name="dataSource" ref="dataSource"/>
    </bean>
```

As shown in the preceding XML, the additional beans added by the `persistence setup` command are:

- `dataSource`: refers to a `javax.sql.DataSource` object, which represents an application's data source. The properties for the data source are contained in the `database.properties` file that was created by `persistence setup`. The `database.properties` file is read by Spring's application context because of the presence of the `<property-placeholder>` element in the `applicationContext.xml` file (refer to the *Creating a Roo project* recipe in *Chapter 1*).

- `entityManagerFactory`: refers to Spring's factory bean, which is responsible for creating JPA `EntityManagerFactory`. You should use `LocalContainerEntityManagerFactoryBean` because it provides maximum control over the configuration of `EntityManagerFactory`.

- `transactionManager`: refers to the `JpaTransactionManager` bean, which is appropriate if your application uses a single `EntityManagerFactory`, that is, only a single database or transactional resource.

The `<annotation-driven>` element of Spring's `transaction` schema (`spring-tx-3.0.xsd`) suggests that you should use Spring's `@Transactional` annotation to mark methods as transactional. The value `aspectj` of the `mode` attribute means that the AspectJ transaction aspect is weaved into the class at load-time or compile-time. If you want to use Spring's AOP framework for proxying the `@Transactional` annotated beans (which are usually your service classes), then specify the value of the `mode` attribute as `proxy` or don't specify the `mode` attribute at all.

If you keep the `mode` attribute value as `aspectj` (which is recommended) then you should take care of the following requirements:

- Enable *compile-time* (or *load-time*) *weaving* for your application. You don't need to worry about this because if you package your Roo project into a WAR or JAR (refer to the *Packaging your Roo* project recipe of this chapter), then the AspectJ compiler Maven Plugin (refer to the *Creating a Roo project* recipe of *Chapter 1*) is used to weave the AspectJ transaction aspect (defined in `spring-aspects.jar` file) into the Roo methods annotated with the `@Transactional` annotation.

- Use the `@Transactional` annotation on the concrete class and not on the interface.

There's more...

Now, let's look at how we can use the JNDI-bound data source in applications generated by Spring Roo.

JNDI-bound data source

In most real-world applications, the `javax.sql.DataSource` object is obtained from JNDI and not created from properties defined in a properties file. To access a JNDI-bound data source, instead of relying on Spring to create `DataSource` for the application, use the `jndiDataSource` argument of `persistence setup` to specify the JNDI name of the `DataSource`, as shown here:

```
persistence setup --provider HIBERNATE --database MYSQL --jndiDataSource
jdbc/accountDB
```

If the `jndiDataSource` argument is specified, then Spring Roo adds the `jndi-lookup` element of Spring's `jee` schema to the `applicationContext.xml` file, as shown here:

```
<beans ... xmlns:jee="http://www.springframework.org/schema/jee" ...
xsi:schemaLocation="http://www.springframework.org/schema/jee http://
www.springframework.org/schema/jee/spring-jee-3.0.xsd">
.....
<jee:jndi-lookup id="dataSource" jndi-name="jdbc/accountDB" />
.....
```

The `jndi-lookup` element, shown above, is responsible for accessing the `DataSource` configured in JNDI with the name `jdbc/accountDB` (referred to by the `jndi-name` attribute) and making it available in Spring's application context with bean `id` as `dataSource`.

If you compare the preceding `applicationContext.xml` file with the one shown earlier, you can see that the only difference is how the `dataSource` bean is made available to the Spring's application context.

See also

▸ Refer to the *Creating persistent entities* recipe to see how to create persistent entities

▸ Refer to the *Creating applications that interact with multiple databases* recipe for details on how to develop applications that interact with multiple databases

Viewing database configuration properties

In this recipe we'll see how the `database properties list` command lets us view the list of database properties and their values, as specified in the `database.properties` file.

Getting ready

Refer to the *Setting up a JPA provider for your project* recipe to create a `flight-app` Roo project and to set up a persistence provider using the `persistence setup` command.

 You won't need this recipe if you're using a JNDI-bound data source in your Roo project.

How to do it...

Follow these steps to view database properties:

1. Start the Roo shell from the `C:\roo-cookbook\ch02-recipes` directory.

2. To view database properties defined in the `database.properties` file located in `SRC_MAIN_RESOURCES\META-INF\spring\` directory, you can use the `database properties list` command, as shown here:

   ```
   roo> database properties list

   database.driverClassName = com.mysql.jdbc.Driver
   database.password =
   database.url = jdbc:mysql://localhost:3306/myFlightAppDB
   database.username =
   ```

How it works...

The `database properties list` command is processed by the **JPA add-on**. Instead of using the `database properties list` command you can use the `properties list` command (refer to the *Viewing properties defined in a properties file* recipe of *Chapter 1*), which shows the properties contained in a `properties` file. The end result of using either of the commands is the same, the only difference being that you need to specify the `name` and `path` arguments in the `properties list` command to refer to the `database.properties` file.

There's more...

Instead of using Spring Roo, you can also view the `database.properties` file using an IDE like Eclipse or STS. The whole idea of using Spring Roo's `database properties list` command is to allow developers to look at the database properties without switching to the IDE.

See also

▶ The next recipe, *Managing database configuration properties*, shows how you can add, remove, and modify properties defined in the `database.properties` file of your Roo project.

Managing database configuration properties

In the previous recipe, we saw how we can view the database configuration properties defined in the `database.properties` file using the `database properties list` command. In this recipe, we'll look at how we can add, modify, or remove properties from the `database.properties` file using the `database properties set` and `database properties remove` commands.

The following table shows the properties that we'll add, modify, and remove from the `database.properties` file:

Property	Action
`database.username`	Modified to `database.username = root`
`database.password`	Modified to `database.password = asarin`
`database.url = jdbc\:mysql\://localhost\:3306/myFlightAppDB`	Removed from `database.properties`
`database.modified.url = jdbc\:mysql\://localhost\:3406/myFlightAppDB`	Added to `database.properties`
`database.initialPoolSize=10`	Added to `database.properties`

Getting ready

Refer to the *Setting up a JPA provider for your project* recipe to create the `flight-app` Roo project and to set up a persistence provider using the `persistence setup` command.

Start the Roo shell from the `C:\roo-cookbook\ch02-recipes` directory.

 You won't need this recipe if you're using JNDI-bound data source in your Roo project.

How to do it...

The following steps will show you how to add, modify, or remove properties:

1. The `database properties set` command is useful if you want to modify properties defined in the `database.properties` file, as shown here:

   ```
   roo> database properties set --key database.username --value root
   ```

   ```
   roo> database properties set --key database.password --value
   asarin
   ```

2. The `database properties set` command can also be used to add new properties to the `database.properties` file, as shown here:

   ```
   roo> database properties set --key database.modified.url --value
   jdbc:mysql://localhost:3406/myFlightAppDB
   ```

   ```
   roo> database properties set --key database.initialPoolSize
   --value 10
   ```

3. The `database properties remove` command is for removing an existing property from the `database.properties` file, as shown here:

   ```
   roo> database properties remove --key database.url
   ```

How it works...

The `database properties set` and `database properties remove` commands are processed by **JPA add-on**. Instead of using these commands you can use the `properties set` and `properties remove` command also, as shown in the *Managing properties defined in a properties file* recipe in *Chapter 1, Getting Started with Spring Roo*

It is important to note that if you modify the names of properties in the `database.properties` file, then these modifications must be reflected in the `dataSource` bean defined in the `applicationContext.xml` file of your Roo project.

Instead of using Spring Roo, you can also modify the `database.properties` file using an IDE like Eclipse or STS. Using Roo commands to modify the `database.properties` file allows developers to replay the actions taken from the Roo shell using the `script` command.

See also

▶ Refer to the *Viewing database configuration properties* recipe, described earlier in this chapter, to see how you can view properties defined in the `database.properties` file using the Roo command

Creating persistent entities

In this recipe we look at how Spring Roo simplifies the creation of JPA entities using the `entity` and `field` commands. In this recipe we'll create a `Flight` JPA entity which has a composite primary key. Refer to the *Creating a many-to-one relationship between entities* recipe of *Chapter 3, Advanced JPA Support in Spring Roo* to see how to create persistent entities with surrogate keys.

The following figure shows the attributes of the `Flight` entity and its composite primary key (`FlightKey`):

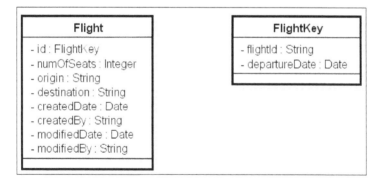

Getting ready

Exit the Roo shell and delete the contents of the `C:\roo-cookbook\ch02-recipes` directory.

Execute the `ch02_jpa_setup.roo` script. It creates a `flight-app` Roo project and sets up Hibernate as the persistence provider using the `persistence setup` command. If you are using a different database than MySQL or your connection settings are different from what is specified in the script, then modify the script accordingly.

Start the Roo shell from the `C:\roo-cookbook\ch02-recipes` directory.

> The `ch02_persistent_entities.roo` script that accompanies
> this book creates the `flight-app` project, sets up Hibernate as
> the persistence provider, modifies the `database.username` and
> `database.password` properties in the `database.properties`
> file, and executes the commands shown in this recipe.

How to do it...

The following steps will demonstrate how to create persistent entities:

1. Create a `Flight` entity in the `sample.roo.flightapp.domain` package using
   the `entity` command:

   ```
   ..roo> entity --class ~.domain.Flight --identifierType ~.domain.
   FlightKey --table FLIGHT_TBL
   ```

2. Add fields to the `Flight` entity using `field` commands:

   ```
   ..roo> field number --type java.lang.Integer --fieldName
   numOfSeats
   ```

   ```
   ..roo> field string --fieldName origin
   ```

   ```
   ..roo> field string --fieldName destination
   ```

   ```
   ..roo> field date --type java.util.Date --fieldName createdDate
   ```

   ```
   ..roo> field date --type java.util.Date --fieldName modifiedDate
   ```

   ```
   ..roo> field string --fieldName createdBy
   ```

   ```
   ..roo> field string --fieldName modifiedBy
   ```

3. Switch focus to the `FlightKey` class (that was auto-generated in the `sample.roo.`
   `flightapp.domain` package when we created the `Flight` entity in Step 1):

   ```
   ..roo> focus --class ~.domain.FlightKey
   ```

4. Add `flightId` and `departureDate` fields to the `FlightKey` class:

   ```
   ..roo> field string --fieldName flightId
   ```

   ```
   ..roo> field date --fieldName departureDate --type java.util.Date
   ```

> The output of the `entity` command is not shown above for brevity.
> We'll discuss the important ITD files generated corresponding to a JPA
> entity in the *How it works...* section.

How it works...

The `entity` command is used to create a JPA persistent entity. It provides a couple of arguments which should be sufficient for most scenarios that you encounter while developing the persistence layer of your enterprise application. For instance, the `mappedSuperclass` argument marks the class with the `@MapperSuperclass` JPA annotation (refer to the *Creating a mapped superclass* recipe in *Chapter 3, Advanced JPA Support in Spring Roo*), the `inheritanceType` argument adds the `@Inheritance` JPA annotation to let you specify the inheritance strategy followed for persisting classes of an inheritance hierarchy, and so on.

The following table describes arguments that you can pass to the `entity` command:

Argument	Description
class	This is a mandatory argument which specifies the fully-qualified name of the persistent entity class. You can use the '~' symbol while specifying the fully-qualified name.
mappedSuperclass	Instructs Roo that the class is a 'mapped superclass'. If specified, the generated class is annotated with the `@MappedSuperclass` JPA annotation.
extends	Identifies the superclass of the entity class.
abstract	Specifies that the generated entity is an abstract entity.
inheritanceType	Specifies the inheritance strategy used for persisting the entity. It accepts one of the following values: `JOINED`, `SINGLE_TABLE`, and `TABLE_PER_CLASS`. If specified, it adds the `@Inheritance` JPA annotation to the entity class.
table	Specifies the name of the table to which the entity is mapped.
identifierField	Specifies the name of the identifier field in the entity. By default the name of the identifier field is id.
identifierType	Specifies the Java type of the identifier field. This argument can accept values pre-defined by Roo, such as `java.lang.Long`, `java.lang.Double`, and so on, or it can take a custom Java type.
	If your entity uses a composite primary key, then you'll use a custom Java type. For instance, the `Flight` entity specifies `FlightKey` as the `identifierType` because it's the composite primary key class of the `Flight` entity. Also note that the composite primary key class is auto-generated when you execute the `entity` command.
identifierColumn	Specifies the table column to which the identifier field is mapped. If your entity uses a composite primary key, then you **must not** use this argument.

Argument	Description
versionField	Specifies the name of the version field in the entity. By default the name of the version field is version.
versionColumn	The table column to which the version field is mapped.
testAutomatically	Instructs Roo to automatically generate integration tests for the entity. In the *Creating integration tests for persistent entities* recipe we'll discuss integration testing of persistent entities in detail.
schema, catalog	Arguments for specifying qualifiers for table names in the database. These arguments translate into schema and catalog attributes of the @Table JPA annotation.
persistenceUnit	Name of the persistence unit, defined in the persistence.xml file, with which the persistent entity is associated.
transactionManager	**[Supported since Spring Roo 1.1.5]** Name of the transaction manager which is used for the persistent entity.

You may have noticed that the field command that we have used for adding fields to the Flight JPA entity is the same field command that we had used to add attributes to our Java class in the *Adding attributes to a Java class* recipe in *Chapter 1, Getting Started with Spring Roo*.

The following code shows the Flight entity which was created by the entity command:

```
@RooJavaBean
@RooToString
@RooEntity(identifierType = FlightKey.class, table= "FLIGHT_TBL")
public class Flight {
    private Integer numOfSeats;
    private String origin;
    private String destination;
    ...
}
```

In the Flight.java code, the @RooJavaBean and @RooToString annotations are the most commonly used Roo annotations. For more information on @RooJavaBean and @RooToString, please refer to the *Creating a Java class* and *Adding attributes to a Java class* recipes in *Chapter 1, Getting Started with Spring Roo*. The @RooEntity annotation provides details about the persistent entity which is the Flight entity in the previous code. The identifierType attribute specifies the identifier type of Flight entity, which is FlightKey—the composite primary key class of the Flight entity. The table attribute specifies the database table to which the Flight JPA entity maps.

You'll notice that the fields of the entity don't use JPA `@Column` annotation to provide a mapping of the fields to the corresponding `FLIGHT_TBL` table columns. Later in this recipe we'll see how `field` command can be used to specify table column mapping for the fields.

The `@RooEntity` annotation introduces a couple of persistence related methods and attributes using the ITD file, `Flight_Roo_Entity.aj`, as shown here:

```
privileged aspect Flight_Roo_Entity {
    declare @type: Flight: @Entity;

    declare @type: Flight: @Table(name = "FLIGHT_TBL");

    @PersistenceContext
    transient EntityManager Flight.entityManager;

    @EmbeddedId
    private FlightKey Flight.id;

    @Version
    @Column(name = "version")
    private Integer Flight.version;

    public FlightKey Flight.getId() {
        return this.id;
    }
    public void Flight.setId(FlightKey id) {
        this.id = id;
    }
    public Integer Flight.getVersion() {
        return this.version;
    }
    public void Flight.setVersion(Integer version) {
        this.version = version;
    }
    ...
}
```

The persistence related methods (such as, `persist`, `remove`, and so on) have been omitted from the previous code listing for brevity. Auto-generated persistence related methods are discussed in the *Controlling auto-generated methods of persistent entities* recipe. As you can see, Spring Roo generates the necessary code to create a fully-functional JPA entity.

The following code in `Flight_Roo_Entity.aj` adds `@Table` and `@Entity` JPA annotations in the `Flight` class:

```
declare @type: Flight: @Entity;
declare @type: Flight: @Table(name = "FLIGHT_TBL");
```

In `Flight_Roo_Entity.aj`, the `FlightKey` field is annotated with the `@EmbeddedId` annotation because it is the composite primary key class of the `Flight` entity. Roo also creates a `version` field in `Flight_Roo_Entity.aj`, which maps to the `version` column of the table to which the `Flight` entity maps. If we create a persistent entity that doesn't use a composite primary key, then instead of `@EmbeddedId`, Spring Roo uses the `@Id` annotation to annotate the primary key.

While generating an entity, Spring Roo also generates a `<entity-name>_Roo_Configurable.aj` ITD, which is responsible for adding Spring's `@Configurable` annotation to the entity. Here, `<entity-name>` is the name of the persistent entity.

The entity instances are typically created outside the Spring's application context by the JPA provider or by using the `new` operator. The use of `@Configurable` annotation is particularly useful in entities because it allows injecting beans configured in Spring's application context into the entity instance. It is because of the `@Configurable` annotation that Spring is able to inject the `EntityManager` instance into persistent entities.

The following code listing shows the `FlightKey` class of the `flight-app` application:

```
@RooToString
@RooIdentifier
public final class FlightKey {
    private String flightId;
    private Date departureDate;
}
```

In the code, the `@RooIdentifier` annotation of Spring Roo is responsible for adding constructors, getter and setter methods for fields, and also provides implementation of the `hashCode` and `equals` methods of the `FlightKey` composite primary key class. Spring Roo generates a `<entity-name>_Roo_Identifier.aj` ITD file corresponding to the `@RooIdentifier` annotation on the composite primary key class. Here, `<entity-name>` is the name of the persistent entity.

The following code shows the methods and attributes defined in the `FlightKey_Roo_Identifier.aj` ITD file:

```
privileged aspect FlightKey_Roo_Identifier {

    declare @type: FlightKey: @Embeddable;

    public FlightKey.new(String flightId, Date departureDate) {}
```

```
    private FlightKey.new() {}

    public String FlightKey.getFlightId() {
      return this.flightId;
    }

    public Date FlightKey.getDepartureDate() {
      return this.departureDate;
    }

    public boolean FlightKey.equals(Object obj) {}

    public int FlightKey.hashCode() {}


}
```

In the code, implementation details of methods and constructors have not been shown for brevity. As the code suggests, `FlightKey_Roo_Identifier.aj` ITD adds the following methods, constructors, fields, and annotations to the `FlightKey` class:

▸ Adds the `@Embeddable` JPA annotation to the `FlightKey` class, which is required because the `FlightKey` class is added to the `Flight` entity using the `@EmbeddedId` JPA annotation

▸ Adds a no-argument constructor to the `FlightKey` class

▸ Adds a constructor that accepts fields defined in the `FlightKey` class as arguments

▸ Adds getter and setter methods for the fields defined in the `FlightKey` class

▸ Adds implementation for the `equals` and `hashCode` methods of the `java.lang.Object` class

The `@RooIdentifier` annotation accepts two attributes—`gettersByDefault` and `settersByDefault`, which allow you to control the creation of getter and setter methods for the fields defined in the `FlightKey` class. `@RooIdentifier` also accepts a third attribute, `dbManaged`, which is useful if the JPA entity was created by Roo using database reverse engineering. We'll discuss the `dbManaged` attribute in detail in the *Creating entities from a database* recipe of *Chapter 3, Advanced JPA Support in Spring Roo*.

There's more...

We'll now look at how to add fields to persistent entities that contain information about the table columns to which the fields map.

Adding table column information in persistent entity fields

Delete the `origin` field from the `Flight.java` file and ensure that Spring Roo is running in the background to remove the `origin` field from AspectJ ITD files.

Now, add the `origin` field to the `Flight` persistent entity using the `field` command, and specify the name of the table column, `FLT_ORIGIN`, to which the `origin` field maps, as the value of `column` argument:

```
~.domain.Flight roo> field string --fieldName origin --column FLT_ORIGIN
```

The presence of the `column` argument indicates that the field is annotated with the `@Column` JPA annotation with the value of the `column` argument representing the value of the `name` attribute of the `@Column` annotation, as shown here:

```
@RooJavaBean
@RooToString
@RooEntity(table = "FLIGHT_TBL")
public class Flight {

    @Column(name = "FLT_ORIGIN")
    private String origin;
}
```

The Roo script `ch02_persistent_fields.roo` that accompanies this book contains commands to create the `flight-app` project consisting of the `Flight` entity and the `FlightKey` class. Additionally, the script adds database column mapping for all the persistent fields defined in the `Flight` entity and `FlightKey` class. It is recommended that you exit the Roo shell, remove all the files from `ch02-recipes` directory, and recreate the `flight-app` Roo project by executing the `ch02_persistent_fields.roo` script.

The class argument in roo commands

We saw in a couple of recipes that the `focus` command is used to switch command reference from one class or interface to another class or interface in the Roo project, followed by Roo commands that apply to that class or interface. Instead of using the `focus` command, you can use the `class` argument of the `roo` command (if supported by the `roo` command) to explicitly specify the class or interface to which the command applies. For instance, we can add a `flightId` field to `FlightKey` class without using the `focus` command, as shown here:

```
...roo>  field string --class ~.domain.Flight --fieldName origin --column
FLT_ORIGIN
```

As we can see from the `field` command, we can specify a fully-qualified name of the class on which the command applies.

▸ Refer to the *Controlling auto-generated methods of persistent entities* recipe to see how you can control Spring Roo generated methods corresponding to a persistent entity

Adding JSR 303 constraints to persistent fields

JSR 303 (bean validation) defines a standard approach for *annotations-based* JavaBeans validation. In this recipe we'll look at how Spring Roo's `field` command can be used to add JSR 303 validation constraints to persistent fields of entities.

The following table shows the validation constraints that apply to fields defined in the `Flight` entity and `FlightKey` class of our `flight-app` project:

Persistent field	Constraint	JSR 303 annotation
`Flight -> createdDate`	Not null	`@NotNull`
`Flight -> createdBy`	Not null	`@NotNull`
`Flight -> numOfSeats`	Not null	`@NotNull`
	Maximum seats 200	`@DecimalMax("200")`
	Minimum seats 100	`@DecimalMin("100")`
`Flight -> origin`	Not null	`@NotNull`
	Maximum length of value of `origin` is 20, minimum length is 3	`@Size(min=3, max=20)`
`Flight -> destination`	Not null	`@NotNull`
	Maximum length of value of `destination` is 20, minimum length is 3	`@Size(min=3, max=20)`
`FlightKey -> flightId`	Not null	`@NotNull`
`FlightKey -> departureDate`	Not null	`@NotNull`

Getting ready

Exit the Roo shell and delete the contents of the `C:\roo-cookbook\ch02-recipes` directory.

Execute the `ch02_jpa_setup.roo` script. It creates a `flight-app` Roo project and sets up Hibernate as a persistence provider using the `persistence setup` command. If you are using a different database than MySQL or your connection settings are different from what is specified in the script, then modify the script accordingly.

Start the Roo shell from the `C:\roo-cookbook\ch02-recipes` directory.

How to do it...

Follow these steps to add JSR 303 constraints:

1. Create the `Flight` entity in the `sample.roo.flightapp.domain` package using the `entity` command:

   ```
   ..roo> entity --class ~.domain.Flight --identifierType ~.domain.
   FlightKey --table FLIGHT_TBL
   ```

2. Add `numOfSeats`, `origin`, `destination`, `createdBy`, `modifiedBy`, `createdDate`, and `modifiedDate` fields to the `Flight` entity, as shown here:

   ```
   ..roo> field number --type java.lang.Integer --fieldName
   numOfSeats --column NUM_OF_SEATS --notNull --decimalMin 100
   --decimalMax 200

   ..roo> field string --fieldName origin --column FLT_ORIGIN
   --notNull --sizeMin 3 --sizeMax 20

   ..roo> field string --fieldName destination --column FLT_
   DESTINATION --notNull --sizeMin 3 --sizeMax 20

   ..roo> field date --type java.util.Date --fieldName createdDate
   --column CREATED_DATE --notNull

   ..roo> field string --fieldName createdBy --column CREATED_BY
   --notNull
   ```

3. Set the Roo prompt on the `FlightKey` primary key class using the `focus` command:

   ```
   ..roo> focus --class ~.domain.FlightKey
   ```

4. Add `flightId` and `departureDate` fields to the `FlightKey` entity, as shown here:

   ```
   ..roo> field string --fieldName flightId --column FLIGHT_ID
   --notNull

   ..roo> field date --fieldName departureDate --type java.util.Date
   --notNull --column FLT_DEP_DATE
   ```

How it works...

In the `field` command you can use arguments such as `notNull`, `nullRequired`, `decimalMax`, `decimalMin`, `regexp`, `sizeMax`, and `sizeMin` to specify the validation constraints that apply to a field. The use of these arguments will result in the generation of fields that are annotated with JSR 303 annotations, as shown here for `Flight` entity:

```
public class Flight {

    @NotNull
    @DecimalMin("100")
    @DecimalMax("200")
    @Column(name="NUM_OF_SEATS")
    private Integer numOfSeats;

    @NotNull
    @Column(name = "FLT_ORIGIN")
    @Size(min = 3, max = 20)
    private String origin;

    @NotNull
    @Column(name = "FLT_DESTINATION")
    @Size(min = 3, max = 20)
    private String destination;
    .....
}
```

There's more...

Using JSR 303 constraints is not limited to domain objects; you can use JSR 303 constraints in any class, irrespective of the tier in which the class is used. For instance, you can use JSR 303 constraints in command or form-backing objects of your web tier.

See also

▶   Refer to the *Creating persistent entities* recipe to see how to create persistent entities and add fields to them

Controlling auto-generated methods of persistent entities

When a persistent entity is created using Roo, a number of methods are auto-generated to simplify usage and testing of the entity. For instance, when the `Flight` entity was created in the *Creating persistent entities* recipe, the corresponding `Flight_Roo_Entity.aj` AspectJ ITD file was created with methods like `persist`, `remove`, `merge`, `flush`, `findFlight`, and so on.

In this recipe we'll look at how to control the generation of entity methods by:

> Specifying the prefix to be used for a method

> Instructing Roo not to generate a particular method

For the purpose of this recipe, we'll instruct Roo to do the following for the `Flight` entity:

> Change the name of the `persist` auto-generated method to `save`

> Change the name of the `findFlight` auto-generated method to `finderForFlight`

> Don't generate `countFlights` and `findFlightEntries` methods

Getting ready

Exit the Roo shell and delete the contents of the `C:\roo-cookbook\ch02-recipes` directory.

Execute the `ch02_jsr303_fields.roo` script. It creates a `flight-app` Roo project and sets up Hibernate as the persistence provider using the `persistence setup` command. The script also creates a `Flight` entity, which has `FlightKey` as its composite primary key class, and adds fields to the `Flight` and `FlightKey` classes. If you are using a different database than MySQL or your connection settings are different from what is specified in the script, then modify the script accordingly.

Start the Roo shell from the `C:\roo-cookbook\ch02-recipes` directory.

How to do it...

The following steps will show you how to control auto-generated methods:

1. Open `Flight.java` file in your favorite IDE.

2. Change the `@RooEntity` annotation to:

```
@RooEntity(identifierType = FlightKey.class,
    persistMethod="save", countMethod="",
```

```
findMethod="finderFor", findEntriesMethod="")
```

3. You'll see the following output on the Roo shell:

   **Updated SRC_MAIN_JAVA\sample\roo\flightapp\domain\Flight_Roo_
   Entity.aj**

How it works...

The @RooEntity annotation of Roo is responsible for managing the methods defined in the corresponding *_Roo_Entity.aj AspectJ ITD. @RooEntity annotation defines attributes which let you specify the prefix to be used for the methods generated by Roo and also to control whether a particular method is generated or not. The @RooEntity annotation also defines attributes which you can use to specify entity identifier and version fields name, type, and table column information.

In the previous code, the @RooEntity annotation specifies the following information:

- identifierType = FlightKey.class: specifies the Flight entity identifier type as FlightKey class. The default value is Long.

- persistMethod = "save": the value 'save' means that instead of generating a persist method, Roo generates a method named save.

- countMethod = "": as the value is "", it means Roo must not generate countFlights method.

- findEntriesMethod = "": as the value is "", it means Roo must not generate findFlightEnteries method.

- findMethod = "finderFor": as the value is finderFor, instead of generating findFlight method, Roo will generate method named finderForFlight.

The follow table describes all the attributes defined by `@RooEntity` annotation:

@RooEntity attributes	Description
`countMethod`, `findAllMethod`, `findEntriesMethod`, `findMethod`, `flushMethod`, `mergeMethod`, `persistMethod`, `removeMethod`	Attributes for specifying the prefix of the generated method. A value of "" means that the method will not be generated by Roo.
`identifierColumn`, `identifierField`, `identifierType`	Attributes for specifying JPA entity identifier information, which includes the name of the table column to which the identifier field maps, the name of the identifier field in the AspectJ ITD file, and the Java type of the identifier field.
`versionField`, `versionType`, `versionColumn`	Attributes for specifying the version field information, which includes name of the table column to which the version field maps, name of the version field in the AspectJ ITD file, and the Java type of the version field.
`finders`	Attribute that specifies names of the methods for which dynamic finder methods are generated by Roo.
`mappedSuperclass`	Instructs Roo to generate a `@MappedSuperclass` annotation instead of `@Entity`. We'll see mapped superclass usage in *Chapter 3, Advanced JPA Support in Spring Roo*.
`inheritanceType`	Inheritance type to be used for the JPA entity.
`persistenceUnit`	The name of the persistence unit, defined in `persistence.xml`, with which the entity is associated.
`transactionManager`	**[Supported since Spring Roo 1.1.5]** The name of the transaction manager associated with the entity.

See also

▸ Refer to the *Creating persistent entities* recipe to see how to create JPA entities using Roo

Creating integration tests for persistent entities

Spring Roo provides a `test integration` command that simplifies the creation of integration tests for persistent entities. In this recipe, we'll look at how to create an integration test for an entity.

Exit the Roo shell and delete the contents of the `C:\roo-cookbook\ch02-recipes` directory.

Execute the `ch02_jsr303_fields.roo` script. It creates a `flight-app` Roo project and sets up Hibernate as persistence provider using the `persistence setup` command. The script also creates a `Flight` entity, which has `FlightKey` as its composite primary key class, and adds fields to the `Flight` and `FlightKey` classes. If you are using a different database than MySQL or your connection settings are different from what is specified in the script, then modify the script accordingly.

Start the Roo shell from the `C:\roo-cookbook\ch02-recipes` directory.

How to do it...

The following steps will show you how to create integration tests:

1. Change the focus of the Roo commands to the `Flight` entity:

   roo> focus --class ~.domain.Flight

2. Execute the `test integration` command:

   ~.domain.Flight> test integration

   Created ...FlightDataOnDemand.java

   Created ...FlightIntegrationTest.java

   Created ...FlightDataOnDemand_Roo_DataOnDemand.aj

   Created ...FlightIntegrationTest_Roo_IntegrationTest.aj

   Created ... FlightDataOnDemand_Roo_Configurable.aj

   Created ... Flight_Roo_Configurable.aj

How it works...

The `test integration` command generates files in the `src\test\java` folder. The output from the `test integration` command shows that the following files are generated:

- ▸ `FlightDataOnDemand.java`: represents a 'data on demand' class which provides the necessary data for automated integration testing of the `Flight` entity.

- ▸ `FlightDataOnDemand_Roo_DataOnDemand.aj`: this AspectJ ITD file defines methods that are added to the `FlightDataOnDemand` class during compilation. The methods defined in this AspectJ ITD file are responsible for dynamically creating 10 instances of the `Flight` entity and storing them in the database—referred to as seed data. These `Flight` instances are used while performing integration testing. The entity instances created by AspectJ ITD comply with the JSR 303 constraints that apply on persistent fields of the entity. By default, a transaction associated with a test method is rolled-back after the test method completes—the reason why you won't see seed data in database tables after the execution of integration tests. Refer to the *Executing persistent entities tests* recipe to see an example usage of Spring's @ `Roolback` annotation to specify that transactions associated with test methods must not be rolled-back.

- ▸ `FlightIntegrationTest.java`: represents the JUnit integration test class for the `Flight` entity.

- ▸ `FlightIntegrationTest_Roo_IntegrationTest.aj`: AspectJ ITD responsible for defining integration testing methods for the `Flight` entity.

- ▸ `FlightDataOnDemand_Roo_Configurable.aj` and `Flight_Roo_Configurable.aj`: AspectJ ITDs that add the `@Configurable` annotation to `FlightDataOnDemand` and `Flight` classes, respectively.

Let's now look at each of these files in detail.

The following listing shows the `FlightDataOnDemand.java` class:

```
import org.springframework.roo.addon.dod.RooDataOnDemand;
import sample.roo.flightapp.domain.Flight;

@RooDataOnDemand(entity = Flight.class)
public class FlightDataOnDemand { }
```

The code listing shows the use of Roo's `@RooDataOnDemand` annotation, which identifies the persistent entity for which the `FlightDataOnDemand` class creates seed data for integration testing. The `@RooDataOnDemand` annotation is responsible for the creation of the corresponding `*_Roo_DataOnDemand.aj` AspectJ ITD file. The `@RooDataOnDemand` accepts two attributes to customize the behavior of seed data generation:

- ▸ `entity`: identifies the persistent entity for which the seed data needs to be created.

- ▸ `quantity`: the number of records to be created for the entity, default being 10. If you want to create more records for integration testing of the entity, then specify an appropriate value of this attribute.

If you are using a performance testing tool like JMeter to test the performance of the JPA layer of your enterprise application, you can modify the `FlightIntegrationTest` JUnit test class and use it as a JUnit Request Sampler (or you can put a wrapper around `FlightIntegrationTest` and use Java Request Sampler) when creating a test plan in JMeter. This lets you quickly get started with testing the performance of your data access code. Based on the performance test requirements for a persistent entity, you can adjust the value of the `quantity` attribute of the `@RooDataOnDemand` annotation. For instance, if you want to test the performance of the data access layer when there are n number of records in the database, then specify the value of `quantity` attribute as n.

The following listing shows the `FlightDataOnDemand_Roo_DataOnDemand.aj` AspectJ ITD file, which defines methods, attributes, and annotations that are weaved into the `FlightDataOnDemand.java` class at compile-time:

```
privileged aspect FlightDataOnDemand_Roo_DataOnDemand {

    declare @type: FlightDataOnDemand: @Component;

    private Random FlightDataOnDemand.rnd =
                    new java.security.SecureRandom();

    private List<Flight> FlightDataOnDemand.data;

    public Flight FlightDataOnDemand.getNewTransientFlight (int
       index) {...}

    public Flight FlightDataOnDemand.getSpecificFlight(int
       index) {...}

    public Flight FlightDataOnDemand.getRandomFlight() {...}

    public boolean FlightDataOnDemand.modifyFlight(Flight obj)
    {...}

    public void FlightDataOnDemand.init() {...}

}
```

The code listing shows that AspectJ ITD does the following:

▸ Adds the `@Component` annotation to the `FlightDataOnDemand` class, so that it is auto-registered with Spring's application context. This enables you to create custom integration tests in which you can autowire one or more `*DataOnDemand` classes.

▸ Creates an instance of the `java.security.SecureRandom` class, which is used for generating a random number.

- Declares a list which holds `Flight` entities generated by the 'data on demand' class. These `Flight` entity instances represent the seed data generated by the 'data on demand' class.

- Defines a `getNewTransientFlight(int index)` method for generating a *unique* `Flight` instance based on the value of the `index` argument. The `getNewTransientFlight` method creates persistent entity instances which comply with the JSR 303 annotations specified for the entity's persistent fields. For instance, the `Flight` entity specifies the `@Size(min = 3, max = 20)` JSR 303 annotation for the `origin` and `destination` fields (refer to the `Flight.java` class); therefore, the `getNewTransientFlight` method attempts (that is, it is not guaranteed, as we'll see soon) to ensure that the size of the `origin` and `destination` fields comply with the corresponding JSR 303 annotation.

- Defines the `getSpecificFlight(int index)` method, which returns the `Flight` entity at the specified `index` from the collection of seed data maintained by the 'data on demand' class.

- Defines the `getRandomFlight()` method, which returns `Flight` entity at a random index (obtained from the `java.security.SecureRandom` instance) in the seed data collection maintained by the 'data on demand' class.

- Defines the `modifyFlight(Flight+obj)` method, which is supposed to modify the `Flight` entity passed as argument and return the success or failure of modification. But it simply returns `false`, that is, it never modifies the passed `Flight` instance.

- Defines an `init()` method, which is responsible for creating the seed data for integration testing of the `Flight` entity. It creates `Flight` entities in the database using the `getNewTransientFlight(int index)` method. The number of `Flight` entities created in the database is determined by the value of the `quantity` attribute of the `@RooOnDemand` annotation.

It is important to note that the `init()` method is internally called by methods defined in the `*_Roo_DataOnDemand.aj` to ensure that a fresh set of seed data is created in the database each time a test method is invoked.

JSR 303 annotations and seed data

The 'data on demand' classes generated by Spring Roo provide limited support for creating entity instances that comply with JSR 303 annotations. As of Spring Roo 1.1.3, it only supports `@NotNull`, `@Past`, and `@Future` JSR 303 constraints, along with some support for maximum and minimum range annotations. If your project uses any other JSR 303 annotation, then it is recommended to create your own setter method for entity fields in the `*DataOnDemand.java` class.

The following listing shows the `FlightIntegrationTest.java` class:

```
import org.junit.Test;
import org.springframework.roo.addon.test.RooIntegrationTest;

@RooIntegrationTest(entity = Flight.class )
public class FlightIntegrationTest {
    @Test
    public void testMarkerMethod() {
    }
}
```

The code listing shows the presence of Roo's `@RooIntegrationTest` annotation, which indicates that an integration test AspectJ ITD is to be created for the `Flight` entity. The `testMarkerMethod` is an example JUnit test method. The `@RooIntegrationTest` annotation accepts an `entity` attribute, which identifies the persistent entity for which the integration test is created—`Flight` in case of the `FlightIntegrationTest` class. Additionally, the `@RooIntegrationTest` annotation defines attributes which let you control the integration test methods that are auto-generated by Roo in the corresponding `*_Roo_IntegrationTest.aj` AspectJ ITD.

The following listing shows the `FlightIntegrationTest_Roo_IntegrationTest.aj` AspectJ ITD file that was generated by Roo corresponding to the `FlightIntegrationTest` class:

```
import org.junit.Test;
import org.junit.runner.RunWith;
import org.springframework.test.context.ContextConfiguration;
import org.springframework.test.context.
        junit4.SpringJUnit4ClassRunner;
privileged aspect FlightIntegrationTest_Roo_IntegrationTest {
  declare @type: FlightIntegrationTest:
        @RunWith(SpringJUnit4ClassRunner.class);

  declare @type: FlightIntegrationTest:
    @ContextConfiguration(locations =
    "classpath:/META-INF/spring/applicationContext.xml");

   declare @type: FlightIntegrationTest:@Transactional;

    @Autowired
    private FlightDataOnDemand FlightIntegrationTest.dod;

    @Test
    public void FlightIntegrationTest.testFindAllFlights() {
    ...
```

```
    }

    @Test
    public void FlightIntegrationTest.testPersist() {
    ...
    }
    ...
}
```

The previous code shows that AspectJ ITD does the following:

- Adds JUnit's `@RunWith` annotation to the `FlightIntegrationTest` class, instructing the use of Spring's `SpringJUnit4ClassRunner` for running the JUnit tests.

- Adds Spring's `@ContextConfiguration` annotation to the `FlightIntegrationTest` class, which specifies the location of Spring's application-context XML file to be used for executing the tests. By default, it is set to use the `applicationContext.xml` file in the `META-INF\spring` folder. If you want to use a different application-context XML for running the tests, then specify the `@ContextConfiguration` annotation in the `FlightIntegrationTest` class.

- Adds Spring's `@Transactional` annotation to the `FlightIntegrationTest` class, which means all the test methods defined in `FlightIntegrationTest` (or weaved into it by AspectJ ITD) are transactional in nature.

- Declares integration test methods, like `testFindAllFlights`, `testPersist`, and so on. The test methods make use of `FlightDataOnDemand` (a 'data on demand' class) instance for creating `Flight` instances (the seed data) for testing the `Flight` entity and for retrieving a random `Flight` instance from the database.

There's more...

In some scenarios you may want to customize the seed data created by `*DataOnDemand.java` class and to control the integration test methods that are auto-generated by Spring Roo.

Customizing seed data creation

If you're using JSR 303 annotations that are not supported by Spring Roo, you'll need to create custom setter methods (defined in `*_Roo_DataOnDemand.aj`) for setting persistent entity field values. The following listing shows some of the setter methods (`setNumOfSeats` and `setOrigin`) auto-generated by Roo for the `Flight` entity; the following is the `FlightDataOnDemand_Roo_DataOnDemand.aj` method:

```
    public Flight FlightDataOnDemand.getNewTransientFlight
    (int index) {
      sample.roo.flightapp.domain.Flight obj = new
                    sample.roo.flightapp.domain.Flight();
```

```
    setEmbeddedId(obj, index);
    setNumOfSeats(obj, index);
    setOrigin(obj, index);
    setDestination(obj, index);
    ...
    return obj;
}

private void FlightDataOnDemand.setEmbeddedId(Flight obj,
  int index) {
    java.lang.String flightId = "flightId_" + index;
    ...
    obj.setId(embeddedIdClass);
}

private void FlightDataOnDemand.setNumOfSeats(Flight obj,
  int index) {
    java.lang.Integer numOfSeats = new Integer(index);
    obj.setNumOfSeats(numOfSeats);
}

private void FlightDataOnDemand.setOrigin(Flight obj,
  int index) {
    java.lang.String origin = "origin_" + index;
    if (origin.length() > 20) {
      origin = origin.substring(0, 20);
    }
    obj.setOrigin(origin);
}
...
```

In the code listing, there are a couple of things to notice about the `Flight` entity that is created:

▶ `@NotNull` JSR 303 annotation is taken care of while creating the `Flight` entity, but the `@DecimalMax` and `@DecimalMin` JSR 303 annotations on the `numOfSeats` field are completely ignored (refer `setNumOfSeats` method in the code listing).

▶ The `@Size` annotation on `origin` and `destination` fields (refer `setOrigin` method in the code listing) is partially supported as the method only checks if the maximum length of the value assigned to `destination` (or `origin`) field is 20. It doesn't check for the minimum length as 3.

▶ The composite key is dynamically created and set (refer to the `setEmbeddedId` method in the previous listing).

To address the issue with JSR 303 support in the auto-generated `Flight` entity instance by `FlightDataOnDemand_Roo_DataOnDemand.aj`, we can write custom `setNumOfSeats`, `setOrigin`, and `setDestination` methods in the `FlightDataOnDemand.java` class, which does the following:

- Checks that the length of `origin` and `destination` fields are within the limits defined by `@Size`
- Provides checks for the `@DecimalMin` and `@DecimalMax` JSR 303 annotations

It is important to note that if you create `setNumOfSeats`, `setOrigin`, and `setDestination` methods in the `FlightDataOnDemand.java` class, then Roo removes these methods from the corresponding `FlightDataOnDemand_Roo_DataOnDemand.aj` AspectJ ITD. This requires that the signature of methods in the `FlightDataOnDemand.java` class is the same as the signature of methods defined in the corresponding `FlightDataOnDemand_Roo_DataOnDemand.aj` AspectJ ITD file. Similarly, you can customize any method of `FlightDataOnDemand_Roo_DataOnDemand.aj` by writing them in the `FlightDataOnDemand.java` class.

The following figure shows how Roo removes `setNumOfSeats`, `setOrigin`, and `setDestination` methods from the `FlightDataOnDemand_Roo_DataOnDemand.aj` file:

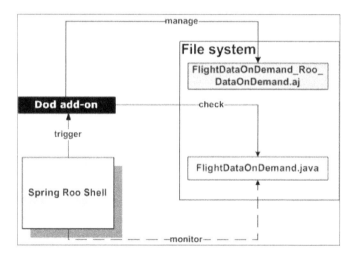

The figure shows that **Spring Roo Shell** monitors the **FlightDataOnDemand.java** class (because it is annotated with Roo's `@RooDataOnDemand` annotation). When any change is made to the **FlightDataOnDemand.java** class, Roo triggers add-on(s) responsible for managing the AspectJ ITD file(s) corresponding to the `FlightDataOnDemand.java` class. In the case of `FlightDataOnDemand`, Roo triggers **Dod add-on** ('data on demand') to update **FlightDataOnDemand_Roo_DataOnDemand.aj** AspectJ ITD, so that the AspectJ ITD is in sync with the `FlightDataOnDemand.java` class. When you add `setNumOfSeats`, `setOrigin`, and `setDestination` methods in the **FlightDataOnDemand.java** class, **Dod add-on** checks if the methods already exist there. If they exist, **Dod add-on** removes those methods from the **FlightDataOnDemand_Roo_DataOnDemand.aj** AspectJ ITD.

It is important to note that modifying a Java class that is annotated with Roo annotations may result in multiple AspectJ ITDs getting affected. For instance, if you remove the `modifiedBy` field from the `Flight.java` class, Roo will update the `Flight_Roo_JavaBean.aj`, `Flight_Roo_ToString.aj`, and `FlightDataOnDemand_Roo_DataOnDemand.aj` AspectJ ITD files to reflect the removal of the `modifiedBy` field.

Controlling integration test methods

We mentioned earlier that the `@RooIntegrationTest` annotation in `*IntegrationTest.java` defines attributes which let you control the integration test methods that are auto-generated by Roo in the `*_Roo_IntegrationTest.aj` AspectJ ITD file. The `@RooIntegrationTest` annotation defines the following attributes to control the auto-generation of integration test methods: `count`, `find`, `findAll`, `findAllMaximum`, `findEntries`, `flush`, `merge`, `persist`, and `remove`. If the value of any of these attributes is specified as `false`, then the corresponding test method is removed from the `*_Roo_IntegrationTest.aj` AspectJ ITD file. For instance, the `testFindAllFlights` method searches for all `Flight` instances in the database, which may not be desirable for performance reasons. To instruct Spring Roo to remove the auto-generated `testFindAllFlights` method from the `FlightIntegrationTest_Roo_IntegrationTest.aj` file, all you need to do is to specify the value of the `findAll` attribute value as `false` in the `@RooIntegrationTest` annotation, as shown here:

```
@RooIntegrationTest(entity = Flight.class, findAll=false)
public class FlightIntegrationTest {
    . . .
}
```

Generating integration tests at the time of entity creation

In this recipe we saw how to create integration tests using the `test integration` command. You can also use the `testAutomatically` argument of the `entity` command to instruct Roo to create integration tests at the time of entity creation, as shown here:

```
roo> entity --class ~.domain.Flight --testAutomatically --identifierType
~.domain.FlightKey --table FLIGHT_TBL
```

Providing custom implementation for integration tests

As with the 'data on demand' class, you can provide a custom implementation for an integration test method in your `*IntegrationTest.java` class. For instance, if you want to modify the `testPersist` Roo-generated test method with a customized `testPersist` method, create a `testPersist` method in the `FlightIntegrationTest.java` file. Adding the `testPersist` method to `*IntegrationTest.java` results in the removal of the `testPersist` method from the corresponding `*_Roo_IntegrationTest.aj` file by Roo. Similarly, you can customize any other test method defined in the `*_Roo_IntegrationTest.aj` file.

See also

- ▶ Refer to the *Creating new 'data on demand' for testing entities* recipe to see how you can create seed data for an entity

- ▶ Refer to the *Executing persistent entities tests* recipe to see how integration and mock tests of entities are executed using Spring Roo

- ▶ Refer to the *Creating mock tests for persistent entities* recipe to create mock static methods defined in entities

Creating new 'data on demand' for testing entities

We saw in the previous recipe that the `test integration` command and `testAutomatically` argument of the `entity` command result in the generation of an integration test and seed data for an entity. In situations where you're creating your own integration tests, you may still want to use the Roo-generated seed data for an entity. So, you are writing your custom integration test class but using a Roo-generated 'data on demand' class. This is where the `dod` command of Spring Roo comes into the picture.

Getting ready

Exit the Roo shell and delete the contents of the `C:\roo-cookbook\ch02-recipes` directory.

Execute the `ch02_jsr303_fields.roo` script. It creates a `flight-app` Roo project and sets up Hibernate as the persistence provider using the `persistence setup` command. The script also creates a `Flight` entity, which has `FlightKey` as its composite primary key class, and adds fields to the `Flight` and `FlightKey` classes. If you are using a different database than MySQL or your connection settings are different from what is specified in the script, then modify the script accordingly.

Start the Roo shell from the `C:\roo-cookbook\ch02-recipes` directory.

How to do it...

Follow these steps to create new 'data on demand':

1. Change the focus of Roo commands to the `Flight` entity:

   ```
   roo> focus --class ~.domain.Flight
   ```

2. Execute the `test integration` command:

   ```
   ~.domain.Flight> test integration
   ```

3. To create a new 'data on demand' class for the `Flight` entity, execute the following `dod` command:

   ```
   ~.domain.Flight> dod --entity ~.domain.Flight --class MyFlightDod


   Created SRC_TEST_JAVA\..MyFlightDod.java
   Created SRC_TEST_JAVA\..MyFlightDod_Roo_Configurable.aj
   Created SRC_TEST_JAVA\..MyFlightDod_Roo_DataOnDemand.aj
   ```

How it works...

The `dod` command accepts two arguments:

- `entity`: the fully-qualified name of the entity for which the 'data on demand' class needs to be created.

- `class`: the name of the 'data on demand' class. This class is annotated with the @ RooDataOnDemand annotation. If this argument is not specified, then by default, the name of the class is `<entity-name>DataOnDemand`, where `<entity-name>` is the simple name of the entity.

The `dod` command generates the corresponding 'data on demand' Java class, `*_Roo_DataOnDemand.aj`, and `*_Roo_Configurable.aj`. Now, you can use the newly created 'data on demand' Java class (`FlightIntegrationTest.java`) in your integration test class, as shown here:

```
package sample.roo.flightapp.domain;

public class FlightIntegrationTest {
  @Autowired
  private MyFlightDod myDod;

  @Test
  public void testMyCustomDodTest() {
    sample.roo.flightapp.domain.Flight obj =
```

```
        myDod.getNewTransientFlight(Integer.MAX_VALUE);
    ..
    obj.persist();
    obj.flush();
    ..
  }
}
```

See also

▶ Refer to the *Creating integration tests for persistent entities* recipe for details on how to create integration tests for entities using Spring Roo

Creating mock tests for persistent entities

In the recipe *Creating integration tests for persistent entities*, we saw how Spring Roo helps with the creation of integration tests. In this recipe we look at how Spring Roo simplifies the generation of a mock test for an entity using the `test mock` command.

Getting ready

Exit the Roo shell and delete the contents of the `C:\roo-cookbook\ch02-recipes` directory.

Execute the `ch02_jsr303_fields.roo` script. It creates a `flight-app` Roo project and sets up Hibernate as the persistence provider using the `persistence setup` command. The script also creates a `Flight` entity, which has `FlightKey` as its composite primary key class, and adds fields to the `Flight` and `FlightKey` classes. If you are using a different database than MySQL or your connection settings are different from what is specified in the script, then modify the script accordingly.

Start the Roo shell from the `C:\roo-cookbook\ch02-recipes` directory.

How to do it...

Follow these steps to create mock tests:

1. Set the focus of Roo on the `Flight` entity, using the `focus` command:

   ```
   roo> focus --class ~.domain.Flight
   ```

2. To create a mock test for the `Flight` entity, execute the following `test mock` command:

   ```
   ~.domain.Flight roo> test mock
   Created SRC_TEST_JAVA\sample\roo\flightapp\domain\FlightTest.java
   ```

How it works...

The execution of the `test mock` command creates a JUnit test, `FlightTest.java`, which is responsible for mock testing of the `Flight` entity, as shown here:

```
package sample.roo.flightapp.domain;

@RunWith(JUnit4.class)
@MockStaticEntityMethods
public class FlightTest {

  @Test
  public void testMethod() {
     int expectedCount = 13;
     Flight.countFlights();

     ..AnnotationDrivenStaticEntityMockingControl.
                 expectReturn(expectedCount);

     ..AnnotationDrivenStaticEntityMockingControl.playback();
      org.junit.Assert.assertEquals(expectedCount,
                                    Flight.countFlights());
  }
}
```

If you are using Spring Roo 1.1.3, then you'll have to add the `@MockStaticEntityMethods` and `@RunWith(JUnit4.class)` annotations in Roo-generated mock tests, as shown.

In the code listing, the `@MockStaticEntityMethods` annotation represents a Spring annotation which supports mock testing of static entity methods, like count and finder methods. Spring defines an `AnnotationDrivenStaticEntityMockingControl` aspect, which applies to methods of a test class annotated with `@MockStaticEntityMethods` and mocks calls to the `static` methods of the persistent entity. Additionally, the `AnnotationDrivenStaticEntityMockingControl` aspect defines the `expectReturn` and `playback` methods to simplify writing mock tests.

As the `AnnotationDrivenStaticEntityMockingControl` aspect applies to any class annotated with `@MockStaticEntityMethods`, it makes it possible to write tests using any testing framework (JUnit or TestNG) for mock testing entities. For testing of instance methods defined in the entity, you'll continue to use the common approaches for mock testing using **EasyMock**, **Mockito**, and so on.

▶   Refer to the *Creating integration tests for persistent entities* recipe to see Spring Roo's support for auto-generation of integration tests for JPA entities

Executing persistent entities tests

In previous recipes we saw how to create mock and integration tests for persistent entities. In this recipe we'll look at how to execute these tests using the `perform tests` command of Spring Roo.

Getting ready

Exit the Roo shell and delete the contents of the `C:\roo-cookbook\ch02-recipes` directory.

Execute the `ch02_jsr303_fields.roo` script. It creates a `flight-app` Roo project and sets up Hibernate as the persistence provider using the `persistence setup` command. The script also creates a `Flight` entity, which has `FlightKey` as its composite primary key class, and adds fields to the `Flight` and `FlightKey` classes. If you are using a different database than MySQL or your connection settings are different from what is specified in the script, then modify the script accordingly.

Install the MySQL 5.5.11 database—this is required because we'll now be executing integration tests. Create a database named "myFlightAppDB" in MySQL server instance and ensure that the connection properties defined in the `database.properties` file of the `flight-app` Roo project can be used to successfully connect to "myFlightAppDB".

Start the Roo shell from the `C:\roo-cookbook\ch02-recipes` directory.

How to do it...

Follow these steps to create and execute tests:

1. Change the focus of Roo commands to `Flight` entity:

    ```
    roo> focus --class ~.domain.Flight
    ```

2. Execute the `test integration` command to create integration tests for the `Flight` entity:

    ```
    ~.domain.Flight> test integration
    ```

3. To execute tests defined in the Roo project, issue the `perform tests` command from the Roo prompt, as shown here:

    ```
    roo> perform tests
    ```

The integration test for the `Flight` entity will fail currently because:

► The auto-generated 'data on demand' class provides limited support for creating entity instances that comply with JSR 303 annotations. As explained in the Creating integration tests for persistent entities recipe, you can write custom setter methods for persistent fields in the `FlightDataOnDemand.java` entity to create `Flight` entities that comply with JSR 303 annotations specified on the persistent fields.

► The query fired by the `countFlights` method in the `Flight_Roo_Entity.aj` AspectJ ITD file doesn't work with MySQL 5.1.1. You need to change the `countFlights` method from:

```
public static long countFlights() {
    return entityManager().createQuery("SELECT COUNT(o)
      FROM Flight o", Long.class).getSingleResult();
}
```

To:

```
public static long countFlights() {
    return entityManager().createQuery("SELECT COUNT(*)
      FROM Flight o", Long.class).getSingleResult();
}
```

As AspectJ ITD files are managed by Spring Roo, you should not change the `countFlights` method in the `Flight_Roo_Entity.aj` file. Instead, either perform push-in refactoring or create a `countFlights` method in the `Flight.java` file.

In push-in refactoring, you use the IDE to push the declarations, methods, attributes, and constructors defined in the AspectJ ITD file to the target Java class. For more information on push-in refactoring, refer to the Removing Roo with *push-in refactoring* recipe of *Chapter 7*.

 When writing `countFlights` method in `Flight.java`, make sure that Roo is running in the background, so that Roo can remove the `countFlights` method from the `Flight_Roo_Entity.aj` file. Additionally, ensure that the signature of `countFlights` method is same as the one defined in the `Flight_Roo_Entity.aj` file.

How it works...

The `perform tests` command is processed by the **maven add-on** of Roo and is responsible for executing all the tests that form part of the Roo project. If you want to directly execute the tests using maven, then exit the Roo prompt and use the `mvn test` command of maven. The results of test execution are saved in the `<project_dir>/target/surefire-reports` directory, where `project_dir` is your Roo project directory.

There's more...

The `ch02_flightapp_testing.zip` file that accompanies this book contains the `flight-app` Eclipse project that we saw in recipes of the previous chapter and this chapter. You can import this project into your Eclipse IDE and view the following changes that I made to the `flight-app` project to demonstrate concepts that we've learned so far:

▶ Defined the `setNumOfSeats` method in `FlightDataOnDemand.java` to create `Flight` entities that meet the constraint specified by the JSR 303 `@Size` annotation for the `numOfSeats` field. Defining the `setNumOfSeats` method in `FlightDataOnDemand.java` results in the removal of the method with the same signature from the `FlightDataOnDemand_Roo_DataOnDemand.aj` file.

▶ Defined `setOrigin` and `setDestination` methods in `FlightDataOnDemand.java` to create `Flight` entities that meet the constraints specified by JSR 303 `@DecimalMax` and `@DecimalMin` annotations on `origin` and `destination` fields. Defining `setOrigin` and `setDestination` methods in `FlightDataOnDemand.java` results in removal of methods with the same signature from the `FlightDataOnDemand_Roo_DataOnDemand.aj` file.

▶ Changed the `@RooIntegrationTest` annotation in `FlightIntegrationTest.java` to instruct Roo not to generate `findAll`, `findEntries`, and `count` test methods.

▶ Autowired `MyFlightDod` reference (a custom 'data on demand' class) in `FlightIntegrationTest.java` and defined a custom `testMyCustomDodTest` method.

▶ Added a `@Rollback(false)` Spring annotation to the `testPersist` method in `FlightIntegrationTest.java` so that the data created by the `testPersist` method is not rolled back after it is executed. This feature could be particularly useful if you want to manually verify the data that was created by the `testPersist` method or if you want to keep the data for further testing.

You can execute the tests defined in the `flight-app` project using the `perform tests` command and check your database to view the seed data that was created by the 'data on demand' class and during the testing of `testPersist` method.

See also

▶ Refer to the *Creating integration tests for persistent entities* recipe to see Spring Roo's support for auto-generation of integration tests for JPA entities

▶ Refer to the *Creating mock tests for persistent entities* recipe to mock static methods defined in entities

Creating applications that interact with multiple databases

As of Spring Roo 1.1.3, both `entity` and `persistence setup` commands support the `persistenceUnit` argument which lets you create enterprise applications which interact with multiple databases. In this recipe we'll create two persistent units:

▶ `flight`: the `flight` persistence unit consists of a single entity, `Flight`. It uses Hibernate as a JPA provider and maps to a MySQL database named "myFlightDB".

▶ `payment`: the `payment` persistence unit consists of a single entity, `Payment`. It uses Hibernate as the JPA provider and maps to a MySQL database named "myPaymentDB".

Getting ready

Exit the Roo shell and delete the contents of the `C:\roo-cookbook\ch02-recipes` directory.

Start the Roo shell from the `C:\roo-cookbook\ch02-recipes` directory.

How to do it...

The following steps will demonstrate how to create an application that interacts with multiple databases:

1. Create the `flight-app` Roo project:

   ```
   ..roo> project --topLevelPackage sample.roo.flightapp --java 6
   --projectName flight-app
   ```

2. Set up the `flight` persistence unit:

   ```
   ..roo> persistence setup --provider HIBERNATE --database MYSQL
   --databaseName myFlightDB --persistenceUnit flight
   ```

3. Create `Flight` entity, which is associated with the `flight` persistence unit:

   ```
   ..roo> entity --class ~.domain.Flight --table FLIGHT_TBL
   --persistenceUnit flight
   ```

4. Add some fields to the `Flight` entity:

   ```
   ~.domain.Flight roo> field string --fieldName origin --column FLT_
   ORIGIN --notNull
   ```

   ```
   ~.domain.Flight roo> field string --fieldName destination --column
   FLT_DESTINATION --notNull
   ```

5. Create an integration test for the `Flight` entity:

   ```
   ~.domain.Flight roo> test integration
   ```

6. Set up the `payment` persistence unit:

   ```
   .. roo> persistence setup --provider HIBERNATE --database MYSQL
   --databaseName myPaymentDB --persistenceUnit payment
   ```

7. Create the `Payment` entity, which is associated with the `payment` persistence unit:

   ```
   .. roo> entity --class ~.domain.Payment --table PAYMENT_TBL
   --persistenceUnit payment
   ```

8. Add fields to the `Payment` entity:

   ```
   ~.domain.Payment roo> field string --fieldName paymentType
   --column PYMT_TYPE --notNull
   ```

9. Create an integration test for the `Payment` entity:

   ```
   ~.domain.Payment roo> test integration
   ```

10. Execute the `perform eclipse` command to import the `flight-app` project into Eclipse IDE:

    ```
    ~.domain.Payment roo> perform eclipse
    ```

11. Execute the integration tests:

    ```
    .. roo> perform tests
    ```

Executing the integration tests at this time will result in failure. We'll shortly see what we need to do to get the tests working when using multiple databases.

How it works...

The concept of a persistence unit is not only useful when the enterprise application interacts with multiple databases but also when you want to logically group entities in your application. Using different persistence units can also be useful if you want to use different persistence providers for different logical groups of entities.

When setting up a persistence provider using the `persistence setup` command you can specify the persistence unit name by specifying the `persistenceUnit` argument. Also, when creating entities using the `entity` command you can use the `persistenceUnit` argument to specify the persistence unit to which the entity belongs. Spring Roo makes use of the `persistenceUnit` argument of the `persistence setup` command to define a different persistence unit in the `/META-INF/persistence.xml` file. The following listing shows the `persistence.xml` file of the `flight-app` project after the execution of the `persistence setup` commands:

```
<persistence ..>
  <persistence-unit name="flight"
```

```
      transaction-type="RESOURCE_LOCAL">
    <provider>
      org.hibernate.ejb.HibernatePersistence
    </provider>
    ..
  </persistence-unit>

  <persistence-unit name="payment"
      transaction-type="RESOURCE_LOCAL">
    <provider>
      org.hibernate.ejb.HibernatePersistence
    </provider>
    ..
  </persistence-unit>
</persistence>
```

In the code, the `name` attribute of the `<persistence-unit>` element reflects the `persistenceUnit` argument value that you specified in the `persistence setup` command. As we have specified Hibernate as the JPA provider for both `flight` and `payment` persistent units, the `<provider>` element contains `org.hibernate.ejb.HibernatePersistence` as the JPA provider. If you want to use different JPA providers for your persistence unit, then specify it using the `provider` argument of the `persistence setup` command.

As we are using different persistence units, the entities created using the `entity` command use the `persistenceUnit` attribute to identify the persistence unit with which the entity is associated. The following code listing shows that the `persistenceUnit` argument value is used in the `@RooEntity` annotation of the `Flight` class:

```
@RooJavaBean
@RooToString
@RooEntity(persistenceUnit = "flight", table = "FLIGHT_TBL")
public class Flight {..}
```

In the code, the value of the `persistenceUnit` attribute of `@RooEntity` is `flight`, which affects the way Roo generates the corresponding `*_Roo_Entity.aj` AspectJ ITD file. The following code listing shows the affect of `persistenceUnit` attribute of `@RooEntity` annotation on the `Flight_Roo_Entity.aj` ITD file:

```
privileged aspect Flight_Roo_Entity {

    @PersistenceContext(unitName = "flight")
    transient EntityManager Flight.entityManager;

    ...
    @Transactional("flight")
    public void Flight.persist() {..}
```

```
        @Transactional("flight")
        public void Flight.remove() {..}
        ...
    }
```

In the code, the @PersistenceContext annotation makes use of the unitName attribute to specify the persistence unit with which the EntityManager persistence context is associated with. Also, notice that the @Transactional annotation now makes use of the flight qualifier to specify the transaction manager required for managing transactions.

As of Spring Roo 1.1.3, you'll have to ensure that the transaction manager, entity manager factory, and data source bean definitions for each persistence unit are configured in the / META-INF/spring/applicationContext.xml file, as shown here:

```
    <bean class="org.apache.commons.dbcp.BasicDataSource"
        destroy-method="close" id="flightDataSource">
        ....
    </bean>
    <bean class="org.apache.commons.dbcp.BasicDataSource"
        destroy-method="close" id="paymentDataSource">
        ....
    </bean>

    <bean
      class="org.springframework.orm.jpa.JpaTransactionManager"
      id="flightTransactionManager">
      <qualifier value="flight"/>
      <property name="entityManagerFactory"
            ref="flightEntityManagerFactory"/>
    </bean>

    <bean
        class="org.springframework.orm.jpa.JpaTransactionManager"
        id="paymentTransactionManager">
        <qualifier value="payment"/>
        <property name="entityManagerFactory"
            ref="paymentEntityManagerFactory"/>
    </bean>

    <tx:annotation-driven mode="aspectj"
        transaction-manager="flightTransactionManager"/>
    <tx:annotation-driven mode="aspectj"
        transaction-manager="paymentTransactionManager"/>
```

```
<bean
    class="org.springframework.orm.jpa.
    LocalContainerEntityManagerFactoryBean"
    id="flightEntityManagerFactory">
    <property name="persistenceUnitName" value="flight"/>
    <property name="dataSource" ref="dataSource"/>
</bean>
<bean class="org.springframework.orm.jpa.
        LocalContainerEntityManagerFactoryBean"
        id="paymentEntityManagerFactory">
    <property name="persistenceUnitName" value="payment"/>
    <property name="dataSource" ref="dataSource"/>
</bean>
```

The code shows that different transaction managers, entity manager factories, and data source beans are configured for each persistence unit. The transaction manager bean definitions make use of the `<qualifier>` element, so that `@Transactional` annotations can refer to the target transaction manager using a qualifier. Also, the `LocalContainerEntityManagerFactoryBean` is passed the persistence unit name with which it is associated, using the `persistenceUnitName` property.

To ensure that integration tests work, you'll also need to specify the transaction manager to use for the test methods annotated with the `@Transactional` annotation. To achieve this, all you need to do is specify the `@Transactional` annotation in your test class, as shown here for `PaymentIntegrationTest` class:

```
@RooIntegrationTest(entity = Payment.class)
@Transactional("payment")
public class PaymentIntegrationTest {

    @Test
    public void testMarkerMethod() {
    }
}
```

See also

▶ Refer to the *Creating persistent entities* recipe to see how to create persistent entities which belong to a single persistence unit

Packaging your Roo project

If you are using Roo only to create the persistence layer of your enterprise application, then you may want to package your Roo project as a JAR file and use it. This recipe shows how you can package your Roo project and how Roo ensures that your packaged JAR file is independent of Roo-specific annotations and AspectJ ITDs.

Getting ready

Exit the Roo shell and delete the contents of the `C:\roo-cookbook\ch02-recipes` directory.

Execute the `ch02_jsr303_fields.roo` script. It creates a `flight-app` Roo project and sets up Hibernate as persistence provider using the `persistence setup` command. The script also creates a `Flight` entity, which has `FlightKey` as its composite primary key class, and adds fields to the `Flight` and `FlightKey` classes. If you are using a different database than MySQL or your connection settings are different from what is specified in the script, then modify the script accordingly.

Start the Roo shell from the `C:\roo-cookbook\ch02-recipes` directory.

How to do it...

To package your Roo project into a JAR file, execute the `perform package` command from the Roo shell:

```
roo> perform package


[INFO] ----------------------------------------------------------
[INFO] Building flight-app 0.1.0.BUILD-SNAPSHOT
[INFO] ----------------------------------------------------------
...
[INFO] --- aspectj-maven-plugin:1.2:compile (default) @ flight-app ---
...
[INFO] --- aspectj-maven-plugin:1.2:test-compile (default) @ flight-app
---
...
[INFO] Building jar: ...\target\flight-app-0.1.0.BUILD-SNAPSHOT.jar
[INFO] ----------------------------------------------------------
[INFO] BUILD SUCCESS
[INFO] ----------------------------------------------------------
```

How it works...

The perform package command packages the Roo project using maven. Alternatively, you can also use the mvn package command of maven to package the Roo project. It is important to note that when using the perform package command, tests defined in the Roo project are not executed.

The output from executing perform package shows that AspectJ compiler Maven Plugin is used to compile the main and test Java classes of the flight-app project. The compile goal of AspectJ compiler Maven Plugin weaves AspectJ ITDs and aspects defined in the spring-aspects.jar file into the main Java classes of the project. The test-compile goal weaves AspectJ ITDs and aspects defined in the spring-aspects.jar file into the test classes of the project.

The perform package command creates the flight-app project's JAR file in the target directory.

The following figure shows an example of how Flight.class is created by the AspectJ compiler Maven Plugin by weaving AspectJ ITDs that apply to the Flight.java class:

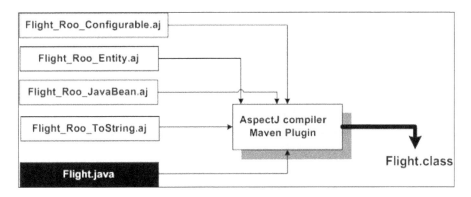

The figure shows that **AspectJ compiler Maven Plugin** weaves **Flight_Roo_Configurable.aj**, **Flight_Roo_Entity.aj**, **Flight_Roo_JavaBean.aj**, and **Flight_Roo_ToString.aj** AspectJ ITDs into **Flight.java** to create **Flight.class**.

There's more...

To verify that your generated class file contains declarations from corresponding AspectJ ITDs, you can also use the javap command. The javap command examines a .class file and outputs the attributes, methods, and constructors that form part of the class.

To use `javap`, you need to first set the `PATH` environment variable to point to the `bin` directory of your Java SE installation, as shown here:

```
C:\> set PATH=%PATH%;C:\Program Files\Java\jdk1.6.0_23\bin
```

Now, go to the directory which contains your Roo project (`ch02-recipes` in our case) and execute the `javap` command to view the details of the compiled `Flight` class, as shown here:

```
C:\roo-cookbook\ch02-recipes> javap -classpath target\classes sample.roo.
flightapp.domain.Flight
```

```
public class sample.roo.flightapp.domain.Flight ...
{
  transient javax.persistence.EntityManager entityManager;

  ...

  public void clear();
  public static long countFlights();
  public static final javax.persistence.EntityManager
    entityManager();
  public static java.util.List findAllFlights();

  ...

  public void flush();
  public java.lang.String getCreatedBy();
  public java.util.Date getCreatedDate();
  public java.lang.String getDestination();
  public sample.roo.flightapp.domain.FlightKey getId();
  public java.lang.String getModifiedBy();
  public java.util.Date getModifiedDate();
  public java.lang.Integer getNumOfSeats();
  public java.lang.String getOrigin();
  public java.lang.Integer getVersion();
  public sample.roo.flightapp.domain.Flight merge();
  public void persist();
  public void remove();

  ...

}
```

The output shows that methods defined in AspectJ ITDs are now part of the compiled `Flight` class file.

See also

- Refer to the *Creating integration tests for persistent entities* recipe to see Spring Roo's support for auto-generation of integration tests for JPA entities.

3
Advanced JPA Support in Spring Roo

In this chapter, we will cover:

- ▶ Viewing candidate dynamic finder methods
- ▶ Adding dynamic finder methods to an entity
- ▶ Creating a many-to-one (or one-to-one) relationship between entities
- ▶ Creating a one-to-many (or many-to-many) relationship between entities
- ▶ Creating a mapped superclass
- ▶ Customizing Roo-generated identifier definitions
- ▶ Generating database metadata
- ▶ Creating entities from a database

Introduction

In the previous chapter, we looked at how Spring Roo simplifies developing enterprise applications that make use of JPAs for persistence. In this chapter, we continue our discussion of JPAs and look at recipes that let us add dynamic finder methods, create relationships between entities, and perform database reverse engineering to auto-generate JPA entities.

Viewing candidate dynamic finder methods

A dynamic finder method is a finder method for which you don't need to write a JPA query. It fetches entity instances from the database based on one or more persistent fields of the entity class. The implementation of these dynamic finder methods is auto-generated by Roo when you add their names to a persistent entity. As Roo doesn't create a DAO layer of an application, dynamic finder methods are defined in the entity class. In this recipe, we will look at the finder list command, which introspects a persistent entity and suggests names of possible dynamic finder methods that can be added to the given persistent entity.

Getting ready

Create a sub-directory `ch03-recipes` inside the `C:\roo-cookbook` directory.

Execute the `ch03_persistent_entities.roo` script to create a `flight-app` Roo project. The script sets up Hibernate as a persistence provider and creates a `Flight` entity, which has `FlightKey` as its composite primary key class. Additionally, the script adds fields to the `Flight` and `FlightKey` classes. If you are using a different database than MySQL or your connection settings are different than what is specified in the script, then modify the script accordingly.

Start Roo shell from the `C:\roo-cookbook\ch03-recipes` directory.

How to do it...

To use the `finder list` command to view dynamic finder methods, follow the given steps:

1. Set the focus of the subsequent commands on the `Flight` entity using the `focus` command:

   ```
   roo> focus --class ~.domain.Flight
   ```

2. Execute the `finder list` command to view the list of candidate dynamic finder methods for the `Flight` entity, as shown here:

   ```
   ~.domain.Flight roo> finder list

   .....

   findFlightsByCreatedDateBetween(Date minCreatedDate, Date
   maxCreatedDate)
   findFlightsByCreatedDateGreaterThan(Date createdDate)

   . . . . .

   findFlightsByDestination(String destination)
   findFlightsByDestinationEquals(String destination)
   findFlightsByDestinationIsNotNull()
   findFlightsByDestinationIsNull()
   ```

```
findFlightsByDestinationLike(String destination)
findFlightsByDestinationNotEquals(String destination)
```

How it works...

The `finder list` command displays names of the candidate dynamic finder methods for an entity. By default, the dynamic finder methods suggested by the `finder list` command search for entity instances based on only one persistent field of the entity. For instance, in the output of the `finder list` command you will not find a dynamic finder method name which finds the `Flight` entity instances based on both the `createdDate` and `modifiedDate` fields. If an entity inherits from a *mapped superclass*, then the dynamic finder methods corresponding to the inherited fields are also displayed by Roo.

The dynamic finder methods suggested by the `finder list` command are dependent upon the type of the field. For instance, the `createdDate` is of type `java.util.Date` and can participate in *greater than*, *less than*, and *between* comparisons; therefore, `findFlightsByCreatedDateBetween`, `findFlightsByCreatedDateGreaterThan`, and so on, are shown as candidate dynamic finder methods, and these methods accept the `createdDate` field as the argument. On the other hand, the `destination` field is of type `String`, which doesn't participate in *greater than*, *less than*, and *between* comparisons; therefore, Roo doesn't suggest dynamic finder methods for finding the `Flight` instances based on *greater than*, *less than*, and *between* comparisons of `destination` field.

There's more...

Let's now look at how to instruct Roo to:

- Provide a list of candidate dynamic finder methods, which fetch entities based on more than one persistent field
- Restrict suggested dynamic finder method names based on a filter criteria

Listing dynamic finder methods for multiple persistent fields

If you want Roo to list finder method names that fetch entities based on multiple persistent fields, you should use the `depth` argument of the `finder list` command. The `depth` argument accepts a numeric value, which determines the number of persistent fields the dynamic finder method uses to search for entities in the database. For instance, if you want `Flight` instances to be searched based on both the `origin` and `destination` fields, then the value of the `depth` argument must be 2. The default value of the `depth` argument is 1, therefore; when we executed the `finder list` command, without specifying `depth` argument, it listed dynamic finder method names that fetch entities based on only one persistent field. The following `finder list` command shows the affect of the `depth` argument on the suggested list of dynamic finder method names:

```
~.domain.Flight roo> finder list --depth 2
findFlightsByDestinationAndOrigin(String destination, String origin)
```

```
findFlightsByDestinationAndOriginEquals(String destination, String
origin)
```

. . . . .

As the output suggests, two persistent fields now form part of listed candidate dynamic finder method names. Similarly, if you want your finders to span a n number of persistent fields, then specify n as the value of a `depth` argument.

Limiting list of dynamic finder methods, based on a filter criteria

As you increase the value of the `depth` argument, the number of candidate dynamic finder method names listed by Roo increases exponentially due to the number of possible combinations for method arguments. In such cases, it is desired to filter candidate dynamic finder method names based on a filter criteria. The `finder list` command provides a `filter` argument, which accepts a comma separated list of strings that must be present in the dynamic finder method name. Dynamic finder method names which don't contain the strings specified by the `filter` argument are omitted from the displayed list of candidate dynamic finder method names. This makes it easy for you to locate dynamic finder methods that you want to add to a persistent entity.

 Note that there should be no spaces in the comma-separated list of strings specified as the value of the `filter` argument.

The following `finder list` command shows the `filter` argument usage:

```
~.domain.Flight roo> finder list --depth 2 --filter
destinationlike,originlike

findFlightsByDestinationLikeAndOriginLike(..)

findFlightsByDestinationLikeOrOriginLike(..)

findFlightsByOriginLikeAndDestinationLike(..)

findFlightsByOriginLikeOrDestinationLike(..)
```

The output now shows only four methods that contain the text specified in the `filter` argument. Similarly, you can add additional text to the `filter` argument to narrow down the list of candidate dynamic finder method names that are displayed by the `finder list` command.

See also

▸ Refer to the *Adding dynamic finder methods to an entity* recipe below to see how Spring Roo simplifies adding dynamic finder methods to an entity

Adding dynamic finder methods to an entity

The `finder list` command shows the candidate dynamic finder method names whose implementations Roo can automatically generate. In this recipe, we will look at how to add dynamic finder methods to a persistent entity using the `finder add` command. As an example, we will add the `findFlightsByDestinationLikeAndOriginLike` method to a `Flight` entity.

Getting ready

Refer to the *Viewing candidate dynamic finder methods* recipe, to create the `flight-app` Roo project.

Start the Roo shell from the `C:\roo-cookbook\ch03-recipes` directory.

How to do it...

To add dynamic finder methods, follow the given steps:

1. Set the focus of subsequent commands on the `Flight` entity using a `focus` command:

   ```
   roo> focus --class ~.domain.Flight
   ```

2. Add the `findFlightsByDestinationLikeAndOriginLike` dynamic finder method to the `Flight` entity using the `finder add` command:

   ```
   .. roo> finder add findFlightsByDestinationLikeAndOriginLike

   Updated SRC_MAIN_JAVA\sample\roo\flightapp\domain\Flight.java

   Created SRC_MAIN_JAVA\sample\roo\flightapp\domain\Flight_Roo_
   Finder.aj
   ```

How it works...

The `finder add` command adds a dynamic finder method implementation to a persistent entity. This feature saves the effort of writing your own JPA-QL queries for the finder methods. The `finder add` command adds the name of the finder method to the `finders` attribute of the `@RooEntity` annotation (refer to *Chapter 2* for more details). The presence of the `finders` attribute in the `@RooEntity` annotation triggers the creation of a `*_Roo_Finder.aj` ITD file (if it doesn't already exist for the entity) and auto-generation of the finder method implementation in the `*_Roo_Finder.aj` ITD file. `*_Roo_Finder.aj` adds finder method implementation to the corresponding JPA entity class.

The following figure shows how Roo adds dynamic finder methods to a JPA entity when the `finder add` command is executed:

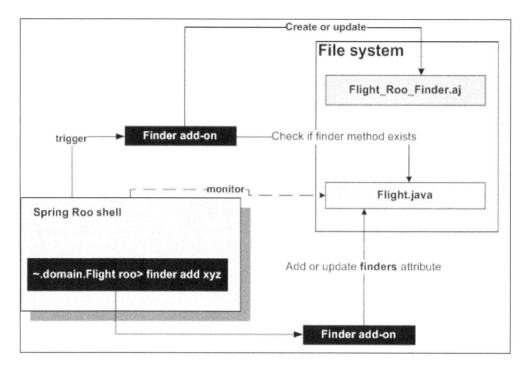

The given figure shows that when the `finder add xyz` command is executed, the **Finder add-on** of Roo adds the `xyz` method name to the `finders` attribute of the `@RooElement` annotation in the `Flight.java` file. As Spring Roo monitors Java files that are annotated with Roo's annotations, Roo uses the Finder add-on to add the `xyz` dynamic finder method implementation to the `Flight_Roo_Finder.aj` file. If `Flight_Roo_Finder.aj` doesn't exist, the Finder add-on creates it. Now, if you define the `xyz` method in the `Flight.java` file (because you may want to customize the implementation of the `xyz` method generated by Roo), the Finder add-on removes it from the `Flight_Roo_Finder.aj` file.

The following code shows the modified `@RooEntity` annotation of the `Flight` entity, after the `finder add` command is executed:

```
@RooEntity(identifierType = FlightKey.class,
table = "FLIGHT_TBL",
finders = { "findFlightsByDestinationLikeAndOriginLike"})
public class Flight { ... }
```

The following code shows the auto-generated implementation of the `findFlightsByDestinationLikeAndOriginLike` finder method in the `Flight_Roo_Finder.aj` file:

```
import javax.persistence.EntityManager;
import javax.persistence.TypedQuery;
...
 public static TypedQuery<Flight>
   Flight.findFlightsByDestinationLikeAndOriginLike(
     String destination, String origin)
{

    if (destination == null || destination.length() == 0)
       throw new IllegalArgumentException("The destination
           argument is required");
    ...
    if (origin == null || origin.length() == 0)
       throw new IllegalArgumentException("The origin argument
           is required");
    ...
    EntityManager em = Flight.entityManager();
    TypedQuery<Flight> q = em.createQuery("SELECT Flight FROM
      Flight AS flight WHERE LOWER(flight.destination) LIKE
      LOWER(:destination)  AND LOWER(flight.origin) LIKE
      LOWER(:origin)", Flight.class);
    q.setParameter("destination", destination);
    q.setParameter("origin", origin);
    return q;
}
```

The given code shows the following:

- ▶ The finder method expects that both the `origin` and `destination` arguments must be supplied to the finder method or an exception is thrown. In general, the dynamic finder method implementation generated by Roo requires that the arguments passed to the method are not `null`. If an argument type is `String`, the dynamic finder method implementation requires that the argument must not be `null` or blank, as shown in this code.
- ▶ JPA-QL for the finder method is auto-generated.
- ▶ The return type of the finder method is `javax.persistence.TypedQuery<Flight>`. You can call the `getResultList` method of the `TypedQuery` object from your web controller class to execute the `SELECT` query and obtain the result.

There's more...

Let's now look at how we can add a custom finder method to an entity, perform integration testing of dynamic finder methods, and use a `@RooEntity` annotation to trigger auto-generation of a dynamic finder method implementation:

Adding custom finder methods

You may want to add custom finder methods if the dynamic finder methods offered by Roo don't meet your application's requirements. In such cases, you can either perform push-in refactoring of Roo-generated dynamic finder methods and modify their implementation (not their name or signature) in the corresponding persistent entity Java class or you can define the method in the persistent entity Java class (which will result in removing the method from the `*_Roo_Finder.aj` AspectJ ITD) or you can create your own AspectJ ITD to introduce your custom finder methods into the persistent entity Java class.

If you want to change the implementation of a dynamic finder method, then you can either use push-in refactoring or you can define the method in persistent entity Java class. The effects of using push-in refactoring or defining the method in persistent entity Java class are the same. In push-in refactoring, you use the IDE to move a declaration from AspectJ ITD file to the target Java class and then modify it. And, in case you decide to define the method in the Java class itself, you will probably do a copy-paste from AspectJ ITD to the Java class, and let Roo remove the method declaration from AspectJ ITD.

The following figure shows what happens when you use push-in refactoring to move a method declaration from AspectJ ITD to the target Java clss:

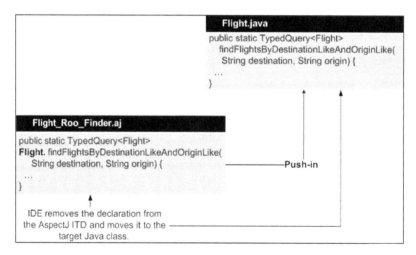

The given figure shows that when you perform push-in refactoring of the `findFlightsByDestinationLikeAndOriginLike` method, the IDE simply moves the method from the AspectJ ITD file to the target `Flight.java` class. So, if you have to customize a method such as `findFlightsByDestinationLikeAndOriginLike` by writing it in the `Flight.java` class, it will be much simpler if you perform push-in refactoring or simply copy the method from the AspectJ ITD file and paste it in the `Flight.java` class (followed by removing the `Flight.` that is prefixed to the method name). Copy-pasting from AspectJ ITDs to target Java classes isn't efficient if you are planning to move all the declarations in all the AspectJ ITDs to target Java classes. This is where push-in refactoring is helpful, as we will see in *Chapter 7, Developing Add-ons and Removing Roo from Projects*.

If you want to add a custom finder method whose name or signature is different from the dynamic finder methods offered by Roo, then you can either define the method in the persistent entity Java class or you can create a new AspectJ ITD and declare your method in it. Both these approaches are fine, and it depends upon how comfortable you are with writing AspectJ ITDs. Roo generates AspectJ ITDs so that cross-cutting concerns are separate from the Java classes. So, if you feel that writing finder methods in your persistent entity Java class pollutes it, you should consider writing AspectJ ITDs. It is important to note that the custom AspectJ ITDs that you create in your project are not managed by Roo.

The following code shows an example of the `Flight_MyCustom_Finder.aj` AspectJ ITD, which introduces the `searchFlights(SearchCriteria criteria)` finder method into `Flight.java`:

```
import javax.persistence.EntityManager;
import javax.persistence.TypedQuery;

privileged aspect Flight_MyCustom_Finder {

  public static TypedQuery<Flight> Flight.searchFlight(
      SearchCriteria criteria) {
    EntityManager em = Flight.entityManager();
    TypedQuery<Flight> q = em.createQuery("SELECT Flight ..",
      Flight.class);
    q.setParameter("destination", criteria.getDestination());
    q.setParameter("origin", criteria.getOrigin());
    return q;
  }
}
```

As the given code shows, you can create your own AspectJ ITD and add custom finder methods to JPA entities. As custom AspectJ ITDs are not managed by Roo, if you create the `searchFlight` method in the `Flight.java` class, Roo will not remove it from the `Flight_MyCustom_Finder.aj` file.

Integration testing of dynamic finder methods

Roo doesn't create integration tests for the auto-generated dynamic finder methods. To test finder methods, write the test method in the `*IntegrationTest.java` file corresponding to the persistent entity.

Adding dynamic finders through @RooEntity annotation

The `@RooEntity` annotation accepts a `finders` attribute, which contains an array of string values identifying names of dynamic finder methods that must be generated for the persistent entity. The `finders add` command adds the finder method name to the `finders` attribute, which in turn results in the generation of dynamic finder method by Roo. As the addition of finder method name to `finders` attribute triggers generation of dynamic finder method implementation, instead of using the `finder add` command you can directly add the name of the finder method to the `finders` attribute using IDE, which in turn will trigger Roo to generate the finder method implementation.

See also

▸ Refer to the *Controlling auto-generated methods of persistent entities* recipe in *Chapter 2, Persisting Objects Using JPA* to know more about the elements supported by the `@RooEntity` annotation

▸ Refer to the *Viewing candidate dynamic finder methods* recipe to see how the `finder list` command is used to show the names of candidate dynamic finder methods

Creating a many-to-one (or one-to-one) relationship between entities

In real-world applications, domain entities have relationships between them. In this section, we look at how Roo simplifies creating a many-to-one (or one-to-one) relationship between JPA entities.

The following figure shows the relationship between the `FLIGHT_TBL` and `FLIGHT_DESC_TBL` tables, which we will use as a reference to model our *many-to-one* relationship:

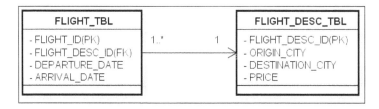

In the given figure, the `FLIGHT_TBL` table contains *scheduled* flight details and the `FLIGHT_DESC_TBL` table contains details of all the flights that an airline offers. Each record in the `FLIGHT_TBL` table refers to *exactly one* `FLIGHT_DESC_TBL` record. As there can be multiple flights from one city to another, the relationship between `FLIGHT_TBL` and `FLIGHT_DESC_TBL` is *many-to-one*. The `FLIGHT_TBL` table is mapped to the `FLIGHT_DESC_TBL` table by the `FLIGHT_DESC_ID` foreign key. It is expected that if a `FLIGHT_TBL` record is deleted, then the deletion is limited to the `FLGHT_TBL` only.

The following figure shows JPA entities corresponding to the FLIGHT_TBL and FLIGHT_DESC_TBL tables:

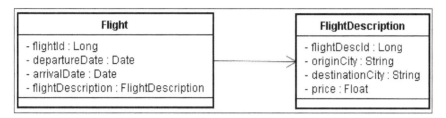

In the given figure, the flightId and flightDescId attributes represent primary keys of the Flight and FlightDescription JPA entities, respectively.

Getting ready

Exit the Roo shell and delete the contents of the C:\roo-cookbook\ch03-recipes directory.

Start the Roo shell from the C:\roo-cookbook\ch03-recipes directory.

Execute the ch03_jpa_setup.roo script which creates the flight-app Roo project, sets up Hibernate as the persistence provider, and configures MySQL as the database for the application. If you are using a different database than MySQL or your connection settings are different than what is specified in the script, then modify the script accordingly.

How to do it...

To create the Flight and FlightDescription JPA entities with a many to one relationship, follow the steps given here:

1. Create the Flight JPA entity (including integration tests) corresponding to the FLIGHT_TBL table:

   ```
   .. roo> entity --class ~.domain.Flight --identifierColumn FLIGHT_
   ID --identifierField flightId --identifierType java.lang.Long
   --table FLIGHT_TBL --testAutomatically
   ```

2. Add attributes to the Flight entity:

   ```
   ~.domain.Flight roo> field date --type java.util.Date --fieldName
   departureDate --column DEPARTURE_DATE
   ```

   ```
   ~.domain.Flight roo> field date --type java.util.Date --fieldName
   arrivalDate --column ARRIVAL_DATE
   ```

3. Create the FlightDescription entity (including integration tests) corresponding to the FLIGHT_DESC_TBL table:

```
~.domain.Flight roo> entity --class ~.domain.FlightDescription
--identifierColumn FLIGHT_DESC_ID --identifierField flightDescId
--identifierType java.lang.Long --table FLIGHT_DESC_TBL
--testAutomatically
```

4. Add attributes to the `FlightDescription` entity:

```
~.domain.FlightDescription roo> field string --fieldName origin
--column ORIGIN_CITY --notNull
```

```
~.domain.FlightDescription roo> field string --fieldName
destination --column DESTINATION_CITY --notNull
```

```
~.domain.FlightDescription roo> field number --type java.lang.
Float --fieldName price --column PRICE --notNull
```

5. Set the focus of the Roo commands on the `Flight` entity and use the `field reference` command to create a many-to-one relationship between the `Flight` and `FlightDescription` entities, as shown here:

```
~.domain.FlightDescription roo> focus --class ~.domain.Flight
```

```
~.domain.Flight roo> field reference --fieldName flightDescription
--type ~.domain.FlightDescription --joinColumnName FLIGHT_DESC_ID
--notNull
```

How it works...

As we are not using composite primary keys for the entities, the following things you'll notice about the `entity` commands that we have used for creating `Flight` and `FlightDescription` entities:

- ▶ `identifierField`: An optional argument has been used to give a custom name to the identifier field of the entities. For instance, the name of identifier field of the `Flight` entity is `flightId` and that of `FlightDescription` is `flightDescId`. If we had not used the `identifierField` argument, then by default Roo would have assigned `id` as the name of the entity's identifier field.

- ▶ `identifierColumn`: An *optional* argument has been used to set the name of the table column to which the identifier field maps. This argument instructs Roo to add the `@Column` JPA annotation to the identifier field. If you don't specify the `identifierColumn`, by default the name of the mapping column is derived by splitting the camel-case name and adding *underscore* as the separator. For instance, if you don't specify the `identifierColumn` argument for an identifier field named `myOwnIdField` field, the name of the table column is assumed to be `my_own_id_field`. In the context of this recipe, the `identifierColumn` will not have any effect because the name of the table column, derived from the identifier field name, is the same as the name assigned by the `identifierColumn` argument.

The following code snippet from the `Flight.java` file shows the `Flight` entity that was created in this recipe:

```
@RooJavaBean
@RooToString
@RooEntity(identifierField = "flightId", identifierColumn = "FLIGHT_
ID", table = "FLIGHT_TBL")
public class Flight {
 ..
}
```

The given code shows that the `@RooEntity` annotation contains the `identifierField`, `identifierColumn`, and the `table` attributes with values that we specified for these arguments in the `entity` command. As mentioned in the *Creating persistent entities* recipe of *Chapter 2, Persisting Objects Using JPA* the elements of the `@RooEntity` annotation are used for generating the corresponding `*_Roo_Entity.aj` AspectJ ITD. The following code shows the identifier field as defined in the `Flight_Roo_Entity.aj` AspectJ ITD:

```
privileged aspect Flight_Roo_Entity
{
    .....
    @Id
    @GeneratedValue(strategy = GenerationType.AUTO)
    @Column(name = "FLIGHT_ID")
    private Long Flight.flightId;
    .....
}
```

In this code, the identifier field is annotated with the `@Column` annotation because of the presence of the `identifierColumn` argument in the `@RooEntity` annotation. The name `flightId` of the identifier field is derived from the value of the `identifierField` argument of the `@RooEntity` annotation.

Now, coming to the `field reference` command that is used for adding an attribute referring to another object in a relationship. In our next example, the `field reference` command adds the reference to the `FlightDescription` object in the `Flight` class. As only a reference to a related object is defined using `field reference`, you can consider that it defines *many* sides of a *many-to-one* relationship.

The `field reference` command is similar to the `field other` (described in *Adding attributes to a Java class* recipe of *Chapter 1, Getting Started with Spring Roo*) command because both the commands are used for defining a reference to custom Java objects. The only difference is that the `field reference` command is specifically meant for defining JPA relationships between entities. The following code from `Flight.java` shows the code introduced by executing the `field reference` command:

```
@NotNull
@ManyToOne
@JoinColumn(name = "FLIGHT_DESC_ID")
private FlightDescription flightDescription;
```

As we can see from the given code, the `field reference` command has added a *many-to-one* JPA relationship between the `Flight` and `FlightDescription` entities.

The following table describes the arguments that can be passed to the `field reference` command:

Argument	Description
`fieldName` (mandatory)	Name of the attribute, which refers to the related entity. In our example, `flightDescription` is the name of the attribute.
`type` (mandatory)	Type of the related entity. In our example, `FlightDescription` is the type of the related entity.
`joinColumnName`	The column which acts as the *foreign key* for the related entity. In our example, the `FLIGHT_DESC_ID` is the column in the `FLIGHT_TBL` (represented by the `Flight` JPA entity), which acts as the foreign key to the `FLIGHT_DESCRIPTION_TBL` table (represented by the `FlightDescription` JPA entity).
`cardinality`	Cardinality of the relationship between JPA entities. By default, cardinality is `MANY_TO_ONE`. If you are creating a one-to-one relationship, then specify `ONE_TO_ONE` as the value of the `cardinality` argument.
`fetch`	JPA fetch strategy for related entity. The possible values are `EAGER` and `LAZY`. The value of the `fetch` argument translates into the value of the `fetch` element of a `@ManyToOne` or a `@OneToOne` annotation.
`referencedColumnName`	Identifies the column in the table of the related entity to which this join column links. The value of this argument is used as a value of the `referencedColumnName` attribute of the `@JoinColumn` JPA annotation.

Even though the Roo shell displays MANY_TO_ONE, MANY_TO_MANY, ONE_TO_MANY, and ONE_TO_ONE as possible values of the `cardinality` argument of the `field reference` command, it only accepts MANY_TO_ONE and ONE_TO_ONE. The reason for this is that `field reference` only makes sense in case of a one-to-one relationship or when the entity is on the *many* side of a many-to-one relationship.

There's more...

Let's now look at how Roo supports testing entities that participate in relationships with other entities and at how to add a custom dynamic finder method corresponding to the many-to-one relationship field.

Testing JPA entities that participate in relationships

Testing entities that participate in relationships can get a bit tricky sometimes because integration tests may not be able to check relationship constraints. For instance, the testRemove method of FlightDescriptionIntegrationTest (refer to the FlightDescriptionIntegrationTest_Roo_IntegrationTest.aj AspectJ ITD) doesn't test for the scenario in which one or more Flight entity instances are associated with the FlightDescription instance being removed.

To effectively test entities that participate in relationships, you may want to modify auto-generated test methods and *data on demand* classes. For instance, in our example scenario, the data on demand class of the FlightDescription (refer to the getNewTransientFlightDescription method defined in the FlightDescriptionDataOnDemand_Roo_DataOnDemand.aj AspectJ ITD) only creates FlightDescription instances, and doesn't create any associated Flight instances. As a result of this, the testRemove method will never be able to test a scenario in which one or more Flight instances are associated with the FlightDescription instance being removed. So, to perform effective testing of the FlightDescription entity, you'll need to do the following:

▶ Define the getNewTransientFlightDescription method in the FlightDescriptionDataOnDemand.java class, which creates the FlightDescription objects that are associated with one or more Flight instances

▶ Define the testRemove method in the FlightDescriptionIntegrationTesting class to first remove all the related Flight entities, before attempting to remove the FlightDescription entity

If entities are not related, data on demand classes are independent of each other. But, if the entities are related, then creating test data becomes a bit of a involved task. For instance, the Flight entity has a *many-to-one* relationship with FlightDescription; which means that the data on demand class for the Flight entity should create records in the FLIGHT_ TBL table, which have a foreign key reference to the FLIGHT_DESC_TBL table records. It is mandatory to assign a foreign key reference to the Flight records in the FLIGHT_TBL table because the FlightDescription relationship is annotated with @NotNull.

Now, the question is how the data on the demand class of the `Flight` entity can discover the `FlightDescription` instances (that were created in the `FLIGHT_DESC_TBL` table by the `getNewTransientFlightDescription` method of the `FlightDescriptionDataOnDemand_Roo_DataOnDemand.aj` AspectJ ITD) so that the `Flight` instances (created by the `getNewTransientFlight` method of the `FlightDataOnDemand_Roo_DataOnDemand.aj` AspectJ ITD) in the `FLIGHT_TBL` can specify the foreign key reference to the `FlightDescription` instances? It's simple! It can be done by using the data on the demand class of the `FlightDescription` entity because it maintains the list of records that it created in the `FLIGHT_DESC_TBL` table. This is exactly what Spring Roo does while generating data on demand classes—it creates dependency between data on demand classes of related entities to create test data.

The following code from the `FlightDataOnDemand_Roo_DataOnDemand.aj` file shows the `Flight` data on the demand class:

```
privileged aspect FlightDataOnDemand_Roo_DataOnDemand
{
    . .

    @Autowired
    private FlightDescriptionDataOnDemand
        FlightDataOnDemand.flightDescriptionDataOnDemand;

    public Flight FlightDataOnDemand.
        getNewTransientFlight(int index)
    {
        sample.roo.flightapp.domain.Flight obj =
                new sample.roo.flightapp.domain.Flight();
        obj.setArrivalDate(obj, index);
        obj.setDepartureDate(obj, index);
        obj.setFlightDescription(obj, index);
        return obj;
    }

    private void FlightDataOnDemand.
        setFlightDescription(Flight obj, int index) {
    sample.roo.flightapp.domain.FlightDescription
    flightDescription = flightDescriptionDataOnDemand.
        getRandomFlightDescription();
    obj.setFlightDescription(flightDescription);
    }
    . . .
}
```

In the given code, the `FlightDescriptionDataOnDemand` object is autowired into the `FlightDataOnDemand` object. As the `Flight` entity has a many-to-one relationship with the `FlightDescription`, data on demand class of the `Flight` entity uses the data on demand class of the `FlightDescription` to obtain a reference to an existing `FlightDescription` instance and set it in the `Flight` instance. This ensures that the test data created during integration testing of the many-to-one relationship is as per the relationship that exists between related entities.

It is important to note that `@NotNull` and `@ManyToOne(..., optional=false)` mean the same thing. It is possible to specify that a relationship between entities must exist either by using `@NotNull` (JSR 303: Bean Validation annotation) or by specifying `false` as the value of the `optional` element of the `@ManyToOne` JPA annotation. In either case, the data on demand class of the entity will ensure that the data on demand class of the related entity is used to enforce a foreign key constraint on the test data created for integration testing.

Dynamic finder method for a many-to-one relationship field

As with other persistent fields, you can use the `finder list` and `finder add` commands to view and add finder method(s) corresponding to the relationship field. For instance, if you execute the `finder list` command against the `Flight` entity, then one of the finders is for the `flightDescription` relationship field, as shown here:

```
~.domain.Flight roo> finder list
..
findFlightsByFlightDescription(FlightDescription flightDescription)
```

Also, you can use the `depth` argument of the `finder list` command to view dynamic finder methods based on the relationship field and other persistent fields of the entity.

See also

► The *Creating a one-to-many (or many-to-many) relationship between entities* recipe that follows

Creating a one-to-many (or many-to-many) relationship between entities

In the previous recipe, we saw how the many-to-one (or one-to-one) relationship is established between entities using the `field reference` command. In this recipe, we'll extend the same example to show how a one-to-many (or many-to-many) relationship can be created using the `field set` command. The following class diagram shows a one-to-many relationship between the `FlightDescription` and `Flight` entities:

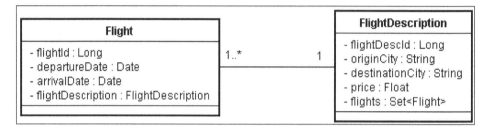

In the given figure, you'll notice that we have added a `flights` field of type `Set<Flight>` to the `FieldDescription` entity, reflecting the one-to-many relationship between the `FlightDescription` and the `Flight` entity.

Getting ready

Exit the Roo shell and delete the contents of the `C:\roo-cookbook\ch03-recipes` directory.

Start the Roo shell from the `C:\roo-cookbook\ch03-recipes` directory.

Execute the `ch03_relationship_many_to_one.roo` script, which creates the `flight-app` Roo project, sets up Hibernate as a persistence provider, configures MySQL as the database for the application, creates the `Flight` and `FlightDescription` JPA entities, and defines a many-to-one relationship between the `Flight` and `FlightDescription` entities. If you are using a different database than MySQL or your connection settings are different than what is specified in the script, then modify the script accordingly.

How to do it...

To create a one to many (or many to many) relationship between the `FlightDescription` and `Flight` entities, follow the steps given here:

1. Set the focus of the Roo commands on the `FlightDescription` entity:

    ```
    .. roo> focus --class ~.domain.FlightDescription
    ```

2. Create a one-to-many relationship between the `FlightDescription` and `Flight` entities using the `field set` command:

```
~.domain.FlightDescription roo> field set --fieldName flights
--type ~.domain.Flight --cardinality ONE_TO_MANY --mappedBy
flightDescription
```

How it works...

The `field set` command is used to create the *many* side of a one-to-many JPA relationship within an entity. If the relationship between two entities is many-to-many, then the `field set` command is used for both the entities in the relationship. The following table describes some of the important arguments that can be specified for the `field set` command:

Argument	Description
`fieldName` (mandatory)	Name of the relationship field that you want to add to the entity. The type of the field is `java.util.Set`.
	In case of our example, the `fieldName` argument is specified as `flights`, which results in an additional field named `flights` to the `FlightDescription` entity.
`type` (mandatory)	Identifies the type of the related entity (which is on the *many* side of a one-to-many relationship) contained in the `Set` defined by the `fieldName` argument.
	In our example, the `type` value is specified as `~.domain.Flight`, which means that the `Set` (defined by the `fieldName` argument) contains elements of type `Flight`, as shown here:
	`private Set<Flight> flights = new HashSet<Flight>();`
`mappedBy`	The value of the `mappedBy` argument refers to the owner of the relationship. It translates into the value of the `mappedBy` element of the JPA `@OneToMany` or `@ManyToMany` annotation.
	In our example, the value of the `mappedBy` argument is `flightDescription`; therefore, the `flights` field created by the `field set` command is annotated with a `@OneToMany` annotation whose `mappedBy` attribute value is `flightDescription`.
`cardinality`	Cardinality of the relationship between JPA entities. By default, cardinality is `MANY_TO_MANY`. As we want to create a one-to-many relationship between the `FlightDescription` and `Flight` entity, the value of the `cardinality` argument is specified as `ONE_TO_MANY`.
`fetch`	TheJPA fetch strategy for related entity. The possible values are `EAGER` and `LAZY`. The value of the `fetch` argument translates into the value of the `fetch` element of the `@ManyToMany` or `@OneToMany` annotation.

Even though the Roo shell displays MANY_TO_ONE, MANY_TO_MANY, ONE_TO_MANY, and ONE_TO_ONE as possible values of the cardinality argument of the field set command, it only accepts MANY_TO_MANY and ONE_TO_MANY. The reason for this—field set only makes sense in the case of a many-to-many relationship or when the entity is on the one side of a one-to-many relationship.

The execution of the field set command against the FlightDescription entity results in the following field added to it:

```
@OneToMany(cascade = CascadeType.ALL,
    mappedBy="flightDescription")
private Set<Flight> flights = new HashSet<Flight>();
```

The given code shows that the field set command simply adds a relationship field to the entity.

There's more...

field set and field reference commands don't provide the option to specify the cascade effect that applies to the related entity. The behavior of the commands is as described here:

- @ManyToMany or @OneToMany annotated JPA relationship field created using the field set command has the value of the cascade element as CascadeType. ALL, which means the entity operations such as refresh, persist, merge, and so on, are propagated to a related entity.

- @ManyToOne and @OneToOne annotated JPA relationship field created using the field reference command don't have the cascade element specified, which means entity operations such as refresh, persist, merge, and so on, are *not* propagated to an associated entity.

In scenarios where you want to specify the cascade effect, you can modify the corresponding JPA annotation in your Java source file.

See also

- Refer to the *Creating a many-to-one (or one-to-one) relationship between entities* recipe to see how a field reference command is used for a creating many-to-one (or one-to-one) relationship

Creating a mapped superclass

In this recipe, we'll look at how to create an entity which inherits a *mapped superclass*. The fields of a mapped superclass are stored into the table to which the inheriting entity is mapped. The mapped superclass itself is *not* mapped to any table. In this recipe, we'll create the `Flight` entity, which extends the `AuditFields` class. The `AuditFields` class represents a *mapped superclass*; the fields of `AuditFields` are stored into the table to which the `Flight` entity is mapped.

The following figure shows the relationship between the `Flight` entity and the `AuditFields` mapped superclass:

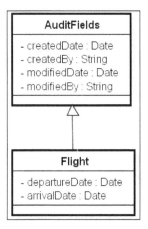

Getting ready

Exit the Roo shell and delete the contents of the `C:\roo-cookbook\ch03-recipes` directory.

Start the Roo shell from the `C:\roo-cookbook\ch03-recipes` directory.

Execute the `ch03_jpa_setup.roo` script which creates the `flight-app` Roo project, sets up Hibernate as persistence provider, and configures MySQL as the database for the application. If you are using a different database than MySQL or your connection settings are different than what is specified in the script, then modify the script accordingly.

How to do it...

To create an entity which inherits a *mapped superclass*, follow the given steps:

1. Create the `AuditFields` class using the `entity` command and add fields to it:

   ```
   .. roo> entity --class ~.domain.AuditFields --mappedSuperclass
   ```

```
~.domain.AuditFields roo> field date --type java.util.Date
--fieldName createdDate

~.domain.AuditFields roo> field date --type java.util.Date
--fieldName modifiedDate

~.domain.AuditFields roo> field string --fieldName createdBy

~.domain.AuditFields roo> field string --fieldName modifiedBy
```

2. Create the `Flight` entity using the `entity` command and add fields to it:

```
.. roo> entity --class ~.domain.Flight --extends ~.domain.
AuditFields --table FLIGHT_TBL

~.domain.Flight roo> field date --type java.util.Date --fieldName
departureDate --column DEPARTURE_DATE

~.domain.Flight roo> field date --type java.util.Date --fieldName
arrivalDate --column ARRIVAL_DATE
```

How it works...

The `mappedSuperclass` argument of the `entity` command is responsible for creating a mapped superclass. It's a flag type argument; if present, it indicates that the generated class must be annotated with the `@MappedSuperclass` JPA annotation. The following code shows the relevant annotations of the `AuditFields` mapped superclass, as generated by the `entity` command:

```
@RooJavaBean
@RooToString
@RooEntity(mappedSuperclass = true)
public class AuditFields {..}
```

As shown in this code, the `AuditFields` class is annotated with the `@RooEntity` annotation. As we saw earlier, the `@RooEntity` annotation triggers Roo to generate a `*_Roo_Entity.aj` AspectJ ITD file corresponding to the `AuditFields` class. The `mappedSuperclass` attribute of the `@RooEntity` annotation instructs Roo to add a declaration in the corresponding `*_Roo_Entity.aj` that annotates the `AuditFields` class with the `@MappedSuperclass` annotation (instead of the `@Entity` JPA annotation).

When an entity class extends a mapped superclass, the Roo generates a `*_Roo_Entity.aj` Aspect ITD file corresponding to the mapped superclass and defines an identifier field (annotated with `@Id` JPA annotation), along with methods such as `persist`, `merge`, `refresh`, and so on. (that we saw in the *Creating persistent entities* recipe of *Chapter 2*). In this case, the inheriting entity's `*_Roo_Entity.aj` file only defines the static count and finder methods for the entity.

The following code listing shows the `AuditFields_Roo_Entity.aj` file:

```
privileged aspect AuditFields_Roo_Entity
{
    declare @type: AuditFields: @MappedSuperclass;

    @PersistenceContext
    transient EntityManager AuditFields.entityManager;
    @Id
    @GeneratedValue(strategy = GenerationType.AUTO)
    @Column(name = "id")
     private Long AuditFields.id;

    @Version
    @Column(name = "version")
    private Integer AuditFields.version;
    @Transactional
    public void AuditFields.persist()
    {
        if (this.entityManager == null)
          this.entityManager = entityManager();
        this.entityManager.persist(this);
    }

    @Transactional
    public void AuditFields.remove() {...}
     public static final EntityManager
             AuditFields.entityManager() {...}
    ...
}
```

The given code shows that the `AuditFields_Roo_Entity.aj` ITD annotates the `AuditFields` class with the `@MappedSuperclass` annotation. Also, notice that the ITD doesn't annotate the `AuditFields` class with `@Entity` and `@Table` annotation. This code shows that the `*_Roo_Entity.aj` ITD of a mapped superclass is the same as that of an entity—consisting of identifier and version definitions, persist, remove, and so on methods, and a method to obtain the JPA `EntityManager` instance.

As the `Flight` entity inherits from the `AuditFields` class, Roo generates a `Flight_Roo_Entity.aj` ITD that doesn't contain identifier and version definitions or persistence methods for persisting, refreshing, and merging the

`Flight` entity, as shown in the following code listing:

```
privileged aspect Flight_Roo_Entity
{
    declare @type: Flight: @Entity;
```

```
declare @type: Flight: @Table(name = "FLIGHT_TBL");
public static long Flight.countFlights() {..}
public static List<Flight> Flight.findAllFlights(){..}
public static Flight Flight.findFlight(Long id) {..}
public static List<Flight> Flight.findFlightEntries(
    int firstResult, int maxResults) {..}
}
```

The given code shows that the `Flight` entity contains only the `find` and `count` methods and inherits the identity, version definitions, and persistence related methods from the `AuditFields` mapped superclass. As in the case of any other JPA entity, the ITD annotates the `Flight` class with the `@Entity` and the `@Table` annotations.

There's more...

Even though the mapped superclass contains the identifier definition, you can override it in the inheriting entity by using `@AttributeOverride` or `@AttributeOverrides` JPA annotation. The following code shows how the `Flight` entity can override the identifier definition in the `AuditFields` class to map the identifier field to the `FLT_ID` column of `FLIGHT_TBL` table:

```
@RooJavaBean
@RooToString
@RooEntity(table="FLIGHT_TBL")
@AttributeOverride(name="id", column=@Column(name="FLT_ID"))
public class Flight extends AuditFields {..}
```

Creating @Embeddable annotated classes

In the last recipe, we saw that the `Flight` entity inherits the `AuditFields` mapped superclass. You could have modelled the `Flight` entity such that it contained the `AuditFields` instance in the `Flight` entity itself instead of inheriting from it. To do so, you need to create an `AuditFields` class annotated with `@Embeddable` JPA annotation, define the reference to the `AuditFields` class in the `Flight` entity, and annotate the referencing field with the `@Embedded` JPA annotation. Let's see how we can do this in Roo:

1. Create the `AuditFields` class using the `entity` command and add fields to it as shown here:

    ```
    .. roo> embeddable --class ~.domain.AuditFields

    ~.domain.AuditFields roo> field date --type java.util.Date
    --fieldName createdDate

    ~.domain.AuditFields roo> field date --type java.util.Date
    --fieldName modifiedDate

    ~.domain.AuditFields roo> field string --fieldName createdBy

    ~.domain.AuditFields roo> field string --fieldName modifiedBy
    ```

2. Create the `Flight` entity using the `entity` command and add fields to it as shown here:

```
.. roo> entity --class ~.domain.Flight --table FLIGHT_TBL

~.domain.Flight roo> field date --type java.util.Date --fieldName
departureDate --column DEPARTURE_DATE

~.domain.Flight roo> field date --type java.util.Date --fieldName
arrivalDate --column ARRIVAL_DATE
```

3. Using the `field embedded` command, define `AuditFields` as an embedded object in the `Flight` entity as shown here:

```
~.domain.Flight roo> field embedded --fieldName auditFields --type
~.domain.AuditFields
```

The following code shows the `AuditFields` class generated by the `embeddable` command:

```
@RooJavaBean
@RooToString
@Embeddable
public class AuditFields
{
    @Temporal(TemporalType.TIMESTAMP)
    @DateTimeFormat(style = "S-")
    private Date createdDate;

    @Temporal(TemporalType.TIMESTAMP)
    @DateTimeFormat(style = "S-")
    private Date modifiedDate;

    private String createdBy;

    private String modifiedBy;
}
```

The given code shows that the `AuditFields` class is annotated with the JPA `@Embeddable` annotation. It is not annotated with the `@RooEntity` annotation, which means that it doesn't contain identifier and version definitions, and persistence related methods.

The following code shows the `Flight` entity:

```
@RooJavaBean
@RooToString
@RooEntity(table = "FLIGHT_TBL")
public class Flight
{
...
    @Embedded
    private AuditFields auditFields;
}
```

This code shows that the `Flight` entity contains a reference to the `AuditFields` class. The `AuditFields` reference is added by the `field embedded` command and it is annotated with the `@Embedded` JPA annotation.

If you want to override the mapping of the fields defined in the `AuditFields` class, you can use the `@AttributeOverrides` and `@AttributeOverride` JPA annotations. The following code snippet shows how these annotations can be used in the `Flight` entity to map the `createdDate` and `modifiedDate` fields of the `AuditFields` class to the `C_DATE` and `M_DATE` columns of the table to which the `Flight` entity maps:

```
@Embedded
@AttributeOverrides({
  @AttributeOverride(name="createdDate",
    column=@Column(name="C_DATE")),
  @AttributeOverride(name="modifiedDate",
    column=@Column(name="M_DATE"))
})
private AuditFields auditFields;
```

See also

> ▸ Refer to the *Creating persistent entities* recipe of *Chapter 2* to see how to create persistent entities, which do not inherit from a mapped superclass

Customizing Roo-generated identifier definition

So far we have seen recipes where the JPA entity identifier is generated by Spring Roo. By default, entities created by Roo specify the identifier generation strategy as `GENERATIONTYPE.AUTO`, which means that the persistence provider will choose an appropriate strategy for the database. You may want to customize this identifier generation strategy based on your application's requirements.

In this recipe, we'll look at how we can modify a Roo-generated identifier definition to use a database table for generating identifier values.

Getting ready

Exit the Roo shell and delete the contents of the `C:\roo-cookbook\ch03`-recipes directory.

Start the Roo shell from the `C:\roo-cookbook\ch03`-recipes directory.

Execute the `ch03_jpa_setup.roo` script which creates the `flight-app` Roo project, sets up Hibernate as a persistence provider, and configures MySQL as the database for the application. If you are using a different database than MySQL or your connection settings are different than what is specified in the script, then modify the script accordingly.

Now, create a new `Flight` entity with a `Long` type identifier field, as shown here:

```
roo> entity --class ~.domain.Flight --identifierColumn FLIGHT_ID
--identifierField flightId --identifierType java.lang.Long --table
FLIGHT_TBL
```

The following code from the `Flight_Roo_Entity.aj` file shows the identifier definition generated by Spring Roo for the `Flight` entity:

```
privileged aspect Flight_Roo_Entity
{
...
    @Id
    @GeneratedValue(strategy = GenerationType.AUTO)
    @Column(name = "FLIGHT_ID")
    private Long Flight.flightId;

    public Long Flight.getFlightId()
    {
        return this.flightId;
    }

    public void Flight.setFlightId(Long id)
    {
        this.flightId = id;
    }
...
}
```

Now, lets say that we want the `Flight` entity's identifier value generated using a database table named `ID_GENERATOR`. This means we need to annotate our `flightId` field with the `@TableGenerator` and change the identifier generation strategy to `GenerationType.TABLE`.

How to do it...

You can override the Roo-generated identifier definition by defining the identifier (with the same name) in the entity's Java source file (and not in the `*_Roo_Entity.aj` file). The following code shows the modified `Flight.java` file containing the `flightId` identifier definition:

```
...
public class Flight
```

```
{
...
   @Id
   @TableGenerator(name = "Flight_Gen", table = "ID_GENERATOR",
       pkColumnName = "ID_COLUMN", valueColumnName = "ID_VALUE",
       pkColumnValue = "FLIGHT_ID_VALUE", initialValue = 10,
       allocationSize=100)
   @GeneratedValue(strategy = GenerationType.TABLE,
       generator = "Flight_Gen")
   private Long flightId;

 public Long getFlightId()
   {
      return this.flightId;
   }
   public void setFlightId(Long flightId)
   {
      this.flightId = flightId;
   }
...
}
```

How it works...

The `@TableGenerator` JPA annotation specifies the details of the table used for primary key generation. The `@GeneratedValue` JPA annotation specifies the strategy used for generating primary key values. The `GenerationType.TABLE` indicates that the value of the `flightId` primary key is obtained from the database table identified by the `generator` element of the `@GeneratedValue` annotation.

When you an define identifier in the Java source file of an entity, Roo automatically removes the identifier definition from the corresponding `*_Roo_Entity.aj` AspectJ ITD file. If you now check the `Flight_Roo_Entity.aj` file, then you will find that the `flightId` definition has been removed from it.

There's more...

Roo's `entity` command provides limited support for creating different types of identifier definitions. In most scenarios, you will possibly find it compelling to customize the Roo-generated identifier definition by defining the entity identifier in the entity's Java source file.

▸ Refer to the *Creating persistent entities* recipe in *Chapter 2* to know more about creating JPA entities using Spring Roo

Generating database metadata

Roo supports creating JPA entities by introspecting an existing database. If you want Roo to create JPA entities for an existing database, then you may want to know the database metadata used as an input by Roo to create JPA entities corresponding to database tables. In this recipe, we'll look at the `database introspect` command, which lets us view the database metadata in XML format. In the next recipe, *Creating entities from a* database, we will see how this metadata is used by Roo to create JPA entities.

The following figure shows tables and views of a database that we'll introspect using the `database introspect` command:

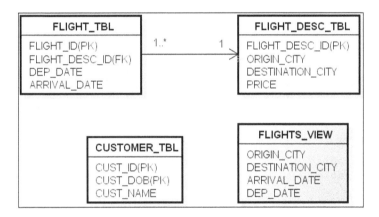

In the given figure, the `FLIGHT_TBL`, `FLIGHT_DESC_TBL`, and `CUSTOMER_TBL` represent database tables, and the `FLIGHTS_VIEW` represents a database view. The relationship between the `FLIGHT_TBL` and `FLIGHT_DESC_TBL` tables is many-to-one. The `CUSTOMER_TBL` uses a composite primary key (consisting of the `CUST_ID` and `CUST_DOB` columns) to uniquely identify a customer. The `FLIGHTS_VIEW` database view combines data from the `FLIGHT_TBL` and `FLIGHT_DESC_TBL` tables based on the `FLIGHT_DESC_ID` column.

Getting ready

Exit the Roo shell and delete the contents of the `C:\roo-cookbook\ch03-recipes` directory.

Start the Roo shell from the `C:\roo-cookbook\ch03-recipes` directory.

Execute the ch03_jpa_setup.Roo script which creates the flight-app Roo project, sets up Hibernate as a persistence provider, and configures MySQL as the database for the application. If you are using a different database than MySQL or your connection settings are different than what is specified in the script, then modify the script accordingly.

Execute the myflightappdb.sql SQL script (that accompanies this book) against the MySQL database. The myflightappdb.sql creates a database named myflightappdb consisting of the FLIGHT_TBL, FLIGHT_DESC_TBL, and CUSTOMER_TBL tables and a FLIGHT_VIEW database view, as shown earlier in this recipe. Ensure that the database. properties file of your Roo project contains the settings to connect to this newly created myflightappdb database.

For the purpose of this recipe, we'll be using the database introspect command to view the metadata of a myflightappdb database created in MySQL database. Now, you're all set to view metadata related to the database you've configured in the database.properties file of your Roo project.

How to do it...

To use the database introspect command to view the database metadata, follow the steps given here:

1. To enable downloading of the driver for the database which we are about to introspect, execute the download accept terms of use command, as shown here:

    ```
    roo> download accept terms of use
    ```

2. Execute the database introspect command, as shown here:

    ```
    roo> database introspect --schema no-schema-required --file mydb.
    xml --enableViews

    Located add-on that may offer this JDBC driver
    1 found, sorted by rank; T = trusted developer; R = Roo 1.1
    compatible
    ID T R DESCRIPTION -----
    01 Y Y 5.1.13.0001 #jdbcdriver driverclass:com.mysql.jdbc.Driver.
    This...
    -----------------------
    [HINT] use 'addon info id --searchResultId ..' to see details
    about a search result
    [HINT] use 'addon install id --searchResultId ..' to install a
    specific search result, or
    [HINT] use 'addon install bundle --bundleSymbolicName TAB' to
    install a specific add-on version
    ```

3. Executing the `database introspect` command for the first time suggests the database driver that we need to download to perform the introspection of the `myflightappdb` database in MySQL. So, download the suggested driver using the `addon install` command, as shown here:

```
roo> addon install id --searchResultId 01

Target resource(s):
-------------------
Spring Roo - Wrapping - mysql-connector-java (5.1.13.0001)

Deploying...done.

Successfully installed add-on: Spring Roo - Wrapping - mysql-
connector-java [version: 5.1.13.0001]
```

4. Re-execute the `database introspect` command as shown here:

```
roo> database introspect --schema no-schema-required --file mydb.
xml --enableViews

Database metadata written to file C:\roo-cookbook\ch03-recipes\
mydb.xml
```

5. Now, open the generated `mydb.xml` file to view the database metadata.

How it works...

The `database introspect` command makes use of the connection properties defined in the `database.properties` file of the Roo project to create metadata information. This implies that you can't simultaneously introspect multiple databases using the `database introspect` command. The command accepts the following arguments:

▶ `schema` (*mandatory*): It is the database schema which you want to introspect. If you want Roo to connect to the database and provide the list of schemas available, then simply press *TAB* after entering the `--schema` argument on the command line. As some of the databases such as MySQL and Firebird don't support the concept of schemas, pressing *TAB* after entering the `--schema` argument on the command line will result in substituting `no-schema-required` as the value of the `schema` argument.

▶ `file` (*optional*): It is the file to which you want to save the database metadata. If you don't specify this argument, the metadata is displayed directly in the Roo console.

▶ `enableViews` (*optional*): It is the flag that indicates whether to include database views in the generated metadata. By default database views are not included in the generated metadata.

The output of the `database introspect` command is an XML file (assuming a `file` argument was specified), which contains details of database tables, including fields and their type, primary key, foreign key, and so on. If you specify the `enableViews` argument, the generated metadata includes database views also.

The following XML fragment shows how the database metadata is presented in the `mydb.xml` file:

```xml
<database name="no-schema-required">
  <table name="customer_tbl">
    <column name="cust_id" primaryKey="true"
      required="true" scale="0" size="10" type="4,INT"/>
    ...
    <unique name="PRIMARY">
      <unique-column name="cust_id"/>
      <unique-column name="cust_dob"/>
    </unique>
  </table>
  <table name="flight_desc_tbl">
      <column name="flight_desc_id" primaryKey="true"
        required="true" scale="0" size="19" type="-5,BIGINT"/>
    ...
      <foreign-key foreignTable="flight_tbl"
        name="FK7E26BB6F365DD59" onDelete="none"
        onUpdate="none">
        <option key="exported" value="true"/>
        <reference foreign="flight_desc_id"
           local="flight_desc_id"/>
      </foreign-key>
      <unique name="PRIMARY">
        <unique-column name="flight_desc_id"/>
      </unique>
  </table>
  <table name="flight_tbl">
  ...
  </table>

  <table name="flights_view">
   <column name="origin_city" primaryKey="false"
     required="true" scale="0" size="255" type="12,VARCHAR"/>
  ...
  </table>
</database>
```

The following table describes the significance of the elements in the given XML:

XML element	Description
`<table>`	Describes a database table or a database view. The `name` attribute specifies the name of the table or view which the `<table>` element describes.
`<column>`	The `<column>`, sub-element of the `<table>` describes the details of a column in the database table or view. The `name` attribute identifies the column name. The `primaryKey` attribute indicates if the column is one of the primary keys of the table or view.
`<foreignKey>`	Specifies the details of an imported or exported foreign key of a table. The `foreignTable` attribute specifies the name of the table containing the imported or exported foreign key. The `<option>` sub-element specifies whether the foreign key is imported or exported by the table. The `<reference>` sub-element specifies the foreign key column and the local column to which the imported or exported foreign key maps.
`<unique>`	Describes the unique constraint that applies to the table or view. If the `name` attribute value is `PRIMARY`, then it means that the unique constraint describes the primary key of the table.

There's more...

The metadata generated by Roo is used as input for generating JPA entities, as we'll see in the *Creating entities from database* recipe. Errors may be reported when you use the `database introspect` command if the `META-INF/spring/database.properties` file is not found or the connection properties defined in the `database.properties` are incorrect. The following table shows error messages that might be reported by the `database introspect` and the corresponding resolution:

Error message	Resolution
`Connection properties must not be null or empty`	Indicates that the `database.properties` file was not found in the `META-INF/spring` folder
`Unable to get connection from driver`	Indicates that the `database.properties` file was found but it doesn't correctly define the connection properties. Check if the username, password, and other connection properties are correctly specified.

Testing database connection

As the `database introspect` command connects to the database to generate metadata, you can also use this command to validate the database connection after you've executed the `persistenceXsetup` command.

See also

▶ Refer to the *Creating entities from a database* recipe to see how the database metadata is used for auto-generating JPA entities

Creating entities from a database

In many application development scenarios, an application needs to be designed for an existing database or the application development starts after the database has been created. To support such scenarios, Roo provides the `database reverse engineer` command to auto-generate JPA entities from database metadata. As we'll see later in this recipe, Roo provides *incremental* database reverse engineering, that is, you can execute the `database reverse engineer` command each time the database changes occur and leave it up to Roo to update JPA entity definitions based on the changes in the database.

The following figure shows tables of the database that we will reverse engineer using the `database reverse engineer` command:

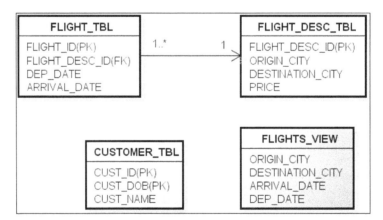

Getting ready

Refer to the *Generating database metadata* recipe to create the Roo project, to create the `myflightappdb` database, tables, and views in MySQL, and install the JDBC driver for MySQL.

How to do it...

To create entities from a database, execute the `database reverse engineer` command as shown here:

```
.. roo> database reverse engineer --package ~.domain.entity.autogen
--schema no-schema-required --enableViews --testAutomatically

Created SRC_MAIN_RESOURCES\dbre.xml

Updated SRC_MAIN_RESOURCES\META-INF\persistence.xml

Created ..\domain\entity\autogen\FlightDescTbl.java

...

Created ..\domain\entity\autogen\CustomerTbl.java
Created ..\domain\entity\autogen\CustomerTblPK_Roo_Identifier.aj
Created ..\domain\entity\autogen\CustomerTblPK.java

...

Created ..\domain\entity\autogen\FlightTbl.java
Created ..\domain\entity\autogen\FlightTbl_Roo_Entity.aj
Created ..\domain\entity\autogen\FlightTbl_Roo_DbManaged.aj
Created ..\domain\entity\autogen\FlightTbl_Roo_Configurable.aj
Created ..\domain\entity\autogen\FlightTbl_Roo_ToString.aj

...

Created ..\domain\entity\autogen\FlightsView.java
Created ..\domain\entity\autogen\FlightsViewPK.java
Created ..\domain\entity\autogen\FlightsViewPK_Roo_Identifier.aj

...
```

As evident from the output, the JPA entities are auto-generated by Spring Roo.

How it works...

The `database reverse engineer` command accepts the following arguments:

- `package`: It is an *optional* argument that specifies the package in which JPA entities are created by Roo. If this attribute is not specified, JPA entities are created in the top-level package of the Roo project.
- `schema`: It is a *mandatory* argument for specifying the database schema name. As some of the databases such as MySQL and Firebird don't support the concept of schemas, pressing *TAB* after entering `--schema` on the command line will result in substituting `no-schema-required` as the value of the `schema` argument.

- ▸ `testAutomatically`: It is an *optional* argument, which instructs Roo to create integration tests for the JPA entities created via the `database reverse engineer` command.

- ▸ `enableViews`: It is an *optional* argument, which instructs Roo to reverse the engineer database views along with database tables. If specified, Roo creates a JPA entity corresponding to each database view.

- ▸ `includeTables`: It is an *optional* argument, which specifies the tables for which JPA entities are created by Roo. By default the JPA entities corresponding to all the tables in the database are created by Roo. The value of the `includeTables` argument specifies a space-separated list of tables enclosed within double quotes, as shown here:

  ```
  .. roo> database reverse engineer --schema no-schema-required
  --includeTables "FLIGHT_TBL FLIGHT_DESC_TBL"
  ```

- ▸ `excludeTables`: It is an optional argument, which specifies the tables for which the JPA entities must not be created by Roo. The value of the `excludeTables` argument specifies a space-separated list of tables enclosed within double quotes, as shown here:

  ```
  .. roo> database reverse engineer --schema no-schema-required
  --excludeTables "FLIGHT_TBL FLIGHT_DESC_TBL"
  ```

Let's now look at some of the interesting things that happened when we executed the `database reverse engineer` command:

- ▸ A `dbre.xml` file is generated in the `SRC_MAIN_RESOURCES` directory of the Roo project. This file contains database metadata in XML format, as described in the *Generating database metadata* recipe.

- ▸ A Java class is generated corresponding to each of the tables and views in the database. The name of the Java source file is `<table-name>.java`, where the table-name is the name of the database table in the camel-case with underscores in the table name removed. Each Java class represents a JPA entity corresponding to a database table or view.

- ▸ The `META-INF/persistence.xml` file is updated. Roo modifies (in case you are using Hibernate as the JPA provider) the value of the property `hibernate.hbm2ddl.auto` from *create* to *validate*, so that the database is not modified when Hibernate `SessionFactory` is created. This makes sense because JPA entities in the application have been created from the database and not otherwise.

- ▸ A `*_Roo_DbManaged.aj` ITD file is created corresponding to each JPA entity created by Roo. It defines fields and relationships derived for the JPA entity from the database metadata. As this ITD file contains fields and relationship information, if you reverse engineer the database multiple times, the changes corresponding to the database are restricted to this ITD file, making incremental database reverse engineering possible in Roo applications.

- ▶ If the primary key of a database table consists of multiple columns, Roo creates a composite primary key class and a *_Roo_Identifier.aj AspectJ ITD. For instance, in the case of CUSTOMER_TBL, Roo generates a CustomerTblPK.java and CustomerTblPK_Roo_Identifier.aj AspectJ ITD file.

- ▶ If a database table or view doesn't define a primary key, Roo creates a composite primary key class consisting of all the fields in the database table or view. For instance, the FLIGHTS_VIEW doesn't define a primary key; therefore, Roo creates the FlightsViewPK.java composite primary key class.

The following code shows the FlightDescTbl_Roo_DbManaged.aj ITD, which corresponds to the FLIGHT_DESC_TBL table:

```
privileged aspect FlightDescTbl_Roo_DbManaged
{

    @OneToMany(mappedBy = "flightDescId")
    private Set<FlightTbl> FlightDescTbl.flightTbls;
    @Column(name = "destination_city",
       columnDefinition = "VARCHAR" length = 255)
    @NotNull
    private String FlightDescTbl.destinationCity;
    @Column(name = "origin_city", length = 255)
    @NotNull
    private String FlightDescTbl.originCity;
    ..

}
```

The given code shows that the *_Roo_DbManaged.aj AspectJ ITD contains fields and relationship information derived from the database metadata. This is different from what we saw in earlier recipes where the JPA fields and relationships are contained in Java source files and not in AspectJ ITD files. Also, notice the presence of the @NotNull JSR 303 annotation, which is derived from the fact that the corresponding database column is defined as non-nullable.

As with other AspectJ ITDs, the creation of the *_Roo_DbManaged.aj is managed by a Roo annotation, @RooDbManaged, as shown here for the FlightDescTbl.java class:

```
@RooJavaBean
@RooToString
@RooEntity(table = "flight_desc_tbl")
@RooDbManaged(automaticallyDelete = true)
public class FlightDescTbl {
}
```

In the given code, the `@RooDbManaged` annotation indicates that the `FlightDescTbl` entity is managed by the database reverse engineering process of Roo. As shown in this code, the `FlightDescTbl` class is empty and only contains class-level annotations. The `@RooDbManaged` annotation controls the creation of the `*_Roo_DbManaged.aj` ITD. The `automaticallyDelete` attribute of the `@RooDbManaged` annotation specifies whether the entity should be removed if the table is removed from the database. The default value is `true`, which means that the JPA entity will be removed from the Roo project if you delete the corresponding database table followed by executing the `database reverse engineer` command.

There's more...

Let's now look at how we can install JDBC drivers for Oracle and DB2 databases, override JPA fields and relationships generated by the database reverse engineering process, perform incremental database reverse engineering, and how composite primary cases are handled by Roo.

Installing JDBC drivers for Oracle and DB2

The database reverse engineering process of Roo requires a JDBC driver to be available as an OSGi bundle. Roo provides an `addon create wrapper` command, which you can use to wrap the JDBC driver inside an OSGi compliant bundle for use with the database reverse engineering process. Roo provides OSGi compliant bundles for most of the JDBC drivers, which can be installed by using the `addon install` command. As open-source JDBC drivers for Oracle and DB2 are not available, to use Roo's database reverse engineering process against these databases, you first need to convert the non-OSGi JDBC driver JAR files of these databases into OSGi compliant bundles.

In *Chapter 7*, we'll look at how the `addon create wrapper` command is used to convert a non-OSGi JDBC driver JAR or any other Maven artifact into OSGi compliant bundles.

Modifying auto-generated JPA fields/relationships

If you want to make a modification to the JPA fields and relationships generated by the database reverse engineering process, then define them in the JPA entity class itself. The field and relationship that you define in the JPA entity class will be automatically removed by Roo from the corresponding `*_Roo_DbManaged.aj` ITD file.

 If you define all the JPA fields and relationships in your entity class, then Roo will automatically delete the corresponding `*_Roo_DbManaged.aj` ITD file.

Incremental database reverse engineering

You can use the database reverse engineering process throughout the lifecycle of your project. If modifications are made to the database, then execute the `database reverse engineer` command, without using the `schema` and `package` arguments. The database reverse engineering process updates the `dbre.xml` file, which in turn results in the addition, deletion, and modification of JPA entities, their fields and relationships.

The `dbre.xml` file is managed by Roo but you can modify it, before modifying the database, to see the impact of changes to the Roo-generated JPA entities. It should be noted that when you re-execute the `database reverse engineer` command, then your custom changes to the `dbre.xml` file will be overwritten.

Database table with composite primary key

If your database table has a composite primary key, then the database reverse engineering process takes care of creating a primary key class which gets annotated with JPA `@Embeddable` annotation (via the `*_Roo_Identifier.aj` ITD). The primary key class is then introduced into the JPA entity class (via the `*_Roo_Entity.aj` ITD) and is annotated with the JPA `@EmbeddedId` annotation.

See also

▸ Refer to the *Generating database metadata* recipe to see how to view metadata information of database tables

4
Web Application Development with Spring Web MVC

In this chapter, we will cover:

- ▶ Auto-generating Spring MVC controllers and JSPX views from JPA entities
- ▶ Packaging, deploying, and using Roo-generated Spring MVC application
- ▶ Modifying Roo-generated views
- ▶ Round-tripping support in Spring Roo for web controllers and views
- ▶ Creating a Spring MVC controller for a specific JPA entity
- ▶ Manually creating a Spring MVC controller for a JPA entity
- ▶ Adding static views to Roo-generated web applications
- ▶ Internationalizing Roo-generated web applications
- ▶ Adding or modifying themes generated by Roo
- ▶ Adding JSON support to domain objects and controllers
- ▶ Creating and executing Selenium tests for web controllers

Introduction

In *Chapter 2, Persisting Objects Using JPA* and *Chapter 3, Advanced JPA Support in Spring Roo*, we looked at how domain layer of an application can be quickly developed using a JPA add-on of Spring Roo. In this chapter, we'll look at how Spring Roo simplifies developing the web layer of an enterprise application using Spring Web MVC. We'll also look at how Spring Roo lets you quickly test your web application locally.

 You can use Roo in developing your enterprise application's persistence layer even if the web framework that you want to use is not supported by Roo. For instance, if you are developing a web application using Wicket, you can still use Roo to generate the persistence layer of your application. Similarly, if you are developing a Swing application, you can use Roo for creating the persistence layer.

Auto-generating Spring MVC controllers and JSPX views from JPA entities

Spring Roo comes with a Web MVC add-on, which supports creating Spring MVC controllers and JSPX views from Roo-managed JPA entities. Spring Roo provides multiple commands, processed by a Web MVC add-on, to help with the auto-generation of the Spring MVC controllers and JSPX views. By default the controllers generated by Roo support creating, reading, updating, and deleting JPA entities from the data store.

The following commands are provided by Roo for creating controllers:

- `controller all`: It is used for scaffolding a Spring Web MVC controller for each JPA entity in the application for which a controller doesn't already exist. The `controller all` command doesn't give you any control over application functionality supported by generated controllers.

- `controller scaffold`: It is used for scaffolding a Spring Web MVC controller corresponding to a JPA entity. Unlike `controller all` command, the `controller scaffold` command provides optional arguments, which allow you to control some of the application functionalities supported by the generated controller. For instance, you can specify that methods for creating, updating, and deleting the JPA entity are not generated for the controller.

- `controller class`: It is used for manually creating a controller. The `controller class` command generates the skeleton of a controller, leaving the implementation of the controller to the developer.

In this recipe, we'll look at the `controller all` command and discuss in detail what happens behind the scenes when you execute the `controller all` command. Creating a Spring MVC controller for a specific JPA entity recipe shows usage of the controller scaffold command and manually creating a Spring MVC controller for a JPA entity recipe shows how to use the controller class command to manually implement a controller.

Getting ready

Create a sub-directory `ch04-recipe` inside the `C:\roo-cookbook` directory.

Copy the `ch04_web-app.roo` script into the `ch04-recipe` directory.

Execute the `ch04_web-app.roo` script that creates a `flight-app` Roo project, sets up Hibernate as a persistence provider, configures MySQL as the database for the application, creates `Flight` and `FlightDescription` JPA entities, and defines a many-to-one relationship between `Flight` and `FlightDescription` entities. If you are using a different database than MySQL or your connection settings are different than what is specified in the script, then modify the script accordingly.

Start the Roo shell from the `C:\roo-cookbook\ch04-recipe` directory.

How to do it...

To create views using the `controller all` command follow the given steps:

1. Execute `controller all` command, specifying ~.web as the value of the package argument, as shown here:

```
.. roo> controller all --package ~.web

Created SRC_MAIN_JAVA\..\web
Created SRC_MAIN_JAVA\..\web\FlightDescriptionController.java
Created SRC_MAIN_WEBAPP\WEB-INF\spring
Created SRC_MAIN_WEBAPP\WEB-INF\spring\webmvc-config.xml
Created SRC_MAIN_JAVA\..\web\ApplicationConversionServiceFacto
ryBean.java
Created SRC_MAIN_JAVA\..\web\FlightDescriptionController_Roo_C
ontroller.aj
Created SRC_MAIN_JAVA\..\web\
ApplicationConversionServiceFactoryBean_Roo_ConversionService.
aj
Created SRC_MAIN_JAVA\..\web\FlightDescriptionController_Roo_
Controller_Finder.aj

..

Created SRC_MAIN_WEBAPP\images
```

```
Created SRC_MAIN_WEBAPP\styles
Created SRC_MAIN_WEBAPP\WEB-INF\classes
Created SRC_MAIN_WEBAPP\WEB-INF\classes\alt.properties
Created SRC_MAIN_WEBAPP\WEB-INF\classes\standard.properties
Created SRC_MAIN_WEBAPP\WEB-INF\layouts
Created SRC_MAIN_WEBAPP\WEB-INF\layouts\default.jspx
Created SRC_MAIN_WEBAPP\WEB-INF\layouts\layouts.xml
Created SRC_MAIN_WEBAPP\WEB-INF\views
Created SRC_MAIN_WEBAPP\WEB-INF\views\flightdescriptions
Created SRC_MAIN_WEBAPP\WEB-INF\views\flights
```

The output of the `controller all` command shows the creation of JSPX views, controllers, directories for images, styles, and so on. Note that only a partial output has been shown in the given code for brevity.

2. As many dependencies are added to the pom.xml file of the `flight-app` project during processing of the `controller all` command, execute the perform eclipse command of Roo to update the .classpath file of the Eclipse project:

   ```
   ..roo> perform eclipse
   ```

3. Import the flight-app project into the Eclipse IDE to view the files and directories that form part of the application.

How it works...

As the output of executing the `controller all` command shows, controllers, views, and so on, are created. To summarize, the following table describes the various directories that are created in the `flight-app` Roo project:

Directory	Description
`sample\roo\ flightapp\web` folder in `SRC_MAIN_JAVA`	Contains the scaffolded controllers (and their ITDs) corresponding to each JPA entity in the application. This folder is created based on the value of the package argument of the `controller all` command.
`SRC_MAIN_WEBAPP\ WEB-INF\spring`	Contains the web application context XML file for the `flight-app` application that is loaded by Spring's `DispatcherServlet`. The name of the web application context XML file is `webmvc-config.xml`.
`SRC_MAIN_WEBAPP\ images`	Contains images used by the JSPX views generated by Roo.
`SRC_MAIN_WEBAPP\ styles`	Contains CSS stylesheets used by the JSPX views generated by Roo. By default it contains two CSS stylesheets: `standard.css` and `alt.css`.

Directory	Description
SRC_MAIN_WEBAPP\ WEB-INF\classes	Roo creates the following two property files, which identify the resources that make up a theme: `standard.properties` and `alt.properties`.
SRC_MAIN_WEBAPP\ WEB-INF\layouts	Contains a tiles configuration XML file, `layouts.xml`, which contains tiles definitions. It also contains a layout template JSPX file, `default.jspx`, which is used as a template by the tiles definitions in the `layouts.xml` file.
SRC_MAIN_WEBAPP\ WEB-INF\views	Contains non-JPA entity specific JSPX views of the Roo-generated web application. For instance, it contains an `index.jspx` file, which shows the home page of the `flight-app` application and an `uncaughtException.jspx` file, which is rendered when an unexpected exception occurs in the web application. To simplify creating a custom home page of the web application, the directory also contains an `index-template.jspx` file.

The directory also contains a tiles configuration XML file, `views.xml`, which extends the tiles definitions defined in the `layouts.xml` file. The tiles definitions in the `views.xml` file are meant for showing non-JPA entity specific JSPX pages such as the home page and the page when unexpected exceptions occur during request processing. You should note that a Roo-generated web application makes use of `Apache Tiles 2` framework to simplify developing user interfaces. |
| SRC_MAIN_WEBAPP\ WEB-INF\views\ flightdescriptions

and

SRC_MAIN_WEBAPP\ WEB-INF\views\ flights | `flightDescriptions` and `flights` directories contain JSPX views corresponding to `FlightDescription` and `Flight` JPA entities, respectively. Each directory also contains a tiles configuration XML file, `views.xml`, which contains tiles definitions for showing JPA entity specific web pages. By default, Roo creates JSPX views for performing CRUD operations on a JPA entity. |
| SRC_MAIN_WEBAPP\ WEB-INF\tags | Contains tags that are installed by Roo to simplify developing JSPs. The tags are XML-only in nature, that is, they are not backed by a Java source code, making it possible to easily modify the behavior of these tags. We will see in the round-tripping support in Spring Roo for web controllers and the views recipe how the `id` attribute of these tags helps achieve round-tripping support in a Roo-generated web application. |

Directory	Description
`SRC_MAIN_WEBAPP\` `WEB-INF\i18n`	Contains resource bundles for the web user interface to support internationalization. By default Roo generates a `messages.properties` and an `application.properties` file. The `messages.properties` file contains translations that are applicable to all web user interfaces generated by Roo. The `application.properties` file contains application-specific translations. This is the reason why you will find translations containing words such as `Flight` and `Flight Description` only in the `application.properties` file. The modifying Roo-generated views and The internationalizing Roo-generated web application recipes describe in detail how these property files are managed by Roo and the role they play in internationalizing a Roo-generated web application.

Apart from creating directories and files, first-time execution of the `controller all` command also converts the nature of the Roo project from a normal Java project to a web project. The change in the nature of the project is reflected by the `<packaging>` element of the `pom.xml` file of the `flight-app` project, as shown here:

```
<project xmlns="http://maven.apache.org/POM/4.0.0 ..>
   ..
   <artifactId>flight-app</artifactId>
   <packaging>war</packaging>
   <version>0.1.0.BUILD-SNAPSHOT</version>
   <name>flight-app</name>
</project>
```

The value `war` of the `<packaging>` element suggests that the project is a web project and not a normal Java project. A normal Java project has the value of a `<packaging>` element as `jar`. We will see in *Packaging your web application* recipe how the value of a `<packaging>` element affects the output of a `perform package` Roo command.

The first-time execution of a `controller all` command also results in the creation of a `web.xml` file—the web application deployment descriptor.

We will now look in detail at the various artifacts generated by a `controller all` command. Let's first look at the configuration information contained in a Roo-generated `web.xml` file.

Configuration information defined in web.xml

The `web.xml` file configures `DispatcherServlet`, root web application context, exception pages, and so on. In this section, we'll look at the configurations defined in the `web.xml` file of the `flight-app` project:

contextConfigLocation initialization parameter

The `contextConfigLocation` context initialization parameter identifies Spring's root web application context XML file(s), as shown here:

```
<context-param>
    <param-name>contextConfigLocation</param-name>
    <param-value>
        classpath*:META-INF/spring/applicationContext*.xml
    </param-value>
</context-param>
```

The META-INF/spring/`applicationContext.xml` file contains bean definitions that are shared by all servlets and filters defined in the `flight-app` web application. These bean definitions are available to application contexts loaded by `DispatcherServlet`. As we saw in the *Creating a Roo project recipe* of *Chapter 1, Getting Started with Spring Roo* and in *Setting up a JPA provider for your project* recipe of *Chapter 2, Persisting Objects Using JPA* an `applicationContext.xml` file contains bean definitions for configuring data sources, services, transactions, and so on, and needs to be shared across the web application.

If you create additional application context XML files, which contain bean definitions that you want to share across the web application, then you can add them to the value of the `contextConfigLocation` parameter using commas or space separated values, as shown here:

```
<param-value>
    classpath*:META-INF/spring/applicationContext*.xml,
    META-INF/spring/mycontext.xml
</param-value>
```

ContextLoaderListener

The root web application context, identified by the `contextConfigLocation` context initialization parameter, is loaded by the `ContextLoaderListener`, which implements `javax.servlet.ServletContextListener`, as shown here:

```
<listener>
    <listener-class>
        org.springframework.web.context.ContextLoaderListener
    </listener-class>
</listener>
```

DispatcherServlet

The `webmvc-config.xml` file created by Roo identifies the web application context of the Roo-generated web application. The `webmvc-config.xml` file contains tile definitions, handler (or controller) definitions, handler mappings, view and exception resolution strategies, and so on. The `DispatcherServlet` of Spring is responsible for loading the `webmvc-config.xml` file and dispatching requests to appropriate handlers, resolving views, exceptions, and so on. In the web.xml of the `flight-app`, `DispatcherServlet` is configured to load `webmvc-config.xml`, as shown here:

```
<servlet>
   <servlet-name>flight-app</servlet-name>
   <servlet-class>
       org.springframework.web.servlet.DispatcherServlet
   </servlet-class>
   <init-param>
       <param-name>contextConfigLocation</param-name>
       <param-value>
           /WEB-INF/spring/webmvc-config.xml
       </param-value>
   </init-param>
   <load-on-startup>1</load-on-startup>
</servlet>
```

As shown in the given code, the `DispatcherServlet` accepts the `contextConfig Location` initialization parameter that identifies the Spring's web application context XML file. The scope of the application context loaded by the `DispatcherServlet` is limited to the requests that are mapped to the `DispatcherServlet`.

If you want to modularize your application, then consider creating a different web application context for each module and configure a `DispatcherServlet` for each module in the `web.xml` file.

OpenEntityManagerInViewFilter

As you might be lazy about loading JPA entities in your web application, Roo configures the `OpenEntityManagerInViewFilter` servlet filter in web.xml to bind the JPA EntityManager to the thread in which a request is handled, as shown here:

```
<filter>
   <filter-name>
         Spring OpenEntityManagerInViewFilter
   </filter-name>
   <filter-class>org.springframework.orm.jpa.support.
       OpenEntityManagerInViewFilter
   </filter-class>
</filter>
```

The `OpenEntityManagerInViewFilter` assumes that the `EntityManagerFactory` for looking up the `EntityManager` instance is registered with the root web application context and has the name `entityManagerFactory`. If you change the id of the `LocalContainerEntityManagerFactory` bean defined in META-INF/spring/ `applicationContext.xml` file, then add a `entityManagerFactoryBeanName` initialization parameter to the `OpenEntityManagerInViewFilter` definition in web.xml to inform it about the `LocalContainerEntityManagerFactory` bean.

HiddenHttpMethodFilter

HTTP specification defines four methods: GET, POST, PUT, and DELETE, but HTML only supports GET and POST methods. As the semantics of different HTTP methods differ, in the REST approach it is recommended to use an appropriate HTTP method for sending an HTTP request. For instance, if you want to delete Flight instances from the database, then you should use the DELETE HTTP method and if you are updating Flight instances, then use a PUT HTTP method. The HTTP method with which the HTTP request was made is obtained using the getMethod() method of javax.servlet.HttpServletRequest.

So, to perform PUT and DELETE operations in your web application, you can do a normal POST and along with it send an additional request parameter with the name _method whose value is either PUT or DELETE. Spring provides a HiddenHttpMethodFilter servlet filter, which reads the value of the _method parameter, creates an HttpServletRequest Wrapper and overrides the getMethod method of HttpServletRequest to return the value of the _method parameter—making it possible to perform PUT and DELETE HTTP operations in your web application.

Spring Roo automatically configures HiddenHttpMethodFilter in the web.xml file generated for the web application, as shown here for the flight-app application:

```
<filter>
    <filter-name>HttpMethodFilter</filter-name>
    <filter-class>org.springframework.web.filter.
        HiddenHttpMethodFilter
    </filter-class>
</filter>
```

The Spring Web MVC's form tag library provides built-in support for dealing with different HTTP methods. For instance, the following form tag will result in performing an HTTP POST and send an additional request parameter named _method whose value is PUT:

```
<form:form method="put">
        <input type="submit" value="Delete Flight"/>
</form:form>
```

In the given code, the method attribute of the form tag identifies the value that needs to be set for the _method request parameter when the form is submitted.

As Roo-generated JSPX files make heavy use of custom tags installed in the SRC_MAIN_WEBAPP\WEB-INF\ tags folder, you will mainly find usage of the Spring MVC's form tag library in these custom tags.

Exception pages

By default, Roo configures exception pages for situations when unexpected exceptions occur or a resource is not found (HTTP status code 404), as shown here for unexpected exceptions:

```
<error-page>
      <exception-type>java.lang.Exception</exception-type>
      <location>/uncaughtException</location>
</error-page>
```

As the Roo-generated application uses `Apache Tiles 2` framework, the `<location>` element is not mapped to the actual HTML or JSPX view that is shown in response to the exception. Later in this recipe, we'll see how Spring's exception resolvers are used by Roo-generated web applications to resolve exceptions to logical views.

Now, that we have seen configurations that form part of the `web.xml` file generated by Roo for the `flight-app` application, let's now look at the web application context XML file: `webmvc-config.xml`, which is loaded by `DispatcherServlet`. The web application context, loaded by `DispatcherServlet`, is the place where request handlers, exception resolvers, theme and locale change interceptors, and so on, are registered.

Beans and configurations defined in webmvc-config.xml

The `webmvc-config.xml` file contains configurations and bean definitions that are loaded by `DispatcherServlet`. Let's now look at the `webmvc-config.xml` file in detail:

Controller auto-detection

In Roo-generation web applications, controllers are auto-detected using the `<component-scan>` element of Spring's `context` schema, as shown here:

```
<context:component-scan base-package="sample.roo.flightapp"
      use-default-filters="false">
    <context:include-filter expression=
      "org.springframework.stereotype.Controller"
    type="annotation" />
</context:component-scan>
```

The `base-package` attribute specifies a comma separated list of packages, which are scanned by Spring for classes annotated with `@Repository`, `@Component`, `@Controller`, and `@Service` annotations. The `use-default-filters` attribute specifies if auto-detection of classes annotated with `@Repository`, `@Component`, `@Controller`, and `@Service` are enabled or disabled. By default, auto-detection is enabled. The value `false` indicates that auto-detection of these annotated classes are disabled. As the web application context loaded by `DispatcherServlet` should contain controller or handler components, the `<include-filter>` element specifies that only classes annotated with `@Controller` annotation are auto-detected by Spring.

If you manually create controllers in a different package, then add the package containing these controllers to the `base-package` attribute's value.

Annotation-driven development support and conversion service

Spring's `mvc` schema provides an `<annotation-driven>` element, which configures annotation-driven development support for Spring MVC applications, as shown here in the `flight-app` web application:

```
<mvc:annotation-driven
    conversion-service="applicationConversionService"/>

<bean id="applicationConversionService" class="sample.roo.flightapp.
web.ApplicationConversionServiceFactoryBean"
/>
```

It is an `<annotation-driven>` element, which ensures that incoming requests are mapped to controllers (annotated with `@Controller` annotation) and to a particular `@RequestMapping` annotated method of the controller. The `conversion-service` attribute configures Spring's `ConversionService` where custom converters and formatters are registered. Before we go into the details of what other Spring features are configured by the `<annotation-driven>` element, let's take a quick look at *Converter* and *Formatter* SPIs introduced in Spring 3 for type conversion and formatting purposes.

In your application, you can either use a Converter SPI or a Formatter SPI to perform type conversions. A *Converter* SPI is suitable when you want to perform general-purpose type conversions from one Java type to another Java type. For instance, when you want to convert `java.util.Number` to `java.long.Date`, you can use a Converter SPI. The *Formatter* SPI addresses the conversion requirements typical of web applications, where you need to convert a `String` value to a particular Java type when an HTML form is submitted and to convert a Java type to a `String` value for displaying it to the user when the form is rendered. You can say that the Formatter SPI is a simplified version of the Converter SPI, and is more suitable for web application environments where localization of `String` values is also required.

You can access conversion and formatting functionalities using the unified `ConversionService` API provided by Spring. The `ConversionService` is backed by a registry of *converters* and *formatters*, which are applied when you perform a type conversion using `ConversionService`. `GenericConversionService` is a concrete implementation of `ConversionService`, which is appropriate for use in most applications. We will see later in this recipe, how the `flight-app` application makes use of the `GenericConversionService` API to perform a general-purpose type conversion at runtime.

If the `conversion-service` attribute is not specified, the `<annotation-driven>` element registers a default `FormattingConversionService` (which extends `GenericConversionService`) for performing conversions to and from `java.lang.Number`, `java.util.Date`, `java.util.Calendar`, and `java.long.Long`. Also, full support for date and time formatting is installed if the Joda Time (`http://joda-time.sourceforge.net/`) library is found in the application's classpath.

In a Roo-generated `flight-app` application, you will find a dependency of the application on the `Joda Time` library in the `pom.xml` file; therefore, formatting support for the `Joda Time` library is installed for your Roo-generated web application.

The `<annotation-driven>` element makes use of the `FormattingConversion ServiceFactoryBean` as a factory for creating a `FormattingConversionService` instance. The use of the `FormattingConversionService` ensures that type conversion and formatting is applied for common types such as numbers and dates during data binding to fields of controller model objects (also referred to as command objects). It is important to note that it is the `FormattingConversionService` that provides support for the `@DateTimeFormat` (refer to `Flight.java`) and for `@NumberFormat` annotations.

To wire custom converters and formatters into the `ConversionService` instance, the `conversion-service` attribute of the `<annotation-driven>` element sets the `ConversionService` instance that is configured with custom converters and formatters, as shown here:

```
<mvc:annotation-driven
      conversion-service ="myConversionService" />


<bean id="myConversionService" class= "..format.
FactoryConversionServiceFactoryBean">
    <property name="converters">
        <list>
            <bean class="com.flight.myCustomConverter"/>
        </list>
    </property>
</bean>
```

The given configuration shows that you can set custom converters using the `converters` property of the `FormattingConversionServiceFactoryBean` class. If you take a quick look at the `FormattingConversionServiceFactoryBean`, you will find that it doesn't support a `formatters` property to allow configuring custom formatters. So, how do we register custom formatters? To register custom formatters, you will need to extend the `FormattingConversionServiceFactoryBean` class and override its `installFormatters` method to set your custom formatters.

In our Roo-generated `flight-app` application, the `conversion-service` attribute refers to the Roo-generated `ApplicationConversionServiceFactoryBean`, which extends Spring's `FormattingConversionServiceFactoryBean`. the `ApplicationConversionServiceFactoryBean` defines converters, which convert `Flight` and `FlightDescription` JPA entity instances into `String` values consisting of entity instance property names and their values.

The following code listing from the `ApplicationConversionServiceFactoryBean.java` file shows the Roo-generated `ApplicationConversionServiceFactoryBean` class:

```
import org.springframework.format.FormatterRegistry;
import org.springframework.format.support.
        FormattingConversionServiceFactoryBean;
import org.springframework.roo.addon.web.mvc.controller.
        RooConversionService;

@RooConversionService
public class ApplicationConversionServiceFactoryBean extends
    FormattingConversionServiceFactoryBean
{

    @Override
    protected void installFormatters(FormatterRegistry registry)
    {
        super.installFormatters(registry);
    }
}
```

In the given code, the `ApplicationConversionServiceFactoryBean` represents an application-wide `ConversionService` with which application converters and formatters are registered. You can register your custom formatters and converters inside the `installFormatters` method.

The `@RooConversionService` triggers a generation of a `*_Roo_ConversionService.aj` AspectJ ITD file. The `*_Roo_ConversionService.aj` defines converters for JPA entities in the application. These converters convert a JPA entity instance into a `String` representation consisting of entity field names and their values. The `String` representation of a JPA entity instance is used for displaying the entity instance as a `String` on the Roo-generated web pages. The following code listing shows the `ApplicationConversionServiceFactoryBean_Roo_ConversionService.aj` file of the `flight-app` application:

```
privileged aspect ApplicationConversionServiceFactoryBean_Roo_
ConversionService
{
    static class
      ApplicationConversionServiceFactoryBean.FlightConverter
        implements Converter<Flight, String>
    {
        public String convert(Flight flight)
        {
            return new StringBuilder().
              append(flight.getDepartureDate()).append(" ").
                append(flight.getArrivalDate()).toString();
        }
```

```
    }
    static class ApplicationConversionServiceFactoryBean.
      FlightDescriptionConverter implements
        Converter< FlightDescription, java.lang.String>
    {
      public String convert(FlightDescription
        flightDescription)
      {
          ...
      }
    }

    public void ApplicationConversionServiceFactoryBean.
      installLabelConverters(FormatterRegistry registry)
    {
      registry.addConverter(getFlightConverter());
      registry.addConverter(getFlightDescriptionConverter());
    }

    public void ApplicationConversionServiceFactoryBean.
      afterPropertiesSet()
    {
      super.afterPropertiesSet();
      installLabelConverters(getObject());
    }
}
```

In the given code, the AspectJ ITD file introduces the following methods and static classes into the `ApplicationConversionServiceFactoryBean.java`:

▸ `FlightConverter` static class: It is the converter for the `Flight` entity. It implements Spring's `Converter` interface and provides implementation of its `convert` method. The `convert` method converts the `Flight` entity instance to `String`.

▸ `FlightDescriptionConverter` static class: It is the converter for the `FlightDescription` entity. It implements Spring's `Converter` interface and provides implementation of its `convert` method. The `convert` method converts the `FlightDescription` entity instance to `String`.

▸ `installLabelConverters`: It registers converters for `Flight` and `FlightDescription` JPA entities with Spring's `FormatterRegistry`, which extends Spring's `ConverterRegistry` for registering converters.

▸ `afterPropertiesSet`: This is the method that is invoked to initialize the `ApplicationConversionServiceFactoryBean`. The method invokes the `installLabelConverters` to register converters for JPA entities.

By default, the `<annotation-driven>` element also configures *JSR 303 – Bean Validation* if a JSR 303 provider is found in an application's classpath. As we will see later in this recipe, JSR 303 validation is used for validating model objects (also referred to as command objects) of Spring MVC controllers.

 In the Roo-generated `flight-app` application, you'll find dependency of the application on the Hibernate Validator library in the `pom.xml` file; therefore, you can be sure that JSR 303 support is installed for your application.

If instead of using JSR 303 validation you want to use a custom validator based on Spring's Validation API for validating model objects, then configure it using the `validator` property of the `<annotation-driven>` element.

ResourceHttpRequestHandler

As web applications need to serve static resources such as images, CSS, and JS files, Roo configures Spring's `ResourceHttpRequestHandler` via the `<resources>` element of the `mvc` schema, as shown here:

```
<mvc:resources location="/,
    classpath:/META-INF/web-resources/"
    mapping="/resources/**" />
```

The `location` attribute specifies the locations from which to serve resources. It accepts comma-separated values for resource locations. The `/` value refers to the web application root and the `classpath:/META-INF/web-resources` value indicates that static resources can also be served from the `META-INF/web-resources` directory of any JAR file in the classpath. It is important to note that a resource is searched in the order of locations specified in the `location` attribute.

The `mapping` attribute specifies the URL mapping pattern of the incoming resource request to which the `ResourceHttpRequestHandler` applies.

DefaultServletHttpRequestHandler

Roo maps the `DispatcherServlet` to / (refer to the `web.xml` file of the `flight-app` application), to which the default servlet of the servlet container is also mapped. As the default servlet of a servlet container is responsible for serving static resources, mapping `DispatcherServlet` to / overrides the default resource serving behavior. To address the static resource serving issue arising from mapping `DispatcherServlet` to /, Roo makes use of the `<default-servlet-handler>` element of the `mvc` schema to configure Spring's `DefaultServletHttpRequestHandler`, which delegates a resource serving to the servlet container's default servlet, as shown here:

```
<mvc:default-servlet-handler />
```

Theme and locale change interceptors

As most web applications are expected to support multiple *locales* and *themes*, Roo configures Spring's `LocaleChangeInterceptor` and `ThemeChangeInterceptor` beans in the web application context XML to simplify changing locale and the theme of the web application, as shown here:

```
<mvc:interceptors>
    <bean class="org.springframework.web.servlet.theme.
        ThemeChangeInterceptor"/>
    <bean class="org.springframework.web.servlet.i18n.
    LocaleChangeInterceptor"
        p:paramName="lang" />
</mvc:interceptors>
```

In the given code, the `<interceptors>` element of Spring's `mvc` schema is used to configure interceptors for pre/post-processing requests before/after the request is handled by controllers. By default, `ThemeChangeInterceptor` inspects the request parameter named `theme` to determine the theme to be applied and `LocaleChangeInterceptor` inspects the request parameter named `locale` to determine the current locale associated with the incoming request.

ParameterizableViewController

In a Spring MVC application, controllers are responsible for processing the incoming request and returning a *logical* view name and view data. The `DispatcherServlet` hands over the logical view name to Spring's `ViewResolver` (configured in the web application context), which resolves the actual view corresponding to the logical view name. The `DispatcherServlet` then renders the actual view. So, does it mean that even if a web application needs to show a static web page, we will need to create a Spring MVC controller for it? Well, this is where the `ParameterizableViewController` built-in controller of Spring MVC comes into picture. The `ParameterizableViewController` simply returns a *pre-configured* view name, which is resolved by the `ViewResolver` and rendered by the `DispatcherServlet`. This saves the effort of creating a custom controller, which does nothing but return the name of view to be rendered. You can either directly configure a `ParameterizableViewController` in your web application context or use Spring's `mvc` schema's `<view-controller>` element to do it for you.

In case of our `flight-app` application, Roo makes use of the `<view-controller>` element for static views, such as the home page of the `flight-app` application and the various exception pages, as shown here:

```
<mvc:view-controller path="/" view-name="index" />
<mvc:view-controller path="/uncaughtException" />
```

In the `<view-controller>` element the `view-name` attribute identifies the name of the view mapped to the URL path identified by the `path` attribute. So, if the URL used to access the `flight-app` application is `http://localhost:8080/flight-app/`, the view name corresponding to this URL is `index`.

If the `view-name` attribute is not specified for the `view-controller` element (as in the given code for an uncaught exception related `<view-controller>` element), then the `RequestToViewNameTranslator`, configured for the `DispatcherServlet`, is used to resolve the name of the view. The `RequestToViewNameTranslator` is configured in the web application context and is used by the `DispatcherServlet` to determine the view name *if* no view name is returned by the controller handling the request. As no `RequestToViewNameTranslator` is configured in the web application context by Roo, the default implementation: the `DefaultRequestToViewNameTranslator`, is used for determining the view name. The `DefaultRequestToViewNameTranslator` simply removes the leading and trailing slashes and any file extension associated with the URI, and the resulting value is used as the view name. So, if we attempt to invoke the `ParameterizableViewController` corresponding to the uncaught exception view-controller element using the following URL: `http://localhost:8080/flight-app/uncaughtException`, then the `DefaultRequestToViewNameTranslator` will simply return a `uncaughtException` as the name of the view that should be rendered by the `DispatcherServlet`.

View resolution

Spring Web MVC applications require a `ViewResolver` to resolve actual view from the logical view name returned by controllers. When creating Spring Web MVC applications, Roo configures Spring's `UrlBasedViewResolver` (an implementation of the `ViewResolver` interface) in the web application context, which returns the actual view. As every view in Spring Web MVC is represented by a class that implements a `View` interface, the `UrlBasedViewResolver` must be informed about the actual `View` class that it must generate corresponding to the logical view name. The following fragment shows the Roo-generated `UrlBasedViewResolver` configuration for the `flight-app` application:

```
<bean class="org.springframework.web.servlet.view.
    UrlBasedViewResolver" id="tilesViewResolver">
  <property name="viewClass"
      value="org.springframework.web.servlet.view.tiles2.
          TilesView" />
</bean>
```

The `UrlBasedViewResolver` resolves a view name to a URL, without requiring you to explicitly map each view name to a URL. For instance, if the view name is `mypage`, then the `UrlBasedReviewResolver` can be used to attach a prefix (using the `prefix` property) `/WEB-INF/jsp` and a suffix (using the `suffix` property) `.jsp` to the view name to create a URL pointing to the `mypage.jsp` page in the `/WEB-INF/jsp` folder of your web application. Here, view name is `mypage` and the URL to which it is mapped by the `UrlBasedViewResolver` is `/WEB-INF/jsp/mypage.jsp`. As the Roo configured `UrlBasedViewResolver` doesn't make use of the `suffix` and the `prefix` properties, the URL for the actual view is the same as the name of the logical view returned by the controller.

If you want to redirect or forward a request to another URL in a Spring MVC controller implementation, then instead of returning a view name you can return a `String` value with a prefix as `redirect:` or `forward:`. If a controller returns a redirect or forward URL, then the `UrlBasedViewResolver` *doesn't* perform view resolution. Instead, it redirects or forwards requests to the URL returned by the controller.

As Roo uses a Apache Tiles 2 framework to simplify JSP development, the `viewClass` property of the `UrlBasedViewResolver` is set to `TilesView`. Tiles support is configured in the web application context using Spring's `TilesConfigurer`, as we will see shortly. The name of the tile definition to which `TilesView` corresponds to is the *actual-view URL* resolved by the `UrlBasedViewResolver`. In case of the `flight-app`, we discussed that the *actual-view* URL generated by the `UrlBasedViewResolver` is the *same* as the logical name of the view; therefore, the name of the tile definition is also the *same* as the logical name of the view returned by the controller.

To get a complete picture of how views are resolved in Roo-generated web applications, consider the controller configured by the following `<view-controller>` element:

```
<mvc:view-controller path="/" view-name="index" />
```

We discussed earlier that the `ParameterizableViewController` configured by the given `view-controller` element will return the view name as `index`. As no `suffix` or `prefix` properties of the `UrlBasedViewResolver` are configured, the actual view URL is also an `index`. Now, `TilesView` refers to the tile definition, which has the same name as the *actual-view* URL value generated by the `UrlBasedViewResolver`; therefore, the name of the tile definition is also `index`. To summarize, the `ParameterizableViewController` configured we saw earlier will result in showing the view whose tile definition name is `index` (you will find this tile definition name in the `WEB-INF/views/views.xml` file).

Tiles definitions

Tiles definitions are defined in XML files and configured in the web application context using `TilesConfigurer`, as shown here:

```
<bean class="org.springframework.web.servlet.view.
      tiles2.TilesConfigurer" id="tilesConfigurer">
  <property name="definitions">
    <list>
      <value>/WEB-INF/layouts/layouts.xml</value>
      <value>/WEB-INF/views/**/views.xml</value>
    </list>
  </property>
</bean>
```

The `definitions` property of the `TilesConfigurer` specifies the tiles definitions XML files. The path to these files can also use wildcard characters. For instance, the `/WEB-INF/views/**/views.xml` path loads tiles definitions from all `views.xml` files, which are inside the `/WEB-INF/views/` directory.

Exception handling

In a typical web application, it is required to gracefully handle exceptions thrown by controllers. When an exception is thrown by a controller, the `DispatcherServlet` makes use of Spring's `HandlerExceptionResolver` for resolving exceptions. Roo configures the `SimpleMappingExceptionResolver` (an implementation of the `HandlerException Resolver`) as the exception resolver for the `flight-app` application, as shown here:

```
<bean
    class="org.springframework.web.servlet.handler.
      SimpleMappingExceptionResolver"
    p:defaultErrorView="uncaughtException">
    <property name="exceptionMappings">
      <props>
        <prop key=".DataAccessException">dataAccessFailure</prop>
      ....
      </props>
    </property>
</bean>
```

The `SimpleMappingExceptionResolver` maps exception class names to error view names. In the given code, this mapping is set via the `exceptionMappings` property. You can either specify the fully-qualified class name of the exception or you can use a *substring* to match multiple exception class names to an error view. For instance, the `.DataAccessException` will map to the `my.custom.DataAccessException` as well as the `org.springframework.dao.EmptyResultDataAccessException`, and in both cases the `DispatcherServlet` will attempt to render the `dataAccessFailure` view. The `defaultError` view attribute of the `SimpleMappingExceptionResolver` identifies the view to which an exception is resolved if no exception mapping is found.

Miscellaneous configuration

Spring Roo also configures the following classes in `webmvc-config.xml`:

- `ReloadableResourceBundleMessageSource`: Spring is a built-in `MessageSource` implementation, which loads resource bundles from `WEB-INF/i18n` folder.

- `ResourceBundleThemeSource`: Spring is a built-in `ThemeSource` implementation for loading the `ResourceBundle` for each theme supported by the web application. In the context of the `flight-app` application, this configuration loads the `alt.properties` and `standard.properties` theme files.

- `CookieThemeResolver`: Spring is a built-in `ThemeResolver` implementation, which stores a cookie in the browser for identifying the theme chosen by the user.

- `CookieLocaleResolver`: Spring is a built in `LocaleResolver` implementation, which stores a cookie in the browser for identifying the locale chosen by the user.

▶ `CommonsMultipartResolver`: Spring is a built-in `MultipartResolver` implementation, which makes use of the `Jakarta Commons FileUpload 1.2` (`http://commons.apache.org/fileupload/`) or higher to support uploading files in web applications.

Now, that we know the configurations created by Spring Roo in our `flight-app` application; let's look at the controller classes generated by Roo.

Roo-generated controllers

Roo generates a controller for each JPA entity corresponding to which a controller doesn't already exist. For instance, in case the of the `flight-app` application, Roo creates the `FlightController` and the `FlightDescriptionController` controllers corresponding to the `Flight` and the `FlightDescription` JPA entities, respectively. The following code from the `FlightController.java` file shows the `FlightController` generated by Spring Roo:

```
@RooWebScaffold(path = "flights", formBackingObject = Flight.class)
@RequestMapping("/flights")
@Controller
public class FlightController {}
```

The `@Controller` annotation indicates that the `FlightController` is a Spring MVC controller component.

The `@RequestMapping` *class-level* annotation maps incoming requests to controller classes. The URI to which the controller map is specified by the value specified in the `@RequestMapping` annotation. For instance, the `FlightController` maps to the `/flights` URI. As we will see soon, `@RequestMapping` annotation can also be used at a *method-level* to narrow down the mapping specified at the class-level.

The `@RooWebScaffold` Roo annotation instructs Roo to generate an ITD containing CRUD operations for the `Flight` JPA entity (identified by the `formBackingObject` attribute) and creates JSPX views for performing CRUD operations on the `Flight` JPA entity. The `path` attribute identifies the sub-directory inside the `/WEB-INF/views/` in which view artifacts (JSPX views and tiles definitions XML) are created for the `FlightController`. Refer the *Creating a Spring MVC controller for a specific JPA entity* recipe to see a detailed list of the `@RooWebScaffold` annotation attributes.

The following code shows the AspectJ ITD created for `FlightController`:

```
import javax.validation.Valid;
privileged aspect FlightController_Roo_Controller
{
    @RequestMapping(method = RequestMethod.POST)
    public String FlightController.create(@Valid Flight flight,
    ...)
```

```
    {
        if (bindingResult.hasErrors())
            {
                . . .
                return "flights/create";
            }
        . . .
        flight.persist();
        return "redirect:/flights/" + ...;
    }
    . . .
}
```

The following are the important points to notice about the given code:

▶ The `method` attribute of the `@RequestMapping` method-level annotation specifies that the `create` method of a `FrontController` is invoked if an HTTP POST request is received by the controller. The `create` method represents the controller method in which the `Flight` entity is persisted in the database.

▶ The return value from the `create` method is either a `flight/create` or `redirect:flights/...` `String` value. If the return value is `flight/create`, then the `flight-app` application shows the web page, which maps to the `flight/create` tiles definition name. If the return value is `redirect:flights/`, then it is interpreted as a redirect URL (as mentioned earlier), to which the `DispatcherServlet` redirects the request.

▶ You may notice that the `Flight` parameter of the `create` method is annotated with a `@Valid` JSR 303-bean validation annotation. The use of the `@Valid` annotation results in invoking validation of the `Flight` entity before it is persisted in the database.

The following `createForm` method, defined in the `FlightController_Roo_Controller.aj` ITD, highlights another way in which the `@RequestMapping` annotation is used:

```
@RequestMapping(params = "form", method = RequestMethod.GET)
public String FlightController.createForm(Model uiModel)
{
    ..
    return "flights/create";
}
```

The `createForm` method shows the HTML form in which the user enters details required for creating the `Flight` entity in the database. The `createForm` method is invoked if the request received by the `FlightController` handler contains a request parameter named `form` (as specified by `params` attribute) and the request method used for the request is HTTP `GET` (as specified by the `method` attribute).

The following `delete` method, defined in the `FlightController_Roo_Controller.aj` ITD, shows yet another way of using the `@RequestMapping` annotation:

```
@RequestMapping(value = "/{flightId}",
    method = RequestMethod.DELETE)
public String FlightController.delete(
        @PathVariable("flightId") Long flightId, ..)
{
    ..
}
```

The `delete` method deletes a `Flight` JPA entity from the database. The `value` attribute of the *method-level* `@RequestMapping` narrows down the mapping specified by the `@RequestMapping` annotation at the *class-level*. We earlier saw that the class-level `@RequestMapping` for the `FlightController` specifies `/flights` as the URI to which the `FlightController` maps. This means, the `delete` method maps to the `/flights/{flightId}` URI-template. Now, the `{flightId}` is a variable whose value is determined from the submitted request. When the value of the `{flightId}` variable is substituted in the URI-template, then it becomes a URI. So, where does the value of the `{flightId}` variable come from? It comes from the request URI. For instance, if the request URI is `/flights/1`, then the value of the `{flightId}` variable is 1. As you will notice in the given code, the `@PathVariable` annotation has been used for the method parameter named `flightId`. The annotation `@PathVariable("flightId")` retrieves the value of the `{flightId}` variable and binds it to the `Long` type `flightId` method parameter.

> The `@PathVariable` not only binds the value of the URI variables to method parameters, but also performs type conversion.

If you look at the code for the `FlightController_Roo_Controller.aj` or the `FlightDescriptionController_Roo_Controller.aj` ITD, then you will find that the controller methods responsible for processing the HTTP `POST`, `PUT`, and `DELETE` methods return a redirect URL (specified using `redirect:` prefix), that is, the Spring MVC controllers automatically implement the `PRG` (Post-Redirect-Get) pattern.

There's more...

In this recipe, we saw that Spring Roo does a lot of work behind the scenes to give us a fully-functional Spring Web MVC application. Depending upon your choice of web frontend, you can also use Roo's built-in support for Flex and GWT to create web applications. In the next chapter, we will look at Spring Roo's support for creating web applications using Flex, GWT, and the Spring Web Flow framework.

See also

- Refer to the *Getting started with Flex application development* and *Scaffolding Flex application from JPA entities* recipes to see how Spring Roo simplifies developing Flex applications.

- Refer to the *Scaffolding GWT application from JPA entities* recipe to see how Spring Roo can be used to develop GWT based applications

- Refer to the *Getting started with Spring Web Flow* recipe for details on how Spring Roo supports developing applications with the Spring Web Flow framework

Packaging, deploying, and using a Roo-generated Spring MVC application

The task of developing the Spring MVC application is incomplete without packaging, deploying, and using it. In this recipe, we will look at how a Roo-generated Spring Web MVC application is packaged, deployed, and run.

Getting ready

Delete the contents of `ch04-recipe` sub-directory inside the `C:\roo-cookbook` directory.

Copy the `ch04_web-app.roo` script into the `ch04-recipe` directory.

The Execute the `ch04_web-app.roo` script that creates the `flight-app` Roo project, sets up Hibernate as the persistence provider, configures MySQL as the database for the application, creates `Flight` and `FlightDescription` JPA entities, and defines many-to-one relationships between the `Flight` and `FlightDescription` entities. If you are using a different database than MySQL or your connection settings are different than what is specified in the script, then modify the script accordingly.

Start Roo shell from the `C:\roo-cookbook\ch04-recipe` directory.

How to do it...

For packaging, deploying, and using a Roo-generated Spring Web MVC application follow the given steps:

1. Execute the `controller all` command to create controllers and views corresponding to JPA entities in the `flight-app` project, as shown here:

```
roo> controller all --package ~.web
```

2. Package the `flight-app` web application using the `perform package` command of Roo:

   ```
   roo> perform package
   ```

3. Executing the `perform package` command will create a WAR file named `flight-app-0.1.0.BUILD-SNAPSHOT.war` in the `target` directory of your `flight-app` project. You can now deploy the WAR file to your application server.

4. If you want to directly run the `flight-app` project as a dynamic web application in an embedded Tomcat instance, then exit the Roo shell and execute the following maven command:

   ```
   ..ch04-recipe> mvn tomcat:run
   ```

   Now, you can access the `flight-app` application by accessing the following URL: `http://localhost:8080/flight-app`

   If you see the following web page, then it means you have successfully deployed the `flight-app` application on the embedded Tomcat instance:

5. Create a new **Flight Description** by selecting the **Create new Flight Description** option from the menu and entering values the for **Origin**, **Destination**, and **Price** into their relevant field, as shown in the following screenshot:

Save the entered **Flight Description** by clicking the **Save** button.

6. Now, select **Create new Flight** option from the menu and select **Departure Date** and **Arrival Date**, as shown in the following screenshot:

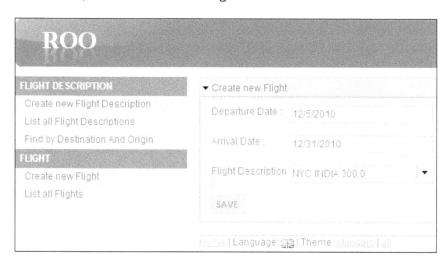

As the **Departure Date** and **Arrival Date** fields are date type fields, a popup calendar is shown to simplify entering dates for these fields. You may notice that the **Flight Description** field is a drop-down field, which shows all **Flight Descriptions** that you have created. Roo shows a drop-down of **Flight Descriptions** because there exists *many-to-one* relationships between `Flight` and `FlightDescription` JPA entities.

Now, save **Flight** details by clicking the **Save** button.

7. You can view the newly created **Flight Description** and **Flight** details by clicking the **List all Flight Descriptions** and **List all Flights** menu options, respectively. You can also search for a **Flight Description**, based on origin and destination, by clicking the **Find by Destination And Origin** menu option. The **Find by Destination And Origin** option is available because we had defined a finder method (refer `ch04_web_app.roo` script) for our `FlightDescription` JPA entity.

8. By default two themes are installed in the Roo-generated `flight-app` application: `standard` and `alt` (represented by the `standard.properties` and `alt.properties` files of the `flight-app` project). The default theme of the `Flight-app` application is `standard`. You can change the theme of the `Flight-app` application by selecting the `alt` theme, as shown in the following screenshot:

9. As the screenshot shows, selecting the `alt` theme moves menu options to the right and the main content of the page is moved to the left. As mentioned earlier, theme selected by a user is saved in the browser cookie; therefore, if you close the browser and reopen it, you will find that the `alt` theme is applied by default on the web pages of the `Flight-app` application.

How it works...

The `perform package` command runs maven's `package` command, which does the packaging of the project. The project is packaged as a WAR file because the packaging (as per the `<packaging>` element the in `pom.xml` file) specified for the `flight-app` project is `war`. It is important to note that when the `perform package` command is executed, tests are *not* executed. It executes maven's `package` command and specifies that the tests are skipped, as shown here:

```
..ch04-recipe>mvn package -Dmaven.test.skip
```

As mentioned earlier, the `perform command` of Roo can be used to execute maven commands. You can execute maven's `package` command (and execute tests) from the Roo shell, as shown here:

```
.. roo> perform command --mavenCommand package
```

>
> **Don't run an embedded Tomcat instance from a Roo shell**
>
> You can run the `flight-app` project as a web application in the embedded Tomcat instance using Roo's `perform command`, but you should *not* do it because it will result in the creation of a different process, which you can't stop using *CTRL-C* and also you can't execute Roo commands from the Roo shell.

The `flight-app` project's `pom.xml` file configures `Tomcat Maven Plugin` (`http://mojo.codehaus.org/tomcat-maven-plugin/index.html`), which makes it possible to run the `flight-app` project as a dynamic web application in an embedded Tomcat instance. The following XML fragment shows the configuration of the Tomcat Maven Plugin:

```
<plugin>
    <groupId>org.codehaus.mojo</groupId>
    <artifactId>tomcat-maven-plugin</artifactId>
    <version>1.0</version>
</plugin>
```

You can configure the plugin to affect the behavior of the embedded Tomcat instance. For instance, if you want to change the default 8080 HTTP port to 8090, then you can do so by supplying the `maven.tomcat.port` system property when running the project on the Tomcat instance, as shown here:

..ch04-recipe> mvn tomcat:run –Dmaven.tomcat.port=8090

There's more...

Roo also provides a `perform assembly` command, which executes an `assembly` goal of Maven Assembly Plugin (`http://maven.apache.org/plugins/maven-assembly-plugin/`, configured in the `pom.xml` file of the Roo project). You should use the `perform assembly` command only if you want to distribute your project as an archive, such as ZIP, TAR, WAR, JAR, and so on. This distributable archive contains configuration files, project documentation, and runtime dependencies of the project.

Running Roo project in embedded Jetty container

The Roo configures the `Jetty Maven Plugin` (`http://docs.codehaus.org/display/JETTY/Maven+Jetty+Plugin`) in the `pom.xml` file to support running the Roo project as a web application in an embedded Jetty container. To run the `flight-app` project in an embedded Jetty container, all you need to do is to execute the `jetty:run` goal of the plugin from the directory containing your project's `pom.xml` file:

..ch04-recipe> mvn jetty:run

If you want to change the default 8080 HTTP port to 8090 on which the Jetty container listens for HTTP requests, then you can configure it by specifying the `jetty.port` system property, as shown here:

..ch04-recipe> mvn jetty:run –Djetty.port=8090

See also

▶ Refer to the *Modifying Roo-generated views* recipe for details about the JSPX views generated by Roo and how you can customize its layout.

▶ Refer to the *Adding or modifying themes generated by Roo* recipe to see how you can customize default themes installed by Roo and how to add new themes to the Roo-generated web application

> ▸ Refer to the *Internationalizing Roo-generated web applications* recipe, for the internationalization support that Spring Roo provides

Modifying Roo-generated views

In most application scenarios, you'd like to modify the layout of the views generated by Roo or to change the placement of different form elements or add new form elements to the view. In this recipe, we will look at how you can modify the home page of the `flight-app` application.

The following screenshot shows the modified home page of the `flight-app` application:

The following are the modifications that we'll be doing to the Roo-generated `flight-app` application to display the home page, as shown in the given screenshot:

> ▸ Change the home page of the web application to show the name of the application as `Flight Application`
>
> ▸ Change the home page of the web application to describe the flight Application in detail, instead of the benefits of Roo.
>
> ▸ Change the banner image that shows up at the top of every web page
>
> ▸ Change the categorization of the menu to show the **Create new Flight Description** and **Create new Flight** options under the **CREATE** category, the **List all Flight Descriptions** and the **List all Flights** under the **VIEW** category, and the **Find by Destination and Origin** under the **FIND** category.

Getting ready

Delete the contents of the `ch04-recipe` sub-directory inside the `C:\roo-cookbook` directory.

Copy the `ch04_web-app.roo` script into the `ch04-recipe` directory.

Execute the `ch04_web-app.roo` script that creates the `flight-app` Roo project, sets up Hibernate as the persistence provider, configures MySQL as the database for the application, creates `Flight` and `FlightDescription` JPA entities and defines many-to-one relationships between the `Flight` and `FlightDescription` entities. If you are using a different database than MySQL or your connection settings are different than what is specified in the script, then modify the script accordingly.

Start the Roo shell from the `C:\roo-cookbook\ch04-recipe` directory.

Execute the `controller all` command to create controllers and views corresponding to the JPA entities in the `flight-app` project, as shown here:

```
.. roo> controller all --package ~.web
```

As many dependencies are added to the `pom.xml` file of the `flight-app` project during the processing of the `controller all` command, execute the `perform eclipse` command of Roo to update the `.classpath` file of the eclipse project.

```
.. roo> perform eclipse
```

Now, import the project into your Eclipse IDE.

How to do it...

To modify Roo-generated views follow the steps given here:

1. Open the `SRC_MAIN_WEBAPP\WEB-INF\i18n\application.properties` and modify the value of the `application_name` property from `Flight-App` to `Flight Application`, as shown here:

   ```
   application_name=Flight Application
   ```

   Now, add the following properties to the `application.properties` file:

   ```
   menu_category_create_label=Create
   menu_category_view_label=View
   menu_category_find_label=Find
   ```

2. Open the `SRC_MAIN_WEBAPP\WEB-INF\views\menu.jspx` file and perform the following changes:

   - Add a new `<menu:category>` tag (inside the `<menu:menu>` tag) with the `c_create` as the `id` attribute value, as shown here:

     ```
     <menu:category id="c_create"></menu:category>
     ```

   - Move the `<menu:item>` with the `id` attribute values `i_flight description_new` and `i_flight_new` inside the newly added `<menu:category>` tag, as shown here:

     ```
     <menu:item id="i_flightdescription_new"
     ```

```
messageCode="global_menu_new"
url="/flightdescriptions?form"
z="DFDc4F2kZR5ysns4ZeMk5pr3E84=" />
<menu:item id="i_flight_new" messageCode="global_menu_new"
url="/flights?form"
z="opwPKDFqpdHotAZ0M/SeEslICC4=" />
```

❑ Add a new <menu:category> tag with c_view as the id attribute value as shown here:

```
<menu:category id="c_view"></menu:category>
```

❑ Move <menu:item> with the id attribute values i_flightdescription_list and i_flight_list inside the newly added <menu:category> tag, as shown here:

```
<menu:item id="i_flightdescription_list"
messageCode="global_menu_list"
url="/flightdescriptions?...."
z="cvk+gcfsrOjH0bM6HiDsKdYX2gY=" />
<menu:item id="i_flight_list" messageCode="global_menu_list"
url="/flights?...."
z="sxdeS3ThjFWc2xKcFfdI4iiZms4=" />
```

❑ Add a new <menu:category> tag with c_find as the id attribute value, as shown here:

```
<menu:category id="c_find"></menu:category>
```

❑ Move <menu:item> with the id attribute value fi_flightdescription_destinationandorigin inside the newly added <menu:category> tag, as shown here:

```
<menu:item id="fi_flightdescription_destinationandorigin"
messageCode="global_menu_find"
url="/flightdescriptions?find=...."
z="SiTmEGC8Kg6mdn8j47EUsKdsOn4=" />
```

❑ Add a new attribute render and set its value to false for existing <menu:category> tags with the id attribute values c_flightdescription and c_flight, as shown here:

```
<menu:category id="c_flightdescription"
z=".." render= "false"/>
<menu:category id="c_flight" z=".." render="false"/>
```

3. Open the SRC_MAIN_WEBAPP\WEB-INF\i18n\messages.properties and modify the welcome_text property value, as shown here:

> welcome_text=Flight Application allows you to perform CRUD
> operations on Flight and FlightDescription JPA entities. It also
> allows you to search for a FlightDescription based on origin and
> destination.

4. Copy `banner-graphic.png` (from the files that accompany this chapter) to the `SRC_MAIN_WEBAPP\images` directory.

5. As of Spring Roo 1.1.5, changes to the JSPX files are not actively monitored by the Roo shell; therefore, restart the Roo shell. You will now find the value of the `z` attribute of the `<menu:category>` tags with ids `c_flightdescription` and `c_flight` is changed to `user-managed`.

How it works...

Roo-generated web application makes use of the `messages.properties` and the `application.properties` resource bundles to support internationalization of the web user interface. The `application.properties` file contains labels for menu and form fields that are displayed on various web pages of the Roo-generated web application. The labels contained in the `application.properties` file are derived from the name of JPA entities and their fields. Also, the name of the web application, as displayed on the home page of the application, is contained in the `application.properties` file. The `messages.properties` contains generic messages which are applicable to all Roo-generated web applications and are not specific to a single web application. For instance, labels for the **Save** button and **Reset** button are specified in the `messages.properties` file. Refer to the *Internationalizing Roo-generated web applications* recipe for details on how you can use these property files to internationalize or localize Roo-generated Spring Web MVC applications.

Not all files generated by Roo are managed by Roo when changes occur in your JPA entities. For instance, the `application.properties` file is modified by Roo only when you add new JPA entities to your domain model or add new fields to them. Removing a field or a JPA entity will not automatically remove the label properties corresponding to the field or the JPA entity from the `application.properties` file. But modifying the name of a field in a JPA entity will result in adding new properties to the `application.properties` file. As Roo never tries to manage existing label properties defined in the `application.properties` file, you can safely change them. The `messages.properties` file contains generic labels; therefore, it is never managed by Roo once it is generated.

The `menu.jspx` file and the JSPX files contained inside the `WEB-INF/views` folder is managed by Spring Roo. If you add, modify, or delete fields from JPA entities, then Roo is responsible for updating the corresponding JSPX views (inside the `WEB-INF/views`) to reflect the change. The `menu.jspx` file is managed by Roo to ensure that when new Spring Web MVC controllers are created or finder methods are added to a JPA entity for which a controller already exists, additional menu options are added to `menu.jspx`.

Let's now look at how we achieved the modified home page based on the actions that we performed on the Roo-generated `flight-app` project:

Changing the displayed application name and welcome text

To change the application name and welcome text, we first need to find the JSPX view, which shows the home page of the web application and then find the property in the `application`
`.properties` file, which is used by the JSPX view to show the application name and welcome text. Alternatively, you can look at the property keys of the labels that you want to change in the `application.properties` file, followed by using your IDE to search for JSPX files, which make use of those property keys.

Let's first find the JSPX view that shows the home page of the `flight-app` application. In the `webmvc-config.xml` file, the following `<view-controller>` element suggests that when the request is received at the web application root `/`, then the view name is `index`:

```
<mvc:view-controller path="/" view-name="index"/>
```

Now, the following `UrlBasedViewResolver` in `webmvc-config.xml` suggests that we need to find the tile definition named `index` in the tiles definitions XML file to find the view:

```
<bean class="org.springframework.web.servlet.view.
    UrlBasedViewResolver" id="tilesViewResolver">
  <property name="viewClass"
    value="org.springframework.web.servlet.view.
        tiles2.TilesView"/>
</bean>
```

The following `TilesConfigurer` configuration in `webmvc-config.xml` suggests where to look for tiles definitions XML to find tiles definition named `index`:

```
<bean class="org.springframework.web.servlet.view.
    tiles2.TilesConfigurer" id="tilesConfigurer">
  <property name="definitions">
    <list>
      <value>/WEB-INF/layouts/layouts.xml</value>
      <value>/WEB-INF/views/**/views.xml</value>
    </list>
  </property>
</bean>
```

A quick scan of XML configuration files specified by `TilesConfigurer` shows that the `index` tiles definition is defined in the `SRC_MAIN_WEBAPP/WEB-INF/views/views.xml` file, as shown here:

```
<definition name="index" extends="default">
  <put-attribute name="body"
    value="/WEB-INF/views/index.jspx" />
</definition>
```

As we'll see in the *Adding static views to Roo-generated web application* recipe, the
`<put-attribute>` element refers to the JSPX file responsible for showing the main content
(which excludes the header, footer, and menu) of the page. So, the `/WEB-INF/views/`
`index.jspx` is the file, which shows the home page of the `flight-app` application.

The following code shows the contents of the `index.jspx` file:

```
<div xmlns:spring="http://www.springframework.org/tags"
    xmlns:util="urn:jsptagdir:/WEB-INF/tags/util" .. >

  <spring:message var="app_name" code="application_name" .../>
  <spring:message var="title"
    code="welcome_titlepane" arguments="${app_name}" .../>

  <util:panel id="title" title="${title}">
    <h3>
      <spring:message code="welcome_h3"
          arguments="${app_name}" />
    </h3>
    <p>
      <spring:message code="welcome_text" />
    </p>
  </util:panel>
</div>
```

The `<message>` tag of Spring's tag library retrieves messages and labels from the resource
bundle, which are Roo-generated `application.properties` and `messages.properties`
files in case of the `flight-app` application. The `code` attribute identifies the property key
whose value needs to be obtained from the resource bundle. The `var` attribute identifies the
variable to which the returned property value is assigned. The `arguments` attribute specifies
the arguments that need to be passed to the `<message>` tag, which are typically used by the
`<message>` tag implementation to fill placeholders specified in the message or label retrieved
from the resource bundle.

The `<panel>` tag is one of the custom tags installed by Roo when the `controller all`
command was executed. The `<panel>` tag is used to show a collapsible panel. To see the
implementation of the `<panel>` tag, refer to the `/WEB-INF/tags/util/panel.tagx` file.

The following table shows the properties file in which the messages and labels, as specified by the `<message>` tags in the `index.jspx` file, are located and their value:

Code	Property value
application_name	Defined in `application.properties`.
	Value: `Flight-app`.
welcome_titlepane	Defined in `messages.properties`.
	Value: `Welcome to {0}`.
welcome_h3	Defined in `messages.properties`.
	Value: `Welcome to {0}`.
welcome_text	Defined in `messages.properties`.
	Value: `Spring Roo provides interactive, lightweight, ...`

The `{0}` in the value of the `welcome_titlepane` and the `welcome_h3` represents a placeholder, which is filled by the value specified in the `arguments` attribute of the `<message>` element.

The given table shows that if we change the `application_name` property, then it will change the application name as shown on the home page. And if we change the `welcome_text` property, then it will change the default welcome text.

Changing menu options

The `menu.jspx` file shows the menu options in the Roo web application. The following table describes the tags that make up the `menu.jspx` file:

Tags	Description
`<menu>`	The `<menu>` custom tag (defined in `menu.tagx`) defines a menu.
`<category>`	The `<category>` tag (defined in `category.tagx`) defines the top-level categories in the menu.
`<item>`	The `<item>` tag (defined in `item.tagx`) defines items within the menu categories.

The following attributes are applicable to all the tags installed by Spring Roo (which includes the `<menu>`, `<item>`, and `<category>` tags for menu):

▸ `id`: The `id` attribute is used by Roo to check existence of elements in JSPX files. For Roo-generated views, the value of the `id` attribute is derived from the JPA entity name and field names. For example, the menu item **Create new Flight Description**, created by the `<menu:item>` element, has the `id` attribute value `i_flightdescription_new`, and is derived from the name of the `FlightDescription` JPA entity. If you remove the `<menu:item>` element with id `i_flightdescription_new`, then Roo finds out that the element has been removed and adds it to the JSPX file *again*.

In some cases, the value of the `id` attribute is also used by tag implementations to determine the message or label that should be used in the implementation of a tag. For example, if the `messageCode` attribute is not specified, `i_flightdescription_new` id of the `<menu:item>` element is used by the `item.tagx` implementation to find the label associated with the menu item.

▸ `render`: The `render` attribute specifies whether the contents of the tag should be rendered or not. By default, the value of the `render` attribute is `true`, that is, the contents of the tag, including enclosing tags, should be rendered. Set the value to `false`, if you don't want the contents of the tag and its enclosing tags to be rendered.

▸ `z`: The `z` attribute is used internally by Spring Roo to check if the developer has made any modifications to the tag. It is this, `z` attribute that allows Roo to perform round tripping. The value of the `z` attribute represents a hash key for a tag used in the JSPX file and is calculated based on the tag name, attributes present in the tag, and their values. The `z` attribute is never used in the calculation of the hash key. Also, the order in which the attributes are specified in the tag is not considered for the hash key calculation.

▸ If you make any modification to a tag (by adding attributes, modifying attribute values, or deleting an attribute), then Roo finds this out because the hash key of the tag now will not match with the Roo calculated hash key for the tag. In case of a mismatch, Roo simply sets the value of `z` to `user-managed`.

Significance of z attribute of Roo installed JSP tags

Let's consider the following element in `menu.jspx` to understand the relevance of the `z` attribute:

```
<menu:item id="i_flightdescription_new"
    messageCode="global_menu_new"
    url="/flightdescriptions?form"
    z="DFDc4F2kZR5ysns4ZeMk5pr3E84="/>
```

The given `<item>` element shows a menu option labelled **Create new Flight Description**. The `url` attribute of the `<item>` tag identifies the web controller responsible for handling the web request when the **Create new Flight Description** menu option is clicked. As the `url` attribute value is `/flightdescriptions?form` and it matches the value of the `@RequestMapping` class-level annotation of the `FlightDescriptionController` (refer to the `FlightDescriptionController.java` file), the `FlightDescriptionController` handles the request when the **Create new Flight Description** menu option is clicked. If you change the `url` attribute (and the corresponding `@RequestMapping` class-level annotation in the `FlightController.java`) to, let's say, `/fds?form`, then Roo will automatically update the `<item>` element's z attribute value to `user-managed`, which means Roo no longer manages this element. Later in this recipe, we will look at how you can switch an element back to the Roo-managed mode from the `user-managed` mode.

Understanding a Roo-generated JSPX file

Let's consider the `/WEB-INF/views/flights/create.jspx` view, which shows the form for creating the `Flight` entities. The following code shows the content of `create.jspx`:

```
<div xmlns:field="urn:jsptagdir:/WEB-INF/tags/form/fields"
xmlns:form="urn:jsptagdir:/WEB-INF/tags/form" xmlns:jsp="http://java.
sun.com/JSP/Page" xmlns:spring="http://www.springframework.org/tags"
..>

    <form:create id="fc_sample_roo_flightapp_domain_Flight"
        modelAttribute="flight"
        path="/flights" render="${empty dependencies}"
        z="/JE8B/QGFrFLKszYDOjyDJjnTPc=">
      <field:datetime
          dateTimePattern="${flight_departuredate_date_format}"
          field="departureDate"
          id="c_sample_roo_flightapp_domain_Flight_departureDate"
          z="BtcAuQvStTt55J3J6zFybfhkSxA="/>
      ....
      <field:select field="flightDescription"
          id=".." itemValue="flightDescId"
          items="${flightdescriptions}"
          path="/flightdescriptions" required="true"
          z="MPt8rEJwJ7fZPqUZPDn6K7+A8OE="/>
    </form:create>
    ....
</div>
```

A couple of interesting things to notice about the `create.jspx` file generated by Roo are as follows:

- The `<create>` custom tag (refer to `/WEB-INF/tags/form/create.tagx`) is used for creating an HTML form. If you look at the `create.tagx` file, you will find that it makes use of Spring's `form` tag library to create a form. The `render` attribute specifies that the form should not be rendered if there are certain dependencies that we need to create before creating the `Flight` entity. Soon we will see from where the `dependencies` variable is coming from.

- The `<datetime>` custom tag (refer to `/WEB-INF/tags/form/fields/datatime.tagx`) is used to create a text field for entering departure the date of the flight. The `field` attribute identifies the `Flight` JPA entity's field for which the text field has been created. The text field is associated with a `dijit` (Dojo's UI JavaScript library) date calendar to simplify entering a date into the field.

- The `<select>` custom tag (refer to `/WEB-INF/tags/form/fields/select.tagx`) is used to create a drop-down box for selecting the flight description associated with the flight that we are about to create. Again, the `field` attribute identifies the `Flight` JPA entity's field for which the drop-down box has been created. The `required` attribute specifies whether or not it is mandatory to select a flight description for creating a `Flight` entity. As the value of the `required` attribute is `true`, you must select a flight description from the drop-down to create the `Flight` entity.

As we can see, Roo intelligently decided that the `<datetime>` tag should be used for creating fields corresponding to the `Date` type, such as the `departureDate` field of the `Flight` entity. Roo also interpreted the `@ManyToOne` relationship between the `Flight` and `FlightDescription` JPA entities and created a drop-down box (using the `<select>` tag) for selecting flight descriptions. As the `@ManyToOne` relationship between the `Flight` and `FlightDescription` entities is also annotated with `@NotNull` (JSR-303 annotation), Roo translates that dependency on the user interface side by setting the `required` attribute to `true` for the `<select>` tag.

Now, let's look at how the `dependencies` variable is used by the `<create>` tag to decide whether to render the create `Flight` form or not. One of the things that you will notice when you go about creating a `Flight` entity is that it will ask you to first create `FlightDescription`, as shown in the following screenshot:

As shown in the screenshot, instead of displaying the **Create new Flight** form, the web application displays a note saying that we need to first create flight descriptions. The decision to show the note is taken by the `dependencies` variable, as shown again here:

```
<form:create id="fc_sample_roo_flightapp_domain_Flight"
      modelAttribute="flight"
      path="/flights" render="${empty dependencies}"
...
```

The `dependencies` variable is added to the request by the `FlightController`. The `FlightController` identifies the dependencies of the `Flight` JPA entity based on the relationships in which it participates. As the `Flight` entity has a not null many-to-one relationship with the `FlightDescription` entity, the `FlightController` adds it as a dependency in the `dependencies` variable, as shown here in the contents of the `FlightController_Roo_Controller.aj` file:

```
@RequestMapping(params = "form", method = RequestMethod.GET)
    public String FlightController.createForm(Model model)
    {
        model.addAttribute("flight", new Flight());
        addDateTimeFormatPatterns(model);
        List dependencies = new ArrayList();
        if (FlightDescription.countFlightDescriptions() == 0)
        {
            dependencies.add(new String[]{"flightDescription",
                "flightdescriptions"});
        }
        model.addAttribute("dependencies", dependencies);
        return "flights/create";
    }
```

The `createForm` method is responsible for rendering the form for creating the `Flight` entity instances. The given code shows that if no `FlightDescription` entity instances are found, the `createForm` method adds a `String[]` to the `dependencies` model attribute. The `dependencies` attribute contains the dependencies, which are not currently available for creating the `Flight` instances. The form for creating `Flight` entities is rendered only if the `dependencies` attribute is empty, something which we have already seen.

We saw earlier that we can switch an element in the JSPX file from the Roo-managed mode to the `user-managed` mode. In some scenarios, you may want to switch back from the `user-managed` mode to the Roo-managed mode. Let's look at how we can do so:

Switching elements from user-managed to Roo-managed mode

We saw that Spring Roo does a lot of heavy lifting to create the user interface of the web application. This includes creating JSPX files, installing custom tags, creating Spring Web MVC controllers, creating web application context XML file, creating the web application deployment descriptor, creating tiles definitions, installing themes, and so on. We also saw that the value of the `required` attribute of the `<select>` tag for showing flight descriptions was set to `true` because the `Flight` JPA entity participates in a not null many-to-one relationship with the `FlightDescription` entity.

Let's assume that we want the text field of the `departureDate` field also to be mandatory to create the `Flight` entity. You have the option to annotate the `departureDate` field of the `Flight` JPA entity with `@NotNull` JSR-303 annotation and let Roo take care of setting the `required` attribute's value to `true` for the `departureDate` text field. Let's further assume that we don't want to make any changes to the `Flight` entity and a date must be entered in the `departureDate` field when creating the `Flight` entity from the user interface. We can do this by simply setting the `required` attribute's value to `true`, as shown here:

```
<field:datetime
    dateTimePattern="${flight_departuredate_date_format}"
    field="departureDate" required="true"
    id="c_sample_roo_flightapp_domain_Flight_departureDate"
        z="BtcAuQvStTt55J3J6zFybfhkSxA="/>
```

As we have changed the default value of the `required` attribute from `false` to `true`, we have effectively modified the element; therefore, Roo will go ahead and set the value of the z attribute to `user-managed`. A `user-managed` element in Spring Roo doesn't participate in round tripping; therefore, if you make any modifications to the `departureDate` field of the `Flight` entity, then Roo will *not* make any corresponding modifications to the `departureDate` element in the `create.jspx` file. For instance, if you remove the `departureDate` field from the `Flight` entity, then Roo will not remove the `departureDate` element from `create.jspx`. If you want your modified form element to be Roo-managed again, all you need to do is set the value of the z attribute to `?`. The value of `?` instructs Roo to re-calculate the value of the z attribute based on the current attributes and their values, making it possible for Roo to figure out if changes happen to the form element in the future.

As we just discussed, you can take control of Roo-managed form elements in JSPX views by adding or modifying one or more attributes. It is recommended that after you make changes to a form element, revert back to the Roo-managed mode by setting the value of the z attribute to `?`. In Roo-managed mode any modification to the JPA entities is taken care of by Roo, saving the effort to make adjustments to the views.

See also

▶ Refer to the *Round-tripping support in Spring Roo for web controllers and views* recipe to see examples of round tripping support in Roo

▶ Refer to the *Adding static views to Roo-generated web application* recipe to find out how you can add your custom web pages to Roo-generated web applications

▶ Refer to the *Creating a Spring MVC controller for a specific JPA entity* recipe for details on how you can instruct Roo not to generate views for certain functionalities.

Round-tripping support in Spring Roo for web controllers and views

In Roo-generated applications, you can change JPA entities and let Roo take care of making necessary changes to the controllers and views. In this recipe, we look at an example scenario, which demonstrates how changes to a JPA entity are propagated to corresponding controllers and views.

Getting ready

Delete the contents of the ch04-recipe sub-directory inside the C:\roo-cookbook directory.

Copy the ch04_web-app.roo script into the ch04-recipe directory.

Execute the ch04_web-app.roo script that creates the flight-app Roo project, sets up Hibernate as the persistence provider, configures MySQL as the database for the application, creates Flight and FlightDescription JPA entities, and defines a many-to-one relationship between the Flight and FlightDescription entities. If you are using a different database than MySQL or your connection settings are different than what is specified in the script, then modify the script accordingly.

Start the Roo shell from the C:\roo-cookbook\ch04-recipe directory.

Execute the controller all command to create controllers and views corresponding to JPA entities in the flight-app project, as shown here:

```
.. roo> controller all --package ~.web
```

Execute the perform eclipse command to update the project's classpath settings, as shown here:

```
.. roo> perform eclipse
```

Now, import the project into your Eclipse IDE.

The following code from the FlightDescription.java file shows the FlightDescription entity, which we will modify in this recipe to get a feel of Roo's round-tripping capabilities:

```
@RooJavaBean
@RooToString
@RooEntity(identifierField = "flightDescId",
```

```
    identifierColumn = "FLIGHT_DESC_ID",
    table = "FLIGHT_DESC_TBL",
    finders = {"findFlightDescriptionsByDestinationAndOrigin" })
public class FlightDescription
{

    @NotNull
    @Column(name = "ORIGIN_CITY")
    private String origin;

    @NotNull
    @Column(name = "DESTINATION_CITY")
    private String destination;

    @NotNull
    @Column(name = "PRICE")
    private Float price;
}
```

How to do it...

To see round-tripping support for web controllers and views, follow the steps given here:

1. Open the `FlightDescription.java` file in your editor.

2. Remove the `finders` attribute and its value from the `@RooEntity` annotation, and save the `FlightDescription.java` file. The Roo shell shows the actions taken by Roo in response to the deletion of the `finders` attribute, as shown here:

    `Updated SRC_MAIN_WEBAPP\WEB-INF\views\menu.jspx`

    `Deleted SRC_MAIN_JAVA\...\web\FlightDescriptionController_Roo_Controller_Finder.aj`

    `Deleted SRC_MAIN_JAVA\...\domain\FlightDescription_Roo_Finder.aj`

3. Change the name of the `origin` field to `originCity`, `destination` field name to `destinationCity` and save the `FlightDescription.java` file. The Roo shell shows the following actions taken by Roo in response to our changes:

    `Updated ...\WEB-INF\views\flightdescriptions\list.jspx`

    `Updated ...\WEB-INF\views\flightdescriptions\show.jspx`

    `Updated ...\WEB-INF\views\flightdescriptions\create.jspx`

    `Updated ...\WEB-INF\views\flightdescriptions\update.jspx`

    `Updated ...\WEB-INF\i18n\application.properties`

    `Updated ...\domain\FlightDescription_Roo_JavaBean.aj`

    `Updated SRC_MAIN_JAVA\...\web\ApplicationConversionServiceFactoryBean_Roo_ConversionService.aj`

    `Updated SRC_MAIN_JAVA\...\domain\FlightDescription_Roo_ToString.aj`

4. Remove the `@NotNull` JSR 303 annotation from the `price` field and save the `FlightDescription.java` file. Now, Roo shell shows the following output in response to the change:

```
Updated...\WEB-INF\views\flightdescriptions\create.jspx
Updated...\WEB-INF\views\flightdescriptions\update.jspx
```

How it works...

Let's now look at what Spring Roo did when we made modifications to `Flight Description.java`. The following adjustments were made by Spring Roo in the `flight-app` project when the `finders` element was removed:

▸ Spring Roo removed the `FlightDescription_Roo_Finder.aj` ITD, which contained the implementation of the finder method.

> If a JPA entity defines multiple finder methods, then removing a single finder method from the `finders` attribute of the `@RooEntity` annotation will only remove the corresponding finder method from the ITD file.

▸ When the `FlightDescriptionController_Roo_Controller_Finder .aj` ITD was created initially, it contained a method for showing the form (refer to `/WEB-INF/views/flightdescriptions/findFlightDescriptions ByDestinationAndOrigin.jspx`), which allows searching for a `FlightDescription` based on origin and destination cities. It also contained a method to search the `FlightDescription` instances and display returned results (refer to `/WEB-INF/views/flightdescriptions/list.jspx`). Now, as the finder method has been removed, the controller methods to show the search form and search results are removed. It is important to note that in Spring Roo 1.1.3, the method responsible for searching entity instances is not created in `FlightDescriptionController_Roo_Controller_Finder.aj`. This bug is resolved in Spring Roo 1.1.4 and above.

> It is important to note that even though the `findFlight DescriptionsByDestinationAndOrigin.jspx` file is no longer required in the `flight-app` application, Spring Roo doesn't remove it. You will need to manually remove the JSPX file from your Roo project. This is because Spring Roo doesn't automatically delete JSPX files that are no longer required in the application.

▸ As the finder method has been removed, the menu option **Find by Destination and City** is also removed from the `menu.jspx` file.

When the `origin` and the `destination` field names are modified, then the following modifications are performed by Roo:

▶ In the `FlightDescription_Roo_JavaBean.aj` ITD, the getter and setter methods for the `origin` and the `destination` fields are replaced with the getter and setter methods for `originCity` and `destinationCity`, respectively.

▶ In the `FlightDescription_Roo_ToString.aj` ITD, the `toString` method is modified to include the value of the `destinationCity` and `originCity` fields, instead of the `origin` and the `destination` fields.

▶ In the *Auto-generating Spring MVC controllers and JSPX views from JPA entities* recipe we discussed how the Roo-generated `ApplicationConversionService FactoryBean` is configured by the `<mvc:annotation-driven>` element defined in the web application context XML. We saw earlier that the `*_Roo_ ConversionService.aj` file of the `flight-app` project introduces static classes into the `ApplicationConversionServiceFactoryBean` class that represent converters for the `Flight` and the `FlightDescription` JPA entities.

▶ The following code shows the `FlightDescriptionConverter` static class defined in `ApplicationConversionServiceFactoryBean_Roo_Conversion Service.aj`, which returns the converter for the `FlightDescription` entity:

```
import org.springframework.core.convert.converter.Converter;

privileged aspect ApplicationConversionServiceFactoryBean_Roo_
ConversionService {
  ...
  static class ApplicationConversionServiceFactoryBean.
     FlightDescriptionConverter implements
     Converter<FlightDescription, java.lang.String>  {
       public String convert(FlightDescription
        flightDescription){
        return new StringBuilder().
         append(flightDescription.getOrigin()).
         append("").
         append(flightDescription.getDestination()).
         append(" ").
         append(flightDescription.getPrice()).toString();
      }
  }
  ...
}
```

In the given code, the FlightDescriptionConverter static class implements Spring's Converter. It converts the FlightDescription JPA entity into a String representation. The String representation of FlightDescription is created by simply concatenating the values of each of its fields.

As we modified the names of the origin and the destination fields to originCity and destinationCity, Roo modifies the FlightDescription Converter class to use the modified getter methods for the fields. The changes that occurred due to these modifications can be outlined as follows:

▸ The application.properties file is modified to add new properties, which act as labels, for the originCity and the destinationCity fields, as shown here:

```
label_sample_roo_flightapp_domain_flightdescription_
destinationcity=Destination City
label_sample_roo_flightapp_domain_flightdescription_
origincity=Origin City
```

As you may have guessed, the property names are derived from the package in which the JPA entity resides, that is the JPA entity name and the name of the field. It is also important to note that once a property is added to the application.properties file, it is never removed or modified by Roo. Roo always creates new properties in the application.properties file. So, if you frequently modify your JPA entity fields, it will result in unwanted proliferation of properties in the application.properties file, which you will need to remove manually.

▸ JSPX views: the create.jspx, update.jspx, show.jspx, and the list.jspx files in /WEB-INF/views/flightdescriptions/ are modified to reflect the change in name of the fields of the FlightDescription JPA entity. It is important to note that if a field defined in the JSPX view is not Roo-managed, that is, the value of the z attribute is 'user-managed' then Roo will not make any modification to the field in response to changes in JPA entities.

When the @NotNull JSR 303 annotation is removed from the price field of FlightDescription, then Roo cascades this change to the /WEB-INF/views/flightdescriptions/create.jspx and the /WEB-INF/views/flightdescriptions/update.jspx views. The only change that Roo makes to these views is to remove the required attribute from the <input> custom tag element that shows the price field on the web user interface.

There's more...

The round-tripping support for JSPX views in Roo is quite sophisticated and takes care of the following changes in the Roo-managed JPA entity:

▸ Change in name of fields

▸ Change in type of fields

▸ Change in the JSR 303 annotation associated with fields

- Removal of fields
- Addition of new fields

If you want a particular element of a JSPX to remain unmodified even if the corresponding field in the Roo-managed JPA entity is modified, then you can manually set the z attribute value to `user-managed`. The sideeffect of this change is that Roo will create a *new* element in the JSPX views if you add or modify the corresponding JPA entity field.

See also

- Refer to the *Modifying Roo-generated views* recipe to find how you can modify a view created by Spring Roo
- Refer to the *Adding static views to Roo-generated web application* recipe to see how Roo supports adding static views to a Spring MVC web application.

Creating a Spring MVC controller for a specific JPA entity

The `controller all` command let's you create controllers for all JPA entities for which a corresponding controller doesn't exist. If you want to control the web request path to which the controller is mapped or the operations supported by the controller, then you should use the `controller scaffold` command.

Getting ready

Delete the contents of the `ch04-recipe` sub-directory inside the `C:\roo-cookbook` directory.

Copy the `ch04_web-app.roo` script into the `ch04-recipe` directory.

Execute the `ch04_web-app.roo` script that creates the `flight-app` Roo project, sets up Hibernate as the persistence provider, configures MySQL as the database for the application, creates `Flight` and the `FlightDescription` JPA entities, and defines a many-to-one relationship between the `Flight` and `FlightDescription` entities. If you are using a different database than MySQL or your connection settings are different than what is specified in the script, then modify the script accordingly.

Start the Roo shell from the `C:\roo-cookbook\ch04-recipe` directory.

How to do it...

The following steps show how to use the `controller scaffold` command to create controllers for JPA entities:

1. Execute the `controller scaffold` command to create `FlightController`, as shown here:

    ```
    ..roo> controller scaffold --class ~.web.FlightController --entity
    ~.domain.Flight --path /myflightpath --disallowedOperations update,delete
    ```

2. Execute the `perform eclipse` command to update the classpath settings, and import the project in your Eclipse IDE.

How it works...

The following table describes the purpose of each of the arguments passed to the `controller scaffold` command:

Argument	Description
class (mandatory)	Fully-qualified name of the controller class, which you want to create.
entity (optional)	Fully-qualified name of the Roo-managed JPA entity class (a class annotated with `@RooEntity` annotation), which is used as a form-backing object by the generated controller. The value of this argument translates into the value of the `formBackingObject` attribute of the `@RooWebScaffold` annotation.
path (optional)	Identifies the sub-directory inside `/WEB-INF/views/`, which contains the JSPX views corresponding to the controller. The value of this argument translates into the value of the `path` attribute of the `@RooWebScaffold` annotation. The value of the `path` argument also translates into the value of the `@RequestMapping` class-level annotation in the generated controller.
disallowedOperations (optional)	Comma-separated list of operations, which is not supported by the generated controller. For instance, if the value is `update,delete`, then the generated controller doesn't contain methods to update and delete the JPA entity corresponding to which the controller was generated. The only valid values for this argument are `update`, `delete`, and `create`.

The following code from the `FlightController.java` file shows the `FlightController` created by the `controller scaffold` command:

```
@RooWebScaffold(path = "myflightpath", formBackingObject = Flight.
class, update = false, delete = false)
@RequestMapping("/myflightpath")
@Controller
public class FlightController {
}
```

As the given code shows, the value of the `path` attribute of the `@RooWebScaffold` annotation and the `@RequestMapping` annotations are derived from the value of the `path` argument of the `controller scaffold` command. The value of the `disallowedOperations` argument of the `controller scaffold` command is used in the `@RooWebScaffold` annotation to specify the operations that are not supported by the generated controller.

The following table describes the elements of the `@RooWebScaffold` annotation:

Element	Description
path	Specifies the folder inside `/WEB-INF/views/`, which contains the JSPX views created corresponding to the controller.
formBackingObject	Specifies the JPA entity class, which the controller uses as the form-backing object.
update	Indicates if the update operation is defined by the `*_Roo_Controller.aj` AspectJ ITD of the controller. If `true`, Roo creates the JSPX view for updating the corresponding Roo-managed JPA entity. Default value is `true`.
create	Indicates if the create operation is defined by the `*_Roo_Controller.aj` AspectJ ITD of the controller. If `true`, Roo creates the JSPX view for creating the corresponding Roo-managed JPA entity. Default value is `true`.
delete	Indicates if the delete operation is defined by the `*_Roo_Controller.aj` AspectJ ITD of the controller. If `true`, the Roo generated JSPX view provides an option to delete the corresponding Roo-managed JPA entity. Default value is `true`.
exposeFinders	Exposes finder methods defined in the Roo-managed JPA entity. If the finder methods are exposed, a `*_Roo_Controller_Finder.aj` ITD is created that contains methods for rendering the form for entering search criteria, and for searching entity instances and showing search results. Default value is `true`.

Element	Description
exposeJson	Indicates that if the corresponding Roo-managed JPA entity is annotated with the @RooJson class-level annotation, then expose controller functionality (create, update, show, and delete) using JSON. The default value is true.
	Refer to the *Adding JSON support to domain objects and controllers* recipe for details on how to add JSON support to Roo-managed JPA entities and Spring Web MVC controllers.

The following table describes methods that form part of the *_Roo_Controller.aj ITD, assuming that all controller operations were generated:

Method	Description
createForm	Shows the form for creating the entity.
	Creates a new instance of the form-backing object (which is the Roo-managed JPA entity specified by the formBackingObject attribute of the @RooWebScaffold annotation), adds dependencies required for persisting the Roo-managed JPA entity (these dependencies include entities that participate in the relationship, such as FlightDescription is required for persisting a Flight entity), and adds date/time patterns (if required).
create	Persists Roo-managed entity exposed by the controller. Also performs JSR 303 (if available) validation on the entity instance. Adds date/time patterns (if required).
show	Shows details of a persisted entity instance. Adds date/time patterns (if required).
list	Shows the list of persistent entity instances. Adds date/time patterns (if required). Also adds support for pagination of data.
updateForm	Shows the form for updating an entity instance. Adds date/time patterns (if required).
update	Persists changes to an entity instance. Adds date/time patterns (if required).
delete	Deletes an entity instance.

There's more...

As shown in this recipe, the controller scaffold command provides options to help create a customized controller. Even if you have created controllers using the controller all command, you can still customize the controller by setting the attributes of the @ RooWebScaffold annotation.

Let's now see how you can override the auto-generated methods in the `*_Roo_Controller.aj` file:

Overriding auto-generated controller methods

In some scenarios, you may want to override the auto-generated methods of the `*_Roo_Controller.aj` file to provide custom implementation. To override a method defined in ITD, all you need to do is to define a method with the same or different arguments and return types, but with the same name, in your controller Java file.

Let's say that in our `flight-app` web application we need to address the following requirements:

▸ Currently, when a `Flight` entity instance is updated the `FlightController` shows the updated entity instance in a read-only view. This default functionality needs to be changed such that after update, the controller shows the list of `Flight` instances.

▸ To address this requirement, we need to override the default behavior of the `update` method defined in the `FlightController_Roo_Controller.aj` ITD. To override the default behavior of the `update` method, all you need to do is to define an `update` method (with the same or different arguments and return types) in the `FlightController.java` file, as shown here:

```
@RequestMapping(method = RequestMethod.PUT)
public String update(@Valid Flight flight, ..) {
    ....
    return "redirect: /myflightpath/list";
}
```

In the given code, the `update` method redirects the user to `myflightpath/list` (instead of `/myflightpath/{flightId}`) after persisting changes to the `Flight` entity.

 In Spring Roo 1.1.3, if you attempt to override a method defined in the `*_Roo_Controller.aj` file by defining it in your `*Controller.java` file, then Roo complains that the method is already defined in your `*Controller.java` file. This issue is resolved in Spring Roo 1.1.4 and later versions.

See also

▸ Refer to the *Manually creating a Spring MVC controller for a JPA entity* recipe for manually creating a controller.

▸ Refer to the *Auto-generating Spring MVC controllers and JSPX views from JPA entities* recipe for details on how the `controller all` command is used for generating entities.

Manually creating a Spring MVC controller for a JPA entity

If you want to create a custom controller, then Roo offers a `controller class` command that creates the skeleton structure of a controller and a JSPX view to let you quickly get started.

Let's consider that in our `flight-app` application we have the following entities:

- ▸ `Customer`: Represents a customer in the flight booking application
- ▸ `Address`: Represents the address of the customer

For the sake of simplicity, let's assume that there is a one-to-one bidirectional relationship between `Customer` and `Address` entities, the `Customer` being the owner of the relationship. The `Customer` entity has only one field: the `customerName` and the `Address` entity has two fields: `addressLine1` and `addressLine2`.

Let's say the `flight-app` application requires that the `Customer` and the corresponding `Address` entities are created from the same form. When the user enters the customer's name and clicks the **Add address** button (as shown in the next screenshot), then the form is expanded to show the table for entering address information for the customer, and for saving the customer's details. The following screenshot shows the form for entering information:

In the given screenshot, clicking the **Save** button creates a `Customer` and also the corresponding `Address` entity instance.

As we have seen earlier, Roo generates views, which allow creating or updating only a single entity at a time. In this scenario, we need to create both `Customer` and `Address` entities simultaneously. This not only requires us to create a custom view but also a custom controller.

Getting ready

Delete the contents of the `ch04-recipe` sub-directory inside the `C:\roo-cookbook` directory.

Copy the `ch04_manual_controller.roo` script into the `ch04-recipe` directory.

Execute the `ch04_manual_controller.roo` script which creates the `flight-app` Roo project, sets up Hibernate as the persistence provider, configures MySQL as the database for the application, creates `Flight`, `FlightDescription`, `Customer`, and `Address` JPA entities, defines the many-to-one relationship between `Flight` and `FlightDescription` entities and a one-to-one relationship between the `Customer` and `Address` entities. If you are using a different database than MySQL or your connection settings are different than what is specified in the script, then modify the script accordingly.

Start the Roo shell from the `C:\roo-cookbook\ch04-recipe` directory.

How to do it...

To see how to use a manually created Spring Web MVC controller for the given application requirement, follow the given steps:

1. Execute the `web mvc setup` command to set up the Spring Web MVC artifacts, and to convert the Roo project into a web project:

   ```
   .. roo> web mvc setup
   ```

2. Execute the `controller class` command, as shown here:

   ```
   .. roo> controller class --class ~.web.CustomerController
   --preferredMapping /customer


   Created SRC_MAIN_JAVA\sample\roo\flightapp\web\CustomerController.
   java

   Created SRC_MAIN_WEBAPP\WEB-INF\views\customer

   Created SRC_MAIN_WEBAPP\WEB-INF\views\customer\index.jspx

   Updated SRC_MAIN_WEBAPP\WEB-INF\i18n\application.properties


   Created SRC_MAIN_WEBAPP\WEB-INF\views\menu.jspx

   Created SRC_MAIN_WEBAPP\WEB-INF\tags\menu\menu.tagx

   Created SRC_MAIN_WEBAPP\WEB-INF\tags\menu\item.tagx

   Created SRC_MAIN_WEBAPP\WEB-INF\tags\menu\category.tagx


   Created SRC_MAIN_WEBAPP\WEB-INF\views\customer\views.xml
   ```

3. As many dependencies were added to the `pom.xml` file of the `flight-app` project during processing of the `web mvc setup` command, execute the `perform eclipse` command of Roo to update the `.classpath` file of the Eclipse project:

   ```
   .. roo> perform eclipse
   ```

   Now, import the `flight-app` project in Eclipse IDE.

4. In the `Customer.java` file, make the association between the `Customer` and `Address` entities as mandatory by setting the `optional` attribute value of the `@OneToOne` JPA annotation to `false`. Also, set the `cascade` attribute value of `@OneToOne` to `CascadeType.ALL`. The following listing shows the modified `@OneToOne` annotation in `Customer.java`:

```
import javax.persistence.CascadeType;
..
@RooEntity(table = "CUSTOMER_TBL")
public class Customer {

    @NotNull
    @Column(name = "CUST_NAME")
    private String customerName;

    @OneToOne(optional= false, cascade=CascadeType.ALL)
    @JoinColumn(name = "CUSTOMER_ID")
    private Address address;
}
```

5. In the `Address.java` file, make the association between the `Address` and `Customer` entities as mandatory by setting the `optional` attribute value of the `@OneToOne` annotation to `false`. As the `Customer` entity is the owner of the relationship, set the `mappedBy` attribute value of the `@OneToOne` JPA annotation to `address`. The following listing shows the modified `@OneToOne` annotation in `Address.java`:

```
...
@RooEntity(table = "ADDRESS_TBL")
public class Address {

    @NotNull
    @Column(name = "ADDRESS_LINE1")
    private String addressLine1;
    ...
@OneToOne(optional=false, mappedBy = "address")
    private Customer customer;
}
```

As in Spring Roo 1.1.5, the `field reference` command doesn't support any argument, which lets you specify the owner of the one-to-one bidirectional relationship; therefore, you need to edit your Java source for specifying the `mappedBy` attribute value of the `@OneToOne` annotation. On the other hand, the `field set` command does provide a `mappedBy` argument for specifying the relationship owner.

6. Replace the `CustomerController.java` file in the `sample.roo.flightapp.web` package of `SRC_MAIN_JAVA` folder with the one contained in the source code folder of this chapter.

7. Replace the `index.jspx` file in the `/WEB-INF/views/customer/` folder with the `index.jspx` file contained in the source code folder of this chapter.

8. Exit the Roo shell and use the following maven command to deploy the `flight-app` project as a dynamic web application in an embedded Tomcat instance:

   ..ch04-recipe> mvn tomcat:run

   Now, you can access the `flight-app` application by accessing the following URL: `http://localhost:8080/flight-app`

   If you see the following web page, then it means you have successfully deployed the `flight-app` application on the embedded Tomcat instance:

In the given screenshot, selecting the **Customer Controller View** menu option will take you to the form for creating the `Customer` and `Address` entities.

How it works...

The `controller class` command is used for creating a manual controller. It accepts the following arguments:

- `class`: The fully qualified name of the controller class that you want to create.
- `preferredMapping`: The request path to which the controller maps. The value of the `preferredMapping` argument is used to derive the value of @ `RequestMapping` class-level annotation of the generated controller. The value of the `preferredMapping` is also used to create a sub-folder inside the `/WEB-INF/views/` to contain the JSPX views and the tiles definitions XML file corresponding to the generated controller.

As the output suggests, the following actions are performed by Roo when the `controller class` command is executed:

- Creates a skeleton `CustomerController` web controller, leaving the controller implementation details to be provided by the developer.

- ▸ Creates the `customer` sub-folder inside `/WEB-INF/views/`.

- ▸ Creates a skeleton `index.jspx` view inside the `/WEB-INF/views/customer` folder, leaving view details to be provided by the developer.

- ▸ Creates a tiles definitions XML file, `views.xml`, inside the `/WEB-INF/views/customer` folder. It contains a single tile definition `customer/index`, which corresponds to the `index.jspx` view. As we will see shortly, the skeleton `CustomerController` implementation makes use of the `customer/index` tile definition to show the `index.jspx` view.

- ▸ Adds the *Customer Controller View* label to the `application.properties` file, which is used by the `menu.jspx` file to display a menu option for invoking the `CustomerController` web controller.

- ▸ Adds a menu option labelled *Customer Controller View* to the `menu.jspx` file for invoking the `CustomerController` web controller.

It is important to note that no AspectJ ITD file is created when the `controller class` command is executed.

The following code from the `CustomerController.java` file shows the `CustomerController` generated by the `controller class` command:

```
@RequestMapping("/customer/**")
@Controller
public class CustomerController {

  @RequestMapping
  public void get(ModelMap modelMap, ..) { }

  @RequestMapping(method = RequestMethod.POST, value = "{id}")
  public void post(@PathVariable Long id, ..) { }

  @RequestMapping
  public String index() {
     return "customer/index";
  }
}
```

As the given code shows, the generated controller leaves it up to the developer to write the implementation of the controller. The method `index()` is invoked when you click the **Customer Controller View** menu option. The `index()` method simply returns `customer/index`, which shows the `index.jspx` view.

The Roo-generated `CustomerController` is hardly of any use, so you need to write it's functionality. The `CustomerController.java` file that accompanies the source code of this chapter contains the necessary functionality for creating the `Customer` and `Address` entities. Let's now take a look at the methods defined in the supplied `Customer Controller.java` file:

The `index()` method of the `CustomerController` sets the `Customer` JPA entity as the form-backing object and adds another model attribute, which identifies whether to show the address section of the form or not. The following code from the `CustomerController.java` file shows the `index()` method:

```
@RequestMapping
public String index(Model model) {
  model.addAttribute("showAddressSection", false);
  Customer customer = new Customer();
  customer.setAddress(new Address());
  model.addAttribute("customer", customer);
  return "customer/index";
}
```

The `index()` method sets the `showAddressSection` and `customer` model attributes. The `showAddressSection` attribute is used as a flag by the `index.jspx` view to decide whether to show or hide the address section of the form. The `customer` model attribute represents the `Customer` JPA entity, which acts as the form-backing object.

Now, when the **Add address** button is clicked by the user, the following `showAddress` method of the `CustomerController` is invoked:

```
@RequestMapping(method = RequestMethod.POST,
    params = "user-action=showAddressForm")
public String showAddress(@Valid Customer customer,
    BindingResult result, Model model, ..) {
  if (result.hasErrors()) {
    model.addAttribute("customer", customer);
  } else {
    model.addAttribute("showAddressSection", true);
    model.addAttribute("customer", customer);
  }
  return "customer/index";
}
```

The `@RequestMapping` annotation in the given code specifies that the `showAddress` method is invoked when the request type is HTTP POST and the value of the `user-action` request parameter is the `showAddressForm`. If no binding or validation errors occur, then the `showAddressSection` model attribute is set to `true`.

If the `showAddressSection` model attribute value is `true`, then it means the `index.jspx` view will show the address section of the form to allow users to enter an address for the customer. Now, the user can enter address information and click the **Save** button to persist the `Customer` and the associated `Address` JPA entity instance. The following `create` method of the `CustomerController` is invoked when the user clicks **Save** button:

```
@RequestMapping(method = RequestMethod.POST,
    params = "user-action=create")
  public String create(@Valid Customer customer, ..) {
    customer.persist();
    return "customer/index";
}
```

The `@RequestMapping` annotation in the given code indicates that the `create` method is invoked when the request type is HTTP POST and the value of the `user-action` request parameter is `create`.

The following code shows the modified `/WEB-INF/views/customer/index.jspx` file:

```
<?xml version="1.0" encoding="UTF-8" standalone="no"?>
<jsp:root xmlns:c="http://java.sun.com/jsp/jstl/core"
    xmlns:spring="http://www.springframework.org/tags"
    xmlns:form=http://www.springframework.org/tags/form" ..>
<form:form modelAttribute="customer"
        action="customer" method="POST">
  <form:errors cssClass="errors" delimiter="&lt;p/&gt;" />
  <c:choose>
    <c:when test="${not showAddressSection}">
      <spring:message text="Customer name" />:
      <form:input path="customerName" />
      <input type="submit" value="Add address" />
      <input type="hidden" name="user-action"
            value="showAddressForm" />
    </c:when>
    <c:otherwise>
      <spring:message text="Customer name" />:
        <form:input path="customerName" onclick="blur();" />
        <input type="submit" value="Add address"
           disabled="disabled" />
      <input type="hidden" name="user-action"
            value="create" />
    <table>
      <thead>
        <tr>
          <td colspan="2">Address</td>
        </tr>
      </thead>
      <tr>
       <td>
        <label for="addressLine1">
```

```
            Address Line 1
        </label>
        </td>
        ...
    </form:form>
</jsp:root>
```

The given `index.jspx` file shows that we can create our JSPX views without using custom tag library installed by Spring Roo or we can create our custom tag library and use it for creating JSPX views. The `index.jspx` makes use of Spring's `form` tag library to create the HTML form. The `showAddressSection` model attribute is used to show or hide the address section of the form. The `user-action` hidden input field is set to an appropriate value, `showAddressForm` or `create`, depending upon whether the user clicks the **Add address** or the **Save** button.

There's more...

We saw how we can use Roo-generated JPA entities and write our custom JSPX views and web controllers to create a web application. Now, we look at a particular limitation with views that are generated by Roo for the `@OneToMany` relationship:

Scaffolding Spring Web MVC application for a one-to-many relationship

Spring Roo doesn't scaffold an HTML element for the *one* side of a one-to-many relationship. Let's look at this in the context of an example:

In the `flight-app` application, a `Booking` entity instance represents a booking on a flight by a customer. On a particular flight, many bookings are possible; therefore, the relationship between the `Flight` and `Booking` entities is one-to-many. The `ch04_one_to_many.roo` script that accompanies this book does the following:

▸ Creates `Flight` and `Booking` entities

▸ Creates a one-to-many relationship between `Flight` and `Booking` entities

▸ Creates controllers and JSPX views for the entities

Exit the Roo shell and delete the contents of `ch04-recipe`. Execute the `ch04_one_to_many.roo` script and run the generated Spring Web MVC application using maven (as described in the *Packaging, deploying, and using Roo-generated Spring MVC application* recipe).

Now, create a `Booking` instance using the **Create new Booking** menu option of the generated web application, as shown in the following screenshot:

Once you have created a `Booking` instance, you are ready to create a new `Flight` instance and associate a `Flight` with the newly created `Booking` instance. To create a new `Flight` instance, select the **Create new Flight** instance menu option, which shows the form for creating `Flight` instances, as shown in the following figure:

As the given screenshot shows, Spring Roo didn't scaffold an HTML element to select multiple `Booking` instances, to help create a one-to-many relationship between `Flight` and `Booking` entity instances. So, how do we create the relationship between entities in case the relationship is one-to-many? To use the scaffolded Spring Web MVC application to manage relationships between `Booking` and `Flight` entities, specify the `@ManyToOne` annotated field in the `Booking` entity (the *many* side of the relationship) to create a many-to-one relationship between the `Booking` and `Flight` entities. Now, you can create the `Flight` instances (without specifying the related `Booking` instances), and manage the relationship between the `Booking` and `Flight` instances from the form for creating the `Booking` (the *many* side of relationship) instances.

If you don't want to add the `@ManyToOne` annotated field to the `Booking` entity, you can modify the `/WEB-INF/flights/create.jspx` view (which displays the form for creating the `Flight` instances) to add a field, which shows a multi-select list box that displays the `Booking` instances. The following `<field:simple>` custom tag (installed by Roo) in `create.jspx` shows the message: **This relationship is managed from the Booking side** when you select the menu option to view the form for creating the `Flight` instances:

```
<field:simple field="bookings"
    id="c_sample_roo_flightapp_domain_Flight_bookings"
    messageCode="entity_reference_not_managed"
    messageCodeAttribute="Booking" z="..."/>
```

You can replace the `<field:simple>` tag with the `<field:select>` tag (installed by Roo), which displays a multi-select list box:

```
<field:select field="bookings"
    id="c_sample_roo_flightapp_domain_Flight_bookings"
    itemValue="id" items="${bookings}" multiple="true"
    path="/bookings"/>
```

If you look at the `FlightController_Roo_Controller.aj` file, you will find a `@ModelAttribute` annotated method, which stores all `Booking` instances in a model attribute named `bookings`. In the given code, the `bookings` model attribute is referenced by the `items` attribute of the `<field:select>` tag to display the `Booking` instances in a multi-select list box.

See also

> ▸ Refer to the *Creating a one-to-many (or many-to-many) relationship between entities* recipe of *Chapter 3*

Adding static views to a Roo-generated web application

A static view in a Spring Web MVC application is a view for which you don't explicitly create a controller class. We saw earlier that the Spring Web MVC application scaffolded by Roo configures static views using the `<view-controller>` element of Spring's `mvc` schema. The static views don't have an explicit controller, but behind the scenes Spring's built-in `ParameterizableViewController` is used for rendering static views. Refer to the *Auto-generating Spring MVC controllers and JSPX views from JPA entities* recipe for details on pre-configured static views in the Roo generated web application.

In this recipe, we will look at the `web mvc install view` command of Roo, which creates a static view.

Getting ready

Delete the contents of `ch04-recipe` sub-directory inside the `C:\roo-cookbook` directory.

Copy the `ch04_web-app.roo` script into the `ch04-recipe` directory.

Execute the ch04_web-app.roo script that creates the flight-app Roo project, sets up Hibernate as the persistence provider, configures MySQL as the database for the application, creates the Flight and FlightDescription JPA entities and defines a many-to-one relationship between the Flight and FlightDescription entities. If you are using a different database than MySQL or your connection settings are different than what is specified in the script, then modify the script accordingly.

Start the Roo shell from the C:\roo-cookbook\ch04-recipe directory.

Execute the controller all command to create controllers and views corresponding to the JPA entities in the flight-app project, as shown here:

```
.. roo> controller all --package ~.web
```

Execute the perform eclipse command to update the project's classpath settings, as shown here:

```
.. roo> perform eclipse
```

Now, import the flight-app project into your Eclipse IDE.

How to do it...

To add static views to a Roo-generated web application execute the web mvc install view command, as shown here:

```
.. roo> web mvc install view --path /static/views --viewName help --title
Help
Created SRC_MAIN_WEBAPP\WEB-INF\views\static\views
Created SRC_MAIN_WEBAPP\WEB-INF\views\static\views\help.jspx
Managed SRC_MAIN_WEBAPP\WEB-INF\i18n\application.properties
Managed SRC_MAIN_WEBAPP\WEB-INF\views\menu.jspx
Created SRC_MAIN_WEBAPP\WEB-INF\views\static\views\views.xml
Managed SRC_MAIN_WEBAPP\WEB-INF\spring\webmvc-config.xml
```

How it works...

The following table describes the arguments that the web mvc install view command accepts:

Argument	Description
path	Specifies the sub-folder inside the /WEB-INF/views/ folder in which the view is created.
viewName	The name of the view JSPX file.
title	Specifies the name of the menu option with which the static view is accessible.

As the output from the `web mvc install view` command suggests, the following actions are taken by Spring Roo in response to executing the command:

▸ Creates a `/static/views` directory inside the `/WEB-INF/views` folder. Roo uses the value of the `path` argument to determine the directory to create.

▸ Creates a `help.jspx` file inside the `/WEB-INF/views/static/views` directory. The value of the `viewName` argument is used as the name of the JSPX file.

▸ Adds a property with value *Help* to the `application.properties`, that is, the value of the `title` argument is used as the value of the newly added property. The property is used by `menu.jspx` to show a **Help** menu option. The **Help** menu option allows access to the newly created `help.jspx` view.

▸ Creates a `/WEB-INF/views/static/views/views.xml` tiles definitions XML file, containing a single tiles definition for showing the `help.jspx` view, as shown here:

```
<tiles-definitions>
    <definition extends="default" name="static/views/help">
      <put-attribute name="body"
         value="/WEB-INF/views/static/views/help.jspx"/>
    </definition>
</tiles-definitions>
```

▸ Adds a `<view-controller>` element to the `webmvc-config.xml` to allow access to the `help.jspx` view without requiring to write a controller, as shown here:

```
<mvc:view-controller path="/static/view/help"/>
```

See also

▸ Refer to the *Manually creating a Spring MVC controller for a JPA entity* recipe for details on how to create a custom controller and view

Internationalizing Roo-generated web applications

Roo supports internationalization of the complete UI by using resource bundles for labels and messages. In this recipe, we will look at the `web mvc install language` command of Roo and see how it simplifies internationalizing the Roo-generated web user interface.

Getting ready

Delete the contents of `ch04-recipe` sub-directory inside the `C:\roo-cookbook` directory.

Copy the `ch04_web-app.roo` script into the `ch04-recipe` directory.

Execute the `ch04_web-app.roo` script that creates the `flight-app` Roo project, sets up Hibernate as the persistence provider, configures MySQL as the database for the application, creates the `Flight` and `FlightDescription` JPA entities and defines a many-to-one relationship between the `Flight` and `FlightDescription` entities. If you are using a different database than MySQL or your connection settings are different than what is specified in the script, then modify the script accordingly.

Start the Roo shell from the `C:\roo-cookbook\ch04-recipe` directory.

Execute the `controller all` command to create controllers and views corresponding to the JPA entities in the `flight-app` project, as shown here:

```
.. roo> controller all --package ~.web
```

Execute the `perform eclipse` command to update the project's classpath settings, as shown here:

```
.. roo> perform eclipse
```

Now, import the project into your Eclipse IDE.

How to do it...

For internationalizing the Roo-generated web user interface execute `web mvc install language`, as shown here:

```
.. roo> web mvc install language --code es
Created SRC_MAIN_WEBAPP\WEB-INF\i18n\messages_es.properties
Created SRC_MAIN_WEBAPP\images\es.png
Managed SRC_MAIN_WEBAPP\WEB-INF\views\footer.jspx
```

How it works...

The `web mvc install language` command accepts a single argument: `code`, which identifies the language code for which the support needs to be added to the web application. The `code` argument accepts a pre-defined language code, depending upon the languages supported by Spring Roo. Spring Roo contains translations for the standard messages and labels for the following language codes: `de` (German), `en` (English), `es` (Espanol), `it` (Italian), `nl` (Dutch), and `sv` (Swedish).

When the `web mvc install language` command is executed, Roo processes the command by taking the following actions:

- Creates the `messages_es.properties` in `/WEB-INF/i18n/` folder
- Copies an image icon (`es.png`) for the language in the `images` directory
- Updates `/WEB-INF/views/footer.jspx` to show the image icon for the language

To check if the support for the Espanol language is correctly installed, deploy and run the `flight-app` application. The following screenshot shows the home page of the `flight-app` application, after the Espanol language support is added:

As the given screenshot shows, an additional image icon is displayed to allow users to change the language of the web application to Espanol. When a user clicks the image icon corresponding to a language, the `lang` request parameter is set in the request, which is used by `LocaleChangeInterceptor` (configured in the `/WEB-INF/spring/webmvc-config.xml`) for changing the current locale.

The `CookieLocaleResolver` configured in the `/WEB-INF/spring/webmvc-config.xml` stores a cookie named `locale` in the browser, so that users don't need to change their preferred language every time they access the web application.

There's more...

In the Auto-generating Spring MVC controllers and the JSPX views from the JPA entities recipe, we discussed that the `messages.properties` contains messages and labels that are common to all Roo-generated web applications and the `application.properties` contains application-specific messages and labels.

As Roo can't provide translations for application-specific messages and labels, the `web mvc install language` command doesn't create an `application_<language-code>.properties` file. It is left up to the developer to create an `application_<language-code>.properties` file for specific language codes and provide translations.

See also

▶ Refer to the *Auto-generating Spring MVC controllers and JSPX views from JPA entities* recipe for `LocaleChangeInterceptor` and `CookieLocale Resolver` configuration

Adding or modifying themes generated by Roo

A theme is a collection of CSS and image files that define the overall look and feel of the web application. Spring Web MVC framework provides built-in support for defining and applying themes. In the *Auto-generating Spring MVC controllers* and *JSPX views from JPA entities* recipes, we touched upon themes support in Roo-generated Spring Web MVC applications. In this recipe, we'll see in detail how to add new themes to Roo-generated Spring Web MVC applications and to modify default themes installed by Roo.

In this recipe, we'll make the following modifications to the Roo-generated `flight-app` web application:

- ▸ Add a new custom theme
- ▸ Modify existing themes to show different background color of menu headings, and different header images
- ▸ Add a new *standard* theme, which is applied if the language is *es* (that is, Espanol)

Getting ready

Delete the contents of `ch04-recipe` the sub-directory inside the `C:\roo-cookbook` directory.

Copy the `ch04_web-app.roo` script into the `ch04-recipe` directory.

Execute the `ch04_web-app.roo` script that creates the `flight-app` Roo project, sets up Hibernate as the persistence provider, configures MySQL as the database for the application, creates the `Flight` and `FlightDescription` JPA entities and defines a many-to-one relationship between the `Flight` and `FlightDescription` entities. If you are using a different database than MySQL or your connection settings are different than what is specified in the script, then modify the script accordingly.

Start the Roo shell from the `C:\roo-cookbook\ch04-recipe` directory.

Execute the `controller all` command to create controllers and views corresponding to the JPA entities in the `flight-app` project, as shown here:

```
.. roo> controller all --package ~.web
```

Execute the `perform eclipse` command to update the project's classpath settings, as shown here:

```
.. roo> perform eclipse
```

Now, import the `flight-app` project into your Eclipse IDE.

How to do it...

To add new themes and modify existing themes follow the steps given here:

1. Create the `custom.properties` file in the `/WEB-INF/classes` folder and set the following properties:

   ```
   styleSheet=resources/styles/custom.css
   header_image=resources/images/custom_image.png
   ```

   The `custom.properties` file represents the file that defines the *custom* theme that we want to add to the `flight-app` application.

2. Create the `standard_es.properties` file in the `/WEB-INF/classes` folder and set the following properties:

   ```
   styleSheet=resources/styles/standard_es.css
   header_image=resources/images/standard_es_image.png
   ```

   The `standard_es.properties` file represents the file that defines a *standard* theme when the language is *es*.

3. Update the `alt.properties` file in the `/WEB-INF/classes` folder so that it has the following properties:

   ```
   styleSheet=resources/styles/alt.css
   header_image=resources/images/alt_image.png
   ```

   The `alt.properties` file represents the file that defines an *alternate* theme. This theme is installed by Roo.

4. Update the `standard.properties` file in the `/WEB-INF/classes` folder so that it has the following properties:

   ```
   styleSheet=resources/styles/standard.css
   header_image=resources/images/standard_image.png
   ```

   The `standard.properties` file represents the file that defines a standard theme. This theme is installed by Roo.

5. Copy the `alt_image.png` (banner image for alternate theme), the `custom_image.png` (banner image for newly added custom theme), the `standard_es_image.png` (banner image for newly added standard theme when the language is es) and the `standard_image.png` (banner image for standard theme) images that accompany this chapter to the `SRC_MAIN_WEBAPP/images/` folder of the `flight-app` application.

6. Create a copy of `SRC_MAIN_WEBAPP/styles/alt.css` (CSS for alternate theme) and name it `custom.css` (CSS for newly added custom theme). Change the background color of the menu headings by modifying the `background` element of the #menu h2 definition, as shown here:

   ```
   #menu h2 {
   ```

```
    color: #fff;
    background: #3f0;
    text-transform: uppercase;
    font-weight:bold;
    font-size: 12px;
}
```

7. Change the `background` element of the `#menu h2` definition in the `standard.css` (CSS for standard theme) file, as shown here:

```
#menu h2 {
    color: #fff;
    background: #06c;
    text-transform: uppercase;
    font-weight:bold;
    font-size: 12px;
}
```

8. Create a copy of `SRC_MAIN_WEBAPP/styles/standard.css` and name it `standard_es.css` (CSS for newly added standard theme when the language is es). Change the background color of the menu headings by modifying the `background` element of the `#menu h2` definition, as shown here:

```
#menu h2 {
    color: #fff;
    background: #f0f;
    text-transform: uppercase;
    font-weight:bold;
    font-size: 12px;
}
```

9. Modify the `/WEB-INF/tags/util/theme.tagx` file to add the hyperlink for switching to the custom theme (or you can copy the `theme.tagx` file that accompanies the source code of this chapter):

```
...
<c:out value=" | " />
<spring:url var="url_theme3" value="">
    <spring:param name="theme" value="custom" />
    <c:if test="${not empty param.page}">
        <spring:param name="page" value="${param.page}" />
    </c:if>
    <c:if test="${not empty param.size}">
        <spring:param name="size" value="${param.size}" />
    </c:if>
</spring:url>
```

```
<spring:message code="global_theme_custom"
    var="theme_custom" />
```

```
<a href="${url_theme3}" title="${theme_custom}">${theme_custom}</
a>
```

The `<spring:message>` tag in the given code displays the **custom** link, which allows switching the theme to custom.

10. Add the following property to the `/WEB-INF/i18n/messages.properties` file:

    ```
    global_theme_custom=custom
    ```

    This property is used by the `theme.tagx` to display the **custom** link.

11. Update the `/WEB-INF/views/header.jspx` file to use the `header_image` property defined in the theme files for the banner image (or use the `header.jspx` file that accompanies this chapter):

    ```
    <spring:theme code="header_image" var="headerImg"/>
    <spring:url value="/${headerImg}" var="banner" />
    ```

12. Add language support for es (Espanol) using the `web mvc install language` command, as shown here:

    ```
    ..roo> web mvc install language --code es
    ```

13. Deploy the `flight-app` application to embed a Tomcat instance using maven, as shown here:

    ```
    .. recipe> mvc tomcat:run
    ```

How it works...

Let's take a deep dive into how themes are configured and used in Spring MVC applications:

In `webmvc-config.xml`, `ResourceBundleThemeSource` is configured by Spring Roo. When using the `ResourceBundleThemeSource` all theme resources (images and CSS) are defined in a properties file (a theme source), which resides in the classpath root (that is, the `/WEB-INF/classes` directory). So, each properties file in the `/WEB-INF/classes` constitutes a theme definition file. Now, by default Roo creates two properties file in `/WEB-INF/classes` directory: `standard.properties` and `alt.properties`. We can say that we have two themes installed by default in the Roo-generated Spring Web MVC applications. So, what does these property files contain? Each properties file contains information about the CSS and images that form part of the theme. The `alt.properties` file contains the following property:

```
styleSheet=resources/styles/alt.css
```

The `standard.properties` file contains the following property:

```
styleSheet=resources/styles/standard.css
```

As you can see, both `alt.properties` and `standard.properties` define a `styleSheet` property, which refers to a CSS file. Depending upon the theme you choose in the Roo-generated web application, an appropriate style sheet is applied to the web application.

The next question that you may ask is—how the Spring Web MVC application comes to know which theme to apply? Well, this is where the following Roo-generated `CookieThemeResolver` configuration comes into play:

```
<bean class="org.springframework.web.servlet.theme.
  CookieThemeResolver"
  id="themeResolver" p:cookieName="theme"
  p:defaultThemeName="standard"/>
```

The `cookieName` attribute specifies the name of the cookie, which contains the theme that applies to the web application. If no cookie is found, then the configuration uses the theme identified by the `defaultThemeName` attribute, which happens to be standard; therefore, the theme defined by `standard.properties` is used by default by the Roo-generated Spring Web MVC application.

Now, we know how themes are defined using property files and how a theme is configured for Spring Web MVC application. Let's now see how theme resources are accessed by JSPX views:

JSPX views access theme resources such as images and CSS defined in property files using the `<theme>` tag of Spring's tag library, as shown here:

```
<spring:theme code="header_image" var="headerImg"/>
```

The `code` attribute identifies the name of the property, which you want to access from the theme properties file. The `var` attribute of the `<theme>` tag specifies the name of the variable in which the property value is stored. The theme property file from which the property is read is dependent upon the current theme that applies to the web application. For instance, if the current theme is standard, then the `header_image` property is read from the `standard.properties` file, if the current theme is custom, then `header_image` property is read from the `custom.properties` file, and so on.

The `ResourceBundleThemeSource` supports configuring localized themes also. For instance, the `standard_es.properties` file in `/WEB-INF/classes` defines theme resources, which apply when the language is es and the theme is standard.

Now, coming to how you add your custom theme name at the bottom of the web page of the Roo-generated web application. All you need to do is to modify the `theme.tagx` file, which is responsible for showing all the theme hyperlinks. When you select the theme of your choice, the `ThemeChangeInterceptor` comes into picture, which allows for changing the current theme on every request.

The following screenshot shows how the home page of the `flight-app` application looks when the current theme is the modified standard theme:

In the given screenshot, you'll notice the change in the background color of the menu headings such as **FLIGHT DESCRIPTION** and **FLIGHT**. You'll also notice that instead of the default header image, an image containing text **IMAGE (Standard)** is displayed. As we have copied different images for each theme, a different image is displayed, which identifies the theme, which currently applies to the web application.

The following screenshot shows the home page of the `flight-app` application when we select the Espanol language from the footer, without changing the current standard theme:

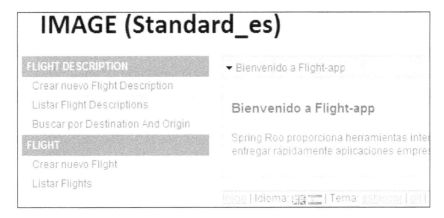

Again, notice the change in the background color of the menu headings and the change in the header image.

The following screenshot shows the home page of the `flight-app` web application when the chosen language is *English* and the theme is custom:

There's more...

In some scenarios, you may have additional properties files in your `/WEB-INF/classes` directory. For instance, you may have a `log4j.properties` file inside `/WEB-INF/classes` for use by the `log4j` library. In such scenarios, you may want to keep your theme properties files in a different folder than the classpath root. You can do so by using the `basenamePrefix` property of `ResourceBundleThemeSource`. For instance, consider the following configuration of the `ResourceBundleThemeSource` in `webmvc-config.xml` file:

```
<bean class="org.springframework.ui.context.support.
    ResourceBundleThemeSource" id="themeSource"
    p:basenamePrefix="themes."/>
```

The value `themes.` of the `basenamePrefix` attribute effectively says that `ResourceBundleThemeSource` should look for themes inside the `/WEB-INF/classes/themes` directory.

See also

▸ Refer to the *Auto-generating Spring MVC controllers and JSPX views from JPA entities* recipe to know more about configurations defined in the `webmvc-config.xml` file

Adding JSON support to domain objects and controllers

Let's say that you have developed the persistence layer of your application using Roo. Now, you want to expose the CRUD operations and dynamic finder methods defined in the Roo-generated JPA entities to the outside world via a RESTful interface.

Roo supports exposing CRUD operations and dynamic finders of JPA entities via RESTful interfaces that use JSON documents for exchanging data. As JSON is used by Roo-generated RESTful interfaces, you can modify JSPX pages of the Roo-generated Spring Web MVC application to use Ajax to interact with these RESTful interfaces.

Roo provides two commands for adding JSON support to existing classes in the Roo project:

- ▸ `json add`: Adds JSON support to the class specified using the `class` argument
- ▸ `json all`: Adds JSON support to all the classes annotated with the `@RooJavaBean` annotation

The `json add` and `json all` commands add the `@RooJson` annotation to Java classes. the `@RooJson` annotation results in the creation of a `*_Roo_Json.aj` AspectJ ITD corresponding to the class annotated with the `@RooJson` annotation. In this recipe, we'll look at the `*_Roo_Json.aj` AspectJ ITD and at the `@RooJson` annotation.

It is important to note that `@RooJson` annotation allows you to control auto-generation of JSON related methods in the corresponding `*_Roo_Json.aj` ITD file.

Getting ready

Delete the contents of the `ch04-recipe` sub-directory inside the `C:\roo-cookbook` directory.

Copy the `ch04_web-app.roo` script into the `ch04-recipe` directory.

Execute the `ch04_web-app.roo` script that creates the `flight-app` Roo project, sets up Hibernate as the persistence provider, configures MySQL as the database for the application, creates the `Flight` and `FlightDescription` JPA entities, and defines a many-to-one relationship between the `Flight` and `FlightDescription` entities. If you are using a different database than MySQL or your connection settings are different than what is specified in the script, then modify the script accordingly.

Start the Roo shell from the `C:\roo-cookbook\ch04-recipe` directory.

Execute the `controller all` command to create controllers and JSPX views corresponding to JPA entities in the `flight-app` project, as shown here:

```
.. roo> controller all --package ~.web
```

Execute the `perform eclipse` command to update the project's classpath settings, as shown here:

```
.. roo> perform eclipse
```

Now, import the `flight-app` project into your Eclipse IDE.

How to do it...

To add the `json` support execute the `json add` command against the `Flight` JPA entity:

```
~.domain.Flight roo> json add --class ~.domain.Flight
Updated SRC_MAIN_JAVA\...\domain\Flight.java
Created SRC_MAIN_JAVA\...\domain\Flight_Roo_Json.aj
Created SRC_MAIN_JAVA\...\web\FlightController_Roo_Controller_Json.aj
```

Alternatively, add the `@RooJson` annotation to the `Flight.java` class. Adding the `@RooJson` annotation to the `Flight` entity has the same effect as executing the `json add` command against the `Flight` entity. Adding the `@RooJson` annotation will result in auto-generation of `Flight_Roo_Json.aj` and `FlightController_Roo_Controller_Json.aj` AspectJ ITDs.

How it works...

Executing the `json add` command annotates the class (specified via `class` argument) with the `@RooJson` annotation. If a class is annotated with the `@RooJson` annotation, Roo creates a `*_Roo_Json.aj` AspectJ ITD, which defines methods for converting objects of the class to JSON documents and vice versa.

We saw that when the `json addon` command was executed against the `Flight` entity, it also resulted in the creation of a `FlightController_Roo_Controller_Json.aj` AspectJ ITD. This ITD is created if the value of the `@RooWebScaffold`'s `exposeJson` attribute in the `FlightController.java` class is true. If the `@RooWebScaffold`'s `exposeJson` attribute is not specified, the default value is `true`.

If the value of the `exposeJson` attribute is `true` and the JPA entity used as the form-backing object by the web controller is annotated with the `@RooJson` annotation, Roo creates a `*_Roo_Controller_Json.aj` ITD corresponding to the web controller class. This ITD defines JSON-based methods to perform CRUD operations and execute dynamic finder methods of the JPA entity. For instance, the `FlightController_Roo_Controller_Json.aj` ITD introduces JSON-related methods into the `FlightController.java` class for performing CRUD operations on the `Flight` entity.

The following listing shows the methods defined in the `Flight_Roo_Json.aj` ITD file that was created corresponding to the `@RooJson` annotated `Flight` entity:

```
import flexjson.JSONDeserializer;
import flexjson.JSONSerializer;

privileged aspect Flight_Roo_Json {
 public String Flight.toJson() {
   return new JSONSerializer().exclude("*.class").
```

```
            serialize(this);
    }
    public static Flight Flight.fromJsonToFlight(String json) {
      return new JSONDeserializer<Flight>().use(null,
            Flight.class).deserialize(json);
    }
    public static String Flight.toJsonArray(
          Collection<Flight> collection) {
      ...
    }
    public static Collection<Flight>
          Flight.fromJsonArrayToFlights(String json) {
          ...
    }
}
```

In the given code listing, Roo makes use of the Flexj son library to incorporate support for serializing and deserializing JSON documents. The auto-generated JSON methods that are defined in `Flight_Roo_Json.aj` are:

▸ toJson: Converts the current `Flight` object into a JSON document

▸ fromJsonToFlight: Converts the JSON document passed as an argument into the `Flight` object

▸ toJsonArray: Converts a *collection* of `Flight` objects into a JSON document containing an array

▸ fromJsonArrayToFlights: Converts a JSON array document into a collection of `Flight` objects

▸ If you want to customize the names of the JSON methods generated by `@RooJson`, you can use the following attributes of `@RooJson` annotation:

   ❑ fromJsonArrayMethod: For customizing the name of the fromJsonArrayTo*<class_name>* method

   ❑ fromJsonMethod: For customizing the name of the fromJson*<class_name>* method

   ❑ toJsonArrayMethod: For customizing the name of the toJsonArray method

   ❑ toJsonMethod: For customizing the name of the toJson method

The *<class_name>* refers to the name of the JPA entity class to which the JSON method applies. If the value of an element is " ", then the corresponding method is not generated by Roo in the `*_Roo_Json.aj` file.

It is important to note that you can use the json add command to add JSON support to any class. For instance, if you create a MyKlass class and annotate it with @RooJson, then Roo will auto-generate the given methods where the <class-name> is MyKlass.

 Excluding fields from serializing

To exclude a field from serializing to JSON format, all you need to do is to annotate the field or the corresponding getter method with the @JSON(include=false) annotation.

In some JavaScript libraries, such as EXT JS, it is expected that the JSON document contains a root node. You can instruct Roo to set the root node of the generated JSON document either by using the rootName argument of the json add command or by setting the rootName attribute of the @RooJson annotation. When the rootName argument of the json add command is used, the generated @RooJson annotation's rootName attribute is set to the value of the rootName command argument.

The following code snippet shows the Flight_Roo_Json.aj ITD when the rootName attribute of the @RooJson annotation on the Flight.java file is set to myRoot:

```
import flexjson.JSONDeserializer;
import flexjson.JSONSerializer;

privileged aspect Flight_Roo_Json {

 public String Flight.toJson() {
    return new JSONSerializer().
      rootName("myRoot").exclude("*.class").serialize(this);
 }
 . . .
 public static String Flight.toJsonArray(
    Collection<Flight> collection) {
     return new JSONSerializer().
       rootName("myRoot").exclude("*.class").
       serialize(collection);
 }
 . . .
}
```

The given code shows that if the rootName attribute of the @RooJson annotation is specified, the toJson and toJsonArray methods of the *_Roo_Json.aj ITD set the root node of the JSON document to myRoot using the rootName method of the JSONSerializer object of Flexjson. The argument passed to the rootName method is the value set for the rootName attribute of the @RooJson annotation.

The following code shows the `FlightController_Roo_Controller_Json.aj` ITD, which was generated because the value of the `@RooWebScaffold`'s exposeJson attribute is `true` in the `FlightController.java` file:

```
import org.springframework.http.ResponseEntity;
import org.springframework.web.bind.annotation.ResponseBody;

privileged aspect FlightController_Roo_Controller_Json {

  @RequestMapping(value = "/{flightId}",
    method = RequestMethod.GET,
    headers = "Accept=application/json")
  @ResponseBody
  public Object FlightController.
    showJson(@PathVariable("flightId") Long flightId) {
    Flight flight = Flight.findFlight(flightId);
    if (flight == null) {
      HttpHeaders headers= new HttpHeaders();
      headers.add("Content-Type", "application/text");
      return new ResponseEntity<String>(headers,
        HttpStatus.NOT_FOUND);
    }
    return flight.toJson();
  }
  ...
}
```

The given code shows the `showJson` method that the ITD adds to the `FlightController.java` class. The `showJson` method represents one of many JSON related methods defined in the ITD. The `showJson` method returns a `Flight` object as a JSON document. The `showJson` method returns the JSON representation of the `Flight` entity whose identifier is specified via request URI. If the request URI is `/flights/10`, then the `showJson` method returns the JSON representation of the `Flight` entity instance whose identifier value is `10`. the `@ResponseBody` annotation instructs the Spring Web MVC framework to write the response to the HTTP response body. The `headers` attribute of the `@RequestMapping` annotation specifies the request headers that must be present in the web request.

To test the JSON related methods defined in `FlightController_Roo_Controller_Json.aj`, you can use the Poster add-on of Firefox or you can use the `curl` command of Linux.

See also

▶ Refer to the *Creating a Spring MVC controller for a specific JPA entity* and *Auto-generating Spring MVC controllers and JSPX views from JPA entities* recipes to view details of methods generated by Roo

Creating and executing Selenium tests for web controllers

Automated web application testing is an important part of any web application development effort. Spring Roo provides supports for auto-generating Selenium tests for the Spring Web MVC controllers. In this recipe, we'll look at how to generate Selenium tests for web controllers using Roo and how to use the `Selenium maven plugin` to execute them.

Getting ready

Delete the contents of `ch04-recipe` sub-directory inside the `C:\roo-cookbook` directory.

Copy the `ch04_web-app.roo` script into the `ch04-recipe` directory.

Execute the `ch04_web-app.roo` script that creates the `flight-app` Roo project, sets up Hibernate as the persistence provider, configures MySQL as the database for the application, creates the `Flight` and `FlightDescription` JPA entities and defines a many-to-one relationship between `Flight` and `FlightDescription` entities. If you are using a different database than MySQL or your connection settings are different than what is specified in the script, then modify the script accordingly.

Start the Roo shell from the `C:\roo-cookbook\ch04-recipe` directory.

Execute the `controller all` command to create controllers and views corresponding to the JPA entities in the `flight-app` project, as shown here:

```
.. roo> controller all --package ~.web
```

Execute the `perform eclipse` command to update the project's classpath settings, as shown here:

```
.. roo> perform eclipse
```

Now, import the `flight-app` project into your Eclipse IDE.

Install the `Firefox` web browser, which is used by default for executing Selenium tests. If you want to use any other web browser, then refer to the *How it works...* section of this recipe.

How to do it...

The following steps demonstrate how to create Selenium tests:

1. Execute the `selenium test` command to create the Selenium test for `FlightDesciptionController`, as shown here:

```
..roo> selenium test --controller ~.web.
FlightDescriptionController --name testFlightDescriptionController
--serverUrl http://localhost:8080/
Created SRC_MAIN_WEBAPP\selenium
Created SRC_MAIN_WEBAPP\selenium\test-flightdescription.xhtml
Created SRC_MAIN_WEBAPP\selenium\test-suite.xhtml
Managed SRC_MAIN_WEBAPP\WEB-INF\i18n\application.properties
Managed SRC_MAIN_WEBAPP\WEB-INF\views\menu.jspx
Managed ROOT\pom.xml
```

2. Execute the `selenium test` command to create the Selenium test for `FlightController`, as shown here:

    ```
    ..roo> selenium test --controller ~.web.FlightController --name
    testFlightController --serverUrl http://localhost:8080/

    Created SRC_MAIN_WEBAPP\selenium\test-flight.xhtml
    Managed SRC_MAIN_WEBAPP\selenium\test-suite.xhtml
    ```

3. Exit the Roo shell and run the `flight-app` project inside the embedded Tomcat (or jetty) instance, by executing the `tomcat:run` goal:

    ```
    .. recipe> mvn tomcat:run
    ```

4. Open another command prompt and execute the `selenium:selenese` maven goal to execute the Selenium tests, as shown here:

    ```
    .. recipe> mvn selenium:selenese
    ```

How it works...

The `selenium test` command creates the Selenium test for a web controller. The following table describes the arguments accepted by the `selenium test` command:

Argument	Description
`controller`	Specifies the fully-qualified name of the web controller for which the Selenium test needs to be created.
`name`	It is the name given to the generated Selenium test.
`serverUrl`	The URL of the server where the web application is running. The default value of the `serverUrl` argument is `http://localhost:8080/`. The `serverUrl` argument value is used when executing Selenium tests using the Selenium maven plugin.

When the `selenium test` command is executed for the first time, Roo performs the following tasks:

- Creates the `SRC_MAIN_WEBAPP/selenium` folder, in which all Selenium tests are created

- Creates the `test-<JPA-entity-name>.xhtml` file, which represents the Selenium script for testing the web controller. The `<JPA-entity-name>` is the name of the JPA entity managed by the web controller.

- Creates a `test-suite.xhtml` file, which contains the collection of Selenium tests that form part of the web application.

- Adds a new label property to the `application.properties` file with the value of `Selenium Tests`. The label is used by the `menu.jspx` file to show a menu category under which you'll find a hyperlink **Test Suite**. Clicking the **Test Suite** link shows the list of all the Selenium tests that form part of the web application.

- Updates the `pom.xml` file to configure the Selenium maven plugin. The following XML fragment shows the configuration of the Selenium maven plugin:

```
<plugin>
    <groupId>org.codehaus.mojo</groupId>
    <artifactId>selenium-maven-plugin</artifactId>
    <version>1.1</version>
  <configuration>
   <suite>src\main\webapp\selenium\test-suite.xhtml</suite>
   <browser>*firefox</browser>
   <results>
      ${project.build.directory}/selenium.html</results>
   <startURL>http://localhost:4444/</startURL>
  </configuration>
</plugin>
```

The `<configuration>` element configures settings for the Selenium maven plugin. The `<suite>` element identifies the Selenium test suite, which is executed when you run the `selenium:selenese` goal. The `<browser>` element specifies the web browser to use for executing Selenium tests. The value `*firefox` indicates that the tests are executed using the Firefox web browser. If you want to use IE for executing the Selenium tests, then specify `*iexplore` as the value of the `<browser>` element. If you want to use any other browser, then specify `*custom` as the value. The `<startURL>` identifies the URL where the Selenium server is running. The Selenium server acts as a proxy between the browser running the selenium tests and the web application being tested. The `selenium:selenese` goal starts the Selenium server, executes tests defined in the test suite and stops the server when the execution of tests completes. The `<results>` element specifies the location where the Selenium test results are stored. The `${project.build.directory}` variable refers to the `target` directory of your project.

When you execute the `selenium:selenese` goal, the Firexfox web browser is automatically opened and tests defined in the `test-suite.xhtml` are executed. The result of the execution is saved in the `/target/selenium.html` file.

Let's now look at the XHTML files (representing Selenium test scripts) that were created when we executed the `selenium test` command:

Selenium test scripts

The Selenium scripts are simple HTML files. The following listing shows the content of the `test-flightdescription.xhtml` script:

```html
<html ..>
..
<title>testFlightDescriptionController</title>
..
<table border="1" cellpadding="1" cellspacing="1">
 ..
 <tbody>
  <tr>
   <td>open</td>
   <td>
    http://localhost:8080/flight-app/flightdescriptions?
    form&amp;lang=en_IN</td>
   <td></td>
  </tr>
  <tr>
   <td>type</td>
   <td>_origin_id</td>
   <td>someOrigin1</td>
  </tr>
  ..
  <tr>
   <td>clickAndWait</td>
   <td>//input[@id='proceed']</td>
   <td></td>
  </tr>
  ..
 </html>
```

The HTML test script of Selenium consists of multiple table rows (that is, `<tr>` elements) and each row has three columns (represented by `<td>` elements). There is a specific semantic associated with each column. The first column identifies the Selenium command to be executed. For instance, the `open` command instructs Selenium to open a URL and the `type` command enters a value in an input type HTML element. The `type` command may also be used for selecting a value in a drop-down box, selecting a checkbox, and so on. The `clickAndWait` command instructs Selenium to perform a click action and waits for the new page to load in response to the click action. The second column in the table row identifies the target of the Selenium command. For instance, the `test-flightdescription.xhtml, open` command opens the following URL:

```
http://localhost:8080/flight-app/flightdescriptions?form&amp;
lang=en_IN
```

The given URL opens the web page for creating the `FlightDescription` JPA entities. This is the same form, which opens up when you select the **Create new Flight Description** menu option in the `flight-app` web application.

The `type` command shown in the `test-flightdescription.xhtml` enters value for the input field with the `id` value as `_origin_id`. The `id` attribute's value of the **Origin** field on the HTML form for creating the `FlightDescription` entity is `_origin_id`. The `clickAndWait` command makes use of XPath expression to instruct Selenium to click the button whose `id` attribute's value is `proceed`. The `id` attribute's value of the **Save** button on the form for creating the `FlightDescription` entity instances has the value `proceed`.

The third column of the table row in the Selenium script specifies the value that is used by the command for performing its action. For instance, in the `test-flightdescription.xhtml` file, the `type` command sets the value of the input field with the `id _origin_id` to the value `someOrigin1` (the value specified in the third `<td>` element). Depending upon the command, the second and third columns of a table row might be empty. For instance, in the case of the `open` and `clickAndWait` commands, the third column of the table row is empty.

If you look at the `test-flightdescription.xhtml` script in its entirety, it is opening the form for creating new `FlightDescription` entities, entering values for the input fields in the form and clicking the **Save** button. This means, a successful execution of `test-flightdescription.xhtml` means a `FlightDescription` JPA entity is created in the database. Similarly, the `test-flight.xhtml` script creates a `Flight` JPA entity instance.

Selenium test suite

The `test-suite.xhtml` file created by Roo in the `SRC_MAIN_WEBAPP/selenium` folder specifies the tests that are executed by the Selenium maven plugin. The following listing shows the contents of the `test-suite.xhtml` file:

```
<html xmlns="http://www.w3.org/1999/xhtml" lang="en" xml:lang="en">
  ..
  <tr>
    <td>
      <a href="http://localhost:8080/flight-app
        /resources/selenium/test-flightdescription.xhtml">
        testFlightDescriptionController
      </a>
    </td>
  </tr>
  <tr>
    <td>
      <a href="http://localhost:8080/flight-app
        /resources/selenium/test-flight.xhtml">
        testFlightController
      </a>
    </td>
  </tr>
  </table>
 </body>
</html>
```

In the `test-suite.xhtml`, each `<td>` element specifies a Selenium test script that is executed as part of the test suite. The important point to notice is the URL used to specify the location of the test scripts. The `test-flightdescription.xhtml` and the `test-flight.xhtml` are served statically by the `ResourceHttpRequestHandler` handler, which is configured in the `webmvc-config.xml` via the `resources` element of the `mvc` schema, as shown here:

```
<mvc:resources location="/,
    classpath:/META-INF/web-resources/"
    mapping="/resources/**" />
```

Refer to the *Auto-generating Spring MVC controllers and JSPX views from JPA entities recipe* for more information on the configuration of the `<resources>` element.

It is important to note that Selenium tests are executed in the order they are specified in the `test-suite.xhtml` file.

You can view the details of tests that form part of the test suite by deploying your Roo-generated web application and selecting the **Test Suite** menu option under the **SELENIUM TESTS** category, as shown in the following screenshot:

In the case of the flight-app application, selecting the **Test Suite** option shows the test-suite.xhtml, which in turn you can use to view details of the test-flightdescription.xhtml and test-flight.xhtml files.

There's more...

The following are some of the important points to notice about Selenium tests generated by Spring Roo:

- The round-tripping support is not available for Selenium tests generated by Spring Roo. For instance, if you add, remove, or modify an attribute of the Flight JPA entity, then the corresponding Selenium test script test-flight.xhtml is not modified by Roo. You can remove the Roo-generated Selenium test scripts and regenerate them using the selenium test command.

- As we saw, Roo generates Selenium tests only for creating the form-backing object exposed by the controller. So, you can't create a Selenium test for a controller, which doesn't support creation of form-backing objects, that is, the value of the create attribute of the @RooWebScaffold annotation in the controller is false. If you execute the selenium test command against a controller that specifies the value of the @RooWebScaffold's create attribute as false, then the Roo complains that the creation of the Selenium test is not supported by the controller.

- Roo doesn't generate Selenium tests for manually created controllers. So, if you generate a controller, which doesn't have a @RooWebScaffold annotation, then you can't use Roo to generated the Selenium test for it. If you execute the selenium test command against a controller, which isn't annotated with the @RooWebScaffold annotation, then Roo complains that the controller doesn't seem to be a Roo-generated controller.

▸ Roo generates the Selenium tests by introspecting the properties of the form-backing object (which is a JPA entity in case of the Roo generated controllers) exposed by the Roo-generated controllers. The generated Selenium test assumes that the form for creating the JPA entity (exposed by the web controller as a form-backing object) will always be displayed, which is not always the case. For instance, if you access the **Create new Flight** menu option, then it will not show the form to create the `Flight` instance if we haven't already created one or more `FlightDescription` instances. So, if `test-suite.xhtml` specifies execution of `test-flight.xhtml` before the `test-flightdescription.xhtml`, then the `test-flight.xhtml` execution will fail if no `FlightDescription` instances have already been created.

The Spring Roo generated Selenium test doesn't perform a thorough testing of the Roo-generated web application functionality; it only tests the controller functionality that creates the JPA entity instance. It is recommended that you use the Selenium-IDE (available as a Firefox plugin) to record and execute test scripts. If you are looking for a more sophisticated testing approach, then you can use the Selenium-IDE to create a test script, save it as a JUnit4 or TestNG test, modify the test to address specific testing requirements (like, verifying if the JPA entity instance was saved successfully by retrieving it from the database) and execute the JUnit4 or TestNG tests using the maven Surefire plugin.

See also

▸ Refer to the *Creating integration test for persistent entities* recipe of *Chapter 2* for details on how Roo supports auto-generation of integration tests for JPA entities

5
Web Application Development with GWT, Flex, and Spring Web Flow

In this chapter, we will cover:

- ▸ Scaffolding GWT applications from JPA entities
- ▸ Getting started with Flex application development
- ▸ Scaffolding a Flex application from JPA entities
- ▸ Getting started with Spring Web Flow

Introduction

In the previous chapter, we saw that Roo scaffolds Spring Web MVC controllers and JSPX views from JPA entities that are in the application. In this chapter, we'll look at Roo commands that scaffold GWT and Flex front-ends from JPA entities. Additionally, in this chapter, we'll see how we can use Roo to add support for Spring Web Flow in our application.

Scaffolding GWT applications from JPA entities

In this recipe, we'll look at the `gwt setup` command, which scaffolds GWT artifacts from JPA entities.

Getting ready

Create a new directory (`C:\roo-cookbook\ch05-gwt`) in your system. Copy the `ch05_gwt_app.roo` script that accompanies this book to the `ch05-gwt` directory. Start the Roo shell from the `ch05-gwt` directory and execute the `ch05_gwt_app.roo` script using the `script` command. Executing the `ch05_gwt_app.roo` script does the following:

- Creates a `flightapp-gwt` Eclipse project
- Sets up Hibernate as a persistence provider
- Configures MySQL as the database for the application
- Creates `Flight` and `FlightDescription` JPA entities and defines a many-to-one relationship between `Flight` and `FlightDescription` entities

If you are using a different database than MySQL or your connection settings are different from what is specified in the script, then modify the script accordingly.

Install the **Google Plugin for Eclipse IDE** (`http://code.google.com/eclipse/`); it simplifies developing GWT applications using Eclipse IDE.

How to do it...

Follow these steps to scaffold GWT applications:

1. Execute `gwt setup` command, as shown here:

```
..roo>gwt setup
....
Created SRC_MAIN_WEBAPP\WEB-INF\spring
Created SRC_MAIN_WEBAPP\WEB-INF\spring\webmvc-config.xml
Created SRC_MAIN_WEBAPP\WEB-INF\web.xml
Updated ROOT\pom.xml [...]
Created SRC_MAIN_JAVA\sample\roo\flightapp\client
Created SRC_MAIN_JAVA\sample\roo\flightapp\ApplicationScaffold.
gwt.xml
Created SRC_MAIN_JAVA\sample\roo\flightapp\client\managed\request
Created SRC_MAIN_JAVA\sample\roo\flightapp\client\scaffold\request
```

```
Created SRC_MAIN_WEBAPP\index.html

Created SRC_MAIN_WEBAPP\ApplicationScaffold.html

...
```

Note that only partial output has been shown above for brevity.

2. As of Spring Roo 1.1.3, `gwt setup` command creates GAE-specific (Google App Engine) Java files that you must remove from the generated source. To do so, remove the following folders from the `flightapp-gwt` project before going to the next step:

```
src/main/java/sample/roo/flightapp/server/gae
src/main/java/sample/roo/flightapp/shared/gae
src/main/java/sample/roo/flightapp/client/scaffold/gae
```

If you are using Spring Roo 1.1.5, GAE-specific Java files are not generated.

3. Execute the `perform eclipse` command to update the `.classpath` file of the `flightapp-gwt` Eclipse project and to convert the nature of the project to `gwt`:

```
..roo>perform eclipse
```

4. Import the `flightapp-gwt` project into your Eclipse IDE. Add the **Google Web Toolkit** library to the build path (**Project properties | Java Build Path | Add Library**) of the `flightapp-gwt` project, so that the project doesn't show any compilation errors in Eclipse IDE.

5. If you want to run the GWT application using the **GWT Maven plugin** (`http://mojo.codehaus.org/gwt-maven-plugin/`), then exit the Roo shell and execute `gwt:run` goal of the GWT maven plugin, as shown here (alternatively, you may go to the next step):

```
..recipe>mvn clean compile gwt:run
```

Executing the `gwt:run` goal opens the **GWT Development Mode** window, as shown here:

Click the **Launch Default Browser** button in the **GWT Development Mode** window to launch the `flightapp-gwt` application. If not already installed, you'll be prompted to install the **Google Web Toolkit Developer Plugin** for your browser, which is required when you are running a GWT application in development mode.

6. If you want to run the GWT application from your Eclipse IDE, then right-click the **flightapp-gwt** project in Eclipse IDE and select **Google | Web Toolkit Settings...** option. Select the **Web Application** option and check the option **This project has a WAR directory**, as shown here:

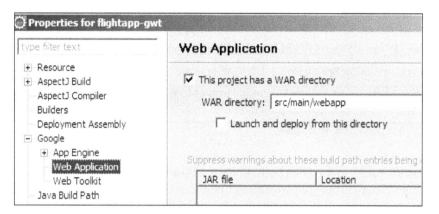

As shown in the screenshot, set the **WAR directory** value to `src/main/webapp`—Maven's standard WAR directory that contains the `Application Scaffold.html` host page. Make sure that the **Launch and deploy from this directory** option is unchecked.

7. Right-click on the **flightapp-gwt** project in Eclipse IDE and select the **Run As | Web Application** option. Select `ApplicationScaffold.html` (or `index.html`) page in the **HTML Page Selection** dialog, as shown in the following figure:

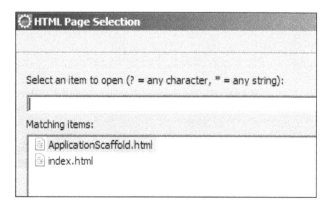

The HTML page that you select on this screen represents a host HTML page that is responsible for loading the GWT application. Both `ApplicationScaffold.html` and `index.html` files are located in the `src/main/webapp` directory of the `flightapp-gwt` GWT application. `index.html` is a simple HTML page that simply loads the `ApplicationScaffold.html` page—the host HTML page of `flightapp-gwt` GWT application.

When you are running the GWT application for the first time, you will be asked to select the location of the WAR directory of the `flightapp-gwt` project, which is `target/flightapp-gwt-0.1.0.BUILD-SNAPSHOT`.

8. The **Run As | Web Application** option starts the embedded Jetty server (bundled with **Google Plugin for Eclipse**) and runs the GWT application in the development mode. In development mode, the GWT application executes like a regular Java application, and is not compiled to JavaScript. This makes it possible to debug the GWT application during the development phase and when the application is ready for production, simply compile the GWT application to create corresponding JavaScript files. In the development mode, Eclipse IDE shows a new **Development Mode** view with the link to access the GWT application, as shown here:

9. Click the URL displayed in the **Development Mode** view to open it in the default web browser or right-click the URL to select the browser in which you want to open it. If the `flightapp-gwt` application is successfully deployed, you'll see the home page of the application, as shown here:

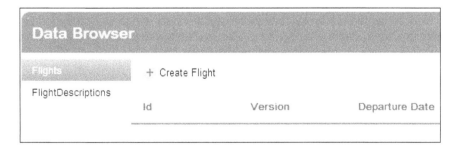

You can now use the **Flights** and **FlightDescriptions** menu options to perform CRUD operations on `Flight` and `FlightDescription` JPA entities.

How it works...

The `gwt setup` command is processed by the GWT add-on of Spring Roo.

You might be wondering, why the Roo-generated GWT user interface doesn't show a link corresponding to the `findFlightDescriptionsByDestinationAndOrigin` finder method in the `FlightDescription` JPA entity? As of Spring Roo 1.1.5, the GWT add-on doesn't add finder functionality to the scaffolded GWT application.

The `gwt setup` command does the heavy lifting of scaffolding GWT Activities, Places, Proxies, and Views for performing CRUD operations on JPA entities. Let's first take a look at the Roo-generated GWT module descriptor file, `ApplicationScaffold.gwt.xml`, which describes a GWT module.

GWT module descriptor

Roo creates `ApplicationScaffold.gwt.xml` in the root package, `sample.roo.flightapp`, of the `flightapp-gwt` project. It defines module dependencies, source paths, properties, deferred binding configurations, and module entry points. Let's look at some of the important elements defined in `ApplicationScaffold.gwt.xml`.

By default, the name of the GWT module is derived from the location of the module descriptor. As Roo creates the `ApplicationScaffold.gwt.xml` file in the `sample.roo.flightapp` package, the name of the module is `sample.roo.flightapp.ApplicationScaffold`. The `ApplicationScaffold.gwt.xml` file renames the module to `applicationScaffold` using the `rename-to` attribute of the `<module>` element, as shown here:

```
<module rename-to="applicationScaffold">
```

The GWT compiler generates JavaScript code in the directory identified by the module name; therefore, the code for our `applicationScaffold` module is generated in the `applicationScaffold` sub-directory of the generated WAR file.

The `<inherits>` element of the module descriptor specifies modules on which the module is dependent upon. For instance, `applicationScaffold` is dependent on `User`, `Logging`, `Activity`, `Places`, and so on, built-in modules of GWT, as shown here:

```
<inherits name='com.google.gwt.activity.Activity'/>
<inherits name='com.google.gwt.place.Place'/>
<inherits name="com.google.gwt.user.User"/>
<inherits name='com.google.gwt.logging.Logging'/>
```

The `<source>` element of the module descriptor specifies package, including its sub-packages (relative to the classpath location of `ApplicationScaffold.gwt.xml` file), which contain Java classes that GWT compiler needs to translate into JavaScript, as shown here for `applicationScaffold` module:

```
<source path='client'/>
<source path='shared'/>
```

The given `<source>` element instructs the GWT compiler to translate Java classes contained in `sample.roo.flightapp.client` and `sample.roo.flightapp.shared` packages, and their sub-packages.

The `<public>` element of module descriptor specifies packages (and their sub-packages) that contain publicly accessible resources, like images and CSS files, as shown here:

```
<public path="public"/>
```

As with the `<source>` elements, the `<public>` element specifies the location of packages relative to the classpath location of the module descriptor file.

The `ApplicationScaffold.gwt.xml` file configures logging for the module, as shown here:

```
<set-property name="gwt.logging.enabled" value="TRUE"/>
<set-property name="gwt.logging.logLevel" value="INFO"/>
<set-property name="gwt.logging.consoleHandler"
    value="ENABLED"/>
<set-property name="gwt.logging.developmentModeHandler"
    value="ENABLED"/>
<set-property name="gwt.logging.simpleRemoteHandler"
    value="DISABLED"/>
...
```

In this code, `gwt.logging.enabled` property enables logging for the `applicationScaffold` module, `gwt.logging.logLevel` property sets the logging level to `INFO`, `gwt.logging.consoleHandler` property enables logger output to appear in the IDE console, `gwt.logging.developmentModeHandler` property enables logger output to appear in the 'Development Mode' console of the IDE and `gwt.logging.simpleRemoteHandler` property disables remote logging of log messages. Later in this recipe, we'll see that `gwt.logging.simpleRemoteHandler` property is set to `ENABLED` to enable logging messages on the server-side.

Roo-generated GWT applications by default provide support for the mobile Safari browser. So, if you are developing a GWT application, it'll work seamlessly on mobile phones that use the mobile Safari browser. If the application is accessed using the mobile Safari browser, then the GWT application will create a web UI suitable for display in mobile devices. To support both desktop and mobile Safari browsers, the `applicationScaffold` module makes use of the deferred binding feature of the GWT compiler.

To use the deferred binding feature, the `<define-property>` element of module descriptor is used to define a new property named `mobile.user.agent`, as shown here:

```
<define-property name="mobile.user.agent"
        values="mobilesafari, none"/>
```

The `values` attribute specifies a comma-separated list of values that the `mobile.user.agent` property can accept.

To set the `mobile.user.agent` property value, the module descriptor makes use of the `<property-provider>` element, as shown here:

```
<property-provider name="mobile.user.agent">
    <![CDATA[
    var ua = navigator.userAgent.toLowerCase();
    ...
]]>
```

The `CDATA` section contains the JavaScript that is used to obtain the value of the `mobile.user.agent` from the *user-agent* information sent by the web browser to the server hosting the GWT application.

Now, the most important part: the deferred binding rule is defined using a replacement technique in the `applicationScaffold` module descriptor file, as shown here:

```
<replace-with
    class="...client.scaffold.ioc.MobileInjectorWrapper">
  <when-type-is
      class="...client.scaffold.ioc.DesktopInjectorWrapper"/>
  <all>
    <when-property-is name="mobile.user.agent"
        value="mobilesafari"/>
  </all>
</replace-with>
```

This configuration instructs the GWT compiler to replace the code of `Desktop Injectorrapper` with `MobileInjectorWrapper` (while generating JavaScript for the `applicationScaffold` module) if the value of `mobile.user.agent` property is `mobilesafari`. This is possible because both `DesktopInjectorWrapper` and `MobileInjectorWrapper` implement the same interface, `InjectorWrapper`. When the GWT compiler executes, it uses deferred binding rules (defined in the module descriptor file) to generate separate `flightapp-gwt` application's JavaScript code for mobile Safari and desktop browsers. This ensures that the desktop and mobile browsers download JavaScript code meant specifically for that browser type. For instance, the mobile Safari browser will not download JavaScript code that is specific to the desktop web browser and vice versa. The classes that need to create an instance of `DesktopInjectorWrapper` or `MobileInjectorWrapper` make use of the `create` static method of the `com.google.gwt.core.client.GWT` class to instruct the GWT compiler to instantiate the `DesktopInjectorWrapper` or `MobileInjectorWrapper` instance using deferred binding.

The code generated for mobile Safari browser follows a similar design approach as the code for the desktop browser; therefore, in this book we'll limit the discussion of Roo-generated code specific to desktop browser.

A module descriptor also describes *entry points* into the GWT application using `<entry-point>` element, as shown here for `applicationScaffold` module:

```
<entry-point
    class="sample.roo.flightapp.client.scaffold.Scaffold"/>
```

The above code suggests that `Scaffold` class represents the entry point for the `applicationScaffold` module. `Scaffold` class implements `com.google.gwt.core.client.EntryPoint` interface of GWT—a mandatory requirement for entry point classes.

The GWT module's entry point

As mentioned earlier, the `Scaffold` class of the `flightapp-gwt` application represents an entry point into the `applicationScaffold` module. The `Scaffold` class implements GWT's `EntryPoint` interface and implements its `onModuleLoad` method to bootstrap the `flightapp-gwt` application, as shown here:

```
Scaffold.java
package sample.roo.flightapp.client.scaffold;

import com.google.gwt.core.client.EntryPoint;
import com.google.gwt.core.client.GWT;

public class Scaffold implements EntryPoint {
    final private InjectorWrapper injectorWrapper =
        GWT.create(DesktopInjectorWrapper.class);

    public void onModuleLoad() {
        injectorWrapper.getInjector().getScaffoldApp().run();
    }
}
```

The first thing to notice in this code is the use of the `create` method of the `com.google.gwt.core.client.GWT` class to create the `DesktopInjectorWrapper` instance. As the `DesktopInjectorWrapper` implementation needs to be replaced by `MobileInjectorWrapper` for the mobile Safari browser, `DesktopInjectorWrapper` is created using the `create` method of the `GWT` class.

The onModuleLoad method is like Java's main method, and is responsible for initializing the flightapp-gwt application. In the Scaffold class, the onModuleLoad method is responsible for creating the application's web UI, registering event handlers with EventBus, and so on. The DesktopInjectorWrapper and MobileInjectorWrapper classes represent a wrapper around GIN's Ginjector implementation.

Dependency injection using GIN

GIN is a dependency injection framework that uses Google Guice framework to support dependency injection in GWT applications. In GWT applications, references to objects that are needed throughout the application can be created using GIN or a factory. The Roo-generated flightapp-gwt GWT application makes use of GIN to create EventBus, ApplicationRequestFactory, and PlaceController—objects that are used across the flightapp-gwt application. The following table describes the importance of these objects in the flightapp-gwt application:

Object	Description
EventBus	The EventBus is used in a GWT application for publishing events and registering event handlers.
ApplicationRequestFactory	A Roo-generated interface that extends GWT's RequestFactory interface. The implementation of this interface is generated by the GWT compiler. The flightapp-gwt application makes use of RequestFactory to interact with the JPA layer.
PlaceController	A GWT Place represents a location in a GWT application. If you select the **Flights** menu option from the UI of the flightapp-gwt application, then it represents a *place*. Now, if you select the **FlightDescriptions** option from the UI, then it represents a different place in the application. GWT's PlaceController is used to navigate from one place to another in the GWT application.

Now that we know what objects are used across the flightapp-gwt application, let's look at how GIN creates these objects and how these objects are injected into objects that depend on them.

To understand how `Ginjector` is used in `flightapp-gwt`, let's look at the following class diagram:

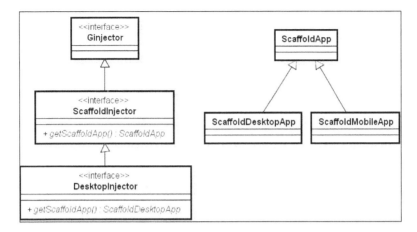

In this class diagram, the `Ginjector` interface is part of GIN API. The `ScaffoldInjector` and `DesktopInjector` are generated by Roo. The following are the important points to notice in the above class diagram:

▶ `ScaffoldInjector` extends the `Ginjector` interface and defines a single method `getScaffoldApp`, which returns an instance of type `ScaffoldApp`.

▶ `ScaffoldApp` is a Roo-generated class that defines the contract for initializing the GWT application for both the desktop and mobile browser.

▶ The `DesktopInjector` extends `ScaffoldInjector` and overrides the `getScaffoldApp` method to return `ScaffoldDestopApp`. This change in return type is perfectly legal because `ScaffoldDesktopApp` is a subclass of the `ScaffoldApp` class.

▶ `ScaffoldDesktopApp` is responsible for creating the web UI, tailored for the desktop web browser, and performing all the initialization work before the application is put into service. Similarly, `ScaffoldMobileApp` is responsible for creating the web UI for the mobile browser.

GIN's `Ginjector` interface is at the heart of the GIN framework and is responsible for performing dependency injection. To use `Ginjector`, a GWT application must do the following:

▶ Define an interface that extends `Ginjector`—this is the `DesktopInjector` interface in the case of `flightapp-gwt`. The GWT compiler is responsible for providing the implementation of this interface.

- ▶ Define one or more methods in the interface to return a top-level object that the rest of the application would use. The `Ginjector` creates the top-level object by injecting dependencies of the lower-level objects based on the bindings configured by the `Ginjector`. In the case of the `flightapp-gwt` application, `ScaffoldDesktopApp` and `ScaffoldMobileApp` represent top-level objects.

- ▶ Define a `GinModule` or `AbstractGinModule` (both are part of GIN API) class that defines bindings for the dependencies. The `ScaffoldModule` class in `flightapp-gwt` defines bindings for `EventBus`, `PlaceController`, and `ApplicationRequestFactory`.

- ▶ Annotate the method, contructor, or field of your classes where you want `Ginjector` to perform dependency injection with the `@Inject` annotation (part of Guice API). In the case of `flightapp-gwt`, `ApplicationDetailsActivites`, `ApplicationMasterActivities`, and so on, make use of the `@Inject` annotation to let `Ginjector` inject dependencies.

Let's now look at the code created by Roo corresponding to each of the activities described previously.

The following code shows the `DesktopInjector` interface:

```
DesktopInjector.java
package sample.roo.flightapp.client.scaffold.ioc;
..
import sample.roo.flightapp.client.scaffold.ScaffoldDesktopApp;
import com.google.gwt.inject.client.GinModules;

@GinModules(value = {ScaffoldModule.class})
public interface DesktopInjector extends ScaffoldInjector {

    ScaffoldDesktopApp getScaffoldApp();
}
```

`DesktopInjector` extends the `ScaffoldInjector` interface (which in turn extends GIN's `Ginjector` interface) and defines a single method—getScaffoldApp, which returns the `ScaffoldDesktopApp` object. So, the responsibility of `Ginjector` implementation generated by the GWT compiler is to return an instance of `ScaffoldDesktopApp` with all its dependencies injected with appropriate implementations.

The @GinModules annotation specifies the class (which implements the GinModule
interface or extends the AbstractGinModule abstract class) responsible for defining
dependencies and their providers. The following code shows the ScaffoldModule class,
which binds EventBus, PlaceController, and ApplicationRequestFactory
dependencies to their respective providers:

```java
ScaffoldModule.java
package sample.roo.flightapp.client.scaffold.ioc;

import com.google.gwt.event.shared.EventBus;
import com.google.gwt.event.shared.SimpleEventBus;
import com.google.gwt.inject.client.AbstractGinModule;
import com.google.gwt.place.shared.PlaceController;
import com.google.inject.Inject;
import com.google.inject.Provider;
import com.google.inject.Singleton;

public class ScaffoldModule extends AbstractGinModule {

  @Override
  protected void configure() {
   bind(EventBus.class).
      to(SimpleEventBus.class).in(Singleton.class);
   bind(ApplicationRequestFactory.class).
      toProvider(RequestFactoryProvider.class).
      in(Singleton.class);
   bind(PlaceController.class).
      toProvider(PlaceControllerProvider.class).
      in(Singleton.class);
  }

  static class PlaceControllerProvider implements
      Provider<PlaceController> {

   private final PlaceController placeController;

   @Inject
   public PlaceControllerProvider(EventBus eventBus) {
    this.placeController = new PlaceController(eventBus);
   }

   public PlaceController get() {
    return placeController;
   }
```

```
    }

    static class RequestFactoryProvider implements
        Provider<ApplicationRequestFactory> {

        ..

    }
}
```

The Roo-generated `ScaffoldModule` class extends `AbstractGinModule` and overrides the `configure` method to associate dependencies with their providers. The `bind` method of `AbstractGinModule` binds a dependency to its provider. The `in(Singleton.class)` instructs that only a single instance of `EventBus`, `PlaceController`, and `ApplicationRequestFactory` are created for the application. The `PlaceControllerProvider` and `RequestFactoryProvider` static inner classes represent provider for the `PlaceController` and `RequestFactory` instances, respectively. `SimpleEventBus` (part of GWT API) is an implementation of `EventBus`.

An important point to notice in this code is the use of `@Inject` annotation by `PlaceControllerProvider` for instructing `Ginjector` to inject an implementation of `EventBus`. So, if you are creating a hierarchy of objects, then define the method in `Ginjector`, which returns the top-level object because the lower-level objects in the hierarchy can make use of `Ginjector`'s dependency injection feature using the `@Inject` annotation.

The following figure summarizes how the `Scaffold` class makes use of the GIN framework to bootstrap the application:

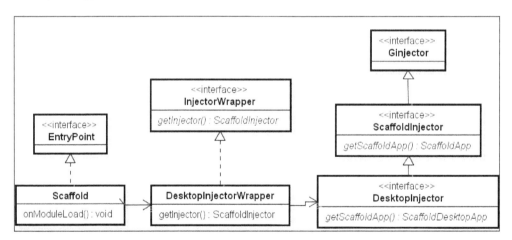

The `Scaffold` class' onModuleLoad method invokes the getInjector method of DesktopInjectWrapper to access Ginjector implementation, followed by a call to getScaffoldApp to obtain an instance of ScaffoldDesptopApp. The following sequence diagram further clarifies the sequence of method invocations between classes:

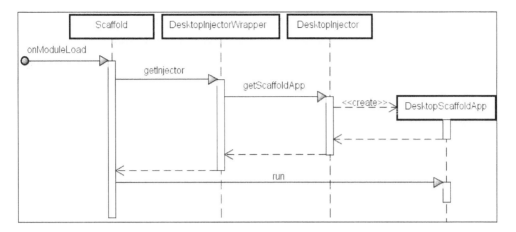

In the above sequence diagram, the call to the `run` method of `DesktopScaffoldApp` results in initialization of the web UI.

Now that we know how the `flightapp-gwt` application makes use of GIN and initializes itself, we'll look at GWT's `EntityProxy` and `RequestFactory` interfaces and how scaffolded code makes use of them.

EntityProxy, RequestContext, and RequestFactory interfaces

An entity proxy represents a client-side (the JavaScript-side) object that mimics an entity on the server-side, which is a JPA entity in the case of the `flightapp-gwt` GWT application. Entity proxies act as means to transfer data between client and the server. In GWT, a client-side object that acts as an entity proxy extends GWT's `EntityProxy` interface and defines `abstract` getter and setter methods for the fields defined in the corresponding server-side entity. In `flightapp-gwt`, we have `Flight` and `FlightDescription` JPA entities; therefore, Roo generates corresponding entity proxies `FlightProxy` and `FlightDescriptionProxy`, respectively. By default, Roo creates `abstract` getter and setter methods in entity proxy for all the attributes defined in the corresponding JPA entity class. The following code shows the `FlightProxy` entity proxy:

```
FlightProxy.java
package sample.roo.flightapp.client.managed.request;

import com.google.gwt.requestfactory.shared.EntityProxy;
import com.google.gwt.requestfactory.shared.ProxyForName;
import org.springframework.roo.addon.gwt.RooGwtMirroredFrom;

@RooGwtMirroredFrom("sample.roo.flightapp.domain.Flight")
@ProxyForName("sample.roo.flightapp.domain.Flight")
public interface FlightProxy extends EntityProxy {
    abstract Long getId();
```

```
abstract Integer getVersion();
abstract Date getDepartureDate();
abstract Date getArrivalDate();
abstract FlightDescriptionProxy getFlightDescription();
abstract void setId(Long id);
...
}
```

Roo's @RooGwtMirroredFrom annotation specifies the fully-qualified class name of the JPA entity for which the FlightProxy entity proxy was created.

 It is the @RooGwtMirroredFrom annotation that keeps the entity proxy in-sync with the corresponding JPA entity.

The GWT's @ProxyForName annotation specifies the server-side entity represented by the entity proxy. Notice that in the above code the getFlightDescription method is defined to return FlightDescriptionProxy because it represents the entity proxy corresponding to the FlightDescription JPA entity.

To invoke server-side services, the GWT application's client-side code needs to have client-side stubs for remote services. The client-side code makes use of service stubs to invoke remote services. A service stub is defined by an interface that extends GWT's RequestContext interface and defines methods with a signature similar to that of the corresponding remote service methods. We'll shortly see the difference between methods defined in the remote service class and the client-side service stub.

By default, Roo generates rich entities and the resulting application doesn't have a service layer; therefore, in the case of the Roo-generated GWT application a service stub defines methods corresponding to the JPA entity class. The following code shows the Roo-generated FlightRequest service stub corresponding to the Flight JPA entity in flightapp-gwt application:

```
FlightRequest.java
package sample.roo.flightapp.client.managed.request;

import com.google.gwt.requestfactory.shared.InstanceRequest;
import com.google.gwt.requestfactory.shared.Request;
import com.google.gwt.requestfactory.shared.RequestContext;
import com.google.gwt.requestfactory.shared.ServiceName;
import org.springframework.roo.addon.gwt.RooGwtMirroredFrom;

@RooGwtMirroredFrom("sample.roo.flightapp.domain.Flight")
@ServiceName("sample.roo.flightapp.domain.Flight")
public interface FlightRequest extends RequestContext {
```

```
    abstract Request<java.lang.Long> countFlights();
    abstract Request<java.util.List<...FlightProxy>>
        findAllFlights();
    ....
    abstract InstanceRequest<...FlightProxy, java.lang.Void>
        remove();
    abstract InstanceRequest<...FlightProxy, java.lang.Void>
        persist();
}
```

As this code shows, a `FlightRequest` service stub extends GWT's `RequestContext` interface. GWT's `@ServiceName` annotation specifies the full-qualified name of the server-side service class corresponding to the client-side service stub, which is the `Flight` JPA entity in the case of the `FlightRequest` stub. The above code shows that the `FlightRequest` service stub defines methods that return the following:

- ▸ `Request<T>` – where `T` represents the actual return type of the corresponding method on the server-side class. For instance, `countFlights` method returns `java.long.Long` in `Flight` JPA entity, and so does the `countFlights` method in `FlightRequest` stub. If a method on the server-side service class returns an entity, then the client-side service stub returns the corresponding entity proxy. For instance, `findAllFlights` method in `Flight` JPA entity returns a `java.util.List<Flight>`, so the `findAllFlights` method in `FlightRequest` stub returns `java.util.List<FlightProxy>`. It is important to note that the methods corresponding to static methods of the server-side service return `Request<T>` type in the client-side service stub.

- ▸ `InstanceRequest<P,T>` – where `P` represents the entity type on which the corresponding server-side service method acts and `T` represents the actual return type of the method. For instance, `persist` method of `Flight` JPA entity acts on `Flight` entity instance and returns `void`; therefore, the return type of the corresponding method in `FlightRequest` stub is `InstanceRequest<FlightProxy, java.lang.Void>`. Note that the only stub methods corresponding to instance methods on the server-side service return `InstanceRequest`.

 It is Roo's `@RooGwtMirroredFrom` annotation that keeps the client-side stub in-sync with the corresponding JPA entity.

Now, let's look at how `RequestFactory` helps with communication between client-side and server-side code.

`RequestFactory` acts as a communication bridge between the entity proxy and the corresponding entity on the server-side. `RequestFactory` manages entity proxies and is responsible for copying server-side entity attribute values to corresponding entity proxy and vice versa. In your GWT application, you are required to define an interface that extends `RequestFactory` interface and provide methods that return client-side stubs for server-side services. Roo creates an `ApplicationRequestFactory` class (we discussed earlier that this was created using GIN), which is shown here:

```
package sample.roo.flightapp.client.managed.request;

import sample.roo.flightapp.shared.scaffold.ScaffoldRequestFactory;

public interface ApplicationRequestFactory extends
    ScaffoldRequestFactory {

    FlightRequest flightRequest();
    FlightDescriptionRequest flightDescriptionRequest();
}
```

The following class diagram shows the inheritance hierarchy of the `ApplicationRequestFactory` class:

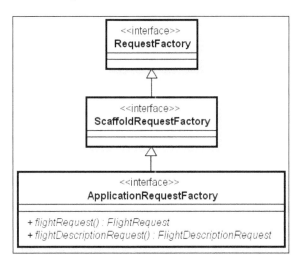

The above figure shows that `ApplicationRequestFactory` extends the Roo-generated `ScaffoldRequestFactory` interface, which in turn extends GWT's `RequestFactory` interface. The hierarchy is created such that if you want to define your custom client-side service stub methods, then you can add them to the `ScaffoldRequestFactory`.

ApplicationRequestFactory is managed by Roo; therefore, you should not modify it manually to add custom client-side service stub methods. Instead, add them to ScaffoldRequestFactory.

The interaction between entity proxy and server-side entity is achieved by configuring GWT's RequestFactoryServlet in the web.xml file of the GWT web application.

 You don't need to configure RequestFactoryServlet in the web.xml file of the flightapp-gwt project because when you execute the gwt setup command, Roo configures GWT's RequestFactoryServlet in the web.xml file.

The following code shows the configuration of RequestFactoryServlet in the web.xml file of the flightapp-gwt application:

```
web.xml
<servlet>
  <servlet-name>requestFactory</servlet-name>
  <servlet-class>
     com.google.gwt.requestfactory.server.RequestFactoryServlet
  </servlet-class>
</servlet>
<servlet-mapping>
  <servlet-name>requestFactory</servlet-name>
  <url-pattern>/gwtRequest</url-pattern>
</servlet-mapping>
```

This configuration shows that by default Roo maps the RequestFactoryServlet to /gwtRequest URL, which you can change. If you change the URL mapping of RequestFactoryServlet, then you also need to change how ApplicationRequestFactory is created by ScaffoldModule—the Roo-generated GIN module we discussed earlier.

RequestFactory requires that the server-side entity must define a no-argument constructor, getId, getVersion, and find<Entity> methods. The getVersion should return the version, getId should return the unique ID associated with entity instance, and the find<Entity> method which accepts entity ID and returns the corresponding entity instance. So, if you create entities using the Roo entity command, then make sure that you don't set the name of the identifier field or version field to anything other than id and version, respectively. When you execute the Roo gwt setup command, and Roo finds that the names of ID and version fields is different from id and version, then it doesn't scaffold the GWT application.

Let's now look at some of the Roo-generated GWT activities and places.

Activities and places

Roo-generated GWT code consists of many base classes and interfaces that attempt to provide a consistent approach to performing CRUD operations on JPA entities. In this section, we'll look at some of the important classes and interfaces and concepts which will give you a starting point to understand the Roo-generated GWT code.

The Roo-generated GWT web UI consists of a **Master display region** and a **Detail display region**. The **Master display region** shows the list of entities that can be managed from the web UI. The widget that shows **Flight** and **FlightDescriptions** in a list represents the **Master display region**. The **Detail display region** shows activities that can be performed on each of the entities displayed in the **Master display region**. The region that shows the list of `Flight` or `FlightDescription` entity instances in the system, the form to create a new entity instance, the form to edit an entity instance, and so on, represents the **Detail display region**.

The following figure shows the **Master display region** and **Detail display region** in the `flightapp-gwt` application:

Let's now look at some of the examples of activities, places and views, in the Roo-generated `flightapp-gwt` application.

Activities are responsible for driving views and handling events generated by user interaction in a display region. It is created by implementing GWT's `Activity` interface or by extending GWT's `AbstractActivity` abstract class. The following diagram shows some of the activities that were generated by Roo for `flightapp-gwt` application:

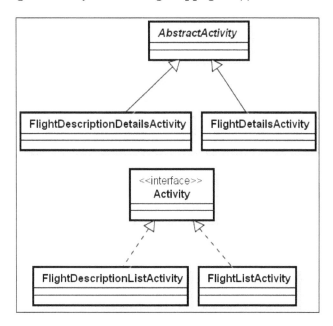

This diagram shows that `FlightDescriptionDetailsActivity` and `FlightDetailsActivity` inherit from the `AbstractActivity` abstract class, and `FlightDescriptionListActivity` and `FlightListActivity` classes implement the `Activity` interface. `<entity-name>DetailsActivity` activities drive views and manage user interactions when an existing entity instance's details are displayed in the **Detail display region**. `<entity-name>ListActivity` activities drive views and manage user interactions when the list of entity instances are displayed in the **Detail display region**.

Places are locations within the display region that can be translated into a URL. An Activity is mapped to a place (changeable into a URL), which makes `Activities` accessible via URL. A place is created by extending GWT's `Place` abstract class. The place implementation class also defines how the place instance can be translated into a URL. `ProxyPlace` and `ProxyListPlace` classes generated by Roo in `flightapp-gwt` are examples of places in GWT. The following figure shows the attributes defined by the `ProxyPlace` and `ProxyListPlace` classes:

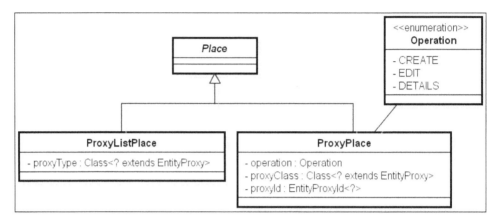

The `ProxyPlace` corresponds to a place in the 'detail' display region and `ProxyListPlace` corresponds to a place in the **Master display region**. When a `ProxyPlace` instance is created, it knows the `EntityProxy` for which the place instance is being created (identified by `proxyClass` attribute), the operation to be performed (identified by `operation` attribute) on the `EntityProxy`, and the unique identifier (identified by `proxyId` attribute of type `EntityProxyId`) of the `EntityProxy`. Similarly, when `ProxyListPlace` is created, it knows about the `EntityProxy` for which the place instance is being created (identified by the `proxyType` attribute).

Each display region is associated with an `ActivityMapper`, which maps each `Place` in the display region to an `Activity`. It is created by implementing GWT's `ActivityMapper` interface. `ActivityMapper` defines a single method `getActivity(Place place)`, which returns an activity corresponding to a place. In the `flightapp-gwt` application, `ApplicationMasterActivities` is an `ActivityMapper` for the **Master display region** and `ApplicationDetailsActivities` is an `ActivityMapper` for the **Detail display region**. The following class diagram shows the `ActivityMapper`s created by Roo in the `flightapp-gwt` project:

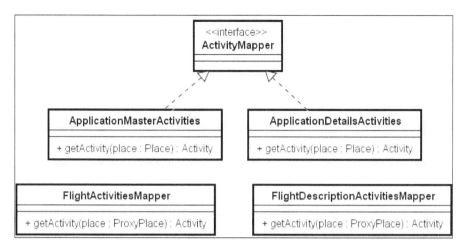

This figure shows that Roo creates `FlightActivitiesMapper` and `FlightDescriptionActivitiesMapper` classes corresponding to the `Flight` and `FlightDescription` JPA entities. Even though these activity mappers don't implement GWT's `ActivityMapper` interface, they act as activity mappers in the `flightapp-gwt` application. These activity mappers return `Activity` instances specific to the `EntityProxy`. The `getActivity` method of an `<entity-name>ActivitiesMapper` class accepts a `ProxyPlace` (which represents a place in the **Detail display region**) argument and returns an `Activity` for that place. The `ApplicationDetailsActivities` activity mapper (which applies to the **Detail display region** of the web UI) is responsible for creating the `FlightActivitiesMapper` and `FlightDescriptionActivities` instances depending upon the JPA entity on which the user actions are to be performed. The `ApplicationMasterActivities` returns either the `FlightListActivity` or `FlightDescriptionListActivity` instance, depending upon the JPA entity selected from the **Master display region**.

An `ActivityManager` is associated with a display region and starts and stops an activity when a user navigates from one place to another. It is created by creating an instance of GWT's `ActivityManager` class by passing an `ActivityMapper` instance and an `EventBus` instance. In `flightapp-gwt`, `ActivityManager` is created for both 'master' and **Detail display region** when the `run` method of `ScaffoldDesktopApp` is executed, as shown in the following sequence diagram:

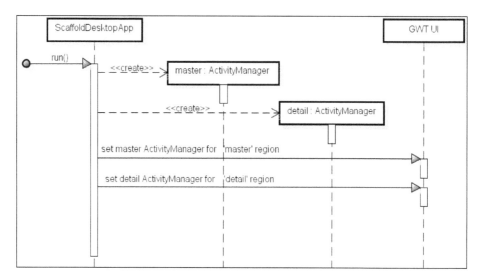

Dealing with entity proxy-specific processing

Roo creates an abstract generic class, `ApplicationEntityTypesProcessor<T>`, for dealing with different entity proxies in the scaffolded GWT application. `ApplicationEntity TypesProcessor<T>` is implemented by classes that perform a functionality based on entity proxy type. The following code listing shows the `ApplicationEntityTypesProcessor<T>` class of the `flightapp-gwt` project:

```
ApplicationEntityTypesProcessor.java
package sample.roo.flightapp.client.managed.request;

public abstract class ApplicationEntityTypesProcessor<T> {

  private final T defaultValue;

  private T result;

  private static void process(
    ApplicationEntityTypesProcessor<?> processor,
    Class<?> clazz) {
    if (FlightProxy.class.equals(clazz)) {
```

```
        processor.handleFlight((FlightProxy) null);
        return;
      }
      if (FlightDescriptionProxy.class.equals(clazz)) {
       processor.handleFlightDescription(
                 (FlightDescriptionProxy) null);
        return;
      }
      processor.handleNonProxy(null);
    }
    . . . .


    public abstract void handleFlight(FlightProxy proxy);

    public abstract void
        handleFlightDescription(FlightDescriptionProxy proxy);

    public T process(Class<?> clazz) {
      setResult(defaultValue);
      ApplicationEntityTypesProcessor.process(this, clazz);
      return result;
    }
    . . . .
  }
```

`ApplicationEntityTypesProcessor<T>` class represents a generic class. The
`handleFlight` and `handleFlightDescription` methods are defined as `abstract`
methods; therefore, subclasses need to provide implementation of these methods.

 You'll find an abstract `handleXXX` method defined for each entity proxy in
the `ApplicationEntityTypesProcessor<T>` class.

The `result` attribute identifies the result to return when the public `process` method of
the `ApplicationEntityTypesProcessor<T>` class is invoked. Note that the return
type of the `result` attribute is a generic type—determined by the generic type associated
with the class. The public `process` method accepts the class or object of the entity proxy
as the argument and internally invokes the private `process` method, which in turn calls the
`handleFlight` or `handleFlightDescription` method, depending upon the entity proxy
object or class.

So, what is the `handleXXX` method expected to do in the implementation class? It simply
sets a return value, which is returned when the public `process` method is called. Let's see
this in the context of an example.

We mentioned earlier that the `ApplicationDetailsActivities` class represents an `ActivityMapper` for the **Detail display region** of the Roo-generated GWT application. The `ApplicationDetailsActivity` returns a `FlightActivityMapper` (specific to the `FlightProxy` entity proxy) or `FlightDescriptionActivityMapper` instance (specific to the `FlightDescriptionProxy` entity proxy) by implementing the `ApplicationEntityTypesProcessor<T>` class.

 `ApplicationDetailsActivities` extends the `ApplicationDetailsActivities_Roo_Gwt` class, which actually implements the `ActivityMapper` GWT interface.

The following code shows how `ApplicationDetailsActivities` makes use of the `ApplicationEntityTypesProcessor<T>` class:

```
ApplicationDetailsActivities_Roo_Gwt.java
public Activity getActivity(Place place) {
....
  final ProxyPlace proxyPlace = (ProxyPlace) place;
    return new ApplicationEntityTypesProcessor<Activity>() {
    @Override
    public void handleFlight(FlightProxy proxy) {
      setResult(new FlightActivitiesMapper(requests,
          placeController).getActivity(proxyPlace));
    }
    @Override
    public void handleFlightDescription(FlightDescriptionProxy
        proxy) {
     setResult(new FlightDescriptionActivitiesMapper(requests,
        placeController).getActivity(proxyPlace));
    }
  }.process(proxyPlace.getProxyClass());
}
```

In this code, the following are the important points to note:

- `ApplicationEntityTypesProcessor<T>` is associated with `Activity` type.
- The `handleFlight` method sets the return value to the `Activity` returned from `FlightActivityMapper`.
- The `handleFlightDescription` method sets the return value to the `Activity` returned from `FlightDescriptionActivityMapper`.
- The `process` method of `ApplicationEntityTypesProcessor<T>` is invoked at the end to obtain the return value set by the `handleFlight` or `handleFlightDescription` method.

This code showed that `ApplicationEntityTypesProcessor<T>` generic class is associated with an `Activity` type and is used to retrieve `Activity` specific to `FlightProxy` or `FlightDescriptionProxy`. Similarly, Roo-generated GWT code makes use of `ApplicationEntityTypesProcessor<T>` class to perform other entity proxy-specific processing, like rendering the list of entities in the **Master display region**.

There's more...

Let's now look at:

- ▶ How to compile and run the Roo-generated GWT application in an embedded Jetty container
- ▶ How to access the mobile version of the Roo-generated `flightapp-gwt` application
- ▶ Round-tripping support in the Roo-generated GWT application
- ▶ How to enable remote logging

Compiling and running the GWT application in an embedded Jetty container

In the Development Mode, the GWT application is not compiled into JavaScript. You can compile the GWT application into JavaScript and run it using an embedded Jetty container by executing `mvn jetty:run-exploded` command, as shown here:

```
C:\roo-cookbook\ch05-gwt> mvn jetty:run-exploded
```

You can now access the `flightapp-gwt` application by entering the following URL: `http://localhost:8080/flightapp-gwt/index.html`

Accessing the mobile version of the GWT application

If you have compiled and deployed the `flightapp-gwt` application using the `mvn jetty:run-exploded` command, then access the mobile version of the `flightapp-gwt` application using the following URL:

```
http://localhost:8080/flightapp-gwt/index.html&m=true
```

If you are running the `flightapp-gwt` application in Development Mode, then use the following URL:

```
http://127.0.0.1:8888/ApplicationScaffold.html?gwt.
codesvr=127.0.0.1:9997&m=true
```

In either case, you'll see the mobile version of the `flightapp-gwt` application, as shown here:

In this screenshot, the **Flights** and **FlightDescriptions** options are clickable, and by selecting them you can get started with performing CRUD operations on JPA entity instances.

Round-tripping support for GWT applications

If you add, modify, or delete any field from a JPA entity in the Roo-scaffolded GWT application, then Roo makes the necessary changes to GWT artifacts accordingly. To see Roo's round-tripping support for the scaffolded GWT application, start the Roo shell from the root directory of the `flightapp-gwt` project and add an `aircraftModel` field to the `FlightDescription` entity using the `field` command or by editing the `FlightDescription.java` file directly from your IDE. In response to the addition of the `aircraftModel` attribute, the Roo shell shows the following actions taken by Roo:

```
Updated ...FlightDescriptionProxy.java

Updated ...FlightDescriptionListView_Roo_Gwt.java

Updated ...FlightDescriptionDetailsView_Roo_Gwt.java

Updated ...FlightDescriptionDetailsView.ui.xml

Updated ...FlightDescriptionEditView_Roo_Gwt.java

Updated ...FlightDescriptionEditView.ui.xml

...
```

The output shows that Roo updates the GWT entity proxy, `FlightDescriptionProxy`, and other GWT artifacts to reflect the modification to the `FlightDescription` JPA entity. The other important thing to notice is that most of the modifications are limited to `*_Roo_Gwt.java` files—files that are managed by Roo. So, if you make changes to files that don't follow the naming convention `*_Roo_Gwt.java`, then such changes will be preserved by Roo (except in the case that you are modifying Java files in the `*.client.managed.*` package). In the Roo-scaffolded GWT application, `*_Roo_Gwt.java` files are equivalent to `*_Roo_*.aj` AspectJ ITD files, that is, Roo attempts to minimize the impact on the scaffolded GWT code by only modifying `*_Roo_Gwt.java` files.

Enabling remote logging

The GWT logging framework emulates Java Logging API, making it possible to log messages from the Java code that resides in the `sample.roo.client` package and its sub-packages. As we mentioned earlier, Java classes contained inside the `sample.roo.client` package and its sub-packages are translated into JavaScript by the GWT compiler. The remote logging capability in GWT enables client code to send log messages to the server-side logging infrastructure. To configure remote logging, set the value of the `gwt.logging.simpleRemoteHandler` property to `ENABLED` in the `ApplicationScaffold.gwt.xml` file:

```
<set-property name="gwt.logging.simpleRemoteHandler"
       value="ENABLED"/>
```

The above configuration enables remote logging of messages. GWT provides a `RemoteLoggingServiceImpl` servlet, which acts as a handler for logging messages received from the client-side. You'll need to configure `RemoteLoggingServiceImpl` servlet in your `web.xml` file, as shown here:

```
<servlet>
  <servlet-name>remoteLogger</servlet-name>
  <servlet-class>
com.google.gwt.logging.server.RemoteLoggingServiceImpl
  </servlet-class>
</servlet>

<servlet-mapping>
  <servlet-name>remoteLogger</servlet-name>
  <url-pattern>
     /applicationScaffold/remote_logging
  </url-pattern>
</servlet-mapping>
```

The important point to note is that the `RemoteLoggingServiceImpl` servlet should be mapped to the `/<module_name>/remote_logging` URL.

As the method names of the Java class in the client-side are obfuscated when the GWT compiler converts them into JavaScript, you need to resymbolize or deobfuscate them by setting the following properties in the `ApplicationScaffold.gwt.xml` file:

```
<set-property name="compiler.emulatedStack" value="true" />
<set-configuration-property
  name="compiler.emulatedStack.recordLineNumbers"
  value="true" />
<set-configuration-property
  name="compiler.emulatedStack.recordFileNames"
  value="true" />
```

Also, you'll need to create a symbol maps directory using the `-extra` option of GWT compiler and place it inside a directory accessible to the server-side code, like the `WEB-INF/classes` directory of the generated WAR file.

See also

> ▸ Refer to the *Auto-generating Spring MVC controllers and JSPX views from JPA entities* recipe in *Chapter 4, Web Application Development with Spring Web MVC* for details on how Roo scaffolds a Spring MVC application from JPA entities

Getting started with Flex application development

In the previous recipe, we saw how we can scaffold a complete GWT application using Roo. In this recipe, we'll see how Roo simplifies setting up Flex for your Roo project. In the next recipe Scaffolding Flex application from JPA entities we'll look at how Roo generates a fully-functional Flex application to perform CRUD operations on JPA entities.

Getting ready

At the time of writing this book, Flex addon is not compatible with Spring Roo 1.1.3 and above; therefore, download Spring Roo 1.1.2.

At the time of writing this recipe, the Flex addon used is the snapshot version dated 15-Aug-2011 from the `Flex Spring Roo addon repository (http://s3browse. springsource.com/browse/maven.springframework.org/snapshot/ org/springframework/flex/roo/addon/org.springframework.flex. roo.addon/1.0.0.BUILD-SNAPSHOT/)`. Download the JAR file named `org. springframework.flex.roo.addon-xx.jar` and copy it to Roo's `bundle` directory or install it using the `osgi start` (explained in *Chapter 7, Developing Add-ons and Removing Roo from Projects*) command.

 Flex add-on is an example of an installable add-on. For more information on installable add-ons, see *Chapter 7, Developing Add-ons and Removing Roo from Projects*.

Create a new directory `C:\roo-cookbook\ch05-flex` in your system and start the Roo shell from the `ch05-flex` directory. Enter the `help` command and check whether you see `flex setup`, `flex remoting scaffold`, and `flex remoting all` commands in the output. If you see the `flex` commands in the output of the `help` command, it means you have successfully installed the Flex addon.

Copy the `ch05_flex_app.roo` script that accompanies this book to the `ch05-flex` directory. Now, execute the `ch05_flex_app.roo` script using the `script` command. Executing the `ch05_flex_app.roo` script creates a `flightapp_flex` Eclipse project, sets up Hibernate as persistence provider, configures MySQL as the database for the application, creates `Flight` and `FlightDescription` JPA entities, and defines a many-to-one relationship between the `Flight` and `FlightDescription` entities. If you are using a different database than MySQL or your connection settings are different than what is specified in the script, then modify the script accordingly.

Though not required, you may also want to download Flash Builder 4 and install it as the Eclipse plugin to simplify editing MXML and ActionScript files generated by Roo in this recipe.

How to do it...

To set up the flex application, follow the steps given here:

1. Execute the `flex setup` command to create Spring BlazeDS integration-related configuration artifacts in the `flightapp_flex` project:

```
... roo> flex setup
Created SRC_MAIN_WEBAPP\WEB-INF\flex
Created SRC_MAIN_WEBAPP\WEB-INF\flex\services-config.xml
...
Created SRC_MAIN_WEBAPP\WEB-INF\spring
Created SRC_MAIN_WEBAPP\WEB-INF\spring\flex-config.xml
Created SRC_MAIN_WEBAPP\WEB-INF\spring\webmvc-config.xml
...
Created SRC_MAIN_WEBAPP\WEB-INF\web.xml
Managed SRC_MAIN_WEBAPP\WEB-INF\web.xml
...
Managed SRC_MAIN_WEBAPP\WEB-INF\spring\webmvc-config.xml
Managed ROOT\pom.xml [Added dependency com.adobe.flex.
framework:flex-framework:4.0.0.14159]
Managed ROOT\pom.xml [Added dependency org.springframework.
flex:spring-flex-core:1.5.0.BUILD-SNAPSHOT]
...
Created ROOT\.flexProperties
Created ROOT\.actionScriptProperties
...
Created ROOT\src\main\flex\flightapp_flex_scaffold.mxml
Created SRC_MAIN_WEBAPP\flightapp_flex_scaffold.html
Created ROOT\src\main\flex\flightapp_flex_scaffold-config.xml
```

2. Include the Maven repository for Spring snapshot versions in your `pom.xml` file so that the Flex add-on can download Flex add-on dependencies that are not yet available in milestone or in the release Maven repository of Spring:

```
<repositories>
  <repository>
    <id>spring-maven-snapshot</id>
    <name>Spring Maven Snapshot Repository</name>
    <url>
      http://maven.springframework.org/snapshot
    </url>
  </repository>
  ...
</repositories>
```

3. Configure the plugin repository for the Flexmojos Maven plugin (refer to the plugin documentation for more details: `http://repository.sonatype.org/content/sites/flexmojos-site/3.8/plugin-info.html`) in the `pom.xml` file, as shown here:

```
<pluginRepositories>
  <pluginRepository>
    <id>flexmojos-repository</id>
    <url>
      http://repository.sonatype.org/content/groups/flexgroup/
    </url>
  </pluginRepository>
  ...
</pluginRepositories>
```

4. Execute the `perform eclipse` command to update the project's classpath settings with the newly added dependencies in `pom.xml` file. It also adds Flex and ActionScript nature to the `flightapp_flex` Eclipse project.

How it works...

The `flex setup` command is processed by the Flex add-on of Roo.

The `flex setup` command configures Spring BlazeDS integration and creates the necessary artifacts that are required for developing a Flex 4 application. The following table describes some of the important directories and files that were created by the `flex setup` command:

Directory / File	Description
SRC_MAIN_WEBAPP\history	Contains `history.css`, `history.js`, and `historyFrame.html` files that are responsible for managing browser history.
SRC_MAIN_WEBAPP\WEB-INF\flex\services-config.xml	The `services-config.xml` is a BlazeDS configuration file that contains channels and corresponding endpoint configurations for the BlazeDS.
SRC_MAIN_WEBAPP\WEB-INF\spring\flex-config.xml	The `flex-config.xml` configures BlazeDS `MessageBroker` as a Spring-managed bean.
SRC_MAIN_WEBAPP\WEB-INF\spring\webmvc-config.xml	Spring's web application context XML, which is loaded by `DispatcherServlet` defined in the `web.xml` file. Additionally, the `webmvc-config.xml` file imports bean definitions from `flex-config.xml`.
ROOT\html-template	The `html-template` directory contains an `index.template.html` file that acts as an HTML template for embedding the Flex application. Roo generates a `flightapp_flex_scaffold.html` file (based on the `index.template.html` file) in the SRC_MAIN_WEBAPP directory for embedding our Flight App Flex application. So, to load our Flight App Flex application, we'll need to load the `flightapp_flex_scaffold.html` page in the web browser.
ROOT\src\main\flex\flightapp_flex_scaffold.mxml	The `flightapp_flex_scaffold.mxml` is the main application MXML file that defines the layout of the application and the initial user interface.
ROOT\src\main\flex\flightapp_flex_scaffold-config.xml	The `flightapp_flex_scaffold-config.xml` XML file overrides the default Flex compiler settings. In the Scaffolding Flex application from JPA entities recipe we'll see that this XML file contains fully-qualified ActionScript class names that correspond to the main views (MXML files) scaffolded by Roo for each JPA entity.

Let's now look at the important configuration files created by Spring Roo.

The `webmvc-config.xml` file is Spring's web application context XML file, and is loaded by `DispatcherServlet` configured in the `web.xml` file of the `flightapp_flex` project. The `webmvc-config.xml` file imports bean definitions in the `flex-config.xml` application context XML file, as shown here:

```
webmvc-config.xml
<beans ....>
  ....
  <import resource="flex-config.xml"/>
</beans>
```

For information on other elements defined in `webmvc-config.xml` file, please refer to *Chapter 4, Web Application Development with Spring Web MVC*.

The `flex-config.xml` makes use of the `<message-broker>` element of Spring's `flex` schema to configure and initialize a BlazeDS `MessageBroker`, as shown here:

```
flex-config.xml
<beans xmlns="http://www.springframework.org/schema/beans"
 xmlns:flex="http://www.springframework.org/schema/flex"
 ...>

 <flex:message-broker mapping-order="1">
   <flex:mapping pattern="/messagebroker/*"/>
   <flex:message-service default-channels="longpolling-amf" />
 </flex:message-broker>

</beans>
```

By default, the `<message-broker>` element considers the `/WEB-INF/flex/services-config.xml` file as the configuration file for BlazeDS `MessageBroker`. If you change the name or location of the `services-config.xml` file in `flightapp_flex`, then use the `services-config-path` attribute of the `<message-broker>` element to specify your BlazeDS configuration XML file.

The `<mapping>` element of the `flex` schema maps incoming requests from the `DispatcherServlet` to `/messagebroker/*` path—the path to which BlazeDS `MessageBroker` channels are mapped in `services-config.xml`, as we'll see shortly.

The `<message-service>` element configures a BlazeDS `flex.messaging.services.MessageService` object that provides a publish-subscribe messaging between producers and consumers of messages in the application. The `default-channels` attribute specifies the message channel(s) used by Flex clients to access `MessageService` or to receive messages from it. The `longpolling-amf` value refers to the `AMFChannel` configured in `services-config.xml`, with polling enabled.

It is important to note that even though Roo configures `MessageService`, it is not used by the Roo-generated Flex application.

The following listing shows the channels configured in the Roo-generated `services-config.xml` file:

```
services-config.xml
<channels>
  <channel-definition id="amf"
        class="mx.messaging.channels.AMFChannel">
```

```
    <endpoint
        url="http://{server.name}:{server.port}/
        {context.root}/messagebroker/amf"
            class="flex.messaging.endpoints.AMFEndpoint"/>
    </channel-definition>
    ...
    <channel-definition id="longpolling-amf"
            class="mx.messaging.channels.AMFChannel">
        <endpoint url="http://{server.name}:{server.port}/
            {context.root}/messagebroker/amflongpolling"
            class="flex.messaging.endpoints.AMFEndpoint"/>
        <properties>
            <polling-enabled>true</polling-enabled>
            ....
        </properties>
    </channel-definition>
    ...
</channels>
```

This code listing shows channel definitions as created by Roo. A `<channel-definition>` element defines a channel. The `id` attribute is a unique identifier of a channel and is used by Flex clients to connect to an endpoint. The `class` attribute identifies the type of the channel. The enclosing `<endpoint>` element defines the endpoint corresponding to the channel. The `url` attribute of the `<endpoint>` element specifies the URL of the server and `class` attribute specifies the endpoint class. Flex components make use of channels to communicate with BlazeDS endpoints. For instance, the above code listing indicates that `AMFChannel` is used by Flex to communicate with the `AMFEndpoint`.

The `{server.name}` and `{server.port}` tokens used by the `url` attribute value are replaced at runtime based on the URL of the server from which the SWF file is downloaded. The `{context.root}` token is replaced with a value that is calculated at compile-time based on the `<contextRoot>` configuration option defined in the `pom.xml` file for the Flexmojos Maven plugin. Later in this recipe, we'll look at the Flexmojos Maven plugin configuration generated by Roo for the `flightapp_flex` project.

The incoming requests to `DispatcherServlet` are routed to the BlazeDS `MessageBroker`, because the `<mapping-pattern>` element value (that is, `/messagebroker/*`) in `flex-config.xml` maps to the `url` attribute value (`http://../messagebroker/..`) of the `<endpoint>` elements in `services-config.xml`.

We saw earlier that the `longpolling-amf` channel is used as the default channel by `MessageService` for transporting messages. The `<polling-enabled>` property of the channel is set to `true`, which means that polling is enabled for the `longpolling-amf` channel.

The following `<services>` element of the `services-config.xml` file shows the application-level default channels configuration:

```
<services>
  <default-channels>
    <channel ref="amf"/>
  </default-channels>
</services>
```

This `<default-channels>` element specifies that if a Flex component doesn't specify the channel to be used, then use the `amf` channel for communication.

Roo also configures server-side logging in `services-config.xml` using the `<logging>` element, as shown here:

```
<logging>
  <target class="flex.messaging.log.ConsoleTarget"
      level="Warn">
    <properties>
      <prefix>[BlazeDS] </prefix>
      <includeDate>false</includeDate>
      <includeTime>false</includeTime>
      <includeLevel>false</includeLevel>
      <includeCategory>false</includeCategory>
    </properties>
    <filters>
      <pattern>Endpoint.*</pattern>
      <pattern>Service.*</pattern>
      <pattern>Configuration</pattern>
    </filters>
  </target>
</logging>
```

The logging configuration specifies where the log messages are written, what types of messages are written, how they are written, and the log messages generated by each category (like Endpoint, Service, and so on) are written. The `class` attribute (of `target` element) value of `flex.messaging.log.ConsoleTarget` means that the log messages are written to standard ouput. `level="Warn"` means that only warning level messages are written. In the above code, the `<properties>` element specifies that log messages are prefixed with `[BlazeDS]` and include date, time, logging level, and category. The `<filters>` element limits the logging to the categories defined by the `<pattern>` sub-elements.

Let's now look at the scaffolded MXML file which serves as the main application file—the MXML file that contains the `Application` component of Flex's Spark component library.

The following code listing shows the `flightapp_flex_scaffold.mxml` file:

```
flightapp_flex_scaffold.mxml
<s:Application xmlns:fx="http://ns.adobe.com/mxml/2009"
     xmlns:s="library://ns.adobe.com/flex/spark"
     xmlns:mx="library://ns.adobe.com/flex/mx"..>
 <fx:Script>
  <![CDATA[
    ...
    protected function
       entityList_doubleClickHandler(event:MouseEvent):void
    {
      ...
    }
  ]]>
 </fx:Script>

 <fx:Declarations>
  <s:ArrayList id="entities">
  </s:ArrayList>

  <s:ChannelSet id="remotingChannels">
   <s:AMFChannel id="amf" url=
    "http://localhost:8080/flightapp_flex/messagebroker/amf"/>
  </s:ChannelSet>
 </fx:Declarations>

 <s:Group id="mainGroup" height="100%" width="100%">
  <s:layout>
   <s:HorizontalLayout/>
  </s:layout>

  <s:Panel id="entityPanel" title="Entity List" height="100%">
   <s:List id="entityList" dataProvider="{entities}"
      width="100%" height="100%"
     toolTip="Double-Click the selected Entity"
     doubleClickEnabled="true"
     doubleClick="entityList_doubleClickHandler(event)"/>
  </s:Panel>
 </s:Group>

</s:Application>
```

This MXML shows the user interface of the `flightapp_flex` application. The `<Panel>` tag creates a Spark `Panel` component which contains a Spark `List` component. The `List` component shows the list of entities that can be managed from the user interface. The list of entities is defined by the `<ArrayList>` tag. Notice that the value of the `dataProvider` attribute of the `<List>` tag is `{entities}` and the `id` attribute value of the `<ArrayList>` tag is `entities`, which means that the list of entities displayed by the `List` component comes from the list defined by the `<ArrayList>` tag. Well, the `<ArrayList>` tag doesn't contain any element; therefore, for now, the list is empty.

> The `<ArrayList>` tag is populated with child elements when we execute `flex remoting all` or `flex remoting scaffold` commands to scaffold a remoting destination corresponding to a JPA entity, as we'll see in the Scaffolding Flex application from the JPA entities recipe.

The `doubleClick` attribute of `<List>` specifies that the `entityList_doubleClickHandler(event)` ActionScript method to be invoked when a user double clicks an item in the list. In the Scaffolding remoting destination from the JPA entities recipe, we'll go through the implementation detail of the `entityList_doubleClickHandler(event)` method.

The `<ChannelSet>` tag creates a `ChannelSet`—a set of channels for communication with the BlazeDS server. We saw earlier that Roo defines the `amf` channel (channel type being `AMFChannel`) as the default application-wide channel in `services-config.xml`; therefore, the Roo-generated `<ChannelSet>` tag creates an `AMFChannel` using the `<AMFChannel>` tag. The `url` attribute of `<AMFChannel>` specifies the corresponding endpoint URL.

> As the `url` attribute of the `<AMFChannel>` tag specifies the location of the BlazeDS server as `localhost`, your Roo-generated `flightapp_flex` application will work only if your BlazeDS server is running locally. To avoid hard-coded endpoint URLs, it is recommended that you externalize `ChannelSet` configuration into an XML file that is parsed when the Flex application is initialized and later used to communicate with the BlazeDS server.

As mentioned earlier, Roo generates a `flightapp_flex_scaffold-config.xml` configuration file that overrides the default Flex compiler settings. Notice that the naming convention followed by the file is: `<MXML file name>-config.xml`, where `<MXML file name>` is the name of the MXML file corresponding to the configuration file which was created. When an MXML file named `myApp.mxml` is compiled, Flex compiler looks for a configuration file named `myApp-config.xml` in the same location as the MXML file, and uses it to override the default compiler options.

The following listing shows the content of the `flightapp_flex_scaffold-config.xml` file:

```
<flex-config xmlns="http://www.adobe.com/2006/flex-config">
    <includes append="true">
    </includes>
</flex-config>
```

As this code shows, `flightapp_flex_scaffold-config.xml` doesn't do anything interesting. In the _Scaffolding Flex application from JPA entities_ recipe, we'll discuss this file in detail once it's updated after the execution of the `flex remoting all` or `flex remoting scaffold` command.

There's more...

We mentioned earlier that Roo configures the Flexmojos Maven plugin in the `pom.xml` file of the `flightapp_flex` project. Let's now look at the Flexmojos plugin configuration in detail.

Flexmojos Maven plugin configuration

Flexmojos Maven plugin offers many features, but for brevity we'll focus only on the `flexmojos:compile-swf` goal, which is responsible for compiling the Flex project's sources (MXML and ActionScript files) and package it into an SWF file. The following listing shows the configuration of Flexmojos Maven plugin in the `pom.xml` file of the `flightapp_flex` project:

```
pom.xml
<plugin>
 <groupId>org.sonatype.flexmojos</groupId>
 <artifactId>flexmojos-maven-plugin</artifactId>
 <version>3.7.1</version>
 <executions>
  <execution>
   <id>compile-scaffold-swf</id>
   <phase>process-resources</phase>
   <goals>
     <goal>compile-swf</goal>
   </goals>
   <configuration>
     <incremental>true</incremental>
     <sourceFile>
       ${basedir}/src/main/flex/${project.name}_scaffold.mxml
     </sourceFile>
     <sourcePaths>
       <path>${basedir}/src/main/flex</path>
     </sourcePaths>
     <output>
```

```
              ${basedir}/src/main/webapp/${project.name}_scaffold.swf
          </output>
          <contextRoot>/${project.build.finalName}</contextRoot>
            <services>
              ${basedir}/src/main/webapp/WEB-INF/
              flex/services-config.xml
            </services>
            <debug>true</debug>
          </configuration>
        </execution>
      </executions>
      <dependencies>
        <dependency>
          <groupId>com.adobe.flex</groupId>
          <artifactId>compiler</artifactId>
          <version>4.0.0.14159</version>
          <type>pom</type>
        </dependency>
      </dependencies>
    </plugin>
```

In this listing, the `<configuration>` element configures the Flexmojos Maven plugin. The `<sourceFile>` element identifies the main application MXML file to be compiled by the plugin, which is the `flightapp_flex_scaffold.mxml` file. The `<sourcePaths>` specifies the base directory or directories where the project's ActionScript files are located, which corresponds to `/src/main/flex`— the directory, which is created when you execute the `flex remoting all` or `flex remoting scaffold` command. The `<output>` specifies the name and location of the generated SWF file, which is `SRC_MAIN_WEBAPP/flightapp_flex_scaffold.swf` for the `flightapp_flex` project. The `<contextRoot>` element specifies the context root of the web application, which corresponds to the value `/flightapp_flex-0.1.0.BUILD-SNAPSHOT`. The value of `<contextRoot>` element is used to replace the `{context.root}` token specified in the endpoint URLs defined in `services-config.xml` file. The `<services>` element specifies the `services-config.xml` file that defines channels and corresponding endpoints.

The `<dependency>` element specifies that the Flexmojos Maven plugin is dependent on Flex compiler. Note that the dependency type is `pom` and not `jar`. As the dependency type is `pom`, dependencies specified in the corresponding `pom` file (which you can find at `https://repository.sonatype.org/content/groups/flexgroup/`) are added to the required dependencies of the Flexmojos Maven plugin.

▸ Refer to the *Scaffolding a Flex application from JPA entities* recipe, to see how to scaffold remoting destinations and Flex user interface using Roo

Scaffolding a Flex application from JPA entities

In the previous recipe, we saw how to set up a project to use Flex and Spring BlazeDS integration. In this recipe, we go a step further and scaffold a complete Flex application that interacts with BlazeDS to perform CRUD operations on the JPA entities.

Getting ready

This recipe is an extension of the previous recipe, *Getting started with Flex application development*; therefore, perform the steps described in the previous recipe to set up the `flightapp_flex` project to use the Flex and Spring BlazeDS integration.

Start the Roo shell from the `C:\roo-cookbook\ch05-flex` directory—the directory in which the `flightapp_flex` project was created when you went through the *Getting started with Flex application development* recipe.

How to do it...

To scaffold a flex application, follow the steps given here:

1. Execute the `flex remoting all` command, as shown here:

```
.. roo> flex remoting all --package ~.flex
Created SRC_MAIN_JAVA\sample\roo\flightapp\flex
Created ..FlightDescriptionService.java
Created ..FlightDescriptionService_Roo_Service.aj
..
Created ROOT\src\main\flex\sample\roo\flightapp\domain
Created ..FlightDescription.as

Updated ROOT\src\main\flex\flightapp_flex_scaffold.mxml
Updated ROOT\src\main\flex\flightapp_flex_scaffold-config.xml

Created ROOT\src\main\flex\sample\roo\flightapp\presentation\
flightdescription
Created ..FlightDescriptionEvent.as
```

```
Created ..FlightDescriptionView.mxml

Created ..FlightDescriptionForm.mxml
```

2. The output shown here has been organized such that the directory which is created by Roo comes first, followed by the files that are created in the directory. The Spring Roo shell will not show the output as it has been shown above. For brevity, the output shows only the files that were created corresponding to the `FlightDescription` JPA entity.

3. Exit the Roo shell and execute `mvn install` from the directory containing the `flightapp_flex` project to build the `flightapp_flex` project:

   C:\roo-cookbook\ch05-flex>mvn install

4. Execute the `tomcat:run` goal (from the directory containing the `flightapp_flex` Roo project) of the Tomcat Maven plugin to start the embedded Tomcat instance:

   C:\roo-cookbook\ch05-flex>mvn tomcat:run

5. Open the web browser and access the `flightapp_flex_scaffold.html` file, which acts as the HTML wrapper for our Flex application: `http://localhost:8080/flightapp_flex/flightapp_flex_scaffold.html`. If `Flash Player 10` or above is not already installed for your web browser, you'll be asked to install it. It is also recommended that you install `Flash Debugger` for your web browser to view any exceptions raised while interacting with the Flex application. If you see the following Flex application user interface, then it means you have successfully deployed your Flex application on Tomcat:

6. This screenshot shows the list of JPA entities that can be managed using the Flex application. As the `flightapp_flex` project contained `Flight` and `FlightDescription` entities, they are shown in the list.

7. To perform CRUD operations on the `FlightDescription` and `Flight` entity instances, double-click the JPA entity name in the list. The following screenshot shows the screen that is displayed when you double-click the **FlightDescription** item in the list:

Entity List	FlightDescription List	
FlightDescription	New FlightDescription	
Flight	Origin	Destination

How it works...

The `flex remoting all` command is processed by the Flex add-on of Spring Roo.

Flex clients interact with server-side BlazeDS remoting destinations (which are Java objects) via BlazeDS `RemotingService`. As we are using Spring BlazeDS integration, remoting destinations are configured as Spring service components, and the `RemotingService` is configured with sensible defaults by the `<message-broker>` element of Spring's `flex` schema (refer `SRC_MAIN_WEBAPP\WEB-INF\spring\flex-config.xml` file). The `package` argument of the `flex remoting all` command specifies the package in which the remoting destinations are created.

It is important to note that Flex clients interact with messaging destinations (which could be a JMS queue or topic) using the `MessageService` and with remoting destinations (Java objects) using the `RemotingService`.

The following table describes the important directories and files that are created when the `flex remoting all` command is executed:

Directory / file	Description
SRC_MAIN_JAVA\sample\roo\flightapp\flex	Contains remoting destinations created by Roo corresponding to each JPA entity in the `flightapp_flex` application for which a remoting destination doesn't exist. This directory is created based on the `package` argument value of the `flex remoting all` command.
ROOT\src\main\flex\sample\roo\flightapp\domain	Contains Roo-generated ActionScript classes that map to JPA entities in the `flightapp_flex` application.
ROOT\src\main\flex\sample\roo\flightapp\presentation\flightdescription	Contains MXML files and ActionScript classes for performing CRUD operations on the `FlightDescription` JPA entity. The name of the directory is derived from the name of the JPA entity.
ROOT\src\main\flex\sample\roo\flightapp\presentation\flight	Contains MXML files and ActionScript classes for performing CRUD operations on the `Flight` JPA entity. The name of the directory is derived from the name of the JPA entity.

When the `flex remoting all` command is executed, it creates a remoting destination (which is also Spring's service component) corresponding to each JPA entity in the application for which a remoting destination doesn't already exist. A remoting destination defines methods to perform CRUD operations on the corresponding JPA entity. The following code listing shows the remoting destination, `FlightDescriptionService` class, created by Roo corresponding to the `FlightDescription` JPA entity:

```
FlightDescriptionService.java
package sample.roo.flightapp.flex;

import org.springframework.flex.roo.addon.RooFlexScaffold;
import sample.roo.flightapp.domain.FlightDescription;
import org.springframework.flex.remoting.RemotingDestination;
import org.springframework.stereotype.Service;

@RooFlexScaffold(entity = FlightDescription.class)
@RemotingDestination
@Service
public class FlightDescriptionService {
}
```

In this code, `@RooFlexScaffold` annotation instructs Roo to generate a corresponding AspectJ ITD file. This AspectJ ITD file introduces methods into the `FlightDescriptionService` class for performing CRUD operations on the `FlightDescription` entity. The `entity` attribute of `@RooFlexScaffold` annotation specifies the JPA entity managed by the `FlightDescriptionService` class. The `@RemotingDestination` annotation of Spring indicates that `FlightDescriptionService` class is exported as a remoting destination.

Spring-managed `MessageBroker` is responsible for routing messages received from the Flex clients to `RemotingService`, which in turn invokes the method on the Spring-managed remoting destination. The `@Service` annotation indicates that `FlightDescriptionService` represents Spring's service component. The use of the `@Service` annotation ensures that `FlightDescriptionService` is auto-registered with Spring's web application context, using the classpath scanning feature of Spring (refer to the `<component-scan>` element defined in the `webmvc-config.xml` file).

The following code listing shows the AspectJ ITD file created corresponding to the `@RooFlexScaffold` annotation in the `FlightDescriptionService` class:

```
FlightDescriptionService_Roo_Service.aj
package sample.roo.flightapp.flex;

import java.lang.Long;
import java.util.List;
import sample.roo.flightapp.domain.FlightDescription;

privileged aspect FlightDescriptionService_Roo_Service {

  public FlightDescription
      FlightDescriptionService.show(Long id) {
    ...
    return FlightDescription.findFlightDescription(id);
  }

  public List<FlightDescription>
      FlightDescriptionService.list() {
    return FlightDescription.findAllFlightDescriptions();
  }
  ...
}
```

This code shows that `FlightDescriptionService_Roo_Service.aj` introduces CRUD operations for the `FlightDescription` JPA entity in the `FlightDescriptionService` class. Though not shown in the above code, pagination support is also introduced for reading the list of `FlightDescription` JPA entities.

The name of the AspectJ ITD file corresponding to the `@RooFlexScaffold` annotation has the following naming convention: <JPA-entity-name>`Service_Roo_Service.aj`, where `<JPA-entity-name>` is the name of the JPA entity specified by the `entity` attribute of the `@RooFlexScaffold` annotation.

Invoking Spring-managed remoting destination methods from the Flex client may require sending and receiving objects. For instance, the `show` method of `FlightDescriptionService` returns a `FlightDescription` object and the `create` method accepts a `FlightDescription` object. Flex allows exchanging data between the Flex client and remoting destination method by auto-converting the ActionScript object to the Java object and vice versa. As the Flex client in the `flightapp_flex` application exchanges flight description details with the `FlightDescriptionService` remoting destination, Roo generates ActionScript classes corresponding to the JPA entity managed by `FlightDescriptionService`. The following code shows the Roo-generated `FlightDescription.as` ActionScript class corresponding to the `FlightDescription` JPA entity:

```
FlightDescription.as
package  sample.roo.flightapp.domain{
[RemoteClass(alias="sample.roo.flightapp.domain.FlightDescription")]
   public class FlightDescription {
       public var destination:String;
       public var id:Number;
       public var origin:String;
       public var price:Number;
       public var version:Number;
   }
}
```

This code shows that the `FlightDescription.as` ActionScript class defines the same attributes as the corresponding `FlightDescription` JPA entity. The `[RemoteClass]` metadata tag specifies the remote Java object to which the ActionScript object maps. The `alias` attribute specifies the fully-qualified class name of the remote Java object to which the ActionScript object maps.

Roo creates ActionScript and MXML files corresponding to each JPA entity so that CRUD operations can be performed on JPA entities from the scaffolded Flex user interface. The following table describes each of these Roo-generated files (located in ROOT\src\main\ flex\sample\roo\flightapp\presentation\flightdescription and ROOT\ src\main\flex\sample\roo\flightapp\presentation\flight directories):

File	Description
`<JPA-entity-name>Event.as`	Subclass of `flash.events.Event` that defines different event types, like create, edit, and delete events that are generated when a JPA entity is created, edited, or modified. In `flightapp_flex` project, `FlightEvent.as` and `FlightDescriptionEvent.as` represent event classes.
`<JPA-entity-name>View.mxml`	MXML file that shows the list of entity instances and options to create, edit, and delete entity instances. In the `flightapp_flex` project, `FlightView.mxml` and `FlightDescriptionView.mxml` MXML files show list of `Flight` and `FlightDescription` entity instances, respectively, and options to create, edit, and delete the entity instances.
`<JPA-entity-name>Form.mxml`	The MXML file that shows the form for creating entity instances. In the `flightapp_flex` project, `FlightForm.mxml` and `FlightDescriptionForm.mxml` files show the form for creating `Flight` and `FlightDescription` JPA entity instances, respectively.

The following code shows the `FlightDescriptionEvent.as` ActionScript class created by Roo:

```
package sample.roo.flightapp.presentation.flightdescription
{
  import flash.events.Event;
  import sample.roo.flightapp.domain.FlightDescription;
  public class FlightDescriptionEvent extends Event {
    public static const CREATE:String =
                          "flightDescriptionCreate";
    public static const UPDATE:String =
                          "flightDescriptionUpdate";
    public static const DELETE:String =
                          "flightDescriptionDelete";

    public var flightDescription:FlightDescription;

    public function FlightDescriptionEvent(type:String,
      flightDescription:FlightDescription,
      bubbles:Boolean = true, cancelable:Boolean = false){
        this.flightDescription = flightDescription;
        super(type, bubbles, cancelable);
      }
    }
  }
}
```

The `FlightDescriptionEvent` class is a subclass of the `flash.events.Event` class and defines three different types of events: `flightDescriptionCreate`, `flightDescriptionUpdate`, and `flightDescriptionDelete`. The `FlightDescription` ActionScript object (which corresponds to the `FlightDescription` JPA entity on the server-side) represents the payload carried by the `FlightDescriptionEvent` event type.

As mentioned earlier, in the `flightapp_flex` application, `flightapp_flex_scaffold.mxml` file defines the initial user interface of the application. When the `flex remoting all` command was executed, we saw in the output that the `flightapp_flex_scaffold.mxml` file was updated. The following code shows the modification that was made by Roo to the `flightapp_flex_scaffold.mxml` file:

```
flightapp_flex_scaffold.mxml
...
<fx:Declarations>
  <s:ArrayList id="entities">
    <fx:String>FlightDescription</fx:String>
    <fx:String>Flight</fx:String>
  </s:ArrayList>


  ...
</fx:Declarations>
...
  <s:Panel id="entityPanel" title="Entity List" height="100%">
   <s:List id="entityList" dataProvider="{entities}"
      width="100%" height="100%"
      toolTip="Double-Click the selected Entity"
      doubleClickEnabled="true"
      doubleClick="entityList_doubleClickHandler(event)"/>
  </s:Panel>
  </s:Group>
```

If you compare this code with the code of the `flightapp_flex_scaffold.mxml` file that we saw in the previous recipe, you'll notice that the only change that happened is the addition of the `<fx:String>` elements to the `<ArrayList>`. Roo creates an `<fx:String>` element corresponding to each JPA entity in the application. By default, the value of the `<fx:String>` element is the simple name of the corresponding JPA entity. As the `<List>` component makes use of `<ArrayList>` as its data provider, the `<List>` component now displays **Flight** and **FlightDescription** list items in the user interface, as shown here:

This screenshot shows that Roo doesn't generate a list item corresponding to the finder method, findFlightDescriptionsByDestinationAndOrigin, defined in FlightDescription JPA entity.

When you double-click an item in the list shown above, it invokes the entityList_doubleClickHandler ActionScript method defined in the flightapp_flex_scaffold. mxml file, which displays the user interface generated either by FlightView.mxml or FlightView.mxml, depending upon the list item double-clicked. The following code shows the entityList_doubleClickHandler method:

```
protected function
   entityList_doubleClickHandler(event:MouseEvent):void {
   . .
   var selectedEntity:String = entityList.selectedItem;
   var selectedEntityPackage:String =
     selectedEntity.toLowerCase();

   var viewClass:Class =
     getDefinitionByName("sample.roo.flightapp.presentation."
     + selectedEntityPackage+"::"+selectedEntity+"View")
     as Class;
   if (viewClass != null) {
    var newView:UIComponent = UIComponent(new viewClass());
     . . .
     mainGroup.addElement(newView);
    }
   . . .
}
```

As MXML files are compiled into ActionScript classes, FlightDescriptionView.mxml and FlightView.mxml files are converted to FileDescriptionView and FlightView ActionScript classes, respectively. The entityList_doubleClickHandler method obtains the selected item value from the list (which is either **FlightDescription** or **Flight**) and appends 'View' string to it—making the concatenated value to FlightDescriptionView or FlightView. The entityList_doubleClickHandler then creates an instance of FlightDescriptionView or FlightView and adds it to the main user interface.

The following sequence diagram summarizes the role played by the `entity_doubleClickHandler` method:

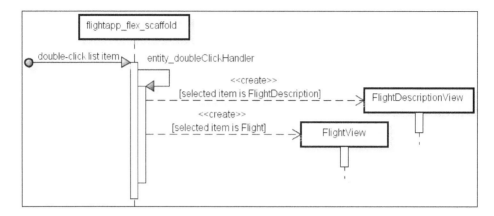

It is important to note that the `entityList_doubleClickHandler` method of the `flightapp_flex_scaffold.mxml` file never directly references either the `FlightView` or `FlightDescriptionView` ActionScript class. In fact, `FlightView` and `FlightDescriptionView` classes are not referenced by any other MXML or ActionScript class in the `flightapp_flex` project. The side-effect of this is that the Flex compiler doesn't include `FlightDescriptionView` and `FlightView` in the generated SWF file. To instruct Flex compiler to include `FlightDescriptionView` and `FlightView` ActionScript classes, Roo adds their fully-qualified name in the `flightapp_flex_scaffold-config.xml` file, as shown here:

```
flightapp_flex_scaffold-config.xml
<flex-config xmlns="http://www.adobe.com/2006/flex-config">
  <includes append="true">
    <symbol>sample.roo.flightapp.presentation.flightdescription.
FlightDescriptionView
    </symbol>
    <symbol>
        sample.roo.flightapp.presentation.flight.FlightView
    </symbol>
  </includes>
</flex-config>
```

The `<symbol>` elements specify the ActionScript classes that should be included in the generated SWF file by the Flex compiler.

The `FlightDescriptionView.mxml` shows a **New FlightDescription** button, and if clicked, it invokes the `showForm` method. The `showForm` method of `FlightDescriptionView.mxml` shows the form (represented by `FlightDescriptionForm.mxml`) for creating `FlightDescription` entity instances, as shown here:

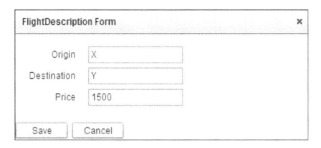

The following sequence diagram shows what happens behind the scenes when you click on the **New FlightDescription** button:

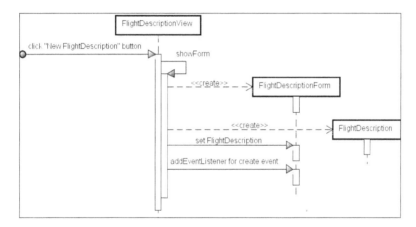

This sequence diagram shows that the `showForm` method creates `FlightDescriptionForm` and `FlightDescription` objects. The `FlightDescription` object (which corresponds to `FlightDescription` JPA entity) acts as the form-backing object that we see in web applications. The `showForm` methods sets the `FlightDescription` object in the `FlightDescriptionForm` instance. Also, `showForm` adds an event listener for the `FlightDescriptionEvent.CREATE` event to `FlightDescriptionForm`.

The following code shows the `showForm` method:

```
private function showForm
   (flightDescription:FlightDescription = null):void {
  var form:FlightDescriptionForm =
    PopUpManager.createPopUp(this, FlightDescriptionForm, true)
```

```
    as FlightDescriptionForm;
..
    form.flightDescription = flightDescription != null ?
    flightDescription : new FlightDescription();

    form.addEventListener(FlightDescriptionEvent.CREATE,
       flightDescriptionView_flightDescriptionCreateEventHandler);
}
```

This code shows that, the `addEventListener` method accepts the type of event that `FlightDescriptionForm` object listens to, which is `FlightDescriptionEvent.CREATE`. The `addEventListener` also accepts the name of the handler method that is invoked when the event is received by the `FlightDescriptionForm` object. So, if the `FlightDescriptionEvent.CREATE` event is received by the `FlightDescriptionForm` object, it results in the invocation of the `flightDescriptionView_flightDescriptionCreateEventHandler` method. We'll come back to the handler method, but first let's look at how the `FlightDescriptionEvent.CREATE` event is generated.

The following sequence diagram shows that the `FlightDescriptionEvent.CREATE` event is generated when the user presses the **Save** button to create a `FlightDescription` JPA entity instance:

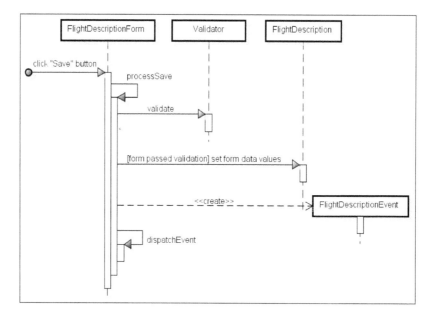

This sequence diagram shows that when the **Save** button is clicked, it results in the invocation of the `processSave` method defined in `FlightDescriptioForm.mxml`. The `processSave` method validates the form data entered by the user using the `mx.validators.Validator`. If the data validation succeeds, form data is set in the `FlightDescription` ActionScript object. The `processSave` method now creates a `FlightDescriptionEvent` event of type `FlightDescriptionEvent.CREATE` and passes the `FlightDescription` ActionScript object as the payload of the event. Invoking the `dispatchEvent` method results in dispatching the newly created event to listeners.

So, after receiving the `FlightDescriptionEvent.CREATE` event, `flightDescriptionView_flightDescriptionCreateEventHandler` is invoked, as explained earlier. The following code shows the `flightDescriptionView_flightDescriptionCreateEventHandler` method, which invokes the `FlightDescriptionService`'s `create` method to create an instance of the `FlightDescription` JPA entity:

```
protected function
  flightDescriptionView_flightDescriptionCreateEventHandler
    (event:FlightDescriptionEvent):void {
    flightDescriptionService.create(event.flightDescription);
}
...
```

The `flightDescriptionService` object in the previous code represents a `mx.rpc.remoting.RemoteObject`, which is used by Flex clients to access remoting destinations. `RemoteObject` is defined in `FlightDescriptionView.mxml` using the `<RemotObject>` tag, as shown here:

```
<s:RemoteObject channelSet="{remotingChannels}"
    destination="flightDescriptionService"
    fault="flightDescriptionService_faultHandler(event)"
    id="flightDescriptionService">
  ...
</s:RemoteObject>
```

In this code, `{remotingChannels}` identifies the `ChannelSet` to use for communication with server-side Java objects. We saw in the previous recipe that remoting channels used by the `flightapp_flex` application are defined in the `flightapp_flex_scaffold.mxml` file using the `<ChannelSet>` tag. The `destination` attribute specifies the remoting destination that is accessed via `RemoteObject`.

There's more...

The Flex Add-on provides round-tripping support, that is, modifications to JPA entities are propagated to MXML and ActionScript files.

Flex Addon doesn't provide any support for controlling the methods that form a part of the Spring-managed remoting destinations. For instance, you can't control the methods that are part of the `FlightDescriptionService_Roo_Service.aj` file using `@RooFlexScaffold` annotation.

If you want that a method in the Spring-managed remoting destination is not accessible to Flex clients, then all you need to do is to either perform push-in refactoring or define the method in the corresponding Java class and add the `@RemotingExclude` annotation of Spring to the method.

Spring Roo makes use of JSR 303 annotations specified in the JPA entity to add Flex validators in the MXML files. For instance, if a JPA entity field specifies `@NotNull` JSR 303 annotation then Roo adds a Flex `StringValidator` or `Numbervalidator` that checks that the field on the form is not blank. Note that Flex addon support for JSR 303 annotations is limited.

See also

▶ Refer to the *Getting started with Flex application development* to see how you can set up Flex for your Roo project

Getting started with Spring Web Flow

In *Chapter 4, Web Application Development with Spring Web MVC* we saw that Roo simplifies building Spring Web MVC applications. In this recipe, we'll look at how Roo sets up your Roo project to use Spring Web Flow—a framework that is built on top of Spring Web MVC.

Spring Web Flow allows modelling a web application as a set of flows, where each flow represents a finite state machine.

 The support for Spring Web Flow is broken in Spring Roo 1.1.3; therefore, you must use Spring Roo 1.1.4 or 1.1.5 to execute this recipe. This recipe has been developed using Spring Roo 1.1.5.

Getting ready

Create a new directory `C:\roo-cookbook\ch05-webflow` in your system and copy the `ch05_webflow_app.roo` script that accompanies this book to the `ch05-webflow` directory.

Start the Roo shell from the `ch05-webflow` directory and execute the `ch05_webflow_app.roo` script using the `script` command. Executing the `ch05_webflow_app.roo` script creates a `flightapp-webflow` Eclipse project, sets up Hibernate as persistence provider, configures MySQL as the database for the application, and creates `Flight`, `FlightDescription`, `Customer`, and `Address` JPA entities. The `Customer` entity has a one-to-one relationship with the `Address` entity and `Flight` has a many-to-one relationship with the `FlightDescription` entity. If you are using a different database than MySQL or your connection settings are different than what is specified in the script, then modify the script accordingly.

How to do it...

To set up the Spring Web Flow framework, follow the steps given here:

1. Execute the `web flow` Roo command to create a Customer flow, as shown here:

   ```
   .. roo> web flow --flowName customer
   Created SRC_MAIN_WEBAPP\WEB-INF\spring
   Created SRC_MAIN_WEBAPP\WEB-INF\spring\webflow-config.xml
   Created SRC_MAIN_WEBAPP\WEB-INF\spring\webmvc-config.xml
   ...
   Created SRC_MAIN_WEBAPP\WEB-INF\views\customer
   Created SRC_MAIN_WEBAPP\WEB-INF\views\customer\flow.xml
   Created SRC_MAIN_WEBAPP\WEB-INF\views\customer\view-state-1.jspx
   Created SRC_MAIN_WEBAPP\WEB-INF\views\customer\view-state-2.jspx
   Created SRC_MAIN_WEBAPP\WEB-INF\views\customer\end-state.jspx
   Created SRC_MAIN_WEBAPP\WEB-INF\views\menu.jspx
   Created SRC_MAIN_WEBAPP\WEB-INF\views\customer\views.xml
   ...
   Updated ROOT\pom.xml [...; added dependency org.springframework.
   webflow:spring-webflo
   w:2.2.1.RELEASE]
   ```

2. Execute the `perform eclipse` command to update the project's classpath settings:

   ```
   .. roo> perform eclipse
   ```

3. You can now import the `flightapp_webflow` project into your Eclipse IDE.

4. Exit the Roo shell and execute the `tomcat:run` goal of the Tomcat Maven plugin from the `ch05-webflow` directory to deploy the `flightapp_webflow` project to the embedded Tomcat container:

   ```
   C:\roo-cookbook\ch05-webflow> mvn tomcat:run
   ```

5. Open the http://localhost:8080/flightapp_webflow URL in your favorite browser. If you see the following page, then it means your application is successfully deployed in the embedded Tomcat container:

6. Click the **Enter Customer flow** menu option to start the sample flow installed by the web flow command. This screenshot shows the first step in the flow when the Customer flow is started:

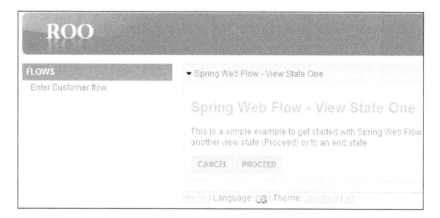

7. The **CANCEL** button ends the Customer flow and the **PROCEED** button takes you to next step in the flow.

How it works...

Spring Web Flow allows creating a web application as a set of flows, where each flow defines a series of states, transitions, and actions. The `web flow` command, processed by the Spring Web Flow add-on, creates artifacts that are required to quickly get started with developing web applications using Spring Web Flow. The `flowName` is an optional argument that specifies the name of the flow which you want to create. If the `flowName` argument is not specified, Roo creates a sample flow.

When the `web flow` command is executed for the first time, it mostly creates files and directories that you've already seen in *Chapter 4, Web Application Development with Spring Web MVC*. In this recipe, we'll focus on files and directories that Roo creates specifically for developing applications with Spring Web Flow. It is important to note that the `web flow` command only creates a sample flow, which gives you the starting point to create your custom flow.

As the output of the `web flow` command shows, Roo not only creates the `webmvc-config.xml` file (which is also created when you execute the `web mvc install` command) but also creates a `webflow-config.xml` file. The `webflow-config.xml` file is the application context XML file that defines Spring Web Flow-specific special beans like `FlowHandler Mapping`, `FlowHandlerAdapter`, and so on. The `webmvc-config.xml` web application context XML defines the beans that we discussed in *Chapter 4, Web Application Development with Spring Web MVC*. Additionally, it now imports the bean definitions in `webflow-config.xml`, using the `<import>` element of Spring's `beans` schema, as shown here:

```
<import resource="webflow-config.xml"/>
```

The value of `flowName` argument is used by Roo to create a directory with the same name in the`/WEB-INF/views` folder, containing flow-related artifacts. By default, Roo only creates an example flow to let you get started with creating your own flow. The following table describes the flow-related artifacts that were created in the `/WEB-INF/views/customer` directory when we executed the `web flow --flowName customer` command:

File name	Description
`flow.xml`	XML file that defines the flow states, transitions, and actions
`view-state-1.jspx`	JSPX file that corresponds to the first view state of the Customer flow
`view-state-2.jspx`	JSPX file that corresponds to the second view state of the Customer flow
`end-state.jspx`	JSPX file that corresponds to the end view state of the Customer flow
`views.xml`	Tiles configuration XML file, which contains tiles definitions for showing JSPX pages in the Customer flow

Let's first look at how we define a flow in a flow definition XML file.

The following listing shows the `flow.xml` file that was created in the `WEB-INF/views/customer` folder:

```
flow.xml
<flow xmlns="http://www.springframework.org/schema/webflow" ..>

    <view-state id="view-state-1" view="customer/view-state-1">
            <transition on="success" to="view-state-2"/>
            <transition on="cancel" to="end-state"/>
    </view-state>

    <view-state id="view-state-2" view="customer/view-state-2">
            <transition on="cancel" to="end-state"/>
    </view-state>

    <end-state id="end-state" view="customer/end-state"/>

</flow>
```

As this code shows, every flow definition XML file begins with the `<flow>` root element. A `<view-state>` element defines a view state—a state in which a view is rendered. The `id` attribute of the `<view-state>` element uniquely identifies the state in the flow definition XML file. As the first state defined in the flow definition, XML file is the start state of the flow, `view-state-1` represents the start state of Customer flow. The `view` attribute of the `<view-state>` element specifies the view that should be rendered to the user. As Roo-generated Spring Web Flow application makes use of Apache Tiles 2 framework, the value of the `view` attribute represents a logical name of the view. The actual view corresponding to the `view` attribute value is determined based on the tiles definition contained in the `WEB-INF/views/customer/views.xml` file. The `<end-state>` element defines the end state of the flow. The `view` attribute defines the logical name of the view that is rendered when the end state of the flow is reached. A flow may define multiple end states and in some cases the end state may not render a view.

The `<transition>` element specifies the state to which the flow is transitioned when an event occurs. The `on` attribute specifies the event that triggers the transition and the `to` attribute specifies the state to which the flow transitions. For instance, if the Customer flow is in `view-state-1` state and `success` event is received, then the flow transitions to `view-state-2` state and if `cancel` event is received, then the flow transitions to `end-state`. As you can see, the state transitions result in navigation from one page to another page in a Spring Web Flow application.

Let's now look at the beans defined in Roo-generated `webflow-config.xml` file for the `flightapp_webflow` project.

Spring Web Flow configuration

The `webflow-config.xml` defines a `HandlerMapping` that returns a `FlowHandler` for initiating execution of a flow, as shown here:

```
<bean class=
"org.springframework.webflow.mvc.servlet.FlowHandlerMapping">
  <property name="order" value="0" />
  <property name="flowRegistry" ref="flowRegistry" />
</bean>
```

The `order` property specifies the priority assigned to the `FlowHandlerMapping` with respect to other `HandlerMapping` implementations configured in the web application context. The value can be anything from `Integer.MIN_VALUE` to `Integer.MAX_VALUE`. The lower the value of the `order` property, the higher the priority of the `HandlerMapping` implementation. So, if a `HandlerMapping` implementation configured in the web application context specifies a value of `order` property more than `0`, then it has a lower priority than `FlowHandlerMapping`. The priority of a `HandlerMapping` implementation comes into play when `DispatcherServlet` attempts to find a handler for processing the request.

The `HandlerMapping` configuration with highest priority (that is, lowest `order` value) is first consulted by `DispatcherServlet` to find a matching handler and `HandlerMapping` configuration that doesn't specify an `order` property is given the lowest priority.

The `flowRegistry` property of `FlowHandlerMapping` specifies a `FlowDefinitionRegistry` that contains a registry of all the flow definitions in the application. The following `<flow-registry>` element of Spring's `webflow` schema defines a flow registry:

```
<webflow:flow-registry id="flowRegistry"
    flow-builder-services="flowBuilderServices"
    base-path="/WEB-INF/views">
  <webflow:flow-location-pattern value="/**/flow.xml" />
</webflow:flow-registry>
```

The `base-path` attribute specifies the location relative to which flow definition XML files are located. The value `/WEB-INF/views` of the `base-path` attribute means that the flow definition XML files are located relative to the `/WEB-INF/views` folder. The `<flow-location-pattern>` specifies the location pattern for finding the flow definition XML files, relative to the `base-path`. The value `/**/flow.xml` means that the `flow.xml` files inside the `/WEB-INF/views` folder or its subfolder represent the flow definition XML files.

Flows are registered in the flow registry with a unique ID, which is determined by the name of the flow definition XML file (if `base-path` attribute is not specified) or by the location of the flow definition XML file relative to the `base-path` attribute value. As the Roo-generated `webflow-config.xml` file makes use of the `base-path` attribute, the unique ID assigned to the flow is determined by the location of the flow definition XML files relative to the `base-path` attribute value. For instance, the Customer flow definition XML file in the `flightapp_webflow` project is located in the `/WEB-INF/views/customer` folder (relative to `base-path`) and the `base-path` attribute is `/WEB-INF/views`. If we subtract the `base-path` value (`/WEB-INF/views`) from the flow definition XML location (`/WEB-INF/views/customer`), then it returns the unique ID of the flow with which it is registered in the flow registry—which is `customer` for the Customer flow.

When a request is received (via `DispatcherServlet`) by the `FlowHandlerMapping`, it checks whether the flow registry contains a flow whose unique ID matches the current request path. If a match is found, then it returns a `FlowHandler` that starts execution of the matched flow, else it returns `null`. When `null` is returned, `DispatcherServlet` consults the next `HandlerMapping` in the web application context to find the handler for processing the request.

The `flow-builder-services` attribute of the `<flow-registry>` element specifies an implementation of `FlowBuilderServices`, which is used for configuring custom services that are required to build flows registered in the flow registry. For instance, if you want to configure a custom `ConversionService` or `ViewFactoryCreator`, you can specify reference to a `FlowBuilderServices` instance as the value of the `flow-builder-services` attribute value. As Roo-generated Spring Web Flow application makes use of Apache Tiles 2 framework, `FlowBuilderServices` is configured with a `ViewFactoryCreator` that maps a URL to a `TilesView` (described in detail in *Chapter 4, Web Application Development with Spring Web MVC*), as shown here:

```
<bean id="mvcViewFactoryCreator" class=
"org.springframework.webflow.mvc.builder.MvcViewFactoryCreator">
  <property name="viewResolvers" ref="tilesViewResolver" />
</bean>
```

The `MvcViewFactoryCreator` is an implementation of the `ViewFactoryCreator`, which creates a `ViewFactory` for rendering Spring Web MVC-based views, like JSPs. The `viewResolvers` property of `MvcViewFactoryCreator` specifies the view resolution strategy. The `tilesViewResolver` (defined in the `webmvc-config.xml` file) represents a `UrlBasedViewResolver` that resolves view names corresponding to URLs. As Roo-generated Spring Web Flow application makes use of Apache Tiles 2 framework, the `UrlBasedViewResolver` resolves a URL to a `TilesView`, as shown here:

```
<bean class=
"org.springframework.web.servlet.view.UrlBasedViewResolver"
  id="tilesViewResolver">
  <property name="viewClass" value=
    "org.springframework.web.servlet.view.tiles2.TilesView"/>
</bean>
```

Refer to *Chapter 4, Web Application Development with Spring Web MVC* for more information on `UrlBasedViewResolver`.

Let's now take a step back and see how request is mapped to a flow and how the view is resolved corresponding to the view state of the Customer flow. If you look at the `menu.jspx` file, you'll find that the menu option **Enter Customer flow** refers to the `/customer` URL, as shown here:

```
<menu:item id="i_flows_customer" messageCode="webflow_menu_enter"
url="/customer" z="..")/>
```

So, when you click the **Enter Customer flow** menu option, `FlowHandlerMapping` attempts to find the flow whose unique ID is `customer` (removing the leading '/' from the request path gives the flow ID to look for). As our Customer flow has a `customer` unique ID, `FlowHandlerMapping` returns a `FlowHandler` instance that starts the execution of Customer flow. As the first `<view-state>` element in `flow.xml` of Customer flow defines the start state of the Customer flow, view corresponding to the first `<view-state>` element is rendered. The `view` attribute of the first `<view-state>` element is `customer/view-state-1`, which represents a logical view name. As the Roo-generated Spring Web Flow application makes use of Apache Tiles 2 framework, the Tiles configuration XML files (including `/WEB-INF/views/customer/views.xml` Tiles configuration XML file) in the application are consulted to find the tiles definition corresponding to the logical view name `customer/view-state-1`. The following listing shows the `/WEB-INF/views/customer/views.xml` file:

```
<tiles-definitions>
  <definition extends="default" name="customer/*">
    <put-attribute name="body"
      value="/WEB-INF/views/customer/{1}.jspx"/>
  </definition>
</tiles-definitions>
```

The `<definition>` element's `name` attribute value is `customer/*`, which matches the logical view name `customer/view-state-1`. So, we now know the tiles definition that applies to the first `<view-state>` element of the Customer flow. Another interesting thing to notice is the use of token `{1}` in the value of `<put-attribute>` element. The token `{1}` refers to the first value that appears in the logical view name after the `customer/` string— which is `view-state-1` for the first `<view-state>` element of the Customer flow. Similarly, if the logical view name is `customer/x/y/z`, then the value of token `{1}` is x, token `{2}` is y, and `{3}` is z. This makes the view rendered for the first `<view-state>` element of the Customer flow as `/WEB-INF/views/customer/view-state-1.jspx`.

Now, coming back to `webflow-config.xml`, the flows are started by `FlowHandler` and executed by `FlowExecutor`, and the following `FlowHandlerAdapter` implementation is configured:

```
<bean class=
"org.springframework.webflow.mvc.servlet.FlowHandlerAdapter">
  <property name="flowExecutor" ref="flowExecutor" />
</bean>
<webflow:flow-executor id="flowExecutor" />
```

The `<flow-executor>` element of Spring's `webflow` schema installs a `FlowExecutor`, which is used by the `FlowHandler` implementation to execute a flow. You can create a custom `FlowHandler` implementation if you like, by extending `AbstractFlowHandler` class.

Developing applications using both Spring Web MVC and Spring Web Flow

You'll also find that the following beans are configured in the `webflow-config.xml` file:

```
<bean class="org.springframework.web.servlet.mvc.annotation.
  AnnotationMethodHandlerAdapter" />

<bean class="org.springframework.web.servlet.mvc.
SimpleControllerHandlerAdapter" />
```

The `AnnotationMethodHandlerAdapter` is used when you are using `@Controller` annotated controllers in Spring Web MVC and `SimpleControllerHandlerAdapter` is used when you are using controllers that implement Spring Web MVC's `Controller` interface.

You might be wondering why these `HandlerAdapter` implementations are configured when we are using Spring Web Flow and not Spring Web MVC. Well, Spring Web Flow is usually used along with Spring Web MVC because not everything in your web application may represent a flow. For instance, in a Flight Booking application, Booking may represent a process spanning a series of steps but creation of a `Flight` entity may not. This is the reason why execution of the `web flow` command not only enables development using Spring Web Flow but also using Spring Web MVC. If you look at `webmvc-config.xml` file, it defines `<annotation-driven>` element of Spring's `mvc` schema, as shown here:

```
<mvc:annotation-driven/>
```

The `<annotation-driven>` element configures `AnnotationMethodHandlerAdapter` and `DefaultAnnotationHandlerMapping` beans to support developing Spring Web MVC applications using annotated controllers. As `webflow-config.xml` explicitly defines `FlowHandlerAdapter`, it overrides the `AnnotationMethodHandlerAdapter` bean configured implicitly by `<annotation-driven>`. This is the reason why the `AnnotationMethodHandlerAdapter` bean is explicitly configured by Roo in the `webflow-config.xml` file.

To see how Spring Web Flow and Spring Web MVC co-exist in the same application, scaffold Spring Web MVC controller for `Flight` and `FlightDescription` JPA entities in `flighapp_webflow` project, as shown here:

```
.. roo> controller scaffold --class ~.controller.FlightController
--entity ~.domain.Flight
```

```
.. roo> controller scaffold --class ~.controller.
FlightDescriptionController --entity ~.domain.FlightDescription
```

Executing `controller scaffold` Roo command will generate Spring Web MVC annotated controllers in the `com.sample.flightapp.controller` package. Also, it will generate JSPX views and a tiles configuration XML file corresponding to the `Flight` and `FlightDescription` JPA entities in `/WEB-INF/views/flights` and `/WEB-INF/views/flightdescriptions` folders, respectively. Now, exit the Roo shell and deploy the `flightapp_webflow` project to the embedded Tomcat container as shown here:

C:\roo-cookbook\ch05-webflow> mvn tomcat:run

Open `http://localhost:8080/flightapp_webflow` URL in your favorite browser. If you see the following page, then it means your application is successfully deployed on the embedded Tomcat container:

As this screenshot shows, the `flightapp_webflow` application consists of both Spring Web Flow flows (created via the `web flow` command) and Spring Web MVC controllers (created via the `controller scaffold` command).

There's more...

Spring Web Flow provides support for associating model attributes with a view state, making it possible to create a flow consisting of form submissions. For instance, you can modify Customer flow such that the user first enters details in a customer form (which binds form field values to the `Customer` JPA entity), followed by address details (which binds form field values to the `Address` JPA entity), and in the end both `Customer` and `Address` entity instances are persisted in the database.

See also

▸ Refer to the *Creating Spring MVC controllers and JSPX views from JPA entities* recipe in *Chapter 4, Web Application Development with Spring Web MVC* to see a description of beans defined in `webmvc-config.xml` file

6
Emailing, Messaging, Spring Security, Solr, and GAE

In this chapter, we will cover:

- ▶ Sending e-mails using JavaMail API
- ▶ Sending and receiving JMS messages
- ▶ Configuring Spring security for your application
- ▶ Using Spring Security with Apache Directory Server
- ▶ Deploying a GWT application on GAE
- ▶ Deploying a Spring Web MVC application on GAE
- ▶ Adding search capability to your domain model with Solr

Introduction

In this chapter, we look at Roo commands that support sending e-mails via JavaMail API, sending and receiving JMS messages, configuring Spring Security for an application, deploying Spring and GWT applications to Google App Engine (GAE), and adding search capability to an application's domain model using Solr search server.

Sending e-mails using JavaMail API

Spring framework provides classes such as `JavaMailSenderImpl`, `SimpleMailMessage`, and so on, which simplify sending e-mails via JavaMail API. In this recipe, we'll look at Roo commands that help with the configuration of these classes. To verify that the emailing feature in our application is working correctly, we'll send an e-mail via Gmail.

Getting ready

Create a new directory `C:\roo-cookbook\ch06-email` in your system. Copy the `ch06_web_app.roo` script to the `ch06-email` directory. If you are using a different database than MySQL or your connection settings are different than what is specified in the script, then modify the script accordingly.

Start the Roo shell from the `ch06-email` directory and execute the `ch06_web_app.roo` script using the `script` command. Executing the Roo script will create a `flightapp-web` eclipse project that represents a Spring Web MVC application consisting of `Flight` and `FlightDescription` JPA entities.

How to do it...

To simplify e-mail sending, follow the steps given here:

1. Execute the `email sender setup` command, by providing `username` and `password` argument values for the Gmail account through which you want to send e-mails. In the following command, replace the `<username>` and `<password>` argument values with the values that reflect your Gmail account username and password, respectively. It is important to note that you don't need to specify `@gmail.com` as the value of username, as it is derived from the `hostServer` argument. If you are using a different mail server for sending e-mails, then modify the argument values accordingly.

   ```
   ... roo> email sender setup --hostServer smtp.gmail.com --port 587
   --protocol SMTP --username <username> --password <password>

   Updated SRC_MAIN_RESOURCES\META-INF\spring\applicationContext.xml

   Updated ROOT\pom.xml [Added dependencies ..., javax.
   mail:mail:1.4.1, javax.activation:activation:1.1.1]

   Created SRC_MAIN_RESOURCES\META-INF\spring\email.properties
   ```

2. Execute the `email template setup` command to specify the sender of the e-mail message and the subject of the e-mail (replace `<username>` with your Gmail account username), as shown here:

```
... roo> email template setup --from <username>@gmail.com
--subject "A new Flight instance has been created"
```

Updated SRC_MAIN_RESOURCES\META-INF\spring\applicationContext.xml

Updated SRC_MAIN_RESOURCES\META-INF\spring\email.properties

3. Add Spring's `MailSender` and `SimpleMailMessage` fields, along with a `sendMessage` method, to `FlightController.java` using the `field email template` command, as shown here:

```
... roo> field email template --class ~.web.FlightController
```

Updated ...flightapp\web\FlightController.java

4. Execute the `perform eclipse` command to update the project's classpath settings:

```
.. roo> perform eclipse
```

5. Import the `flightapp-web` Eclipse project into Eclipse IDE.

6. Open `FlightController_Roo_Controller.aj` file, copy the declaration that introduces `create(...)` method in `FlightController.java` and paste it in the `FlightController.java` file.

 If you are using Spring Roo 1.1.3, then remove the `create` method declaration from `FlightController_Roo_Controller.aj` file. This is required because the create declaration from `FlightController_Roo_Controller.aj` file is not automatically removed in Spring Roo 1.1.3.

The `create` method of the `FlightController` class is invoked when the user enters flight information and submits the request to create a new `Flight` instance. After adding the `create(...)` method, your `FlightController.java` should look as follows:

```
@RooWebScaffold(...)
@RequestMapping("/flights")
@Controller
public class FlightController {

 @Autowired
 private transient MailSender mailTemplate;

 @Autowired
 private transient SimpleMailMessage simpleMailMessage;

 @RequestMapping(method = RequestMethod.POST)
 public String create(@Valid Flight flight,
   BindingResult bindingResult, Model uiModel,
   HttpServletRequest httpServletRequest) {
...
```

```
      flight.persist();
      return "redirect:/flights/" +
        encodeUrlPathSegment(flight.getFlightId().toString(),
        httpServletRequest);
  }

  public void sendMessage(java.lang.String mailTo,
      java.lang.String message) {
    ...
  }
}
```

In the given code, the `create` method has been directly added to the `FlightController.java` by copying it from the `FlightController_ Roo_Controller.aj` AspectJ ITD file. In the ITD, the create method is declared as shown here:

```
public String FlightController.create(...)
```

Make sure that you remove the `FlightController` from the name of the method when you copy it to the `FlightController.java` file. So, this method in `FlightController.java` becomes:

```
public String create(...)
```

When you add the `create(...)` method in `FlightController.java` with the same signature as in `FlightController_Roo_Controller.aj`, then Roo removes the `create(...)` method from `FlightController_Roo_Controller. aj`. Refresh the `flightapp-web` project in Eclipse IDE so that modifications made by Roo are visible.

7. Now, modify the `create(...)` method in `FlightController.java` by adding the following piece of code just after the call to `flight.persist()` method:

```
sendMessage("<username>@gmail.com", "A new instance of Flight
entity with id " + flight.getFlightId() + " has been created.");
```

In this code, replace `<username>` with your Gmail account username.

8. Exit the Roo shell and execute the `tomcat:run` goal of the Tomcat maven plugin from the `ch06-email` directory to deploy the `flightapp-web` project in an embedded Tomcat container, as shown here:

```
C:\roo-cookbook\ch06-email> mvn tomcat:run
```

Access the `flightapp-web` application from the web browser using the following URL: `http://localhost:8080/flightapp-web`. You should now see the following home page of the `flightapp-web` application:

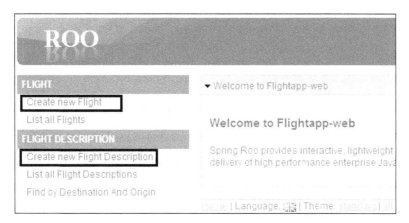

Select the **Create new Flight Description** option from the menu, which shows the form for creating a new `FlightDescription` entity instance. Once you have created the `FlightDescription` instance, select the **Create new Flight** menu option to create a `Flight` instance. The following screenshot shows the form for creating a `Flight` instance:

Enter **Departure Date**, **Arrival Date**, and **Flight Description** information and click the **Save** button. Saving the `Flight` instance will result in sending an e-mail to your Gmail account, with the subject as **A new Flight instance has been created** and the message **A new instance of Flight entity with ID 1 has been created**. As you create more `Flight` instances, an e-mail is sent to your Gmail account for each `Flight` instance created.

How it works...

JavaMail API provides classes such as `Session`, `Transport`, `Authenticator`, and so on, that are used for composing, sending, and reading e-mails. If you want to directly use the JavaMail API to send an e-mail message, then you'll need to know how to use different JavaMail API classes and interfaces. Spring framework abstracts the inner workings of JavaMail API by providing a set of classes and interfaces, which simplifies writing programs that require the functionality of sending e-mails. Also, Spring provides an exception hierarchy, which abstracts exceptions thrown during composing, parsing, and sending e-mails or while authenticating with the mail server.

The following figure shows the important classes and interfaces of Spring that provide e-mail sending functionality. You can find these classes and interfaces in the `org.springframework.mail` and `org.springframework.mail.javamail` packages of the Spring framework.

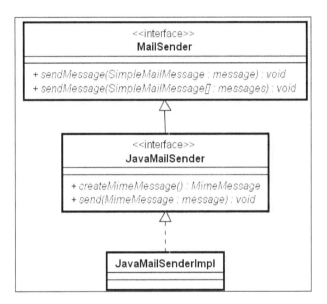

`MailSender` interface is a generic interface that defines e-mail sending functionality. As shown in the given figure, it defines two `send` methods that accept Spring's `SimpleMailMessage` and `SimpleMailMessage[]` objects as arguments.

The `JavaMailSender` interface extends the `MailSender` interface and defines methods specific to sending e-mails using JavaMail API. `JavaMailSender` defines methods such as `createMimeMessage`—for creating a `MimeMessage` instance (which is part of JavaMail API), `send`—for sending a `MimeMessage`, and so on. For the complete list of methods defined by Spring, refer to the Spring API documentation for the `JavaMailSender` interface. Spring provides a concrete implementation of the `JavaMailSender` interface through the `JavaMailSenderImpl` class, which you can use in your application to send e-mails.

It is important to note that the `MailSender` interface defines `send` methods that accept `SimpleMailMessage` or `SimpleMailMessage[]` objects as arguments, and the `JavaMailSender` interface defines `send` methods that accept `MimeMessage` or `MimeMessage[]` objects as arguments. `SimpleMailMessage` is part of Spring framework and is useful for creating simple mail messages consisting of `from`, `to`, e-mail `body`, and so on. If you want to send more refined messages consisting of attachments, inline images, and so on, then you should use `MimeMessage` to create your mail message.

Now that we have a basic understanding of different classes and interfaces that come into the picture when it comes to sending e-mails, let's look at various Spring Roo commands that we used in the `flightapp-web` application for setting up e-mail support and sending e-mails.

Setting up e-mail sending support

The `email sender setup` Roo command sets up e-mail sending support in a Roo project by configuring `JavaMailSenderImpl` in Spring's application context. When the `email sender setup` command is executed, the following actions are performed by Roo:

▶ The `SRC_MAIN_RESOURCES\META-INF\spring\applicationContext.xml` file is updated to configure `JavaMailSenderImpl` as a Spring bean

▶ The `SRC_MAIN_RESOURCES\META-INF\spring\email.properties` file is created, which contains properties for setting up the `JavaMailSenderImpl` instance. The properties defined in the `email.properties` file come from the arguments specified for the `email sender setup` command.

▶ The `pom.xml` file is updated to reflect dependency on JavaMail and Java Activation Framework(JAF) JAR files.

The following listing shows the `JavaMailSenderImpl` configuration in the `applicationContext.xml` file:

```
<bean class="org.springframework.mail.javamail.
  JavaMailSenderImpl" id="mailSender">
  <property name="host" value="${email.host}"/>
  <property name="protocol" value="${email.protocol}"/>
  <property name="port" value="${email.port}"/>
  <property name="username" value="${email.username}"/>
  <property name="password" value="${email.password}"/>
  <property name="javaMailProperties">
    <props>
      <prop key="mail.smtp.auth">true</prop>
      <prop key="mail.smtp.starttls.enable">true</prop>
    </props>
  </property>
</bean>
```

In the given XML, `JavaMailSenderImpl` is configured with properties such as `host`, `protocol`, `port`, and so on. The values of these properties come from the `email.properties` file.

The following listing shows the `email.properties` file:

```
email.host=smtp.gmail.com
email.password=<password>
email.port=587
email.protocol=smtp
email.username=<username>
```

Instead of `<username>` and `<password>`, you'll see username and password values specified for the `email sender setup` command. The `email.properties` file is read by Spring's `PropertyPlaceholderConfigurer` to fill the placeholders defined in the configuration of `JavaMailSender`. The `applicationContext.xml` file uses the `<property-placeholder>` element of Spring's `context` to configure a `PropertyPlaceholderConfigurer`, as shown here:

```
<context:property-placeholder location="classpath*:META-INF/spring/*.
properties"/>
```

The `location` attribute specifies that the `PropertyPlaceholderConfigurer` will look for properties files in the `META-INF/spring` directory of the project.

> In this recipe, we used the `email sender setup` command to set up `JavaMailSenderImpl` for the `flightapp-web` project that represents a Spring Web MVC application. You can use the `email sender setup` command with any Roo project that requires an e-mail sending feature.

Let's now look at how to set up a `SimpleMailMessage` instance:

Setting up a mail message

The `email template setup` command configures `SimpleMailMessage` as a bean in the `applicationContext.xml` file. The `email template setup` command accepts two arguments: `from` and `subject`, identifying the sender and subject of the email, respectively. When the `email sender setup` command is executed, the following actions are performed by Roo:

- Configures `SimpleMailMessage` as a Spring-managed bean in `applicationContext.xml`, as shown here:

```
<bean class="org.springframework.mail.SimpleMailMessage"
    id="templateMessage">
    <property name="from" value="${email.from}"/>
        <property name="subject" value="${email.subject}"/>
```

```
    </bean>
  </beans>
```

The values of ${email.from} and ${email.subject} placeholders come from the email.properties file.

▸ Updates the email.properties file to include email.from and email.subject properties, the values of which come from the value of the from and subject arguments passed to the email template setup command:

```
email.from=<username>@gmail.com
email.subject=A new Flight instance has been created
```

Now that JavaMailSenderImpl and SimpleMailMessage instances are configured in the application context XML file, we'll look at how to send e-mails.

Sending mails

To send an e-mail from your enterprise application you'll require access to both the JavaMailSenderImpl and SimpleMailMessage instances registered with the Spring's application context. Attributes referring to these instances are automatically added to a class by the field email template Roo command. The following code listing shows the FlightController.java class after the field email template command was executed against it:

```java
import org.springframework.mail.MailSender;
....
public class FlightController {

  @Autowired
  private transient MailSender mailTemplate;

  @Autowired
  private transient SimpleMailMessage simpleMailMessage;

  public void sendMessage(java.lang.String mailTo,
    java.lang.String message) {
      simpleMailMessage.setTo(mailTo);
      simpleMailMessage.setText(message);
      mailTemplate.send(simpleMailMessage);
  }
}
```

In the given code, the mailTemplate attribute refers to the JavaMailSenderImpl instance and the simpleMailMessage attribute refers to the SimpleMailMessage instance registered with the Spring's application context. It is important to note that the type of the mailTemplate attribute is MailSender and **not** JavaMailSender. Also, a sendMessage method is added to the FlightController.java for sending e-mails. The sendMessage method accepts arguments that identify the e-mail recipient's address and the text content or body of the e-mail. The sendMessage method makes use of the send(SimpleMailMessage) method of MailSender to send e-mails.

You can now call the `send` method from within the `FlightController.java` class methods to send e-mails. In our example scenario, we called `send` method from the `create` method after a `Flight` instance was persisted, as shown here:

```
@RequestMapping(method = RequestMethod.POST)
 public String create(@Valid Flight flight,
    BindingResult bindingResult, Model uiModel,
    HttpServletRequest httpServletRequest) {
    ...
    flight.persist();
    sendMessage("<username>@gmail.com",
    "A new instance of Flight entity with id "
     + flight.getFlightId()
     + "has been created.");
    return "redirect:/flights/" +
      encodeUrlPathSegment(flight.getFlightId().toString(),
      httpServletRequest);
 }
```

There's more...

Let's now look at how to send e-mails asynchronously, how to send more refined e-mails consisting of attachments, inline images, and so on, and finally how to send e-mails when the JavaMail `Session` is configured in JNDI.

Sending e-mails asynchronously

E-mail sending that we have discussed so far in this recipe, is *synchronous* in nature. Typically, e-mails are sent *asynchronously* by applications—something which can be achieved in Spring via the `@Async` annotation. The `field email template` command supports an `async` argument, that instructs Roo to do the following:

- Create the `sendMessage` method, which is annotated with the `@Async` Spring annotation

- Enable detection of the `@Async` annotated methods using the `<annotation-driven>` element of Spring's `task` namespace, as shown here:

```
<task:annotation-driven executor="asyncExecutor"
      mode="aspectj" />
```

    The `executor` attribute refers to an implementation of the `java.util.concurrent.Executor` interface, responsible for executing the `@Async` annotated method.

- Configure Spring's `ThreadPoolTaskExecutor` in application context XML using the `<executor>` element of Spring's `task` namespace, as shown here:

```
<task:executor id="asyncExecutor"
      pool-size="${executor.poolSize}" />
```

- Spring's `ThreadPoolTaskExecutor` configures a `java.util.concurrent.ThreadPoolExecutor` instance (an implementation of `java.util.concurrent.Executor`) with the thread pool size specified by the `pool-size` attribute value. The `${executor.poolSize}` placeholder's value comes from the `email.properties` file.

- Add the `executor.poolSize` property to the `email.properties` file, as shown here:

  ```
  executor.poolSize=10
  ```

To send mails asynchronously when a `FlightDescription` instance is created, execute the following `field email template` command against the `Flight DescriptionController` class, as shown here:

```
.. roo> field email template --class ~.web.FlightDescriptionController
--async
```

Now, copy the `create(...)` method from `FlightDescriptionController_Roo_Controller.aj` to `FlightDescriptionController.java` and add a call to the `sendMessage(...)` method, as shown here:

```
@RequestMapping(method = RequestMethod.POST)
public String create(@Valid FlightDescription...) {
  ...
  flightDescription.persist();
  sendMessage("<username>@gmail.com",
    "FlightDescription instance created");
  return "redirect:/flightdescriptions/" + ..
}
```

Sending e-mails with attachments

As mentioned earlier, if you want to send mails with attachments, inline images, and so on, then you need to use `MimeMessage` instead of `SimpleMailMessage`. The `field email template` command adds `SimpleMailMessage` and `MailSender` type attributes to the Java class, as shown here:

```
@Autowired
private transient MailSender mailTemplate;

@Autowired
private transient SimpleMailMessage simpleMailMessage;
```

Now, `MailSender` defines methods which accept a `SimpleMailMessage` or `Simple MailMessage[]` object as the argument. `JavaMailSender`, on the other hand, defines methods which accept a `MimeMessage` or `MimeMessage[]` object as the argument. So, we need to change the type of `mailTemplate` attribute from `MailSender` to `JavaMailSender` (a sub-interface of `MailSender`) to send messages of type `MimeMessage`. Also, we need to remove the `simpleMailMessage` attribute from the class because we need mail message of type `MimeMessage` and not `SimpleMailMessage` when sending mail messages with attachments or inline images.

So, how do we go about creating a `MimeMessage`? Spring provides the following utility classes that simplify creating a `MimeMessage`:

* `MimeMessagePreparator`: A callback interface for preparing a `MimeMessage`
* `MimeMessageHelper`: A helper class that provides methods for creating and populating a `MimeMessage`

The following code shows modified `FlightDescriptionController.java` that makes use of `MimeMessageHelper` to send a mail message with an attachment when a new `FlightDescription` instance is created:

```
import javax.mail.MessagingException;
import javax.mail.internet.MimeMessage;
import org.springframework.mail.javamail.JavaMailSender;
import org.springframework.mail.javamail.MimeMessageHelper;
import org.springframework.scheduling.annotation.Async;
...
public class FlightDescriptionController {

  @Autowired
  private transient JavaMailSender mailTemplate;

  @RequestMapping(method = RequestMethod.POST)
  public String create(@Valid FlightDescription
    flightDescription...) {
    ...
    flightDescription.persist();
    sendMessage(..);
    return "redirect:/flightDescriptions/" + ...);
  }

  @Async
  public void sendMessage(java.lang.String mailTo,
    java.lang.String message) throws MessagingException {
    MimeMessage mimeMessage =
      mailTemplate.createMimeMessage();

    MimeMessageHelper helper =
```

```
      new MimeMessageHelper(mimeMessage, true);
    helper.setTo(mailTo);
    helper.setText(message);
    helper.addAttachment("logo.gif",
      new File("C:/logo.gif"));
    mailTemplate.send(mimeMessage);
  }
}
```

In the `FlightDescriptionController.java` we made the following changes:

▸ Changed return type of the `mailMessage` attribute from `MailSender` to `JavaMailSender`

▸ Removed the `simpleMailMessage` attribute of type `SimpleMailMessage` as we need a `MimeMessage` instance to send mails with attachments

▸ Modified the `sendMessage` method to make use of the `MimeMessageHelper` class to create a `MimeMessage` instance and add attachments to it.

Sending e-mails with JavaMail Session configured in JNDI

If JavaMail `Session` is configured in JNDI of your application server, then you'll need to modify the `applicationContext.xml` file of your Roo project to create the `JavaMail SenderImpl` instance using JavaMail `Session` configured in JNDI, as shown here:

```
<beans ... xmlns:jee="http://www.springframework.org/schema/jee" ...
xsi:schemaLocation="http://www.springframework.org/schema/jee http://
www.springframework.org/schema/jee/spring-jee-3.0.xsd">
.....
<jee:jndi-lookup id="mailSession" jndi-name="mail/session" />

<bean class="org.springframework.mail.javamail.JavaMailSenderImpl"
  id="mailSender">
  <property name="session" value="mailSession"/>
</bean>
.....
```

The `jndi-lookup` element of Spring's `jee` namespace, shown in the given code, is responsible for accessing the JavaMail `Session` configured in JNDI with name `"mail/session"` (referred to by the `jndi-name` attribute) and making it available in a Spring application context with bean `id` as `"mailSession"`.

See also

▸ Refer to the next recipe, *Sending and receiving messages with JMS*, to see how you can send and receive messages using JMS

Sending and receiving JMS messages

Spring Roo provides support for developing messaging applications based on JMS (Java Message Service) API. As of Spring Roo 1.1.5, the only JMS provider supported by Roo is embedded `ActiveMQ(http://activemq.apache.org/)`; it is configured in the same JVM as the Java application accessing it.

In this recipe, we'll look at how Spring Roo supports sending and receiving JMS messages using embedded ActiveMQ.

Getting ready

Create a sub-directory `ch06-jms` inside the `C:\roo-cookbook` directory.

Copy the `ch06_web_app.roo` script into the `ch06-jms` directory.

Execute the `ch06_web_app.roo` script that creates `flightapp-web` Roo project, sets up Hibernate as persistence provider, configures MySQL as the database for the application, creates `Flight` and `FlightDescription` JPA entities, and defines many-to-one relationship between `Flight` and `FlightDescription` entities. Also, script makes use of `controller all` command to scaffold a Spring Web MVC application from JPA entities. If you are using a different database than MySQL or your connection settings are different than what is specified in the script, then modify the script accordingly.

Start the Roo shell from the `C:\roo-cookbook\ch06-jms` directory.

In this recipe, we'll look at how to send the newly created `Flight` instance's attributes as a JMS message to a queue destination and use an asynchronous message listener for reading the JMS message from the queue.

How to do it...

To set up flight-app as a JMS messaging application, follow the steps given here:

1. Execute the `jms setup` command to create a new Spring application context XML file for the `flightapp-web` application, which configures embedded ActiveMQ as JMS provider, a JMS destination queue named `myDestination`, and Spring's `JmsTemplate` for sending JMS messages, as shown here:

   ```
   .. roo> jms setup --provider ACTIVEMQ_IN_MEMORY --destinationName
   myDestination --destinationType QUEUE

   Created ..\META-INF\spring\applicationContext-jms.xml

   ...

   Updated ROOT\pom.xml [Added dependency org.apache.
   activemq:activemq-core:5.4.2]
   ```

2. Execute the `field jms template` command to inject Spring's `JmsTemplate` into `FlightController.java`. The `FlightController` makes use of `JmsTemplate` to send JMS messages to embedded ActiveMQ configured in the first step.

```
.. roo> field jms template --class ~.web.FlightController
--fieldName jmsTemplate
```

```
Updated ...\sample\roo\flightapp\web\FlightController.java
```

3. Execute the `jms listener` command to create a `MyListener` JMS message consumer that consumes messages *asynchronously* from the `myDestination` queue created in the first step.

```
... roo> jms listener class --class ~.web.MyListener
--destinationName myDestination --destinationType QUEUE
```

```
Created SRC_MAIN_JAVA\sample\roo\flightapp\web\MyListener.java
Updated SRC_MAIN_RESOURCES\META-INF\spring\applicationContext-jms.
xml
```

4. Execute the `perform eclipse` command to update the project's classspath, as shown here:

```
.. roo> perform eclipse
```

5. Now, import the `flightapp-web` project into your Eclipse IDE.

6. Modify `Flight.java` and `FlightDescription.java` to implement the `java.io.Serializable` interface, as shown here:

```
import java.io.Serializable;
...
public class Flight implements Serializable { .. }
import java.io.Serializable;
...
public class FlightDescription implements Serializable { .. }
```

7. Open the `FlightController_Roo_Controller.aj` file and copy the declaration that introduces the `create(...)` method in `FlightController.java` and adds it directly to `FlightController.java`. The `create` method of the `FlightController` class is invoked when a user enters information in the flight creation HTML form and submits the request to create a new `Flight` instance. After adding the `create(...)` method, your `FlightController.java` should look as follows:

```
@RooWebScaffold(...)
@RequestMapping("/flights")
@Controller
public class FlightController {
```

```
@Autowired
private transient JmsTemplate jmsTemplate;

@RequestMapping(method = RequestMethod.POST)
public String create(@Valid Flight flight,
    BindingResult bindingResult, Model uiModel,
    HttpServletRequest httpServletRequest) {
    ...
    flight.persist();
    return "redirect:/flights/" +
        encodeUrlPathSegment(flight.getFlightId().toString(),
        httpServletRequest);
}

public void sendMessage(java.lang.Object messageObject) {
    jmsTemplate.convertAndSend(messageObject);
}
}
```

In Spring Roo 1.1.3, if you attempt to override a method defined in
`*_Roo_Controller.aj` file by defining it in your `*Controller.java` file, then Roo complains that the method is already defined in the corresponding `*Controller.java` file. This issue is resolved in Spring Roo 1.1.4 and later versions. You can address this issue in Spring Roo 1.1.3 by removing the copied declaration from the `*_Roo_Controller.aj` file.

8. In the given code, the `create` method has been directly added to the `FlightController.java` by copying it from the `FlightController_Roo_Controller.aj` AspectJ ITD file. In the ITD, the `create` method is declared as shown here:

    ```
    public String FlightController.create(...)
    ```

9. Make sure that you remove the `FlightController.` prefix from the name of the method when you copy it to the `FlightController.java` file. So, this method in `FlightController.java` becomes:

    ```
    public String create(...)
    ```

10. Now, modify the `create(...)` method in `FlightController.java` by adding the `sendMessage` method call just after the call to the `flight.persist()` method:

    ```
    sendMessage(flight);
    ```

11. Exit the Roo shell and execute the `tomcat:run` goal of the Tomcat maven plugin from the `ch06-jms` directory to deploy the `flightapp-web` project in an embedded Tomcat container, as shown here:

    ```
    C:\roo-cookbook\ch06-jms> mvn tomcat:run
    ```

12. Access the `flightapp-web` application from the web browser using the following URL: `http://localhost:8080/flightapp-web`. You should now see the following home page of the `flightapp-web` application:

13. Select the **Create new Flight Description** option from the menu that shows you the form for creating a new `FlightDescription` entity instance. Once you have created the `FlightDescription` instance, select the **Create new Flight** menu option to create a `Flight` instance. The following screenshot shows the form for creating a `Flight` instance:

14. Enter **Departure Date**, **Arrival Date,** and **Flight Description** information and click the **Save** button. Saving the `Flight` instance will result in sending a JMS message to the `myDestination` queue containing details of the newly created `Flight` instance and the associated `FlightDescription` instance attributes.

15. The `MyListener` JMS message consumer asynchronously reads the JMS message from the `myDestination` queue and writes it to the standard output, as shown here:

```
JMS message received: DepartureDate: Tue Feb 01 00:00:00 IST
2011, ArrivalDate:Wed Feb 02 00:00:00 IST 2011, FlightDescription:
Origin: NYC, Destination: INDIA
, Price: 1200.0
```

How it works...

The **JMS add-on** of Roo is responsible for processing JMS related commands, which are: `jms setup`, `jms listener`, and `field jms template`.

Spring simplifies integrating an enterprise application with a JMS provider. Spring's `JmsTemplate` class is a helper class, that enables the applications to send and receive JMS messages *synchronously*. The `JmsTemplate` class holds reference to the `javax.jms.ConnectionFactory` instance—used for creating connections with the JMS provider.

 The JMS provider in our example is the embedded (or in-memory) ActiveMQ. It is important to note that Roo only supports embedded ActiveMQ as the JMS provider. If you want to use any other JMS provider or standalone ActiveMQ, then you'll need to change the Roo-generated JMS provider configuration.

Let's look at various commands that we used in the `flightapp-web` application for setting up a JMS provider, and for sending and receiving JMS messages.

Setting up a JMS provider

The `jms setup` command sets up a JMS provider for your enterprise application. The `jms setup` command accepts the following arguments:

- `provider`: A mandatory argument that specifies the JMS provider for which support needs to be added to the application. Roo defines only a single value that this argument can accept, that is, `ACTIVEMQ_IN_MEMORY`, which is meant for setting up embedded ActiveMQ as the JMS provider.

- `destinationName`: An optional argument that specifies the name of the JMS destination accessed by the application. If unspecified, the name of the destination is defaulted to `myDestination`.

- `destinationType`: An optional argument that identifies the type of the JMS destination specified via the `destinationName` argument. Roo defines only two possible values for this argument, which are `QUEUE` (if the JMS destination is of type queue) and `TOPIC` (if the JMS destination is of type topic). If unspecified, the destination type is defaulted to `QUEUE`.

The jms setup command creates an application context XML file: applicationContext-jms.xml in SRC_MAIN_RESOURCES/META-INF/spring directory. The applicationContext-jms.xml file configures embedded ActiveMQ broker, JmsTemplate, JMS ConnectionFactory, JMS destinations, and message listener containers.

The following listing shows the embedded ActiveMQ broker configuration in applicationContext-jms.xml:

```
<beans xmlns="http://www.springframework.org/schema/beans"
    xmlns:amq="http://activemq.apache.org/schema/core" ...>

  <amq:broker persistent="false" useJmx="true">
    <amq:transportConnectors>
      <amq:transportConnector uri="tcp://localhost:61616"/>
    </amq:transportConnectors>
  </amq:broker>
  ...
</beans>
```

The amq namespace refers to ActiveMQ schema, which allows configuring ActiveMQ in Spring's application context XML file. The <broker> element configures an embedded ActiveMQ broker whose name is localhost. If you want to specify a custom name for the broker, then you can do so by using brokerName attribute of <broker> element. The persistent attribute specifies whether the JMS messages received by the ActiveMQ broker are persisted into a data store or not. The value false instructs the broker not to persist messages. If you specify true as the value of the persistent attribute, ActiveMQ configures KahaDB as the default data store for messages. The useJmx attribute specifies if broker's services are exposed via JMX. If the attribute value is true, then you can use JMX clients to invoke ActiveMQ broker's services such as start or stop broker, to add or remove topics and queue JMS destinations, and so on. The <transportConnectors> element defines the *transport connectors* on which ActiveMQ broker listens to a connection from clients. The <transportConnector> element in the given code listing specifies a tcp transport connector that listens on port 61616.

JMS ConnectionFactory is configured in the applicationContext-jms.xml file, as shown here:

```
<amq:connectionFactory brokerURL="vm://localhost"
  id="jmsFactory"/>

<bean class="org.springframework.jms.connection.
CachingConnectionFactory" id="cachingConnectionFactory">
  <property name="targetConnectionFactory">
    <ref local="jmsFactory"/>
  </property>
</bean>
```

The `<connectionFactory>` element of the `amq` namespace configures a JMS `ConnectionFactory`. JMS `ConnectionFactory` is typically configured in the application server and fetched by applications using JNDI. If `ConnectionFactory` is configured in the application server, then you can make use of the `<jndi-lookup>` element of Spring's `jee` schema to obtain it. The `brokerURL` attribute identifies the URL for connecting to ActiveMQ broker. The value of the `brokerURL` attribute is `vm://localhost`, which means that the VM (Virtual Machine) protocol is used by clients to access ActiveMQ broker named `localhost`. The `vm` protocol is used because the client (which is `flightapp-web` application in our case) and broker are located in the same JVM. The use of the VM protocol ensures improved performance because there is no network overhead involved between client and broker communication and the client directly invokes the methods of the broker.

Spring's `CachingConnectionFactory` class is a JMS `ConnectionFactory` adapter that caches instances of JMS `Session`, `MessageConsumer`, and `MessageProducer` for improved performance. The `targetConnectionFactory` property identifies the `ConnectionFactory`, which the `CachingConnectionFactory` instance uses to obtain the JMS `Connection`. The `targetConnectionFactory` property in the given configuration refers to the JMS `ConnectionFactory` created by the `<connectionFactory>` element of the `amq` namespace.

In the `jms setup` command, we also passed JMS destination name (`myDestination`) and type (`QUEUE`), which JMS add-on uses to configure a JMS queue named `myDestination` in the `applicationContext-jms.xml` file, as shown here:

```
<amq:queue id="myDestination" physicalName="myDestination"/>
```

Here, the `<queue>` element of `amq` namespace configures a JMS queue named `myDestination`. The `physicalName` attribute specifies the name of the JMS queue in ActiveMQ. JMS destinations are typically configured in the application server and fetched by applications using JNDI. If JMS destination is configured in the application server, then you can make use of `<jndi-lookup>` element of Spring's `jee` schema to fetch it.

Spring's `JmsTemplate` is also configured in `applicationContext-jms.xml` file, as shown here:

```
<bean class="org.springframework.jms.core.JmsTemplate"
    id="jmsTemplate">
  <property name="connectionFactory"
      ref="cachingConnectionFactory"/>
  <property name="defaultDestination" ref="myDestination"/>
</bean>
```

The `connectionFactory` property refers to the `CachingConnectionFactory` instance. `JmsTemplate` defines `send` methods that accept the JMS `Destination` object or JMS destination name as the parameter. The `defaultDestination` property refers to the JMS destination that is used for sending or receiving messages when the `send` method used doesn't accept the JMS `Destination` object or JMS destination name as the parameter.

To allow the `flighapp-web` application to asynchronously receive JMS messages, the `jms setup` command configures a Spring's *message listener* container in the `applicationContext-jms.xml` file, as shown here:

```
<beans xmlns="http://www.springframework.org/schema/beans"
    xmlns:jms="http://www.springframework.org/schema/jms" ...>
    ...
    <jms:listener-container connection-factory="jmsFactory"
        destination-type="queue" />
    ...
</beans>
```

A message listener container receives messages from the JMS provider and dispatches it to a *message consumer* implementation. The message listener container saves the effort for writing the code that you'll need to write for asynchronous message consumption, which includes registering with the JMS provider, managing transactions, and so on.

In the given configuration, the `<listener-container>` element of Spring's `jms` namespace creates a message listener container. The `connection-factory` attribute identifies the JMS `ConnectionFactory` that the container uses for creating connections with the JMS provider. The `destination-type` identifies the JMS destination type (queue, topic, or durable topic) from which the container receives messages. You can add `<listener>` elements (of Spring's `jms` namespace) inside `<listener-container>` to define the message consumers to which the listener container dispatches the messages for processing.

Let's now look at how we send JMS messages using the `JmsTemplate` class.

Sending message using JMS Template

The `field jms template` command autowires the `JmsTemplate` instance into a class identified by the `class` argument. The `fieldName` argument identifies the name of the field with which `JmsTemplate` is added to the class.

The following code shows the `FlightController.java` file into which we added the `JmsTemplate` field using the `jms template` command:

```
import org.springframework.jms.core.JmsTemplate;
...
public class FlightController {

    @Autowired
    private transient JmsTemplate jmsTemplate;

    public void sendMessage(Object messageObject) {
        jmsTemplate.convertAndSend(messageObject);
    }
}
```

The given code shows that the `jms template` command adds a `JmsTemplate` field and a `sendMessage` method to the `FlightController` class. The `sendMessage` method accepts `Object` type as argument, which represents the object that you want to send as a JMS message to the JMS destination. The `sendMessage` method invokes the `convertAndSend` method of `JmsTemplate`, which *converts* the passed object into a JMS message and sends it to the default destination set by the `setDefaultDestination(...)` method or specified by the `defaultDestination` property of `JmsTemplate` in the application context XML file. In the case of Roo-generated code, the default destination of `JmsTemplate` is specified by the `defaultDestination` property (refer to the `applicationContext-jms.xml` file of the `flightapp-web` project).

So, you might ask—how is the conversion between an object and JMS message performed? Spring provides a `MessageConverter` interface, which you can implement to define how to handle conversion from a Java object to a JMS message and vice versa. Spring provides a built-in `MessageConverter` implementation: `SimpleMessageConverter`, which is used by default by `JmsTemplate` and is responsible for conversion between `String` and JMS `TextMessage`, `byte[]` and JMS `ByteMessage`, `Map` and JMS `MapMessage`, and between the `Serializable` object and JMS `ObjectMessage`. As `Flight` and `FlightDescription` objects in the `flightapp-web` application implement the `Serializable` interface, the `convertAndSend` method of `JmsTemplate` converts them into JMS `ObjectMessage` instances.

Creating a JMS message consumer

The `jms listener` command creates an *asynchronous* JMS message consumer. If you want your application to synchronously consume messages, then you can use one of the `receive` methods of `JmsTemplate`. If you also want to convert the received JMS message into a Java object using `SimpleMessageConverter`, then you can use `receiveAndConvert(...)` method of `JmsTemplate` to receive messages.

The `jms listener` command creates a message consumer and updates the `applicationContext-jms.xml` file to create a new message listener container containing the newly created message consumer as a listener. In the case of `flightapp-web`, the `jms listener` command creates the `MyListener` JMS message consumer and adds the following configuration to the `applicationContext-jms.xml` file:

```
<bean class="sample.roo.flightapp.web.MyListener"
    id="myListener"/>

<jms:listener-container connection-factory="jmsFactory"
        destination-type="queue">
  <jms:listener destination="myDestination"
      method="onMessage" ref="myListener"/>
</jms:listener-container>
```

The `<bean>` element configures `MyListener` message consumer as a Spring bean.

The `<listener>` element of Spring's `jms` namespace defines a message listener to which the message listener container (specified by the enclosing `<listener-container>` element) dispatches JMS messages for processing. The `destination-type` attribute of `<listener-container>` is derived from the value of `destinationType` argument of `jms listener` command. The `ref` attribute refers to the message consumer instance, which is responsible for processing the JMS message. The `destination` attribute (which corresponds to the `destinationName` argument value of the `jms listener` command) identifies the JMS destination from which the message consumer receives JMS messages (via the message container listener) for processing. The `method` attribute specifies the name of the method of the message consumer class, which is responsible for processing the receive JMS message.

So, by executing `jms listener` command for `flightapp-web` we have created a `MyListener` class, which is responsible for processing JMS messages received by the `myDestination` JMS destination. The following code listing from `MyListener.java` shows the Roo-generated `MyListener` class:

```
public class MyListener {

  public void onMessage(Object message) {
      System.out.println("JMS message received: " + message);
  }
}
```

As the given code shows, the Roo-generated message listener doesn't implement any interface or extend any class, and defines an `onMessage` method which accepts the JMS message as argument. The `onMessage` doesn't do anything interesting—it simply prints the message on the standard output.

There's more...

Let's now see how you can send JMS messages asynchronously from your enterprise application:

Sending JMS messages asynchronously

The `field jms template` command supports an `async` argument, which you can use to specify that the Roo-generated `sendMessage` method is annotated with Spring's `@Async` annotation. An `@Async` annotated method of an object is executed asynchronously by Spring using `java.util.concurrent.ThreadPoolExecutor`. If `async` argument is specified, Roo performs the following actions:

  ▶ Creates the `sendMessage` method that is annotated with Spring's `@Async` annotation

- ▶ Enables detection of `@Async` annotated methods in `applicationContext.xml` via the `<annotation-driven>` element of Spring's `task` namespace, as shown here:

```
<task:annotation-driven executor="asyncExecutor"
      mode="aspectj" />
```

  The `executor` attribute refers to an implementation of `java.util.concurrent.Executor` interface, responsible for executing the `@Async` annotated method.

- ▶ Configures Spring's `ThreadPoolTaskExecutor` in `applicationContext.xml` using `<executor>` element of Spring's `task` namespace, as shown here:

```
<task:executor id="asyncExecutor"
      pool-size="${executor.poolSize}" />
```

- ▶ Spring's `ThreadPoolTaskExecutor` configures a `java.util.concurrent.ThreadPoolExecutor` instance (an implementation of `java.util.concurrent.Executor`) with the thread pool size specified by the `pool-size` attribute value. The `${executor.poolSize}` placeholder's value comes from Roo-generated `jms.properties` file, as shown here:

```
executor.poolSize=10
```

See also

- ▶ Refer to the *Sending e-mails using JavaMail API* recipe to see how you can send e-mails from your application

Configuring Spring Security for your application

Roo supports configuring Spring Security for your application via `security setup` command. In this recipe, we'll look at the security related configurations added to your application by Roo when you execute the `security setup` command. In the next recipe, *Using Spring Security with Apache Directory Server*, we'll look at how we can extend the Spring Security configuration to use `Apache Directory Server` for addressing security requirements of a Roo-generated web application and how to incorporate method-level security.

Getting ready

Create a sub-directory `ch06-security` inside the `C:\roo-cookbook` directory.

Copy the `ch06_web_app_security.roo` script into the `ch06-security` directory.

Execute the `ch06_web_app_security.roo` script, which creates the `flightapp-web` Roo project, sets up Hibernate as persistence provider, configures MySQL as the database for the application, creates `Flight`, `FlightDescription`, and `Booking` JPA entities, defines a many-to-one relationship between `Flight` and `FlightDescription` entities, and a many-to-one relationship between `Booking` and `Flight` JPA entities. Also, script makes use of `controller all` command to scaffold Spring Web MVC application. If you are using a different database than MySQL or your connection settings are different than what is specified in the script, then modify the script accordingly.

Start the Roo shell from the `C:\roo-cookbook\ch06-security` directory.

How to do it...

To configure Spring Security for your application through the `security setup` command, follow the steps given here:

1. Execute the `security setup` command to set up Spring Security for the flightapp-web Spring Web MVC application, as shown here:

   ```
   .. roo> security setup
   Updated ROOT\pom.xml [Added property 'spring-security.version'
   with value '3.0.5

   .RELEASE']


   Updated ROOT\pom.xml [Added dependencies org.springframework.
   security:spring-security-core:${spring-security.version}, ...]
   Created SRC_MAIN_RESOURCES\META-INF\spring\applicationContext-
   security.xml
   Created SRC_MAIN_WEBAPP\WEB-INF\views\login.jspx
   Updated SRC_MAIN_WEBAPP\WEB-INF\views\views.xml
   Updated SRC_MAIN_WEBAPP\WEB-INF\web.xml
   Updated SRC_MAIN_WEBAPP\WEB-INF\spring\webmvc-config.xml
   ```

2. Execute the `perform eclipse` command to update project's classpath settings:

   ```
   .. roo> perform eclipse
   ```

3. Import `flightapp-web` Eclipse project into Eclipse IDE

How it works...

The `security setup` command is processed by the **Security add-on** of Roo. The `security setup` command is available only *after* you have installed Spring Web MVC artifacts by executing one of the `controller` commands of Roo. This limits the use of the security add-on only to projects that make use of Spring Web MVC.

Security add-on processes the `security setup` command and performs the following actions:

▶ Adds a property named `spring-security-version` with value 3.0.5 to the `pom.xml` file of the `flightapp-web` project, as shown here:

```
<project ...>
  ...
  <name>flightapp-web</name>
  <properties>
    <roo.version>1.1.2.RELEASE</roo.version>
    <spring.version>3.0.5.RELEASE</spring.version>
    <spring-security.version>
       3.0.5.RELEASE</spring-security.version>
    ...
  </properties>
  ...
</project>
```

The `spring-security-version` property identifies the version of Spring Security framework required by the application. The Spring Security version number property is referenced by the `<dependency>` elements in `pom.xml`, as shown here:

```
<dependency>
  <groupId>org.springframework.security</groupId>
  <artifactId>spring-security-config</artifactId>
  <version>${spring-security.version}</version>
</dependency>

<dependency>
  <groupId>org.springframework.security</groupId>
  <artifactId>spring-security-web</artifactId>
  <version>${spring-security.version}</version>
</dependency>
```

As the given configuration shows, defining the version number of Spring Security required by the `flightapp-web` application as a property in `pom.xml` file can ensure that `pom.xml` defines dependencies on JAR files that belong to the same version of Spring Security.

- Creates an application context XML file: `applicationContext-security.xml` in `SRC_MAIN_RESOURCES/META-INF/spring` directory. The `applicationContext-security.xml` file configures authentication and authorization requirements of the application.

- Adds Spring Security's `DelegatingFilterProxy` servlet filter to the `web.xml` file of the `flightapp-web` application, as shown here:

```
<filter>
  <filter-name>springSecurityFilterChain</filter-name>
  <filter-class>
      org.springframework.web.filter.DelegatingFilterProxy
  </filter-class>
</filter>

<filter-mapping>
  <filter-name>springSecurityFilterChain</filter-name>
  <url-pattern>/*</url-pattern>
</filter-mapping>
```

  The `DelegatingFilterProxy` servlet filter acts as an entry point into Spring Security's web module, which handles web request security. The name of the filter `springSecurityFilterChain` refers to the name of Spring Security's `FlightChainProxy` instance configured in the `applicationContext-security.xml` file. The `DelegatingFilterProxy` filter delegates web request to `FlightChainProxy` instance for performing web request security.

- Creates a login JSPX page `login.jspx` in the `SRC_MAIN_WEBAPP\WEB-INF\views` directory.

- Adds tiles definition for the login page in the `SRC_MAIN_WEBAPP\WEB-INF\views\views.xml` tiles definitions XML file, as shown here:

```
<definition extends="public" name="login">
  <put-attribute name="body"
        value="/WEB-INF/views/login.jspx"/>
</definition>
```

- Configures a `ParameterizableViewController` (via `view-controller` element of `mvc` namespace of Spring) in `webmvc-config.xml` file (located in `SRC_MAIN_WEBAPP\WEB-INF\spring` directory) that dispatches request to `login.jspx` page, as shown here:

```
<mvc:view-controller path="/login"/>
```

- Updates the `pom.xml` file of the `flightapp-web` project to include dependency on Spring Security JAR files, such as `spring-security-core`, `spring-security-config`, and so on.

Let's now look in detail at the `applicationContext-security.xml` file.

Spring Security application context XML file

The `applicationContext-security.xml` file configures Spring Security beans, which are used for authentication and authorization of requests. As we'll see shortly, Roo-generated `applicationContext-security.xml` doesn't do much but gives a good starting point to configure your application-specific security.

AuthenticationManager configuration

Authentication mechanism for the application is configured in `applicationContext-security.xml` via the `<authentication-manager>` element of Spring's `security` namespace, as shown here:

```
<authentication-manager alias="authenticationManager">
  <authentication-provider>
    <password-encoder hash="sha-256"/>
    <user-service>
      <user name="admin" password="..."
            authorities="ROLE_ADMIN"/>
      <user name="user" password="..."
            authorities="ROLE_USER"/>
    </user-service>
  </authentication-provider>
</authentication-manager>
```

Let's look in detail at each of the elements in the given configuration and how they work together to provide authentication services to the application:

- ▶ `<authentication-manager>`: It registers an instance of Spring Security's `AuthenticationManager` implementation that is responsible for providing authentication services. `AuthenticationManager` delegate's authentication to the `AuthenticationProvider` is configured using the `<authentication-provider>` sub-elements.

- <authentication-provider>: It registers an instance of Spring Security's AuthenticationProvider implementation. Spring Security provides a couple of built-in implementations of the AuthenticationProvider interface to simplify incorporating different authentication mechanisms in the application. For instance, if you are using JA-SIG CAS for authentication, you can use CasAuthenticationProvider implementation and if you are using an LDAP server for authentication, you can use LdapAuthenticationProvider, and so on. The AuthenticationProvider implementation usage is specified using the ref attribute of the <authentication-provider> element. If the ref attribute is not specified (as in the case of Roo-generated applicationContext-security.xml), DaoAuthenticationProvider implementation is registered. DaoAuthenticationProvider makes use of Spring Security's UserDetailsService to authenticate users. UserDetailsService loads user details containing username, password, and granted authorities based on the username entered by the application user. DaoAuthenticationProvider authenticates the user by comparing the password entered by the application user with the user details loaded by UserDetailsService.

- <user-service>: It creates an in-memory UserDetailsService instance that reads user details from a properties file or from the nested <user> elements.

- <user>: It defines a user of the application. The name and password attributes identify the username and password required for authentication.

- <password-encoder>: It converts submitted passwords to hashed versions before comparing the submitted password with the one retrieved by UserDetailsService. The hash attribute specifies the hashing algorithm to use for encoding password.

Web request security configuration

The following <http> element shows how web request security is configured in the applicationContext-security.xml file:

```
<http auto-config="true" use-expressions="true">
  <form-login
     login-processing-url="/resources/j_spring_security_check"
     login-page="/login"
     authentication-failure-url="/login?login_error=t"/>
   <logout logout-url="/resources/j_spring_security_logout"/>
   <intercept-url pattern="/choices/**"
       access="hasRole('ROLE_ADMIN')"/>
   <intercept-url pattern="/member/**"
       access="isAuthenticated()" />
   <intercept-url pattern="/resources/**"
       access="permitAll" />
   <intercept-url pattern="/**" access="permitAll" />
</http>
```

Let's now look in detail at how the elements in the given configuration define web request security:

- ▸ `<http>`: It contains the HTTP security configuration elements. It creates an instance of Spring Security's `FilterChainProxy` with bean name as `springSecurityFilterChain`. It is important to note that the name of the `FilterChainProxy` bean is same as the name of the `DelegatingFilterProxy` servlet filter configured in `web.xml` file.

  The `auto-config` attribute automatically configures Spring Security beans, which provide form-based login, logout, and HTTP BASIC authentication services.

  The `use-expression` attribute specifies whether the `access` attributes of the `<intercept-url>` element (discussed later in this recipe) can accept EL expressions.

- ▸ `<form-login>`: It configures Spring Security's `UsernamePasswordAuthenticationFilter` *filter* bean (a bean that implements the `javax.servlet.Filter` interface of Servlet API) and `LoginUrlAuthenticationEntryPoint` bean in an application context. The `UsernamePasswordAuthenticationFilter` filter bean is used by `FilterChainProxy` to perform authentication. `UsernamePasswordAuthenticationFilter` uses the username and password in the submitted request to attempt authentication against the configured authentication provider(s). It is important to note that the names of the request parameters that contain the username and password must be `j_username` and `j_password`, respectively. If you check the Roo-generated `login.jspx` file for parameters that `flightapp-web` project, you'll find that the names of the username and password fields are `j_username` and `j_password`, respectively. The `LoginUrlAuthenticationEntryPoint` bean starts off the form login authentication using `UsernamePasswordAuthenticationFilter`.

  The `login-page` attribute specifies the URL of the login page. The value of this attribute is used by `LoginUrlAuthenticationEntryPoint` to render the login page. The value of the attribute is `/login`, which means that the `<mvc:view-controller path="/login"/>` configured controller in `webmvc-config.xml` is responsible for rendering the login page.

  The `login-processing-url` attribute specifies the URL to which the login form is submitted. The `UsernamePasswordAuthenticationFilter` handles a request submitted to the URL identified by its `filterProcessesUrl` property. The value of the `login-processing-url` attribute is used to set the `filterProcessesUrl` property of `UsernamePasswordAuthenticationFilter`. The value of the `login-processing-url` attribute is `/resources/j_spring_security_check`, which is the same as the value of the `action` attribute of the HTML `<form>` element in the Roo-generated `login.jspx` file of the `flightapp-web` project.

The `authentication-failure-url` attribute specifies the URL to which the user is redirected if login fails. The value of this attribute `/login?login_error=t` means that the `<mvc:view-controller path="/login"/>` configured controller in `webmvc-config.xml` will render the login page again. The `login_error` parameter in the URL is used by the `login.jspx` page to show an authentication failure message on the login page, as shown here:

- ▸ `<logout>`: It configures the `LogoutFilter` filter bean that is responsible for processing logout requests. The `LogoutFilter` handles request submitted to the URL identified by its `filterProcessesUrl` property. The value of `logout-url` attribute is used to set the `filterProcessesUrl` property of `LogoutFilter`. In case of Roo-generated `applicationContext-security.xml`, the value of `logout-url` is `/resources/j_spring_security_logout`. The `footer.jspx` file (located in `/WEB-INF/views` directory) contains the **Logout** hyperlink that is displayed if the user is logged in. The **Logout** hyperlink refers to `/resources/j_spring_security_logout` URL, which means that when the user clicks the **Logout** hyperlink, the request is processed by the `LogoutFilter` filter bean.

- ▸ `<intercept-url>`: It defines the URL pattern and the corresponding access permissions. The `pattern` attribute specifies the URL pattern and the `access` attribute specifies the access permissions. As mentioned earlier, the `<http>` element's `use-expression` attribute is set to `true`; therefore, the `access` attribute can accept *Boolean* EL expressions. If the value returned by the expression is `true`, then access to the URL pattern, specified by the `pattern` attribute, is authorized.

The `hasRole`, `isAuthenticated`, and `permitAll` are examples of built-in expressions. The `hasRole('ROLE_ADMIN')` returns `true` if the role of the authenticated principal is `ROLE_ADMIN`. The `isAuthenticated()` returns `true` if the user is not an anonymous user. The `permitAll` expression always returns `true`.

The `<http>` element registers an implementation Spring Security's `AccessDecisionManager`, which makes access decisions regarding web URL access. An incoming web request is matched against the URL patterns specified by the `<intercept-url>` elements in the order in which they appear within the `<http>` element. If a match is found, it'll be used by `AccessDecisionManager` implementation for making access decisions. As incoming web requests are matched against the URL patterns (specified by the `<intercept-url>` elements) in the order in which they appear within the `<http>` element, more specific URL patterns should be declared before the more general URL patterns.

Using Spring Security with Apache Directory Server

This recipe extends on the previous recipe and shows a fully-functional Flight Booking application developed using Spring Web MVC that makes use of Spring Security to implement web request and *method-level* security. We'll look at modifications or additions that we need to make to configurations and artifacts generated by the `security setup` command to create a security-aware Flight Booking application.

Let's first take a quick look at the security requirements of the Flight Booking application before we delve into the details of how these requirements are met using Spring Security.

Flight Booking application requirements

The Flight Booking application users are authenticated against Apache Directory Server, which contains application users, details and their role information. An authenticated user of the Flight Booking application can either have the role of ROLE_ADMIN_USER or ROLE_APP_USER. Access to application functionality is granted or restricted based on the authenticated user's role.

Web request security requirement of Flight Booking application restricts unauthorized access to menu options. The following screenshot shows the main menu of the Flight Booking application:

The following table defines the access permissions for each menu option (shown in the given screenshot) based on role:

Menu option	Accessible to role
Create new FlightDescription	ROLE_ADMIN_USER
List all Flight Descriptions	
Find by Destination And Origin	
Create new Flight	
List all Flights	
Create new Booking	ROLE_APP_USER
List all Bookings	ROLE_ADMIN_USER

As the given table shows, an application user with the ROLE_ADMIN_USER role can access web pages for Flight, FlightDescription, and Booking JPA entities. An application user with the ROLE_APP_USER role can only access web pages corresponding to the Booking JPA entity.

Even though the **Create new Booking** and **List all Bookings** links are accessible to both ROLE_APP_USER and ROLE_ADMIN_USER roles (as shown in the preceding table), the following security requirements (which will eventually translate into method-level security requirements) must *also* be met by the application:

▸ A user with ROLE_APP_USER role *can* create a new Booking instance, but can't edit or remove an existing Booking instance

▸ A user with ROLE_ADMIN_USER role *can* edit or remove an existing Booking instance, but can't create a new Booking instance

Getting ready

Extract the contents of the `ch06-ldap-security.zip` file into the `C:\roo-cookbook` directory. This will create the `ch06-ldap-security` directory in `C:\roo-cookbook`. The `ch06-ldap-security` directory contains a `flightapp-web` web project that represents the *security-aware* Flight Booking application. This `flightapp-web` project is an extension of the `flightapp-web` project that we created in the previous recipe. It contains modifications to Spring Security generated artifacts, and a couple of additional changes to the address web request and method-level security requirements of the Flight Booking application.

If you are using a different database than MySQL or your connection settings are different than what is specified in `database.properties` file of `flightapp-web` project, then modify the `database.properties` file accordingly.

Open the command prompt and go to the `C:\roo-cookbook\ch06-ldap-security` directory.

How to do it...

To configure security settings with the Spring application, follow the steps given here:

1. Deploy the `flightapp-web` project as a dynamic web application in an embedded Tomcat instance:

   ```
   ..ch06-ldap-security> mvn tomcat:run
   ```

   This will download the dependencies defined in the `pom.xml` file of the `flightapp-web` project. Now, you can access the `flightapp-web` application by accessing the following URL:

   ```
   http://localhost:8080/flightapp-web
   ```

   If you see the following web page, then it means you have successfully deployed the `flightapp-web` application on the embedded Tomcat instance:

2. Select the **Create new Flight Description** menu option, which will show you the login screen of the Flight Booking application, as shown here:

3. Enter **admin** in the **Name** labeled field, **admin** in the **Password** labeled field, and click the **Submit** button to log in to the application. The **admin** user has ROLE_ADMIN_ USER role.

   The **admin** user is associated with the ROLE_ADMIN_USER role; therefore, the **admin** user is shown the form for creating a new FlightDescription instance, as shown here:

4. Enter flight description details as shown in the screenshot and click the **Save** button to create a new FlightDescription instance.

5. Now, select the **Create new Flight** menu option to view the form for creating a new `Flight` instance, as shown here:

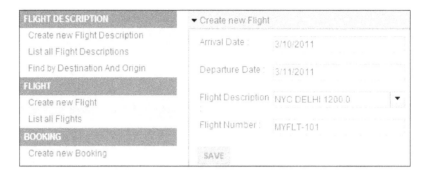

6. Set the date in the **Arrival Date** and **Departure Date** fields, and select the newly created `FlightDescription` from the combo box labeled **Flight Description**. Set the value of the **Flight Number** field to **MYFLT-101**. Now, click the **Save** button to create the new `Flight` instance in the database.

7. In the given form, you may notice that in the Roo-generated Flight Booking Spring Web MVC application we can set arrival and departure dates but can't set *time* of arrival or departure of flights. This is because Roo-generated Spring Web MVC applications make use of the `dijit.form.DateTextBox` component of the Dijit library to render `java.util.Date` type fields of a JPA entity in JSPX views. You can modify this behavior by either modifying Roo-installed `datetime.tagx` tag (refer to the `WEB-INF/tags/form/fields` directory of `flightapp-web`) or by creating your own custom tag that renders a `java.util.Date` JPA field as a form field, which makes use of both `dijit.form.DateTextBox` (for selecting date) and `diji.form.TimeTextBox` (for selecting time). This allows users to select both date and time values for the field.

8. As we have already created the `FlightDescription` instance and associated `Flight` instance, it's time to create a booking on the `MYFLT-101` flight. Select the **Create new Booking** menu option to view the form for creating a new `Booking` instance, as shown here:

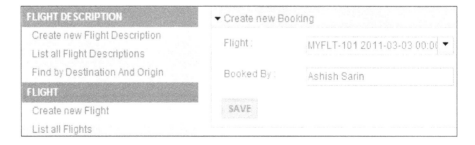

9. Select `MYFLT-101` flight number from **Flight** field and enter a name in the **Booked By** field. If you now click the **Save** button to save the `Booking` instance, you'll receive an **Access denied to admin** message, as shown here:

The access denied message is shown because a user in the `ROLE_ADMIN_USER` role doesn't have access to invoke the `persist` method of the `Booking` JPA entity. Select the **Logout** hyperlink to log out from the Flight Booking application.

10. Now, select the **Create new Booking** option from the menu option. The Flight Booking application will ask you to log in because all menu options are accessible only to authenticated users. Log in with name as **ashish** and password as **ashish**. The user **ashish** has the `ROLE_APP_USER` role.

11. Create a new `Booking` instance, as described in the fifth step. This time the Booking instance is created successfully because `ROLE_APP_USER` has the permission to invoke the `persist` method of the `Booking` JPA entity.

12. Now, select the **Create new Flight Description** menu option. This will show the **Access denied to ashish** message, as shown here:

The access denied message is displayed because web request security of Flight Booking application restricts users from accessing menu options related to `Flight` and `FlightDescription` JPA entities. Also, if you are logged in as **ashish** and attempt to modify or delete an existing `Booking` instance, then you'll be denied access by the application. The reason for this is that the permission to invoke `merge` and `remove` methods of the `Booking` JPA entity is only with users with `ROLE_ADMIN_USER` role.

How it works...

In the *Configuring Spring security for your application* recipe, we discussed Spring Security configuration generated by the `security setup` command. As the `security setup` command created configuration was only helpful in getting us started with adding security to our application, this recipe extends the configuration created by `security setup` command to demonstrate how authentication and authorization can be quickly incorporated into Roo-generated web applications. In this section, we'll look at what modifications or additions we made to configurations and artifacts generated by `security setup` command to create a security-aware Flight Booking application.

Let's start with how we set up Apache Directory Server as the authentication source for the Flight Booking application.

Setting up embedded Apache Directory Server

Spring Security namespace provides an `<ldap-server>` element that configures the location of an external LDAP server against which authentication is to be performed. It can also be used to create an embedded Apache Directory Server instance. If the `url` attribute of the `<ldap-server>` element is specified, then it means that an external LDAP server is being used for authentication. And, if the `url` attribute is not specified, then an embedded instance of Apache Directory Server is created.

The `applicationContext-security.xml` file of the `flightapp-web` project configures embedded Apache Directory Server instances, as shown here:

```
<ldap-server ldif="classpath:application_users.ldif"
        root="dc=sample,dc=com" />
```

The `ldif` attribute specifies the location of the LDIF (LDAP Data Interchange Format) file, which contains user information loaded by the embedded LDAP server. You'll find the `application_users.ldif` file in the `WEB-INF/classes` directory of the `flightapp-web` project. The `root` attribute specifies the root of the LDAP directory tree.

The following figure shows the LDAP directory tree defined by the `application_users.ldif` file:

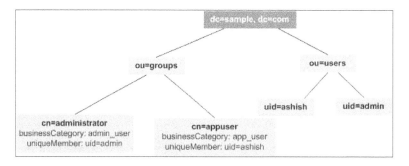

The given figure shows that user groups administrator and appuser are defined under ou=groups, and application users admin and ashish are defined under ou=users. The DN (Distinguished Name) of user ashish is uid=ashish,ou=users,dc=sample, dc=com, and DN of user admin is uid=admin,ou=users,dc=sample,dc=com. DN of administrator group entry is cn=administrator,ou=groups,dc=sample,dc=com, and DN of appuser group entry is cn=appuser,ou=groups,dc=sample,dc=com.

The uniqueMember attribute(s) of an entry defined under ou=groups identifies the application user who belongs to that group. For instance, in the cn=administrator entry, the uniqueMember attribute value is uid=admin,ou=users,dc=sample,dc=com (DN of user admin), which means that the admin user belongs to administrator group. Similarly, ashish belongs to appuser group.

The businessCategory attribute of an entry under ou=groups identifies the role of the users belonging to that group. As the given figure shows, the role of user admin is admin_user and the role of user ashish is app_user.

As Flight Booking application makes use of the embedded Apache Directory Server, the following JAR dependencies have been added to the pom.xml file of the flightapp-web project:

- apacheds-protocol-shared
- apacheds-protocol-ldap
- apacheds-core-entry
- apacheds-core
- apacheds-server-jndi
- shared-ldap

> As Spring Security supports version 1.5.5 of embedded Apache Directory Server, all the given JAR files belong to version 1.5.5.

As we are using Spring Security's LDAP support, spring-security-ldap JAR dependency is also added to the pom.xml file.

Let's now look at configuration, which instructs Spring Security to authenticate against the embedded LDAP server.

Authenticating against the LDAP server

To authenticate against the embedded LDAP server, the following configuration has been added to the applicationContext-security.xml file:

```
<authentication-manager>
  <authentication-provider>
    <ldap-user-service group-search-filter="uniqueMember={0}"
       group-search-base="ou=groups"
```

```
            user-search-base="ou=users"
            user-search-filter="uid={0}"
            group-role-attribute="businessCategory" />
      </authentication-provider>
   </authentication-manager>
```

The `<ldap-user-service>` configures `LdapUserDetailsService` (an implementation of `UserDetailsService` that we discussed earlier), which loads user details containing username, password, and roles from the LDAP server. Authentication is performed by comparing the user entered password with the user details loaded by the `LdapUserDetailsService` instance.

The `<ldap-user-service>` element accepts the following attributes:

- `user-search-base`: Specifies the part of the directory tree under which search for users is performed. The value `ou=users` means that the search will be performed on entries that are defined under DN, which are `ou=users`, `dc=sample`, `dc=com`.

- `user-search-filter`: It specifies the filter criteria used for searching users in the directory tree. The value `uid={0}` means that search is made for the user entry where value of `uid` attribute is equal to username entered by the user in the login form. The value `{0}` is replaced by the username entered by the user in the login form.

- `group-search-base`: It specifies the part of the directory tree under which search for groups is performed. The value `ou=groups` means that the search will be performed on entries that are defined under DN, which are `ou=groups,dc=sample`, and `dc=com`.

- `group-search-filter`: It specifies the filter criteria used for searching groups in the directory tree. The value `uniqueMember={0}` means that a search is made for group entries, where the value of the `uniqueMember` attribute is equal to the DN of the user.

  If user `ashish` attempts to log in to the Flight Booking application, then the value of the `user-search-base` and `user-search-filter` attributes will be used for searching the user. This will result in returning the entry whose DN is `uid=ashish,ou=users,dc=sample,dc=com`. Now, the value of the `group-search-filter` and `group-search-base` attributes will be used to search for the group entry whose `uniqueMember` attribute value is `uid=ashish,ou=users,dc=sample,dc=com`. This will return the `cn=appuser,ou=groups,dc=sample,dc=com` entry because it contains the `uniqueMember` attribute with value `uid=ashish,ou=users,dc=sample,dc=com`.

- `group-role-attribute`: It specifies the attribute of the group entry, which is used as the role name. As the value of `group-role-attribute` is `businessCategory`, if the group entry returned for the authenticating user is `cn=administrator,ou=groups,dc=sample,dc=com`, then the role of the user is `admin_user`—the value of the `businessCategory` attribute of the entry.

It is important to note at this point that Spring Security's LDAP authentication mechanism by default prepends ROLE_ to the name of the role returned after authentication. So, if the `admin` user authenticates with the Flight Booking application, then instead of `admin_user` role, it gets the role ROLE_ADMIN_USER. Similarly, user `ashish` gets the 'ROLE_APP_USER' role.

Let's now look at how web request security is configured for the Flight Booking application.

Configuring web request security

The following `<http>` element of `security` namespace shows how web request security is configured in the `applicationContext-security.xml` file of the `flightapp-web` project:

```
<http auto-config="true" use-expressions="true">
  <access-denied-handler error-page="/accessdenied" />
  <form-login .../>
  <logout logout-url="/resources/j_spring_security_logout" />

  <intercept-url pattern="/flights/**"
    access="hasRole('ROLE_ADMIN_USER')" />

  <intercept-url pattern="/flightdescriptions/**"
    access="hasRole('ROLE_ADMIN_USER')" />

  <intercept-url pattern="/bookings/**"
    access="hasAnyRole('ROLE_APP_USER','ROLE_ADMIN_USER')" />

  <intercept-url pattern="/accessdenied/**"
    access="hasAnyRole('ROLE_APP_USER', 'ROLE_ADMIN_USER')" />
</http>
```

As in the previous recipe, we discussed the `<http>` element of the Roo-generated `applicationContext-security.xml` file; but here we'll only focus on configuration elements specifically added for meeting `flightapp-web` application's web security requirements. In the given code, the following are the elements that we added to configure web request security for the Flight Booking application:

▶ `<access-denied-handler>`: It configures the error page that is shown to the user if access is denied to the requested page. The `error-page` attribute specifies the URL of the error page. The `<mvc:view-controller path="/accessdenied"/>` entry in `webmvc-config.xml` configures `ParameterizableViewController`, responsible for rendering the access denied page—`accessdenied.jspx` in the / `WEB-INF/views` directory.

▶ `<intercept-url>`: It defines the URL pattern and the corresponding access permissions for the Flight Booking application. Let's look at each of the `<intercept-url>` elements defined for the Flight Booking application:

```
<intercept-url pattern="/flights/**"
    access="hasRole('ROLE_ADMIN_USER')" />
```

❑ The pattern `/flights/**` refers to all the web pages that are specific to managing `Flight` JPA entity instances. The `hasRole('ROLE_ADMIN_USER')` expression specifies that pages specific to managing `Flight` JPA entity instances are accessible only to users with the `ROLE_ADMIN_USER` role.

```
<intercept-url pattern="/flightdescriptions/**"
    access="hasRole('ROLE_ADMIN_USER')" />
```

❑ The pattern `/flightdescriptions/**` refers to all the web pages that are specific to managing `FlightDescription` JPA entity instances. The `hasRole('ROLE_ADMIN_USER')` expression specifies that pages specific to managing `FlightDescription` JPA entity instances are accessible only to users with the `ROLE_ADMIN_USER` role.

```
<intercept-url pattern="/bookings/**"
    access="hasAnyRole('ROLE_APP_USER','ROLE_ADMIN_USER')"
/>
```

❑ The pattern `/bookings/**` refers to all the web pages that are specific to managing `Booking` JPA entity instances. The `hasAnyRole('ROLE_APP_USER','ROLE_ADMIN_USER')` expression specifies that pages specific to managing `Booking` JPA entity instances are accessible only to users with the `ROLE_ADMIN_USER` or `ROLE_APP_USER` role.

```
<intercept-url pattern="/accessdenied/**"
    access="hasAnyRole('ROLE_APP_USER', 'ROLE_ADMIN_USER')"
/>
```

❑ The pattern `/accessdenied/**` refers to the web page that shows **Access denied ...** message. The `hasAnyRole('ROLE_APP_USER','ROLE_ADMIN_USER')` expression specifies that the access denied page is accessible to users with the `ROLE_ADMIN_USER` or `ROLE_APP_USER` role. This is important because the access denied page should not be accessible to anonymous users.

Let's now look at how method-level security is configured in the Flight Booking application.

Configuring method-level security

Method-level security in the Flight Booking application is enabled by the `<global-method-security>` element in the `applicationContext-security.xml` file, as shown here:

```
<global-method-security mode="aspectj"
    secured-annotations="enabled"/>
```

The `mode` attribute value specifies whether Spring AOP (which proxies the target object) or AspectJ (in which Spring's AspectJ security aspect is weaved into the class at load-time or compile-time) is used for securing methods. As `Booking` JPA entity is created outside the Spring container, to use Spring's `@Secured` annotation (discussed in the next section) to secure methods defined by `Booking` JPA entity, you need to use AspectJ. The value `aspectj` of the `mode` attribute instructs Spring to weave `AnnotationSecurityAspect` (available in the Spring Security's `spring-security-aspects` JAR file) into classes that make use of the `@Secured` annotation. The `secured-annotations` attribute specifies if the use of the `@Secured` annotations is enabled or disabled for the application context. The value `enabled` means that Spring Security will secure all methods that make use `@Secured` method-level annotation. Spring also supports using JSR-250 security annotations, security expressions (like `hasRole`, `hasPermission`, and so on), and the `<protect-pointcut>` sub-element of the `<global-method-security>` element to implement method-level security. You can use a combination of different approaches to implement method-level security in your application.

As we are using AspectJ mode for implementing method-level security in the Flight Booking application, dependency on `spring-security-aspects` JAR has been added to the `pom.xml` file, and the AspectJ compiler plugin configuration in the `pom.xml` file has been updated to include `spring-security-aspects`, as shown here:

```
<plugin>
 <groupId>org.codehaus.mojo</groupId>
 <artifactId>aspectj-maven-plugin</artifactId>
 ...
 <configuration>
  <outxml>true</outxml>
  <aspectLibraries>
   <aspectLibrary>
    <groupId>org.springframework</groupId>
    <artifactId>spring-aspects</artifactId>
   </aspectLibrary>
   <aspectLibrary>
    <groupId>org.springframework.security</groupId>
    <artifactId>spring-security-aspects</artifactId>
   </aspectLibrary>
  </aspectLibraries>
  ...
 </configuration>
</plugin>
```

The `<aspectLibrary>` element specifies the JAR files that contain aspects. The `spring-aspects` JAR contains aspect for weaving `@Transactional` support and `spring-security-aspects` JAR contains aspect for weaving `@Secured` support in classes.

 You may also notice that Spring Security version 3.1.0 RC1 has been used in the Flight Booking application because `spring-security` schema prior to version 3.1 didn't support `mode` attribute for `<global-method-security>` element.

Now that we have seen how method-level security is configured for the Flight Booking application, we are ready to annotate `Booking` JPA entity methods with the `@Secured` annotation.

Adding @Secured annotation to JPA entity methods

Spring Security's `@Secured` annotation can be used at *method-level* to secure methods from unauthorized access. `@Secured` annotation specifies the user roles that are authorized to invoke the method.

Adding Spring Security's `@Secured` annotation to JPA entity methods in Roo-generated applications is a bit of an involved process. Roo defines JPA entity methods in the `*_Roo_Entity.aj` AspectJ ITD file, which is not recommended to be modified by application developers. To add the `@Secured` annotation to a JPA entity method, perform push-in refactoring (refer to *Chapter 7*) to move the method to the entity's Java class or simply copy the methods from the AspectJ file to entity's Java class. For instance, in the case of the `Booking` JPA entity, the `persist` method is copied from the `Booking_Roo_Entity.aj` file to the `Booking.java` file, as shown here:

```
@RooEntity(identifierColumn = "BOOKING_ID")
public class Booking {
    @PersistenceContext
    transient EntityManager entityManager;
    . . .
    @Transactional
    @Secured("ROLE_APP_USER")
    public void persist() {
        if (this.entityManager == null)
            this.entityManager = entityManager();
        this.entityManager.persist(this);
    }

    public static final EntityManager entityManager() {
        EntityManager em = new Booking().entityManager;
        . . .
        return em;
    }
}
```

The given code shows that the `persist` method is copied from `Booking_Roo_Entity.aj` to the `Booking.java` file. The `@Secured` annotation is added to the `persist` method to make it secure.

It is important to note that copying a method from AspectJ ITD to a Java file *doesn't* require moving dependent methods and attributes also. For instance, moving `persist` method from `Booking_Roo_Entity.aj` to `Booking.java` *doesn't* require moving `entityManager` attribute and `entityManager()` method, as shown in the code. It has been done to simplify understanding the code.

Deploying a GWT application on GAE

GAE (Google App Engine) is the cloud computing platform from Google that provides the infrastructure for deploying your web applications. In this recipe, we'll look at how Roo simplifies developing an application for GAE. We'll also see how a Roo-scaffolded GWT application is created and deployed on GAE. In the *Deploying Spring Web MVC applications on GAE* recipe, we'll see a Spring Web MVC application that can be deployed on GAE.

Getting ready

If you only want to run the GWT application locally using App Engine SDK for Java, then you don't need to sign up with Google App Engine and create an *application identifier*. If you want to deploy the application on GAE, follow the steps mentioned here to create an application identifier for your application.

1. Sign-up for a free Google App Engine account by going to the following URL: `http://appengine.google.com`. Once you are signed in, you'll see the following welcome page:

Go gle app engine

Welcome to Google App Engine

Before getting started. you want to learn more about developing and deploying applications. Learn more about Google App Engine by reading the Getting Started Guide. the FAQ. or the

Create Application

2. Now, you need to create an *application identifier* that uniquely identifies your application and is required for deploying your applications on GAE. Click the **Create Application** button, which will ask you to select your country information and mobile number to generate a verification code, as shown here:

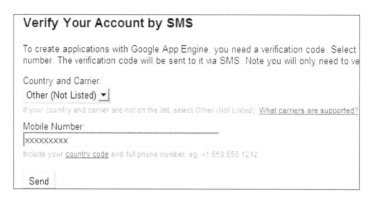

3. Once you have provided the verification code that you received via SMS, you can create the application identifier as shown in the following screenshot:

4. Enter a unique value for the **Application identifier** field and enter a value for **Application title**. As the given screenshot shows, the application identifier name is prepended to **.appspot.com** to form the URL to access your application. So, if your unique identifier is `myappid`, then after deploying the application on GAE you can access it by going to `http://myappid.appspot.com`.

Now, we are all set to create our GWT application, which we want to deploy to GAE.

Create a sub-directory `ch06-gae-gwt` inside the `C:\roo-cookbook` directory and start the Roo shell from `C:\roo-cookbook\ch06-gae-gwt`.

How to do it...

To create a Roo-scaffolded GWT application and deploy it on GAE, follow the steps given here:

1. Create `flightapp-gae-gwt` project using `project` command:

   ```
   ... roo> project --topLevelPackage sample.roo.flightapp --java 6
   --projectName flightapp-gae-gwt
   ```

2. Use `persistence setup` command to setup `DataNucleus` as persistence provider and set `GOOLE_APP_ENGINE` as the database. The `applicationId` argument is optional and if you only want to test the application locally, then you don't need to specify it.

   ```
   ... roo> persistence setup --provider DATANUCLEUS --database
   GOOGLE_APP_ENGINE --applicationId <your application identifier>


   Created SRC_MAIN_WEBAPP\WEB-INF\appengine-web.xml

   Created SRC_MAIN_WEBAPP\WEB-INF\logging.properties

   Updated SRC_MAIN_RESOURCES\log4j.properties


   Updated ROOT\pom.xml [Added property 'gae.home' with value
   '${user.home}/.m2/repository/com/google/appengine/appengine-java-
   sdk/1.4.0/appengine-java-sdk-1.4.0']


   Updated ROOT\pom.xml [Added dependencies com.google.appengine.
   orm:datanucleus-appengine:1.0.7.final..]


   Updated ROOT\pom.xml [Added plugin maven-gae-plugin]

   Updated ROOT\pom.xml [Added plugin maven-datanucleus-plugin]
   ```

   For brevity, the given output only shows GAE-specific actions that are performed by Roo.

3. Create the `FlightDescription` JPA entity and add fields to it, as shown here:

   ```
   ... roo> entity --class ~.domain.FlightDescription
   --identifierType java.lang.Long --testAutomatically


   ... roo> field string --fieldName origin --notNull

   ... roo> field string --fieldName destination --notNull

   ... roo> field number --type java.lang.Float --fieldName price
   --notNull
   ```

4. Scaffold GWT application using the `gwt setup` command:

   ... roo> gwt setup

5. If you want to import `flightapp-gae-gwt` into Eclipse IDE , execute the `perform eclipse` command:

   ... roo> perform eclipse

6. Exit the Roo shell and execute the `gae:run` goal of Maven GAE Plugin to run the `flightapp-gae-gwt` application locally on the Google App Engine development web server that comes bundled with App Engine SDK for Java, as shown here:

   C:\roo-cookbook\ch06-gae-gwt> mvn gae:run

7. The Maven GAE Plugin was configured in the `pom.xml` file of the `flightapp-gae-gwt` project when we executed the `persistence setup` command. A successful start of development server will show the following message: The server is running at http://localhost:8080/

8. Now, open your favorite web browser and go to http://localhost:8080 to access the GWT `flightapp-gae-gwt` web application, which allows you to perform CRUD operations on the `FlightDescription` JPA entity, as shown here:

9. After you have tested the application locally, you can deploy the `flightapp-gae-gwt` application to GAE by executing the `gae:deploy` goal of Maven GAE Plugin, as shown in the following command. If you had not created application identifier and specified it as the value of the `applicationId` argument of the `persistence setup` command, then this step will fail.

```
C:\roo-cookbook\ch06-gae-gwt> mvn gae:deploy


Beginning server interaction for <your-application-identifier>...

...

Email: <email-id>@gmail.com

Password for <email-id>@gmail.com:

...
```

10. As the given output suggests, while deploying your application you need to provide your e-mail address and corresponding password with which you signed up with Google App Engine.

11. Once the `flightapp-gae-gwt` application is successfully deployed on GAE, you can access it via the following URL:

    ```
    http://<your-application-identifier>.appspot.com
    ```

    As the `flightapp-gae-gwt` application is a secured application, you'll be required to log in using your Google Accounts or OpenID credentials.

How it works...

The `persistence setup` command determines that the target deployment environment is Google App Engine if the value of `database` argument is `GOOGLE_APP_ENGINE`. If the value of the `database` argument is `GOOGLE_APP_ENGINE`, then it becomes mandatory to specify `DATANUCLEUS` as the value of the `provider` argument.

You might be wondering why it's mandatory to specify the persistence provider as `DataNucleus` and `GOOGLE_APP_ENGINE` as the database. Well, Google App Engine uses a proprietary *schema-less* object datastore, BigTable, for persisting application data. Java applications can access the BigTable datastore using JPA or JDO via `DataNucleus App Engine plugin` (this is not a Maven plugin but a DataNucleus plugin). DataNucleus is a separate product that allows access to datastores (which includes RDBMS, Excel, XML, LDAP, and so on) using JDO and JPA APIs. Also, the Datanucleus App Engine plugin is developed and maintained by Google and is specifically meant for use with GAE. So, you can say that by using DataNucleus, developers can use JDO or JPA APIs in their applications for accessing or persisting data, irrespective of the datastore(s) used by the application. This could be particularly useful in case your application makes use of distinct types of data sources.

In response to `persistence setup`, Roo performs the following actions:

▶ Creates the `appengine-web.xml` file in the `WEB-INF` directory

▶ Adds dependency on `DataNucleus App Engine plugin in pom.xml`

▶ Configures `Maven GAE plugin in pom.xml`

▶ Configures `Maven DataNucleus plugin in pom.xml`

▶ Creates `logging.properties` configuration for Java logging API

▶ Creates the `persistence.xml` file in the `META-INF` directory, which provides persistence provider (DataNucleus in our case) information

▶ Creates the `applicationContext.xml` file in `META-INF/spring` directory, which contains transaction manager and JPA `EntityManagerFactory` definitions

Let's now look at `appengine-web.xml` file and the plugins configured by Roo.

appengine-web.xml

The `appengine-web.xml` is a configuration file specific to GAE, which specifies application identifier, version of the application, static and resource files in the application, system properties, and so on. The following listing shows the content of `appengine-web.xml` generated by Roo for the `flightapp-gae-gwt` project:

```
<appengine-web-app xmlns="http://appengine.google.com/ns/1.0">
  <application>myappid</application>
  <version>1</version>
  <sessions-enabled>true</sessions-enabled>
  <system-properties>
    <property name="java.util.logging.config.file"
      value="WEB-INF/logging.properties"/>
    <property
      name="appengine.orm.disable.duplicate.emf.exception"
      value="false"/>
  </system-properties>
</appengine-web-app>
```

`<appengine-web-app>` is the root element of `appengine-web.xml`. `<application>` element specifies the application identifier, the value of which comes from the `applicationId` argument of `persistence setup` command.

`<version>` element specifies the version identifier of the application code that you are deploying on GAE. The application version identifier is particularly useful when you want to test your deployed application on GAE before making it the default version, which is accessible to the users. Let's say, you have version **1** of Flight Booking application already deployed on GAE. Now, you make some changes to your application code in order to fix bugs or add/modify application features. To test your modified application on GAE, change the `<version>` element to a different value, let's say **2**, and deploy the application on GAE using `gae:deploy` goal (more on this later) of maven GAE plugin. GAE uses the value of `<version>` element to determine if the existing application code needs to be replaced by the newly deployed application code or to create a new version of the application code. As the version of newly deployed Flight Booking application code is **2** and the existing application code had version **1**, GAE creates a new version of the application, which you can access by going to the following URL: `http://<app-version>.latest.<application-id>.appspot.com`. Assuming that the application identifier of the Flight Booking application is `myappid` and the version deployed is **2**, the URL becomes `http://2.latest.myappid.appspot.com`.

The `<session-enabled>` element enables GAE's session persistence feature, that is, session data is persisted into App Engine's datastore. So, if you set session data in your web application using `setAttribute` method of `HttpSession`, then it is stored in App Engine's datastore. As the session objects are persisted, the objects that you set in the session must implement the `java.io.Serializable` interface.

The `<system-properties>` element defines the system properties available to the application. App Engine supports application logging via Logging API of Java (refer to the `java.util.logging` package). The logging configuration is read from the file, which is specified as the value of `java.util.logging.config.file` system property. In the `appengine-web.xml` file of the `flightapp-gae-gwt` project, the `<property>` sub-element of the `<system-properties>` element specifies that the value of the `java.util.logging.config.file` system property is `WEB-INF/logging.properties`. Similarly, `appengine.orm.disable.duplicate.emf.exception` system property with value `true` instructs App Engine not to raise exceptions when the application attempts to create multiple `javax.persistence.EntityManagerFactory` instances for a persistence unit. By default, App Engine expects that only a single instance of `EntityManagerFactory` exists per persistence unit, and an attempt to create a duplicate `EntityManagerFactory` instance results in exception.

Maven GAE plugin

The Maven GAE plugin simplifies developing Java applications for App Engine by providing goals, which help with downloading and unzipping App Engine SDK, starting and stopping App Engine development server, deploying application to App Engine, retrieving application logs from App Engine, and so on.

The following listing shows Maven GAE plugin specific configuration as defined in `pom.xml` of the `flightapp-gae-gwt` project:

```
<project ...>
    ...
  <properties>
    ...
    <gae.home>
      ${user.home}/.m2/repository/com/google/appengine/
      appengine-java-sdk/1.4.0/appengine-java-sdk-1.4.0
    </gae.home>
  </properties>
  ...
  <plugin>
    <groupId>net.kindleit</groupId>
    <artifactId>maven-gae-plugin</artifactId>
    <version>0.5.7</version>
    <configuration>
      <unpackVersion>1.4.0</unpackVersion>
    </configuration>
    <executions>
      <execution>
        <phase>validate</phase>
        <goals>
          <goal>unpack</goal>
        </goals>
      </execution>
    </executions>
  </plugin>
</project>
```

The `gae.home` property specifies the location of the unpacked version of App Engine SDK.

The sub-element `<unpackVersion>` of plugin `<configuration>` specifies the version of the plugin to unpack. The `<execution>` element specifies that the `gae:unpack` goal of the Maven GAE plugin is executed in the `validate` build lifecycle phase. The `validate` build lifecycle phase is the one in which Maven validates that the project is correct and all the required information to make the build is available. The `gae:unpack` goal unpacks the GAE SDK to the location specified by the `gae.home` property.

Spring Roo 1.1.3 generates `pom.xml`, which makes project dependent on GAE SDK 1.4.0 and Maven GAE plugin 0.5.7, as shown in the listing we just saw. At the time of writing this book, the current version of GAE SDK is 1.5.1 and that of Maven GAE plugin is 0.8.4. To change the version of GAE SDK, modify the `gae.home` property. And, to change the version of Maven GAE plugin, simply modify the value of the `<version>` sub-element of the `<plugin>` element, which configures Maven GAE plugin. If you are using Spring Roo 1.1.5, then the project already uses GAE SDK 1.5.1 and Maven GAE plugin 0.8.4.

The following table specifies some of the goals defined by the Maven GAE plugin:

Goal	Description
gae:run	Runs the project locally on the GAE development web server
gae:deploy	Uploads the application to the GAE server
gae:logs	Retrieves application logs from the GAE server
gae:version	Shows the plugin and GAE SDK versions

Let's now look at the Maven DataNucleus plugin and the role it plays in the GAE application.

Maven DataNucleus plugin

To make a class persistent, DataNucleus expects that the class must implement the `PersistenceCapable` interface of JDO. Why are we talking about JDO now? Well, it's because DataNucleus support for JPA is built on top of JDO. This means that even if you have annotated your domain classes with the `@Entity` JPA annotation, DataNucleus can't persist them. To free developers from implementing the `PersistenceCapable` interface in their domain classes, DataNucleus provides an *enhancer*, which works on the compiled domain classes and implements `PersistenceCapable` interface via bytecode enhancement. The Maven DataNucleus plugin provides a `datanucleus:enhance` goal, which enhances JPA classes annotated with the `@Entity` annotation. The following code shows this:

```
<plugin>
 <groupId>org.datanucleus</groupId>
 <artifactId>maven-datanucleus-plugin</artifactId>
 <version>1.1.4</version>
 <configuration>
  <mappingIncludes>**/*.class</mappingIncludes>
  <enhancerName>ASM</enhancerName>
  <api>JPA</api>
  <mappingExcludes>**/GaeAuthFilter.class</mappingExcludes>
 </configuration>
 <executions>
  <execution>
   <phase>compile</phase>
   <goals>
```

```
        <goal>enhance</goal>
      </goals>
    </execution>
  </executions>
</plugin>
```

In the plugin configuration, the `<execution>` element specifies that
`datanucleus:enhance` goal is executed in the `compile` build lifecycle phase. So, when
Java source files are compiled, the Maven DataNucleus plugin enhances the compiled JPA
domain classes. The `<mappingIncludes>` element specifies the classes that should be
included for enhancement. The `<mappingExcludes>` specifies the classes that should not
be considered for enhancement.

The `<api>` element specifies whether the enhancement is for JPA or JDO. As we are using
JPA in the `flightapp-gae-gwt` project, the value of the `<api>` element is `jpa`. The
`<enhancerName>` element specifies `ASM` as the value, which basically refers to the `ASM`
framework (`http://asm.ow2.org/`) used by DataNucleus for enhancing the bytecode.

Let's now look at the `FlightDescription` entity that was generated by Roo:

Persistent entities

As GAE datastore is not a relational database, you'll find that some of the concepts that apply
while using JPA with relational databases will not apply when using JPA with GAE datastore.

The following code shows the `FlightDescription` JPA entity generated by Roo.

```
@RooJavaBean
@RooToString
@RooEntity
public class FlightDescription {

    @NotNull
    private String origin;

    @NotNull
    private String destination;

    @NotNull
    private Float price;
}
```

The given code shows that we are not using `@Column` and `@Table` JPA annotations to identify
the table into which the entity instances are saved and the table column to which a persistent
entity field maps to. As the GAE datastore is schema-less, you don't need to specify the table
or column information. You can still use the JSR 303 annotations, such as `@NotNull` in this
code, for validating your domain objects.

The following code shows the `FlightDescription_Roo_Entity.aj` AspectJ ITD file:

```
privileged aspect FlightDescription_Roo_Entity {

    declare @type: FlightDescription: @Entity;

    @PersistenceContext
    transient EntityManager FlightDescription.entityManager;

    @Id
    @GeneratedValue(strategy = GenerationType.IDENTITY)
    @Column(name = "id")
    private Long FlightDescription.id;

    @Version
    @Column(name = "version")
    private Integer FlightDescription.version;
    ...
}
```

It is interesting to note that the primary key generation strategy is specified as `GenerationType.IDENTITY`. In GAE, this means that the identifier value is not assigned to the `FlightDescription` entity until the associated transaction completes or you explicitly call the `flush` method of `EntityManager`.

Let's now look at how the `flightapp-gae-gwt` application ensures that only authenticated users can access it.

Authentication and authorization in GAE applications

As with any other web application, web request security constraints for the `flightapp-gae-gwt` application are specified in the `web.xml` file of the application. The following listing shows the `<security-constraint>` element of the `web.xml` file of `flightapp-gae-gwt` application:

```
<security-constraint>
  <display-name>...</display-name>
  <web-resource-collection>
    <web-resource-name>...</web-resource-name>
    <url-pattern>*.html</url-pattern>
  </web-resource-collection>
  <auth-constraint>
    <role-name>*</role-name>
  </auth-constraint>
</security-constraint>
```

The `<url-pattern>` specifies that any URL that matches the `*.html` pattern is secured and would require authentication. In the case of the `flightapp-gae-gwt` application, the home page of the application is `index.html`, which is secured according to the URL pattern specified by the `<url-pattern>` element. As the entry into the `flightapp-gae-gwt` application is restricted, users need to authenticate using their Google Accounts credentials before accessing the application. The `<role-name>` element specifies `*` as the value, which means that any authenticated user can access the application. If you want your application on GAE to be accessible to anonymous users also, then remove the `<security-constraint>` element from the `web.xml` file.

If you remove the `<security-constraint>` element from `web.xml` of the `flightapp-gae-gwt` project and upload the application to GAE servers, you'll find that an attempt to access the `flightapp-gae-gwt` application still asks for authentication. The reason behind this behavior is that the `sample.roo.flightapp.server.gae.GaeAuthFilter` servlet filter configured in the Roo-generated `web.xml` file. `GaeAuthFilter` is a Roo-generated servlet filter, which checks if the user is logged in or not. If the user is not logged in, then it redirects the user to the Google Accounts sign in page. The following code listing from `GaeAuthFilter.java` shows the `GaeAuthFilter` class:

```
import com.google.appengine.api.users.UserService;
import com.google.appengine.api.users.UserServiceFactory;

public class GaeAuthFilter implements Filter {
  ...

 public void doFilter(...) ... {
  UserService userService =
     UserServiceFactory.getUserService();
  ...

  if (!userService.isUserLoggedIn()) {
   String requestUrl = request.getHeader("requestUrl");
   if (requestUrl == null) {
    requestUrl = request.getRequestURI();
   }
   response.setHeader("login",
      userService.createLoginURL(requestUrl));
   response.sendError(HttpServletResponse.SC_UNAUTHORIZED);
   return;
  }
  ...
 }
```

In the given code, `UserServiceFactory` is a GAE-specific class whose `getUserService` method returns an instance of `UserService`. The `UserService` interface defines methods to create login and logout URLs, get details of the currently signed in user, check if the user is logged in, and so on. In this code, `GaeAuthFilter` checks if the user is logged in by calling the `isUserLoggedIn()` method. If the user is not logged in, `GaeAuthFilter` makes use of the `createLoginURL(..)` method of `UserService` to create a login URL and redirects the user to it.

Another interesting point to notice about `GaeAuthFilter` is its mapping. The following listing shows the mapping of GWT's `RequestFactoryServlet` and `GaeAuthFilter` in the `web.xml` file:

```
<filter-mapping>
  <filter-name>GaeAuthFilter</filter-name>
  <url-pattern>/gwtRequest/*</url-pattern>
</filter-mapping>

<servlet-mapping>
    <servlet-name>requestFactory</servlet-name>
  <url-pattern>/gwtRequest</url-pattern>
</servlet-mapping>
```

The `<url-pattern>` elements of `GaeAuthFilter` and GWT's `RequestFactoryServlet` show that a web request sent to `RequestFactoryServlet` is intercepted by `GaeAuthFilter`. This ensures that if the session expires, the application user is redirected to the Google Accounts sign-in page.

`UserService` provides a `getCurrentUser` method that returns a `User` object if the user is logged in. The `User` object contains user id, nickname, and e-mail information of the authenticated user. If your application requires capturing more information about the user, such as their preferences, address, and so on, then you need to save such information as part of your application data.

By default, the only role defined by App Engine is `admin`, which you can specify as the value of the `<role-name>` element. The `admin` role is assigned to users that are application administrators, that is, users that you add using the **Admin Console** of GAE. Admin Console gives you complete control over your deployed application on GAE. It allows you to administer your datastore, test different versions of your application, create application, and so on. You can access Admin Console by going to the following URL: `http://appengine.google.com`. You can use the `isUserAdmin` method of `UserService` to determine if the logged in user belongs to `admin` role or not.

Even though GAE supports only `admin` role, you can still incorporate role-based security in your App Engine applications by introducing application-specific roles. You can save application-specific role information as part of application data. For instance, you can use Spring Security framework with your GWT or Spring Web MVC application to implement web request security and method-level security based on the roles assigned to users.

Deploying a Spring Web MVC application on GAE

As of Spring Roo 1.1.5, the Roo-generated Spring Web MVC application doesn't work on GAE. The reason for this is related to mismatch in the JSTL version used by GAE and by the Roo-generated Spring MVC application. Also, Roo-generated JPA entities support only unowned relationships (refer http://code.google.com/appengine/docs/java/datastore/jdo/relationships.html to learn about owned and unowned relationships). In this recipe, we'll look at a Spring 3.0 Web MVC application (which uses JSTL tags that work on GAE) consisting of `FlightDescription` and `Flight` JPA entities and demonstrates how to create a unidirectional *owned* one-to-many relationship between JPA entities. The `FlightDescription` entity is on the *one* side of one-to-many relationship.

 If you are using Spring Roo 1.2.x, then the Roo-generated Spring Web MVC application can be deployed successfully on GAE.

Getting ready

If you only want to run the Spring Web MVC application locally using App Engine SDK for Java, then you don't need to sign-up with Google App Engine and create an *application identifier*. If you want to deploy the application on GAE, then follow the steps described in the previous recipe and ensure that you modify the application identifier in `WEB-INF/appengine-web.xml` file. It is recommended that you deploy the application on GAE servers, as we'll also discuss some of the features offered by Admin Console.

Extract the `ch06-gae-spring-mvc.zip` file that accompanies this book to the `C:\roo-cookbook` directory. Extracting the ZIP file will create a directory named `ch06-gae-spring-mvc`, which contains the `flightapp-gae-spring-mvc` Eclipse project. The `flightapp-gae-spring-mvc` project makes use of App Engine SDK version 1.4.2 and Maven GAE Plugin 0.8.2.

How to do it...

To deploy a Spring Web MVC application on GAE follow the steps given here:

1. Open the command prompt and go to `C:\roo-cookbook\ch06-gae-spring-mvc` directory. Execute `mvn gae:run` command to deploy the `flightapp-gae-spring-mvc` project on App Engine development web server:

   C:\roo-cookbook\ch06-gae-spring-mvc> mvn gae:run

2. Once the development web server starts successfully, open web browser and go to the following URL: http://localhost:8080. If you see the following page, then it means that your `flightapp-gae-spring-mvc` project is successfully deployed:

Flight Booking Application

Manage Flight Descriptions
Manage Flights

Welcome to Flight Booking application.

3. The given screenshot shows the home page of our Flight Booking application, which currently allows managing `Flight` and `FlightDescription` objects. Selecting the **Manage Flight Descriptions** hyperlink allows users to create and view `FlightDescription` instances. Also, it allows users to child `Flight` instances associated with a `FlightDescription` instance. The **Manage Flights** option allows users to create and delete `Flight` instances.

4. Select **Manage Flight Descriptions** option to view `FlightDescription` instances in the application, as shown here:

5. As we have not yet created any `FlightDescription` instances, the table shows **No record found** message.

6. Select the **Create Flight Description** option to view the form for creating a new `FlightDescription` instance, as shown here:

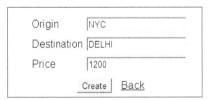

7. Enter the `FlightDescription` details as shown in the given screenshot and click the **Create** button. The newly created `FlightDescription` instance is displayed in the list of `FlightDescription` instances, as shown here:

8. The **View** button corresponding to a `FlightDescription` record shows the `FlightDescription` details along with the `Flight` details, which are associated with the `FlightDescription` instance. The **Delete** button deletes the `FlightDescription` instance along with the associated `Flight` instances.

9. Click the **Home** link to go back to the home page of the application and select the **Manage Flights** link to view the `Flight` instances, as shown here:

10. Select the **Create Flight** link to view the form for creating `Flight` instances, as shown here:

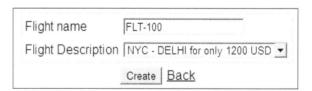

11. Enter **FLT-100** as the value of **Flight name** field and select **NYC – DELHI for only 1200 USD** as the value of **Flight Description** field. Click **Create** button to create `Flight` instance (with `FLT-100` as the flight name), which is a child of `FlightDescription` instance (origin: NYC, destination: DELHI, price: 1200). Similarly, create flights with names `FLT-200`, `FLT-300`, and `FLT-400`. Now, if you go to the `FlightDescription` listing page and click the **View** button, then you'll see the newly created `Flight` instances as a child of the `NYC-DELHI-1200` `FlightDescription` instance, as shown here:

Flight Description		
Origin	**Destination**	**Price**
NYC	DELHI	1200
Associated Flights		
Flight name		
FLT-100		
FLT-200		
FLT-300		
FLT-400		

12. The given screenshot shows the `Flight` instances that are associated with `FlightDescription` instance.

13. If you now delete the `FlightDescription` instance by selecting the **Delete** button (as shown in the next screenshot) corresponding to the `NYC-DELHI-1200` `FlightDescription` instance, then it'll also delete associated `Flight` instances.

Origin	**Destination**	**Price**	**Actions**
NYC	DELHI	1200	View Delete

How it works...

GAE datastore is a non-relational database in which relationships between entities are modeled as either *owned* or *unowned*. An **owned** relationship is based on the concept of parent-child relationship, where the child entity instances cannot exist without a parent. In an **unowned** relationship, entity instances can exist irrespective of their relationship with other entities.

An owned relationship can be best visualized as a tree structure in which the root of the tree is an entity instance, which is the ultimate parent for all the entities. The following figure shows an owned relationship example in which `FlightDescription` is the root entity with `Flight` entity instances as its child entities, and `Booking` entity instances are the child of the `Flight` entity.

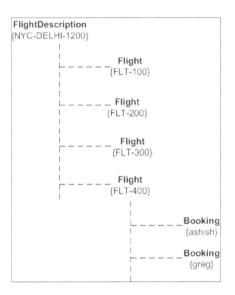

In the given figure, `FlightDescription` (NYC-DELHI-1200) is at the root of the tree. The `Flight` instances (FLT-100, FLT-200, FLT-300, FLT-400) are children of the `FlightDescription` (NYC-DELHI-1200) instance. The `Booking` (ashish, greg) instances are children of the `Flight` (FLT-400) instance. If such a parent-child relationship is defined in the entities stored in the App Engine datastore, then these entities are referred to as part of the same entity group. You can think of an entity group as a tree with a root entity at the top and this root entity doesn't have any parents. In this figure, `FlightDescription` (NYC-DELHI-1200) represents the root entity. The other important point about owned relationships is that except the root entity, all other entities in the entity group cannot be created without a parent. For example, `Flight` instance cannot exist without a `FlightDescription` instance and `Booking` instance cannot exist without a `Flight` instance.

In GAE, creating an owned relationship puts a restriction on the *type* of primary key that you can define for the child entity. The reason for this is that the child entity instance needs to know its parent in the entity group apart from its own entity ID. The type of primary key of the child entity in an owned relationship is either `com.google.appengine.api.datastore.Key` or encoded `String` form of `com.google.appengine.api.datastore.Key`. GAE provides a `KeyFactory` class (discussed later in this recipe), which you can use to create a `Key` instance or to convert a `Key` instance value to `String` (referred to as encoded form of the `Key`) and vice versa.

In an unowned relationship, each entity instance exists independently of each other. For example, the relationship between `Student` and `Course` entities is an example of an unowned relationship. A `Student` entity can exist without a `Course` and a `Course` entity can exist without a `Student`.

In our Flight Booking application, the relationship between `FlightDescription` and `Flight` entities is an example of an owned relationship, where `Flight` entity instances cannot exist without a `FlightDescription` instance. Let's now see how an owned one-to-many relationship has been created between the `FlightDescription` and `Flight` entities in the Flight Booking application.

Owned relationship

The following code listing shows some of the important methods and attributes of the `FlightDescription` entity:

```
import com.google.appengine.api.datastore.Key;
import com.google.appengine.api.datastore.KeyFactory;

@Entity
public class FlightDescription {
   @Id
   @GeneratedValue(strategy = GenerationType.IDENTITY)
   @Basic
   private Key flightDescriptionId;

   @Basic
   @NotNull
   private String origin;
   ...

   @OneToMany
   private List<Flight> flights;

   ...
   @Transactional
   public void persist() {
     if (this.entityManager == null)
        this.entityManager = entityManager();
     this.entityManager.persist(this);
   }

   @Transactional
   public static FlightDescription
        findFlightDescription(String key) {
```

```
        return
        (FlightDescription)entityManager().createQuery("select o
            from FlightDescription o where o.flightDescriptionId =
            :id").setParameter("id",
                KeyFactory.stringToKey(key)).getSingleResult();
    }
    ...
    public String getFlightDescriptionKeyAsString() {
        return KeyFactory.keyToString(flightDescriptionId);
    }
    ...
}
```

The given code shows that `FlightDescription` entity's primary key is of type `com.google.appengine.api.datastore.Key`. The `Key` not only holds the entity's primary key, but also holds information about the entity group to which the entity instance belongs. As the `FlightDescription` represents a root entity (that is, without a parent), the `Key` field will not contain entity group information. The `@OneToMany` annotated `flights` field defines an *owned* relationship between the `FlightDescription` and `Flight` entities.

If it was an *unowned* relationship the `flights` field would have taken the following form:

```
    private List<Key> flights;
```

Here, the `flights` field refers to the primary keys of `Flight` entity instances. Also, the field is not annotated with the `@OneToMany` annotation.

The `findFlightDescription` method of the `FlightDescription` entity takes encoded `String` value of `Key` to find the matching `FlightDescription`. The `KeyFactory` class provides `keyToString` and `stringToKey` to convert `Key` into its encoded `String` form and vice versa. This is particularly useful when you are creating relationships between entities via the user interface of the web application. The query to fetch the `FlightDescription` object makes use of the `KeyFactory` class to obtain `Key` from its `String` representation and use it as part of the query, as shown here again:

```
    entityManager().createQuery("select o
            from FlightDescription o where o.flightDescriptionId =
            :id").setParameter("id",
                KeyFactory.stringToKey(key)).getSingleResult();
```

The `persist` method of `FlightDescription` shows that you don't need to set the value of the primary key. It is set by the App Engine.

The `getFlightDescriptionKeyAsString` method of the `FlightDescription` entity makes use of `KeyFactory` class to return the primary key of the entity as an encoded `String` value.

Let's now look at how `Flight` entity is modeled.

The following code listing shows noteworthy attributes and methods of the `Flight` entity:

```
@Entity
public class Flight {

  @Id
  @GeneratedValue(strategy = GenerationType.IDENTITY)
  @Basic
  private Key flightId;

  @Basic
  @NotNull
  private String flightName;

  private transient String encodedFlightDescriptionId;

  @Transactional
  public void persist() {
    if (this.entityManager == null)
      this.entityManager = entityManager();
    Key parentKey = KeyFactory.stringToKey(
          encodedFlightDescriptionId);

    Key flightKey = KeyFactory.createKey(parentKey,
          Flight.class.getSimpleName(), flightName);

    setFlightId(flightKey);
    this.entityManager.persist(this);
  }

  public String getEncodedFlightDescriptionId() {
    return encodedFlightDescriptionId;
  }

  public String getFlightKeyAsString() {
    return KeyFactory.keyToString(flightId);
  }
}
```

In the given code, `flightId` represents the primary key of the `Flight` entity. The `persist` method of the `Flight` entity makes use of the `createKey` method of the `KeyFactory` class to create the primary key. The `createKey(parent, kind, name)` method accepts primary key information of the **parent** entity (`FlightDescription` is the parent in the case of `Flight` entity), the **kind** (which is similar to the concept of tables in relational databases), and the **name** of the key that uniquely identifies the entity within the *kind*. In the case of the `Flight` entity's primary key, the *kind* refers to the simple name of the entity class: `Flight.class.getSimpleName()` and the *name* of the key is the `flightName` property of the `Flight` entity. So, if you re-create a `Flight` entity with `flightName` as `FLT-100`, then it will overwrite the existing `Flight` (FLT-100) entity instance. GAE datastore doesn't support a composite primary key, but you can still achieve it by concatenating multiple entity field values in creating the *name* of the key.

The `encodedFlightDescriptionId` is the `String` form of the `FlightDescription` primary key who is the parent of `Flight` entity instance. The value of `encodedFlightDescriptionId` is set when the user selects the `FlightDescription` from the user interface for creating the Flight instance, as shown here:

The `<option>` element corresponding to the `FlightDescription` (NYC-DELHI-1200) entity instance is rendered as shown here:

```
<option value="<string value of Key>">NYC-DELHI for only 1200 USD</
option>
```

The `value` attribute specifies the `String` form of the `FlightDescription` primary key (which is of type `Key`). So, when the user clicks the **Create** button, the `String` value of `Key` is bound to the `encodedFlightDescriptionId` field of the `Flight` instance.

The `flightapp-gae-spring-mvc` project contains the `KeyEditor` property editor class that uses `KeyFactory` to perform conversion from `Key` to `String` format and vice versa. The property editor has been used instead of a Spring `ConversionService` implementation because the `ConversionService` implementation doesn't currently work with the `<options>` tag of the Spring `form` tag library.

Let's now look at how we can manage persisted data in GAE datastore using Admin Console.

Managing persisted data using Admin Console

You can view, edit, and delete data persisted by your application in GAE datastore by using Admin Console. Go to `http://appengine.google.com` and sign in to view the applications that you have created, as shown here:

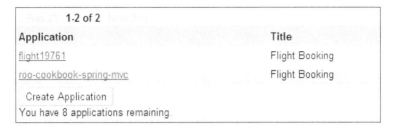

The given screenshot shows the two applications that I have created in GAE. The `roo-cookbook-spring-mvc` application corresponds to the application that we saw in this recipe. Selecting the application will show the Dashboard for the application where you can view different statistics related to your application. We are only interested in viewing the data that we saved in the datastore, so select the Datastore Viewer option from the Dashboard. The Datastore Viewer shows the entities that you saved in the datastore, as shown in the following screenshot:

The given screenshot shows the data for the `FlightDescription` *kind* that we created. You can use the **Query** tab to query the datastore using **GQL**. You can also delete or edit the entity instances. If you change *kind* to `Flight`, then the Admin Console will show the `Flight` entities that you have created, as shown here:

Flight Entities

1-4

ID/Name	VERSION	flightName
name=FLT-100	1	FLT-100
name=FLT-200	1	FLT-200
name=FLT-300	1	FLT-300
name=FLT-400	1	FLT-400

Delete

The given screenshot shows that the *name* set for the primary key of the `Flight` instance is displayed under the **ID/Name** column.

There's more...

If you are designing your entities for App Engine, it is important to note that within a transaction you can only operate on entities which belong to the same entity group. So, if you have `Student` and `Course` entities, which are in different entity groups, then you can't create or update them in a single transaction.

As of Spring Roo 1.1.3, you can only create *unowned* relationship between entities. For instance, if you execute the `field reference` or `field set` command to add a relationship field, then the `*_Roo_JavaBean.aj` AspectJ ITD file corresponding to the JPA entity removes the `@OneToMany` or `@OneToOne` or `@ManyToOne` or `@ManyToMany` annotation from the corresponding field in the JPA entity Java source file, resulting in an *unowned* relationship. The following code fragment shows how the AspectJ ITD file removes the relationship annotation from Java source file:

```
privileged aspect FlightDescription_Roo_JavaBean {

    declare @field: * FlightDescription.flights: -@OneToMany;

    . . .
}
```

The given code shows that if the `FlightDescription` and `Flight` entities were created using Spring Roo, then the `@OneToMany` annotation on the `flights` (which refers to a collection of `Flight` entities) field of `FlightDescription` will be removed by the `FlightDescription_Roo_JavaBean.aj` AspectJ ITD file. The minus sign (`-`) indicates that the `@OneToMany` annotation will be removed from the `FlightDescription.java` file.

See also

▸ Refer to the *Deploying a GWT application on GAE* recipe, to see an example of GWT application for App Engine

Adding search capability to your domain model with Solr

Apache `Solr` is an open-source search platform built on top of the Apache `Lucene` search engine library. Spring Roo's **Solr add-on** provides support for integrating the Roo-generated domain model with Solr platform. In this recipe, we'll look at how Roo makes use of SolrJ Java client library to add domain model data into Solr server for indexing and to search domain model data based on user supplied query parameters.

Getting ready

To see Roo's support for Solr in action, you need to download and run the Solr server, as described here:

1. Download the Solr server version 1.4.0 ZIP file from `Solr website` and unzip the bundle into a directory. Let's call the unzipped directory as `SOLR_HOME`.

2. Go to the `SOLR_HOME\example` directory and start Solr server:

   ```
   C:\...\apache-solr-1.4.0\example> java -jar start.jar
   ```

3. Open the web browser and verify that Solr server has successfully started by going to the following URL: `http://localhost:8983/solr/admin/`

Now, create a sub-directory `ch06-solr` inside `C:\roo-cookbook` directory, copy `ch06_web_app.roo` script and start Roo shell from `C:\roo-cookbook\ch06-solr`.

How to do it...

Follow these step to add search capability:

1. Execute the `ch06_solr.roo` script, as shown here:

   ```
   roo> script --file ch06_web_app.roo
   ```

The script creates a `flightapp-web` Roo project consisting of `Flight` and `FlightDescription` JPA entities.

2. Setup Solr for the `flightapp-web` project using the `solr setup` command:

```
.. roo> solr setup
```

```
Updated ROOT\pom.xml [Added dependency org.apache.solr:solr-solrj:1.4.0]
Created SRC_MAIN_RESOURCES\META-INF\spring\solr.properties
Updated SRC_MAIN_RESOURCES\META-INF\spring\applicationContext.xml
```

3. Make all JPA entities in the project searchable by executing the `solr all` command as shown here:

```
.. roo> solr all
```

```
Updated SRC_MAIN_JAVA\...\FlightDescription.java
Updated SRC_MAIN_JAVA\...\Flight.java
Created SRC_MAIN_JAVA\..\Flight_Roo_SolrSearch.aj
Created SRC_MAIN_JAVA\...\FlightDescription_Roo_SolrSearch.aj
```

4. Create a controller, which is responsible for searching Solr documents, as shown here:

```
.. roo> controller class --class ~.web.
FlightDescriptionSearchController --preferredMapping /
flightdescriptionsearch
```

```
Created SRC_MAIN_JAVA\...\FlightDescriptionSearchController
.java
Created SRC_MAIN_WEBAPP\WEB-INF\views\flightdescriptionsearch
Created SRC_MAIN_WEBAPP\WEB-INF\views\flightdescriptionsearch\
index.jspx
```

Copy `MySolrField.java` and `FlightDescriptionSearchController.java` files from the source code that accompanies this chapter to `sample.roo.flightapp.web` package. Also, replace `/WEB-INF/views/flightdescriptionsearch/index.jsp` with the `index.jsp` file from the source code that accompanies this chapter.

5. Execute the `perform eclipse` command so that you can import the `flightapp-web` project into your Eclipse IDE as shown here:

```
.. roo> perform eclipse
```

6. Exit the Roo shell and execute the `tomcat:run` goal of Maven Tomcat Plugin from `ch06-solr` directory to deploy the `flightapp-web` project in embedded Tomcat container as shown here:

   C:\roo-cookbook\ch06-solr> mvn tomcat:run

7. Open your web browser and go to `http://localhost:8080/flightapp-web`. If you see the following home page of the web application, it means that the `flightapp-web` project is successfully deployed on Tomcat:

   In the given screenshot, **Flight Description Search Controller View** menu option sends request to `FlightDescriptionSearchController` class, which in turn renders the `index.jsp` page located in `/WEB-INF/views/flightdescriptionsearch` folder.

8. At this time make sure that your Solr server is up and running. Now, select **Create new Flight Description** menu option to view the form for creating new `FlightDescription` entities in database, as shown here:

   The given screenshot shows that you need to enter information about the following fields: **Price**, **Origin** and **Destination**. Create two `FlightDescription` instances with the information shown in the following table:

Instance	Price	Origin	Destination
Instance-1	1200	NYC	DELHI
Instance-2	1400	MUMBAI	ATLANTA

9. When you create the `FlightDescription` entity instance, Roo's support for Solr adds the entity data into Solr for indexing and searching. Select the **Flight Description Search Controller View** menu option that searches the Solr server for documents that have a field named `flightdescription_solrsummary_t` and displays it in a tabular format, as shown here:

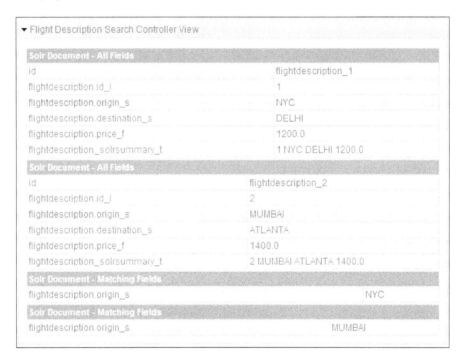

10. The given screenshot shows four tables: two of them are titled **Solr Document – All Fields** and the remaining two are titled **Solr Document – Matching Fields**. **Solr Document – All Fields** titled tables show all the fields of the Solr document that contained the field **flightdescription_solrsummary_t** and **Solr Document – Matching Fields** titled tables show only the `flightdescription.origin_s` field of the Solr document that contains `flightdescription_solrsummary_t` field.

We'll come back to these fields and look at how things work behind the scenes in the *How it works...* section.

How it works...

The integration between Solr search platform and Roo-generated domain model is achieved by:

- ▶ Configuring Solr for Roo project
- ▶ Defining methods to add domain model data to Solr index
- ▶ Defining methods for querying Solr search server

Let's now look at how Roo simplifies Solr integration.

Configuring Solr for Roo project

The `solr setup` command configures Solr for the Roo project. When `solr setup` command is executed, Roo takes the following actions:

- ▶ Adds dependency of project on SolrJ 1.4.0 in `pom.xml` file. SolrJ is used by JPA entities to add entity data to Solr index and for querying the Solr search server.

- ▶ Enables support for `@Async` annotated methods in the project by adding `<annotation-driven>` element of Spring's `task` namespace in `applicationContext.xml` file, as shown here:

```
<task:annotation-driven executor="asyncExecutor"
     mode="aspectj" />
```

  The `executor` attribute refers to an implementation of the `java.util.concurrent.Executor` interface, responsible for executing the `@Async` annotated method.

- ▶ Configures Spring's `ThreadPoolTaskExecutor` in `applicationContext.xml` using `<executor>` element of Spring's `task` namespace, as shown here:

```
<task:executor id="asyncExecutor"
    pool-size="${executor.poolSize}" />
```

  Spring's `ThreadPoolTaskExecutor` configures a `java.util.concurrent.ThreadPoolExecutor` instance (an implementation of `java.util.concurrent.Executor`) with the thread pool size specified by the `pool-size` attribute value. The `${executor.poolSize}` placeholder's value comes from the `solr.properties` file.

- ▶ Configures SolrJ's `CommonsHttpSolrServer` instance (a subclass of SolrJ's `SolrServer` abstract class) in the `applicationContext.xml` file to allow JPA entities to interact with the Solr search server over HTTP protocol:

```
<bean class="org.apache.solr.client.solrj.
  impl.CommonsHttpSolrServer" id="solrServer">
    <constructor-arg value="${solr.serverUrl}"/>
</bean>
```

Behind the scenes, `CommonsHttpSolrServer` makes use of `Apache Commons HttpClient` to interact with the Solr search server. The constructor of `CommonsHttpSolrServer` accepts URL of the Solr search server as an argument. The `<constructor-arg>` element specifies the value of the constructor argument as `${solr.serverUrl}`, which refers to the `solr.serverUrl` property defined in `solr.properties` file.

▸ Creates a `solr.properties` file in the `SRC_MAIN_RESOURCES\META-INF\spring\` directory. The properties file defines an `executor.poolSize` property, which specifies the thread pool size required by `ThreadPoolExecutor`, as shown here:

```
executor.poolSize=10
```

The `solr.properties` file also contains a `solr.serverUrl` property, which identifies the URL where the Solr search server is running, as shown here:

```
solr.serverUrl=http\://localhost\:8983/solr
```

If your Solr server is running on a different host or port, then change the URL in the `solr.properties` file or use the `searchServerUrl` argument of the `solr setup` command to specify the Solr search server URL.

Adding domain model data to Solr index and searching Solr documents

Imagine that you want to search for `FlightDescription` instances where the `origin` field is `NYC`. You can perform this search against the database in which you persist your `FlightDescription` entity instances or you can add the `FlightDescription` instance data into Solr index and search against it. We'll look at how Roo supports adding entity instance data to Solr index, and in the next section, we'll look at how to query that data in Solr search server.

Though there are multiple ways in which you can push data into Solr, Roo makes use of the SolrJ client library to interact with the Solr search server. When the `solr all` Roo command is executed, it adds certain methods (via AspectJ ITD) to JPA entity classes that are fired when an entity is added, removed, or updated. These methods are responsible for adding, updating, and deleting entity data from Solr index using SolrJ client library.

When `solr all` command is executed, the following actions are performed by Roo:

▸ Adds the `@RooSolrSearchable` annotation to JPA entity class that triggers creation of the corresponding `*_Roo_SolrSearch.aj` AspectJ ITD file.

The following code listing shows the `FlightDescription` JPA entity of `flightapp-web` project after `solr all` command was executed:

```
@RooEntity(identifierColumn = "FLIGHT_DESC_
ID", table = "FLIGHT_DESC_TBL", finders = {
"findFlightDescriptionsByDestinationAndOrigin" })
```

```
@RooSolrSearchable
public class FlightDescription {
  ...
}
```

The given code shows that `@RooSolrSearchable` annotation is added to `FlightDescription` entity. If you look at the `Flight` entity, you'll find that the `@RooSolrSearchable` annotation is also added to it.

▶ Creates a `*_Roo_SolrSearch.aj` AspectJ ITD file (corresponding to each JPA entity in the project. `*_Roo_SolrSearch.aj`) that introduces methods into JPA entity class for adding, updating, and removing entity from Solr index. Also, `*_Roo_SolrSearch.aj` defines methods for querying the Solr server using SolrJ client library.

Methods and attributes introduced by *_Roo_SolrSearch.aj AspectJ ITD

Let's now look at methods and attributes introduced by the `FlightDescription_Roo_SolrSearch.aj` file:

▶ `solrServer` attribute that refers to the `CommonsHttpSolrServer` bean configured in `applicationContext.xml` file is shown as follows:

```
@Autowired
transient SolrServer FlightDescription.solrServer;
```

▶ `solrServer()`: A *static* method that returns the `solrServer` attribute introduced by the ITD file is shown as follows:

```
public static final SolrServer FlightDescription.solrServer() {
  SolrServer _solrServer = new FlightDescription().solrServer;
  ..
  return _solrServer;
}
```

▶ `indexFlightDescriptions`: A *static* method that adds a collection of `FlightDescription` entity instances to the Solr index is shown as follows:

```
import org.springframework.scheduling.annotation.Async;
...
...
@Async
public static void
    FlightDescription.indexFlightDescriptions
      (Collection<FlightDescription> flightdescriptions) {
    java.util.List<SolrInputDocument> documents =
        new java.util.ArrayList<SolrInputDocument>();

    for (FlightDescription flightdescription :
        flightdescriptions) {
```

```
        SolrInputDocument sid = new SolrInputDocument();
        sid.addField("id", "flightdescription_" +
            flightdescription.getId());
        sid.addField("flightdescription.id_l",
            flightdescription.getId());
        sid.addField("flightdescription.origin_s",
            flightdescription.getOrigin());
        ...
        sid.addField("flightdescription.price_f",
            flightdescription.getPrice());
        sid.addField("flightdescription_solrsummary_t", ...);
        documents.add(sid);
    }
    try {
      SolrServer solrServer = solrServer();
      solrServer.add(documents);
      solrServer.commit();
    } catch (Exception e) {
        e.printStackTrace();
    }
}
```

The given code shows that the `indexFlightDescriptions` method is annotated with Spring's `@Async` annotation, which means that it is invoked *asynchronously*. The method iterates over all the `FlightDescription` instances (passed as method argument) and creates a list of `SolrInputDocument`. The SolrJ's `SolrInputDocument` class represents a document that you want to feed to Solr server for indexing. The `addField` method of `SolrInputDocument` identifies the field that you want to add to the document.

The field name that is added by Roo to the `SolrInputDocument` has the following naming convention:

```
<entity-simple-name>.<field-name>_<field-type>
```

Here, `entity-simple-name` is the simple name of JPA entity, `field-name` is the name of the field, and `field-type` is the type of the field. So, the `orgin` field is added to `SolrInputDocument` with the name `flightdescription.origin_s` and `price` field is added with the name `flightdescription.price_f`.

If the JPA entity field type isn't `Integer`, `String`, `Long`, `Boolean`, `Float`, `Double`, or `Date`, then the field name with which the JPA entity field is added to `SolrInputDocument` is shown as follows:

```
<entity-simple-name>.<field-name>_t
```

For instance, the `Flight` class in `flightapp-web` project contains the `flightDescription` relationship field of type `FlightDescription`, which is added to `SolrInputDocument` with name `flight.flightdescription_t` (refer to the `Flight_Roo_SolrSearch.aj` AspectJ ITD file).

You might be wondering, why Roo doesn't add JPA entity fields with their exact name in the `SolrInputDocument`. Here is a short description of how Solr works:

`SolrInputDocument` represents a document that you add to Solr search server. The document consists of fields and you need to tell Solr search server, which of these fields should be **indexed**. It is important to note that if a field is *not* indexed, then you can't search or sort documents based on that field. You tell the Solr search server, which fields of a document should be indexed by specifying the fields in `schema.xml` file located in `SOLR_HOME\example\solr\conf` directory. Solr has the concept of *Dynamic Fields*, wherein if a field follows a standard naming convention, then it is automatically indexed by Solr search server. The following XML fragment from the `schema.xml` file defines the dynamic fields that will be automatically indexed by Solr:

```
<dynamicField name="*_s"   type="string"   indexed="true"
   stored="true"/>
<dynamicField name="*_l"   type="slong"    indexed="true"
   stored="true"/>
<dynamicField name="*_t"   type="text"     indexed="true"
   stored="true"/>
<dynamicField name="*_f"   type="sfloat"   indexed="true"
   stored="true"/>
```

The given XML fragment instructs Solr to index any field that matches the pattern `*_s`, `*_l`, `*_t`, or `*_f`. So, now you can see the link between Roo generated field names and the dynamic fields defined by Solr.

The `indexFlightDescriptions` method also adds an id field name to the `SolrInputDocument`. It is *mandatory* for any `SolrInputDocument` to contain a field named id, which *uniquely* identifies the document in Solr index. By default, Roo sets the value of id field to `"flightdescription_" + flightdescription.getId()`. We'll see later in this section that this id field value is used for deleting the document from Solr index.

The `indexFlightDescriptions` method also adds an extra field, `flightdescription_solrsummary_t`, in `SolrInputDocument` so that it can be used to search all documents that have been indexed by Solr for `FlightDescription` JPA entity. Similarly, the `indexFlightDescriptions` method of `Flight_Roo_SolrSearch.aj` AspectJ ITD adds `flight_solrsummary_t` field in `SolrInputDocument` to allow searching for documents indexed by Solr for the `Flight` JPA entity.

The following code in the `indexFlightDescriptions` method adds the `SolrInputDocuments` to Solr index:

```
SolrServer solrServer = solrServer();
solrServer.add(documents);
solrServer.commit();
```

- ▸ `indexFlightDescription`: A *static* method, which adds a `FlightDescription` entity instance to Solr index, which is shown as follows:

```
public static void
  FlightDescription.indexFlightDescription(FlightDescription
    flightdescription) {
    List<FlightDescription> flightdescriptions =
      new ArrayList<FlightDescription>();
    flightdescriptions.add(flightdescription);
    indexFlightDescriptions(flightdescriptions);
}
```

As the given code shows, `indexFlightDescription` method delegates the responsibility of adding `FlightDescription` instance to Solr index to `indexFlightDescriptions` method.

- ▸ `deleteIndex`: A *static* method, which deletes a Solr document corresponding to a `FlightDescription` JPA entity instance is shown as follows:

```
@Async
public static void
  FlightDescription.deleteIndex(FlightDescription
    flightdescription) {
    SolrServer solrServer = solrServer();
    try {
  solrServer.deleteById("flightdescription_" +
    flightdescription.getId());
      solrServer.commit();
    } catch (Exception e) {
      e.printStackTrace();
    }
}
```

In the given code, the `deleteById` method of `SolrServer` deletes the document (from Solr index), which has the `id` attribute value `"flightdescription_"` + `flightdescription.getId()`. The Spring's `@Async` annotation means that the `deleteIndex` method is invoked asynchronously.

- postPersistOrUpdate method, which is invoked when the FlightDescription JPA entity instance is persisted or updated in the database. This method is responsible for adding or updating the Solr index with the modified JPA entity instance data, as shown here:

```
import javax.persistence.PostPersist;
import javax.persistence.PostUpdate;
...
...
@PostUpdate
@PostPersist
private void FlightDescription.postPersistOrUpdate() {
    indexFlightDescription(this);
}
```

The @PostUpdate and @PostPersist JPA annotations indicate that postPersistOrUpdate method is invoked when FlightDescription JPA entity is updated or persisted in the database. The call to indexFlightDescription method suggests that the entity data is updated or added to the Solr index.

- preRemove method, which removes the entity data from Solr index by calling the deleteIndex method:

```
import javax.persistence.PreRemove;
...
...
@PreRemove
private void FlightDescription.preRemove() {
  deleteIndex(this);
}
```

The @PreRemove JPA annotation means that the preRemove method is invoked before the JPA entity instance is removed from the database.

- search(SolrQuery query) method, which allows searching Solr documents that match the search query:

```
public static QueryResponse FlightDescription.search(SolrQuery
query) {
    try {
        return solrServer().query(query);
    } catch (Exception e) {
        e.printStackTrace();
    }
    return new QueryResponse();
}
```

SolrQuery represents a query object, which contains the field information based on which the search has to be performed, the fields to return, and so on. The query method of SolrServer sends the search request to Solr search server using Apache Commons HttpClient and returns a QueryResponse object from which you can extract the Solr documents that matched the search query.

▸ search (String) method that *only* returns Solr document(s) corresponding to FlightDescription entity in Solr search server:

```
public static QueryResponse
   FlightDescription.search(String queryString) {
 String searchString =
   "FlightDescription_solrsummary_t:" + queryString;
    return search(new SolrQuery(searchString.toLowerCase()));
}
```

In the given code, the SolrQuery object is created using the searchString. The searchString specifies the Solr query used for finding matching Solr documents. As searchString already contains the constant value "FlightDescription_solrsummary_t:", which means that you can only search for Solr documents that contain "FlightDescription_solrsummary_t" field. If you remember from the earlier discussion, the "FlightDescription_solrsummary_t" field is only available in Solr documents which have been added corresponding to the FlightDescription entity.

Let's now look at how the FlightDescriptionSearchController controller makes use of search methods defined in the FlightDescription JPA entity to search documents indexed by Solr search server.

Searching Solr documents

FlightDescriptionSearchController defines methods which search for Solr documents corresponding to the FlightDescription entity. The following code listing shows FlightDescriptionSearchController class:

```
@Controller
public class FlightDescriptionSearchController {

  private List<List<MySolrField>> getAllFields() {
    QueryResponse response = FlightDescription.search("*");
    SolrDocumentList documentList = response.getResults();
    return getSolrDocumentFieldList(documentList);
  }

  private List<List<MySolrField>> getMatchingFields() {
    SolrQuery solrQuery = new SolrQuery().
      setQuery("flightdescription_solrsummary_t:*").
```

```
        setParam("fl", "flightdescription.origin_s");
      QueryResponse response =
        FlightDescription.search(solrQuery);
        SolrDocumentList documentList = response.getResults();
        return getSolrDocumentFieldList(documentList);
    }

    private List<List<MySolrField>>
      getSolrDocumentFieldList(SolrDocumentList list) {
        List<List<MySolrField>> matchingDocList
          = new  ArrayList<List<MySolrField>>();
        ...
        return matchingDocList;
      }
  }
```

The `getAllFields` method invokes `search(String queryString)` method of `FlightDescription` entity and passes * as the method argument. As we saw earlier, the `search(String queryString)` method of `FlightDescription` will create the following query: `"FlightDescription_solrsummary_t:*"`, which means search for all Solr documents, which contain `"FlightDescription_solrsummary_t"` field. This query will return all the Solr documents corresponding to `FlightDescription` entity that we added to Solr index.

The `getMatchingFields` method invokes the `search(SolrQuery query)` method passing the `SolrQuery` object, which queries for all Solr documents corresponding to `FlightDescription` JPA entity but specifies that the query result should only contain the `flightdescription.origin_s` field. The `setQuery` parameter of SolrQuery specifies the query and `setParam` specifies that only `flightdescription.origin_s` field should be returned in the result.

The `getResults` method of the `QueryResponse` object returns `SolrDocumentList` representing the list of matching Solr documents returned by the query.

The `getSolrDocumentFieldList` method takes `SolrDocumentList` as the argument and extracts `SolrDocument` instances from it. The method then extracts field names and their values from each `SolrDocument` instance to create a `List<List<MySolrField>>`. The `MySolrField` represents a custom class that we created in `flightapp-web` project to represent a single field-value pair in `SolrDocument`.

The `/WEB-INF/views/flightdescriptionsearch/index.jsp` JSP page displays data returned by `getFields` and `getMatchingFields` methods. This is the reason why selecting **Flight Description Search Controller View** menu option shows two different types of tables. One table type shows all the Solr document fields and the other table type only shows the `flightdescription.origin_s` field.

There's more...

Solr index is updated in @PreRemove, @PostPersist, and the @PostUpdate annotated method. So, what if the transaction fails to commit but the entity data is stored as Solr document in Solr search server? You need to take care of maintaining the integrity yourself, because Roo doesn't help you there.

Let's now look at the attributes that @RooSolrSearchable defines to customize names of Roo-generated methods in *_Roo_SolrSearch.aj AspectJ ITD.

Customizing Roo-generated *_Roo_SolrSearch.aj AspectJ ITD

The following table describes the attributes of @RooSolrSearchable annotation:

Attribute	Description
deleteIndexMethod	Specifies a custom name for the deleteIndex method. Value blank " " instructs Roo not to generate deleteIndex method.
indexMethod	Specifies a custom name for the index methods. Value blank " " instructs Roo not to generate index methods.
postPersistOrUpdateMethod	Specifies a custom name for the postPersistOrUpdate methods. Value blank " " instructs Roo not to generate postPersistOrUpdate methods.
preRemoveMethod	Specifies a custom name for the preRemove method. Value blank " " instructs Roo not to generate preRemove method.
searchMethod	Specifies a custom name for the search method, which accepts SolrQuery as argument. Value blank " " instructs Roo not to generate search method, which accepts SolrQuery argument.
simpleSearchMethod	Specifies a custom name for the search method, which accepts String as argument. Value blank " " instructs Roo not to generate search method, which accepts String argument.

7
Developing Add-ons and Removing Roo from Projects

In this chapter, we will cover:

- ▶ Setting up GnuPG for add-on development
- ▶ Installing an installable add-on
- ▶ Developing a simple add-on
- ▶ Developing an advanced add-on
- ▶ Converting non-OSGi JDBC drivers into OSGi-compliant bundles
- ▶ Removing Roo with push-in refactoring
- ▶ Adding Roo to a project using pull-out refactoring
- ▶ Upgrading to the latest version of Roo

Introduction

In previous chapters, we saw that executing a Roo command kicks-off code generation logic in Roo add-ons. You may want to create a custom add-on for functionality that is not yet supported by base or installable add-ons. For instance, currently there is no Roo add-on that provides support for creating Java portlets using the Spring Portlet MVC. So, we can develop a Roo add-on which is responsible for scaffolding Spring Portlet MVC controllers and JSPs from JPA entities.

In this chapter, we'll look at recipes which show how Roo simplifies installing, developing, and publishing add-ons. Also, we'll take a broad look at the Roo architecture and Roo commands which you'll find useful while developing and testing add-ons.

Setting up GnuPG for add-on development

Roo makes use of GnuPG (http://www.gnupg.org/) to sign add-ons. Signing of add-ons ensures that Roo users download and install only trusted add-ons. The add-on creator module of Roo signs the add-on with his secret PGP key and publishes the public PGP key to a public key server. A Roo user needs to tell Roo explicitly that it trusts an add-on by adding a public PGP key to Roo's key store. This allows Roo to download and install the add-on. If the public PGP key is not added to Roo's key store, the add-on will not be downloaded and installed.

In this recipe, we'll look at how to install GnuPG, create a key-pair (consisting of secret and public keys), and publish the public key to a public key server.

Getting ready

If you are using Windows or UNIX, download and install GnuPG from the following location: http://www.gnupg.org/download/. If you are using Mac, download and install GnuPG for Mac from the following location: http://macgpg.sourceforge.net/.

Installing GnuPG on Windows will create the following installation directory: C:\Program Files\GNU\GnuPG.

How to do it...

The following steps will demonstrate how to set up GnuPG:

1. Open the command prompt and execute the following GnuPG list-secret-keys command to view secret PGP keys that you may have created earlier:

    ```
    C:\Users\Ashish>gpg --list-secret-keys

    gpg: keyring 'C:/Users/Ashish/AppData/Roaming/gnupg\secring.gpg'
    created
    ```

    The output shows that a secring.gpg file is created if it is not found. The secring.gpg file contains key information.

2. Create a new key-pair consisting of a secret PGP key and public PGP key using GnuPG's gen-key command, as shown here:

    ```
    C:\Users\Ashish>gpg --gen-key

    ...

    Please select what kind of key you want:
    ```

```
(1)  RSA and RSA (default)

(2)  DSA and Elgamal

(3)  DSA (sign only)

(4)  RSA (sign only)

Your selection? 1

...
```

Executing the `gen-key` command asks multiple questions, such as for the e-mail ID, real name, kind and length of key, and so on. When asked to `select what kind of key you want`, choose either option 1 (`RSA and RSA (default)`) or 2 (`DSA and Elgamal`), as the key can be used for both encryption and decryption. In the end, you'll be asked to provide a passphrase to protect your secret PGP key. Remember the passphrase, as you'll need to provide it when building your custom add-ons.

3. To verify that the key-pair has been successfully created, execute GnuPG's `list-secret-keys` command:

```
C:\Users\Ashish>gpg --list-secret-keys


C:/Users/Ashish/AppData/Roaming/gnupg\secring.gpg
--------------------------------------------------
sec    2048R/BFB28A4D 2011-04-30

uid                     Ashish Sarin (This is my key)
<ashish.k.sarin@gmail.com>
ssb    2048R/9FCAFB76 2011-04-30
```

If you see the previous output, it means your key-pair has been successfully generated. The `sec` key ID is `BFB28A4D`, which represents the key ID of your public PGP key which you need to publish to a public key server.

4. Now, publish the public key using GnuPG's `send-keys` command, as shown here:

```
gpg --send-keys --keyserver hkp://pgp.mit.edu <public-key-id>
```

Here, `<public-key-id>` is the `sec` key ID that was listed when you executed the `list-secret-keys` command. In my case, `<public-key-id>` is `BFB28A4D`.

How it works...

We saw that GnuPG is used to create a key-pair and publish the public PGP key to a public key server. As most public key servers share keys, you don't need to send keys to all public key servers.

> ▸ Refer to the *Installing an installable* add-on recipe to see how to install add-ons

> ▸ Refer to the *Developing a simple add-on* recipe to see how Spring Roo signs custom add-ons using your secret key

Installing an installable add-on

An add-on that is not part of the Spring Roo distribution is referred to as an installable add-on. So, any add-on that is not a base add-on is an installable add-on. In this recipe, we'll look at how to install an installable add-on and the challenges that you'll face in doing so.

Getting ready

Refer to the *Setting up GnuPG for add-on development* recipe to set up GnuPG on your system.

Create a new directory `C:\roo-cookbook\ch07-service` in your system and start the Roo shell from the `ch07-service` directory.

Executing the `ch07_jpa_setup.roo` script creates a `flight-app` Roo project, sets up Hibernate as a persistence provider, and configures MySQL as the database for the application. If you are using a different database than MySQL or your connection settings are different from what is specified in the script, then modify the script accordingly.

How to do it...

The following steps will demonstrate how to install an installable add-on:

1. Enter the following command in the Roo shell and press *Tab*:

    ```
    roo> addon install bundle --bundleSymbolicName
    ```

    ```
    Display all 308 possibilities? (y or n)
    ```

    Roo asks if it should display the symbolic names of all the available add-ons. Press the *Y* key to instruct Roo to list all the add-ons. You'll find that in the list there are a couple of `gvNIX` (`https://code.google.com/p/gvnix/`) Roo add-ons that have bundle symbolic names starting with "org.gvnix.". For the purpose of this recipe we'll install the gvNIX Service Management add-on whose bundle symbolic name is `org.gvnix.service.roo.addon`. Using the Service Management add-on you can quickly create a service layer of your enterprise application.

2. Now, install gvNIX using the `addon install bundle` command, as shown here:

```
roo> addon install bundle --bundleSymbolicName org.gvnix.service.
roo.addon

...

Downloaded 100% of org.gvnix.service.roo.addon-0.6.0.jar.asc


Download URL 'http://gvnix.googlecode.com/svn/repo/org/gvnix/
org.gvnix.service.roo.addon/0.6.0/org.gvnix.service.roo.addon-
0.6.0.jar' failed


This resource was signed with PGP key ID '0xC5FC814B', which is
not currently trusted
```

The output shows that gvNIX Service Management Roo add-on couldn't be downloaded and installed because it was signed with PGP key ID `0xC5FC814B`, which is not trusted by your Spring Roo installation.

3. Add the PGP key ID `0xC5FC814B` to Roo's key store using the `pgp trust` Roo command, as shown here:

```
roo> pgp trust --keyId 0xC5FC814B
```

4. Now that we have informed Spring Roo to trust the PGP key ID with which the gvNIX Service Management Roo add-on was signed, you can now install the gvNIX Service Management Roo add-on using the `addon install bundle` command, as shown here:

```
roo> addon install bundle --bundleSymbolicName org.gvnix.service.
roo.addon


Target resource(s):
-------------------

   gvNIX - Spring Roo - Addon - Services Management (0.6.0)


Deploying...done.


Successfully installed add-on: gvNIX - Spring Roo - Addon -
Services Management [version: 0.6.0]
```

The output shows that the gvNIX Service Management add-on was successfully installed by Spring Roo and the commands exposed by the gvNIX Service Management add-on are available to the Roo shell. For instance, you'll now find that the following Roo commands are now available to the Roo shell: `service class`, `service import ws`, and `service operation`.

How it works...

The list of add-ons comes from the RooBot's index file. RooBot is a VMWare-hosted service that indexes publicly available OBR (OSGi Bundle Repository) files. An OBR represents a repository of add-ons and an OBR file is an XML file (typically named `repository.xml`), which contains the information about add-ons and the URLs where they are published. Note that an OBR repository need not physically host add-ons, and may only provide an OBR file which contains details of add-ons and the URL at which they are published. A developer provides an OBR file for the Roo add-on that he/she publishes at his/her website. The OBR file is indexed by RooBot, and RooBot ensures that the URL used to download an add-on uses the `httppgp://` (instead of `http://`) URL for signature verification.

Every time you start the Roo shell by executing the `Roo` batch file, the RooBot's index file is downloaded by Spring Roo so that you can search and install add-ons. It is important to note that RooBot does not physically host add-ons. When you execute `addon search` or `addon list command`, Spring Roo refers to RooBot's index file to perform search and listing of available add-ons.

When you attempt to install a Roo add-on using the `addon install bundle` or `addon install id` command, the `httppgp://` URL of the add-on in RooBot's index file is used to download and install the add-on. The use of the `httppgp://` URL requires Spring Roo to first download the PGP signature file (a `.asc` file) and URL of the add-on, and verify that your Spring Roo installation trusts the PGP key ID used to sign the signature file. If your Spring Roo installation doesn't trust the PGP key ID, it will not attempt to download the add-on.

In our recipe, when we first attempted to download gvNIX Service Management Roo add-on, it resulted in an error because the PGP signature file was signed using a PGP key ID which the Spring Roo installation didn't trust. So, we used the `pgp trust` Roo command to add the PGP key ID to Spring Roo's key store and re-attempted to download the gvNIX Service Management Roo add-on. Spring Roo stores trusted keys in the `.spring_roo_pgp.bpg` file in the user's home directory.

There's more...

It is important to note that the `addon` commands (`addon info bundle`, `addon info id`, `addon install bundle`, `addon install id`, `addon list`, `addon search`, `addon upgrade`) work only with add-ons registered with the RooBot index file. For instance, you cannot search for or install a Roo add-on which is not listed with the RooBot index file.

Trusting add-ons by default

If you want to download add-ons without having to add a PGP key ID to Roo's key store, you can do so by executing the `pgp automatic trust` Roo command, as shown here:

```
roo> pgp automatic trust
```

Executing the `pgp automatic trust` command instructs Roo not to verify that the downloaded PGP signature file of the add-on is signed by a trusted PGP key ID. It is important to note that enabling the automatic PGP key trusting feature of Roo can be unsafe.

If you want to turn off the automatic PGP key trusting feature, then simply re-execute the `pgp automatic trust` command.

Installing add-ons not indexed by RooBot

There could be scenarios in which a Roo add-on is not registered with RooBot but you still want to install and use it. If a Roo add-on is meant for internal use within an organization, then you won't publish it to RooBot or you may want to test an add-on thoroughly before registering it with RooBot. In such scenarios, you need to add the OBR URL of the add-on repository to your Roo installation using the `osgi obr url add` command, followed by executing the `osgi obr start` command to download and install the add-on.

Let's look at an example scenario in which you make use of `osgi obr url add` and `osgi obr start` commands to download and install Roo add-ons.

The gvNIX (`https://code.google.com/p/gvnix/`) Google Code project provides multiple Roo add-ons, which deal with Service Management (as discussed earlier), reporting, theming, and so on. Even though gvNIX add-ons are published in RooBot, we can directly download and install them using `osgi obr url add` and `osgi obr start` commands.

To add OBR URL of repository hosting add-ons, you need to locate the OBR XML file that contains a list of add-ons and the URLs where these add-ons are published. In the case of the gvNIX Google Code project, the OBR file name is `repository.xml` and is located in the `repo` directory of the project.

You can carry out the following steps to add an OBR file URL of the gvNIX project to your Roo installation:

- ▶ View the `repository.xml` file by going to the gvNIX Google Code project and selecting the **Source | Browse** option. As we need to add the URL of this `repository.xml` file to the Roo installation using the `osgi obr url add` command, go to the **Source | Browse** option of the gvNIX project on Google Code and open the `repository.xml` file inside `repo` directory.

Google Code presents the content of the `repository.xml` file in HTML format, and the URL that you now see in the browser is not the URL location of the `repository.xml` file.

▶ To get to the real location of `repository.xml` file, select **View raw file** link that shows up in the menu on the right-side of the HTML page. The URL that you'll now see in the browser is `http://gvnix.googlecode.com/svn/repo/repository.xml`.

▶ Now, add the URL to the `repository.xml` file to Roo installation, as shown here:

roo> osgi obr url add --url http://gvnix.googlecode.com/svn/repo/repository.xml

As described here, you can add multiple OBR file URLs to your Roo installation. Once you have added the OBR file URL, you can download and install a Roo add-on defined in the OBR file. For instance, we can now install add-ons listed in the `repository.xml` file of the gvNIX project, as shown here for the Web Report add-on of the gvNIX project:

```
roo> osgi obr start --bundleSymbolicName org.gvnix.web.report.roo.addon
Target resource(s):
-------------------

   gvNIX - Spring Roo - Addon - Web Report (0.6.0)
Deploying...done.
```

As the `osgi obr start` command downloads add-ons using URLs defined in the OBR file, it may be possible that the download URL in OBR file uses `http://` and not `httppgp://`. This could be unsafe, as Spring Roo PGP signature verification is not required when using a `http://` URL for downloading add-ons.

See also

▶ Refer to the *Developing a simple add-on* recipe to see how you can directly install an add-on JAR file

Developing a simple add-on

Roo provides an add-on creator add-on which simplifies developing custom add-ons. You can either create a simple or an advanced add-on using the commands exposed by the add-on creator.

A simple add-on is meant to add project dependencies in the `pom.xml` file or to add configuration artifacts to the project. For instance, in *Chapter 4, Web Application Development with Spring Web MVC* we saw that Roo installs JSP custom tags when scaffolding a Spring Web MVC application. Instead of using Roo-installed JSP custom tags, you can create a simple Roo add-on which replaces Roo-installed JSP custom tags with the tags that you have tailored based on your application requirements.

An advanced add-on, on the other hand, is required in scenarios in which you want to create new Java classes, interfaces, and AspectJ ITD files. For instance, a Portlet add-on will scaffold controllers and JSPs from JPA entities.

In this recipe, we'll look at the `addon create simple` command, which creates a simple Roo add-on that replaces some of the tags installed by Roo for a Spring MVC application with custom tags. We'll also see how we can use the newly created add-on in a Roo project.

As mentioned in *Chapter 1, Getting Started with Spring Roo*, Roo is built on top of the Apache Felix OSGi container and Roo add-ons represent OSGi bundles. As we go through Roo add-on development recipes in this chapter, we'll touch upon some of the OSGi concepts you need to know to understand how add-ons work.

Getting ready

Create a new directory `C:\roo-cookbook\ch07-simple-add-on` in your system and start the Roo shell from the `ch07-simple-add-on` directory.

How to do it...

The following steps will demonstrate how to develop a simple add-on:

1. Execute the `addon create simple` command, as shown here, to create a `com.roo.addon.mysimple` add-on project:

```
roo> addon create simple --topLevelPackage com.roo.addon.mysimple
--description "Mysimple addon" --projectName "Mysimple addon"
Created ROOT\pom.xml
Created ROOT\readme.txt
Created ROOT\legal
Created ROOT\legal\LICENSE.TXT

Created SRC_MAIN_JAVA\...\MysimpleCommands.java
Created SRC_MAIN_JAVA\com\...\MysimpleOperations.java
Created SRC_MAIN_JAVA\...\MysimpleOperationsImpl.java
Created SRC_MAIN_JAVA\...\MysimplePropertyName.java
Created ROOT\src\main\assembly\assembly.xml
```

```
Created SRC_MAIN_RESOURCES\com\roo\addon\mysimple\info.tagx

Created SRC_MAIN_RESOURCES\com\roo\addon\mysimple\show.tagx
```

2. Execute the `perform eclipse` command to create Eclipse IDE-specific configuration files:

```
roo> perform eclipse
```

3. Now, import the `com.roo.addon.mysimple` Eclipse project into the Eclipse IDE.

How it works...

The `addon create simple` command creates a Roo add-on, which contributes commands to the Roo shell and defines operations which are invoked in response to the execution of these commands. The `package` argument specifies the top-level package of the add-on and is also used as the name of the add-on project. The following classes and interfaces are generated by the `addon create simple` command, and the `<last-part-of-top-level-package>` refers to the text after the last index of '.' in the value of `topLevelPackage` argument. In the case of our example, the `topLevelPackage` argument value is `com.roo.addon.mysimple`, which makes value of `<last-part-of-top-level-package>` as `mysimple`:

- `<last-part-of-top-level-package>` Commands.java class: defines methods that are contributed to the Roo shell by the add-on

- `<last-part-of-top-level-package>` Operations.java interface: defines methods that contains the majority of processing logic corresponding to Roo commands

- `<last-part-of-top-level-package>` OperationsImpl.java class: implements the *Operations.java interface

- `<last-part-of-top-level-package>` PropertyName.java enum type: defines the possible values for an argument passed to a Roo command

The add-on generated via the `addon create simple` command gives you the starting point for custom add-on development. The generated add-on doesn't do much, except show the classes and interfaces that you'll typically create in an add-on. You'll need to modify the generated add-on to perform functions specific to your requirements.

Let's begin with looking at the Java classes and interfaces (created by `addon create simple` command) which define commands and operations for the `com.roo.addon.mysimple` add-on.

MysimpleCommands class

The following code listing shows the `MysimpleCommands` class, which defines the commands that the add-on contributes to the Roo shell:

```java
import java.util.logging.Logger;
import org.apache.felix.scr.annotations.Component;
import org.apache.felix.scr.annotations.Reference;
import org.apache.felix.scr.annotations.Service;
import org.springframework.roo.shell.converters.StaticFieldConverter;

@Component
@Service
public class MysimpleCommands implements CommandMarker {

  private Logger log = Logger.getLogger(getClass().getName());

  @Reference private MysimpleOperations operations;

  @Reference private StaticFieldConverter
     staticFieldConverter;

  protected void activate(ComponentContext context) {
    staticFieldConverter.add(MysimplePropertyName.class);
  }

  protected void deactivate(ComponentContext context) {
    staticFieldConverter.remove(MysimplePropertyName.class);
  }
  ...
}
```

The following are some of the important points to note about the `MysimpleCommands` class:

> ▶ `MysimpleCommands` class defines the Roo commands that the mysimple add-on contributes to the Roo shell via `@CliCommand` annotated methods. We'll discuss commands contributed by a mysimple add-on later in this section. When a Roo command is executed from the shell, it results in execution of the corresponding `@CliCommand` annotated method in the `MysimpleCommands` class.

- ▶ MysimpleCommands class is annotated with @Component and @Service Apache Felix annotations. @Component and @Service annotations have source-level retention and are used by Apache Felix Maven SCR Plugin (http://felix.apache.org/site/apache-felix-maven-scr-plugin.html) to generate XML configuration required by OSGi's Service Component Runtime (SCR) - responsible for managing the lifecycle of the MysimpleCommands component and registering it as a service with OSGi service registry. Annotating MysimpleCommands with @Component and @Service annotations ensures that you can access MysimpleCommands object (using @Reference Apache Felix annotation) from other Roo add-ons, if required.

- ▶ MysimpleCommands class implements Roo's CommandMarker interface. CommandMarker is a marker interface, that is, it doesn't declare any methods. Roo looks for components implementing CommandMarker interface to identify components that contribute commands to the Roo shell.

- ▶ @Reference annotation of Apache Felix is like @Autowired annotation of Spring, and is used to resolve service dependencies of a component. MysimpleOperations and StaticFieldConverter are service dependencies of the MysimpleCommands component. MysimpleOperations and StaticFieldConverter services are accessible to MysimpleCommands via the @Reference annotation because the classes implementing MysimpleOperations and StaticFieldConverter interfaces are also annotated with @Service and @Component annotations—making them accessible to other Roo add-ons.

- ▶ MysimpleOperations defines methods that implement the major part of the functionality performed by Roo commands contributed by the add-on. These methods are invoked by the methods defined in the MysimpleCommands class.

- ▶ StaticFieldConverter represents a Spring Converter that provides type-safety for the argument values that are passed from the Roo shell to the corresponding @CliCommand annotated methods in the MysimpleCommands class.

- ▶ As Roo add-ons are deployed as OSGi bundles on the underlying Apache Felix OSGi container, the activate and deactivate methods represent lifecycle methods that are called by the OSGi container to activate and deactivate the Roo add-on, respectively. In the case of the mysimple add-on, the activate method adds MysimplePropertyName enum type to the StaticFieldConverter implementation. In the deactivate method, the mysimple add-on removes the MysimplePropertyName enum type from the StaticFieldConverter implementation.

- ▶ Now that we see the big picture about the role played by the MysimpleCommands class in mysimple add-on, let's look at the methods in the MysimpleCommands class that register commands with the Roo shell and process these Roo commands when they are executed from the Roo shell.

Defining Roo commands

The following code listing shows the methods of the `MysimpleCommands` class that define Roo commands exposed by the mysimple add-on:

```
import org.springframework.roo.shell.CliCommand;
import org.springframework.roo.shell.CliOption;
...


@Reference private MysimpleOperations operations;

@CliCommand(value = "say hello",
  help = "Prints welcome message to the Roo shell")
public void sayHello(
    @CliOption(key = "name", mandatory = true,
      help = "State your name") String name,
    @CliOption(key = "countryOfOrigin", mandatory = false,
      help = "Country of orgin") MysimplePropertyName country) {

    log.info("Welcome " + name + "!");
    ...
}

@CliCommand(value = "web mvc install tags",
  help="Replace default Roo MVC tags used for scaffolding")
public void installTags() {
    .installTags();
}
```

In the preceding code, we can see that:

- The `@Reference` annotation performs autowiring by type and binds the reference to the service that implements the `MysimpleOperations` interface. As `MysimpleOperationsImpl` implements the `MysimpleOperations` interface, reference to the `MysimpleOperationsImpl` object is injected into the `MysimpleCommands` instance.

▸ @CliCommand is a method-level Roo annotation which identifies methods which contribute commands to the Roo shell. The value attribute specifies the name of the command that is contributed by the add-on to the Roo shell. For instance, the mysimple add-on contributes say hello and web mvc install tags commands to the Roo shell. The help attribute specifies the help text that is displayed against the command when you execute the help Roo command. When a Roo command is executed from the Roo shell, the corresponding @CliCommand annotated method is executed by Roo. For instance, if you execute the say hello command from the Roo shell, Roo executes the sayHello method of the MysimpleCommands class, which prints a welcome message on the Roo shell using Java Logging API. Similarly, if you execute the web mvc install tags command, Roo executes the installTags method of the MysimpleCommands class. The installTags method invokes the installTags method of the MysimpleOperationsImpl class, which copies info.tagx and show.tagx tag files into your Roo project. Later in this recipe we'll look in detail at the installTags method of the MysimpleOperationsImpl class.

▸ The @CliOption method-parameter-level Roo annotation specifies the arguments that a Roo command accepts. The key attribute specifies the name of the command argument, the mandatory attribute specifies if the argument is mandatory or optional, and the help attribute specifies the help text associated with the argument. For instance, the say hello command accepts two arguments—name and countryOfOrigin. The name argument is mandatory and countryOfOrigin is optional.

The Java type of an argument can be a simple String or it could be a complex type. In the case of the say hello command, the name argument is of type String and countryOfOrigin is of type MysimplePropertyName. Roo provides converters for common Java types, such as String, Date, Enum, Locale, boolean, and so on. You can also create your custom converters and register them with Roo as an OSGi service. Roo makes use of registered converters to convert the value specified for the argument into the Java type expected by the method. In the case of the mysimple add-on, Roo converts the value entered for the countryOfOrigin argument of the say hello Roo command to the MysimplePropertyName type. We'll see later in this recipe that using MysimplePropertyName (an enum) as the Java type of the countryOfOrigin Roo argument provides tab-completion feature for the argument value. We saw earlier that the MysimplePropertyName class is added to the StaticFieldConverter instance in the activate method. This is to allow StaticFieldConverter to convert the value of the countryOfOrigin argument in the say hello Roo command to the MysimplePropertyName type.

Let's now look at how to make a Roo command unavailable to the Roo shell if certain pre-conditions are not met.

Making Roo commands unavailable

If certain pre-conditions are not met, you may want to make a Roo command unavailable to the Roo shell. For instance, if you have not yet created a Roo project using the `project` command, then Roo doesn't allow you to set up a JPA persistence provider using the `persistence setup` command.

- The `@CliAvailabilityIndicator` is a method-level Roo annotation that lets you specify the pre-conditions that must be met for a Roo command to be available to the Roo shell. The following code shows the methods in the `MysimpleCommands` class that define the availability conditions for the `say hello` and `web mvc install tags` commands:

```
import org.springframework.roo.shell.CliAvailabilityIndicator;
...

@Reference private MysimpleOperations operations;
...

@CliAvailabilityIndicator("say hello")
public boolean isSayHelloAvailable() {
  return true;
}

@CliAvailabilityIndicator("web mvc install tags")
public boolean isInstallTagsCommandAvailable() {
  return operations.isInstallTagsCommandAvailable();
}
```

In the code, `@CliAvailabilityIndicator` annotated methods define the availability of the `say hello` and `web mvc install tags` commands. The value specified in the `@CliAvailabilityIndicator` annotation identifies the name of the Roo command for which the method is executed to determine the command's availability. For instance, the `isSayHelloAvailable` method defines the availability of the `say hello` command and the `isInstallTagsCommandAvailable` method defines the availability of the `web mvc install tags` command. The return type of `@CliAvailabilityIndicator` annotated methods is `boolean` and the method must be a `public` method which doesn't accept any arguments. If the value returned by the `@CliAvailabilityIndicator` annotated method is `true`, then it means that the corresponding command is available, else it is unavailable.

As the `isSayHelloAvailable` method always returns true, the `say hello` command is always available to the Roo shell. On the other hand, the `isInstallTagsCommandAvailable` method consults the `MysimpleOperations` implementation to determine the availability of the `web mvc install tags` command.

Let's now look at the `MysimpleOperationsImpl` class, which defines the majority of the logic executed when the mysimple add-on Roo commands are executed from the Roo shell.

The MysimpleOperations interface and MysimpleOperationsImpl class

The `MysimpleOperations` interface defines three methods as described in the following table:

Method	Description
`boolean isInstallTagsCommandAvailable()`	Checks if the tags sub-directory exists in the `SRC_MAIN_WEBAPP/WEB-INF` directory of your Roo project. Returns `true` if the directory exists.
`String getProperty(String)`	Accepts a system property as an argument and returns its value.
`void installTags()`	Copies `info.tagx` and `show.tagx` tag files from the mysimple add-on to your Roo project.

The `MysimpleOperationsImpl` class implements the `MysimpleOperations` interface. The methods defined in the `MysimpleCommands` class mainly delegate processing of logic to the implementation of the `MysimpleOperations` interface. The following code shows the `MysimpleOperationsImpl` class (methods have not been shown for brevity):

```
import org.springframework.roo.process.manager.FileManager;
import org.springframework.roo.project.ProjectOperations;

@Component
@Service
public class MysimpleOperationsImpl
    implements MysimpleOperations {
  private static final char SEPARATOR = File.separatorChar;

  @Reference private FileManager fileManager;

  @Reference private ProjectOperations projectOperations;
  ...
}
```

The `MysimpleOperationsImpl` class is annotated with `@Component` and `@Service` Apache Flex annotations, which means OSGi's SCR is responsible for managing the lifecycle of the `MysimpleOperationsImpl` component and registering it as a service with the OSGi service registry. Like `MysimpleCommands`, you can access the `MysimpleOperationsImpl` instance from other add-ons using the `@Reference` Apache Felix annotation.

Roo provides many built-in services which simplify add-on development. `FileManager` and `ProjectOperations` types represent services provided by Roo for managing files (like creating, reading, updating files, undo capability, and so on) and performing actions on the Roo project (like adding dependencies to the `pom.xml` file, updating project type, and so on), respectively. `FileManager` service and `ProjectOperations` are provided by the Process Manager and Project core modules of Roo, respectively. It is important to note that add-ons are different from core modules in Roo. The core modules provide vital features of the Spring Roo tool, like file system monitoring, registering commands with the Roo shell, and so on. Roo commands provided by add-ons are executed by Spring Roo users for code generation but Roo commands provided by core modules are primarily meant for accessing internal features of Spring Roo, like obtaining metadata, setting polling speed, and so on.

We saw earlier that the `isInstallTagsCommandAvailable` method of `MysimpleOperations` is invoked by the `isInstallTagsCommandAvailable` method of the `MysimpleCommands` class to check the availability of the `web mvc install tags` command. The following code shows the `isInstallTagsCommandAvailable` method of `MysimpleOperationsImpl`:

```
public boolean isInstallTagsCommandAvailable() {
    return
    projectOperations.isProjectAvailable() &&
    fileManager.exists(projectOperations.getProjectMetadata()
    .getPathResolver().getIdentifier(Path.SRC_MAIN_WEBAPP,
    "WEB-INF" + SEPARATOR + "tags"));
}
```

In the code, the `isInstallTagsCommandAvailable` method makes use of `ProjectOperation` services to check if a Roo project exists. The method also makes use of the `FileManager` service to check if a `tags` sub-directory exists in the `SRC_MAIN_WEBAPP/WEB-INF` directory of your Roo project. If a `tags` directory doesn't exist or you haven't yet created a Roo project, then the method returns `false`. This means the `web mvc install tags` Roo command is not available to the Roo shell if you haven't yet created a Roo project which contains a `tags` sub-directory inside the `SRC_MAIN_WEBAPP/WEB-INF` directory.

We saw earlier that the `installTags` method of `MysimpleCommands` invokes the `installTags` method of `MysimpleOperations`. The following code shows the `installTags` method as implemented by the `MysimpleOperationsImpl` class:

```
import org.springframework.roo.process.manager.MutableFile;
import org.springframework.roo.project.Path;
import org.springframework.roo.project.PathResolver;
import org.springframework.roo.project.ProjectOperations;
import org.springframework.roo.support.util.FileCopyUtils;
import org.springframework.roo.support.util.TemplateUtils;
...
public void installTags() {
```

```
      PathResolver pathResolver =
        projectOperations.getProjectMetadata().getPathResolver();


        createOrReplaceFile(..., "info.tagx");
        createOrReplaceFile(..., "show.tagx");
    }

    private void createOrReplaceFile(String path, String fileName)
    {
      String targetFile = path + SEPARATOR + fileName;

      MutableFile mutableFile = fileManager.exists(targetFile) ?
        fileManager.updateFile(targetFile) :
        fileManager.createFile(targetFile);
      try {
        FileCopyUtils.copy(TemplateUtils.getTemplate(getClass(),
        fileName), mutableFile.getOutputStream());
      } catch (IOException e) {
        throw new IllegalStateException(e);
      }
    }
  }
```

In the code, the `installTags` method copies `info.tagx` and `show.tagx` files from the SRC_MAIN_RESOURCE/com/roo/addon/mysimple directory of the mysimple add-on to the SRC_MAN_WEBAPP/WEB-INF/tags directory of your Roo project. The `createOrReplace` method is the method, which is used by the `installTags` method to copy the files. The following table describes the classes used by the `installTags` and `createOrReplace` methods for copying tag files:

Class	Description
PathResolver	Used to locate files and directories in your Roo project. You can use the `ProjectOperations` service to obtain reference to `PathResolver`.
MutableFile	Represents a file in your Roo project, which you want to create, modify, or delete. You can use the `FileManager` service to obtain reference to the `MutableFile` instance.
FileCopyUtils	Utility class that provides methods for copying resources from the add-on to your Roo project.
TemplateUtils	Utility class that is used to resolve template files in the add-on project. We'll discuss templates in detail later in this recipe.

Let's now look at the `MysimplePropertyName` enum type, which defines constants for the `countryOfOrigin` argument of web mvc install tags command.

MysimpleNameProperty enum type

The following code shows the `MysimpleNameProperty` enum type, which defines constants for the `countryOfOrigin` argument value of the `web mvc install tags` command:

```
public enum MysimplePropertyName {
    AUSTRALIA("Australia"),
    UNITED_STATES("United States"),
    GERMANY("Germany"),
    NOT_SPECIFIED("None of your business!");

    private String propertyName;

    private MysimplePropertyName(String propertyName) {
        Assert.hasText(propertyName, "Property name required");
        this.propertyName = propertyName;
    }
    ...
}
```

In the code, constant `AUSTRALIA` is associated with value `Australia`, `UNITED_STATES` is associated with value `United States`, and so on. We saw earlier that the `countryOfOrigin` argument is of type `MysimplePropertyName`. We can only pass `String` type values for an argument from the Roo shell, so what we should specify as the value of the `countryOfOrigin` argument, and how it'll get converted to `MysimplePropertyName`. When you enter a partial value for the `countryOfOrigin` argument and press the *Tab* key, Roo internally refers to `MysimplePropertyName` to find a matching constant. For instance, if you enter `au` as the value of the `countryOfOrigin` argument, Roo attempts to find the constant that matches `au` in `MysimpleNameProperty` and auto-completes the value. As the matching is case-insensitive, the value `au` of the `countryOfOrigin` argument is completed by the Roo shell as `AUSTRALIA`.

The following diagram summarizes how a simple add-on works:

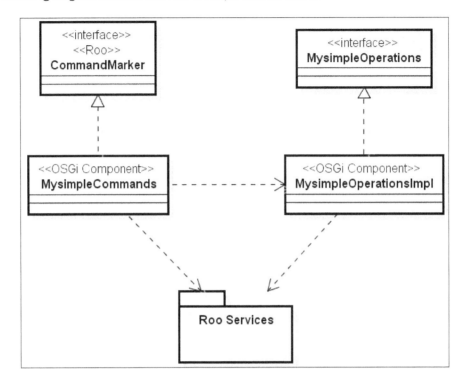

The figure shows that CommandMarker is an interface provided by Roo, and it is implemented by the MysimpleCommands class. The MysimpleCommands class invokes methods of the MysimpleOperationsImpl class to process the commands exposed by the mysimple add-on. The MysimpleCommands and MysimpleOperationsImpl classes use services provided by Roo to perform the desired functionality.

There's more...

In this section we'll look at:

- How to locally deploy the mysimple add-on for testing Roo commands
- How tab-completion support is implemented for Roo commands using constants defined in an enum type and a Java class
- How the @CliAvailabilityIndicator annotation can be used for a method to define availability of multiple Roo commands exposed by the *Command class
- What templates are in add-ons and how they are typically used
- Plugins and dependency configuration in the pom.xml file of an add-on

Deploying and running mysimple add-on

Once you have created an add-on, you may want to test its functionality, before making the add-on available to other developers. In this section, we'll look at how to locally deploy and test the mysimple add-on that we created using the `create addon simple` command.

To use the mysimple add-on, you need to convert it into an OSGi-compliant JAR bundle. To do so, execute `mvn clean install` from the directory which contains your mysimple add-on project, as shown here:

```
C:\roo-cookbook\ch07-simple-add-on> mvn clean install -Dgpg.
passphrase=<thephrase>
```

Here, `<thephrase>` is the password phrase that you provide for signing add-ons using GnuPG (also referred to as GPG). Refer to the *Setting up GnuPG for add-on development* recipe for information on how to set up GnuPG and create a password phrase for signing add-ons.

Executing the `mvn clean install` command creates a `com.roo.addon.mysimple-0.1.0.BUILD-SNAPSHOT.jar` add-on OSGi bundle in the `target` directory of the mysimple add-on project. Now, let's look at how to use the mysimple add-on in a Roo project.

Using the mysimple add-on in a Roo project

The following steps will demonstrate how to use an add-on:

1. Create a new directory `C:\roo-cookbook\ch07-addon-test` in your system and start the Roo shell from this directory.

2. Execute the `ch07_web_app.roo` script to create a `flight-app` Spring Web MVC project.

3. Execute the `osgi start` command to install and activate the mysimple add-on, as shown here:

   ```
   roo> osgi start --url file:///C:/roo-cookbook/ch07-simple-add-on/
   target/com.roo.addon.mysimple-0.1.0.BUILD-SNAPSHOT.jar
   ```

   Here the `url` argument specifies the location of the add-on OSGi bundle you want to install and activate.

   The `osgi start` command installs the mysimple add-on. This command is also used to download and install Roo add-ons that are located on a website by specifying the `http://` or `httppgp://` URL to the add-on JAR file as the value of the `url` argument.

4. To verify that the add-on was successfully installed, type `say` at the Roo shell and press the *Tab* key. Roo should autocomplete the command to `say hello`, as shown here:

   ```
   roo> say hello
   ```

5. Press the *Tab* key again to let Roo show the mandatory `name` argument of the `say hello` command, as shown here:

```
roo> say hello --name
```

6. Enter `Ron` as the value of `name` argument and type `--` followed by the *Tab* key to view the optional arguments of the `say hello` command:

```
roo> say hello --name Ron --
```

7. As the only optional argument of the `say hello` command is `countryOfOrigin`, it is displayed on the Roo shell:

```
roo> say hello --name Ron --countryOfOrigin
```

8. Now, press *Tab* again to view the argument values that can be passed to the `countryOfOrigin` argument. You'll see the following output:

```
roo> say hello --name Ron --countryOfOrigin


AUSTRALIA          GERMANY          NOT_SPECIFIED     UNITED_STATES
```

The output shows that `countryOfOrigin` can accept only one of the four possible values: AUSTRALIA, GERMANY, NOT_SPECIFIED, and UNITED_STATES.

9. Enter `aus` as the value of the `countryOfOrigin` argument and press the *Tab* key to let Roo perform autocompletion of the value, as shown here:

```
roo> say hello --name Ron --countryOfOrigin aus


roo> say hello --name Ron --countryOfOrigin AUSTRALIA
```

As shown, Roo performs autocompletion of value for the `countryOfOrigin` argument. The possible values for the `countryOfOrigin` argument come from the `MysimplePropertyName` enum type.

10. Now, press *Enter* to let the mysimple add-on process the `say hello` command. You'll see an output like the following:

```
~.web.controller roo> say hello --name Ron --countryOfOrigin
AUSTRALIA


Welcome Ron!

Country of origin: Australia

It seems you are a running JDK 1.6.0_23

You can use the default JDK logger anywhere in your add-on to send
messages to the Roo shell
```

When the `say hello` command is executed, it is processed by the `sayHello` method of the `MysimpleCommands` class.

11. Now, execute `web mvc install tags` of the mysimple add-on to install the `info.tagx` and `show.tagx` files to the `flight-app` Roo project:

```
roo> web mvc install tags


Created SRC_MAIN_WEBAPP\WEB-INF\tags\util\info.tagx

Updated SRC_MAIN_WEBAPP\WEB-INF\tags\form\show.tagx
```

The output of executing `web mvc install tags` shows that the `info.tagx` file is added to the `flight-app` project and the `show.tagx` file is replaced. The `web mvc install tags` command is processed by the `installTags` method of the `MysimpleCommands` class, which delegates to the `installTags` method of the `MysimpleOperationsImpl` class.

If you make modifications to the mysimple add-on and want to re-deploy it to Spring Roo, then use the `osgi update` command, as shown here:

```
roo> osgi update --url file:///C:/roo-cookbook/ch07-simple-add-on/target/
com.roo.addon.mysimple-0.1.0.BUILD-SNAPSHOT.jar
```

If you want to uninstall the mysimple add-on, then use the `osgi uninstall` command, as shown here:

```
roo> osgi uninstall --bundleSymbolicName com.roo.addon.mysimple
```

The `bundleSymbolicName` argument identifies the name of the add-on to be uninstalled from Spring Roo. Once an add-on is uninstalled, Roo commands exposed by that add-on are no longer available to the Roo shell.

Tab-completion feature with constant values

The `MysimplePropertyName` enum type defines constants, which represent the possible values that an argument of a Roo command can accept. You are not limited to using enum types to define constants for argument values. Let's say that instead of using the `MySimplePropertyName` enum type we want to use a `Country` class that defines constants for countries. The following code shows the `Country` class that can be used in place of the `MySimplePropertyName` enum type:

```
public class Country {
 public static final Country AUSTRALIA =
     new Country("Australia");
 public static final Country NOT_SPECIFIED =
     new Country("None of your business!");
 public static final Country UNITED_STATES =
     new Country("United States");
```

```
   public static final Country GERMANY =
       new Country("Germany");

   private String countryName;

   public Country(String countryName) {
    this.countryName = countryName;
   }

   public String getCountryName() {
    return countryName;
   }
}
```

The preceding code shows that the `Country` class defines constants for each country representing a possible value of the `countryOfOrigin` argument. Now, to use the `Country` class instead of the `MysimplePropertyName` enum, all you need to do is to replace references to it with `Country` in the `MysimpleCommands` class, as shown here:

```
public class MysimpleCommands implements CommandMarker {
 @Reference private StaticFieldConverter staticFieldConverter;

 protected void activate(ComponentContext context) {
  staticFieldConverter.add(Country.class);
 }

 protected void deactivate(ComponentContext context) {
  staticFieldConverter.remove(Country.class);
 }

 @CliCommand(value = "say hello",
    help = "Prints welcome message to the Roo shell")
 public void sayHello(..., @CliOption(key = "countryOfOrigin",
    mandatory = false,
    help = "Country of orgin") Country country) {

  log.info("Welcome " + name + "!");
  log.warning("Country of origin: " + (country == null ?
    Country.NOT_SPECIFIED.getCountryName() :
    country.getCountryName()));
  ...
 }
 ...
}
```

The preceding code shows that the `Country` class must be added to the `StaticFieldConverter` service and must be specified as the type of `countryOfOrigin` argument in `sayHello` method.

Multiple command availability using @CliAvailabilityIndicator

In mysimple add-on, separate `@CliAvailabilityIndicator` annotated methods are used to indicate availability of the `say hello` and `web mvc install tags` commands. If you want to use a single `@CliAvailabilityIndicator` annotated method to indicate availability of multiple Roo commands offered by the mysimple add-on, then specify the command array in the `@CliAvailabilityIndicator` annotation. For instance, you can define the following method in `MysimpleCommands` to indicate that the `say hello` and `web mvc install tags` commands are always available to the Roo shell:

```
@CliAvailabilityIndicator({"say hello",
   "web mvc install tags"})
public boolean isCommandAvailable() {
      return true;
}
```

In the preceding code the `@CliAvailabilityIndicator` annotation specifies an array of Roo commands (`say hello` and `web mvc install tags`) whose availability is checked by the `isCommandAvailable` method.

Templates in Roo add-ons

Templates in an add-on project are resources that are copied to the Roo project when one or more commands of the add-on are executed. For instance, when you execute the `web mvc install tags` command, the `info.tagx` and `show.tagx` files are copied from add-on to the Roo project. Templates can also be images, XML files, properties files, and so on, which the add-on commands copy to the Roo project.

Templates are located inside the `SRC_MAIN_RESOURCES` directory of an add-on project. For instance, in the case of the mysimple add-on, the `info.tagx` and `show.tagx` files are located in the `SRC_MAIN_RESOURCES/com/roo/addon/mysimple` directory. Add-ons access templates using the `TemplateUtils` class and then copy it to the Roo project using the `FileCopyUtils` class. `TemplateUtils` defines the following two static methods which are used to access templates in the add-on:

- ▸ `String getTemplatePath(Class<?> clazz, String templateFilename)`: this method returns the path to the template file specified via the `templateFilename` argument. The `clazz` argument's package information is used to obtain the sub-directory inside the `SRC_MAIN_RESOURCES` directory that contains the template file.

For instance, if the `clazz` argument represents a class whose package name is `com.roo.addon.mysimple` and the `templateFileName` argument value is `show.tagx`, the `getTemplatePath` method returns the path to the SRC_MAIN_RESOURCES/com/roo/addon/mysimple/show.tagx file. You can also specify the relative path to the template file as the value of the `templateFilename` argument. For instance, if you specify the value of `templateFilename` as WEB-INF/myconfig.xml, then the path to the template file becomes SRC_MAIN_RESOURCES/com/roo/addon/mysimple/WEB-INF/myconfig.xml.

▶ `InputStream getTemplate(Class<?> clazz, String templateFilename)`: this method returns `java.io.InputStream` to the template file. In the case of the mysimple add-on, the `createOrReplaceFile` method of the `MySimpleOperationsImpl` class makes use of the `TemplateUtils` class to obtain `InputStream` to the `info.tagx` and `show.tagx` files.

In some add-ons, a template file may be an XML file which the add-ons need to modify before copying it to the Roo project. To modify XML templates, Roo provides an `XMLUtils` class which add-ons can use to modify the content of XML template files. Let's look at a scenario that shows how add-ons can modify the content of an XML template file before copying it to the Roo project.

The following `config.xml` file shows a Spring application context XML file which represents a template XML file of an add-on:

```
beans xmlns="http://www.springframework.org/schema/beans"
xmlns:context="http://www.springframework.org/schema/context" ...>
    <context:component-scan base-package=""/>
    ...
</beans>
```

In the `config.xml` file, the `<component-scan>` element of Spring's `context` namespace specifies the packages (via the `base-package` attribute) that are scanned by Spring. The classes in these packages (and their sub-packages) that are annotated with the `@Component`, `@Service`, and `@Repository` Spring annotations are auto-registered with Spring's application context. As the add-on copies the `config.xml` file to a Roo project when a Roo command is executed, the add-on doesn't know in advance the value that needs to be specified for the `base-package` attribute. This is the reason why the value of the `base-package` attribute is empty in the `config.xml` file.

The following code shows how an add-on can read the `config.xml` file, modify it, and then write the modified `config.xml` to the Roo project:

```
import org.springframework.roo.metadata.MetadataService;
import org.springframework.roo.project.PathResolver;
import org.springframework.roo.project.ProjectMetadata;
import org.springframework.roo.support.util.XmlUtils;
import org.w3c.dom.Document;
```

```java
import org.w3c.dom.Element;
import java.io.ByteArrayOutputStream;
import java.io.OutputStreamWriter;


@Component
@Service
public class FileWriterOperationsImpl
 implements FileWriterOperations {
@Reference private MetadataService metadataService;
 ...
 public void copyApplicationContextXML() {
  ProjectMetadata projectMetadata =
  (ProjectMetadata) metadataService.get(ProjectMetadata.
                              getProjectIdentifier());

  InputStream templateInputStream =
      TemplateUtils.getTemplate(getClass(),
                                "config.xml");
  Document config;
  try {
    config = XmlUtils.getDocumentBuilder().
                          parse(templateInputStream);
  } catch (Exception ex) {...}

  Element rootElement = (Element) config.getDocumentElement();

  XmlUtils.findFirstElementByName("context:component-scan",
    rootElement).setAttribute("base-package",
                  projectMetadata.getTopLevelPackage().
                  getFullyQualifiedPackageName());

  ByteArrayOutputStream outputStream =
      new ByteArrayOutputStream();

  XmlUtils.writeXml(XmlUtils.createIndentingTransformer(),
                    outputStream,
                    config);
  String xmlContent = outputStream.toString();

  FileCopyUtils.copy(xmlContent, new OutputStreamWriter(...));
 }
 ...
}
```

The `FileWriterOperationsImpl` class is similar to the `MysimpleOperationsImpl` class of the mysimple add-on. It defines the `copyApplicationContextXML` method which is responsible for copying the `config.xml` file from the add-on to the Roo project.

The `MetadataService` class represents a service provided by Roo for retrieving metadata information for the Roo project, Java types, fields, methods, and so on. Metadata is obtained from Roo's `MetadataService` using a metadata identification string, which has the format: `MID:<fully-qualified-class-name>#<instance-identification-key>`, where `<fully-qualified-class-name>` is the metadata type and `<instance-identification-key>` is the Java type to which the metadata applies. If the metadata is not associated with a Java type, then the metadata string format is: `MID:<fully-qualified-class-name>`. If the metadata identification string has the format `MID:<fully-qualified-class-name>#<instance-identification-key>`, then it is referred to as an instance-level metadata identification string. If the metadata identification string has the format `MID:<fully-qualified-class-name>`, then it is referred to as a class-level metadata identification string. In the `FileWriterOperationsImpl` class, `ProjectMetadata` represents a metadata type which holds the Roo project's details, like project name, top-level package name, dependencies, and so on. The `getProjectIdentifier()` method of `ProjectMetadata` returns a metadata identification string for the Roo project and is then passed to `MetadataService` to retrieve the `ProjectMetadata` instance.

The `TemplateUtils` class is used to obtain `java.io.InputStream` to the `config.xml` file. The `XmlUtils` class is then used to parse the `config.xml` file to build the `org.w3c.dom.Document` instance. The `findFirstElementByName` method of `XmlUtils` is used to find the first occurrence of the `<context:component-scan>` element in `config.xml`. The `findFirstElementByName` method returns an instance of `org.w3c.dom.Element`. The `setAttribute` method of `Element` is used to set the value of the `base-package` attribute of the `<context:component-scan>` element to the top-level package of the Roo project. The `writeXml` method of `XmlUtils` writes the `Document` object to `java.io.OutputStream`. The `createIndentingTransformer` method of `XmlUtils` creates a `javax.xml.transform.Transformer` instance, which indents entries in the `Document` object by 4 characters. If you want to perform a custom transformation of XML, you can create a custom `Transformer` implementation and pass it to the `writeXml` method of `XmlUtils` class.

Let's say you have a Roo project named `flight-app` whose top-level package is `com.sample.flightapp`. Now assume that you execute a Roo command which results in the execution of the `copyApplicationContextXML` method of the `FileWriterOperationsImpl` class of the add-on. The `copyApplicationContextXML` method will read the `config.xml` template file, set the `base-package` attribute of the `<context:component-scan>` element to `com.sample.flightapp` and write the modified `config.xml` to the `flight-app` Roo project.

Now let's look at some of the important configurations defined in the `pom.xml` file of the mysimple add-on project.

The pom.xml file

The `pom.xml` file of an add-on created via the `addon create simple` command contains the following configurations:

▶ The core Spring Roo modules on which a simple add-on depends is configured in the `pom.xml` file. If your add-on makes use of other add-ons, then you'll need to configure it in the `pom.xml` file.

▶ By default Google Code is configured as the SCM (Software Configuration Management) repository for the add-on.

▶ The Maven assembly plugin is configured for packaging the add-on. You can execute `perform assembly` Roo command or `assembly:single` goal of the assembly plugin to package the add-on as a ZIP file. The assembly description, `assembly.xml`, is located in the `src/main/assembly` folder of add-on.

▶ The Maven release plugin is configured for releasing the add-on. Once you are done with local testing of your add-on, you can release the add-on to Google Code (or the SCM you configured in the `pom.xml` file) by executing the `mvn release:prepare release:perform` Maven command.

▶ The Maven GPG plugin is configured to sign add-on project artifacts using GnuPG.

▶ The Maven bundle plugin is configured to package an add-on as an OSGi compliant bundle. You'll find that the `<packaging>` element's value is specified as `bundle` in the `pom.xml` file of add-on, which means that the add-on is packaged as an OSGi bundle.

OSGi commands for troubleshooting

Once you have deployed an add-on, you can check if it was successfully installed or not by using the following OSGi commands from the Roo shell:

▶ `osgi ps`: lists the OSGi bundles and their status. If you have successfully installed the mysimple add-on, then executing the `osgi ps` command should show the mysimple add-on as active, as shown here:

```
[Active] [1] Mysimple addon (0.1.0.BUILD-SNAPSHOT)
```

▶ `osgi log`: shows the OSGi container logs. If your add-on fails to install successfully, you can refer to the container logs to troubleshoot installation issues.

▶ `osgi scr list`: lists services and components registered with the OSGi container. If you have successfully installed the mysimple add-on, then executing the `osgi scr list` command should show commands and operation types, as shown here:

```
[181] [active] com.roo.addon.mysimple.MysimpleOperationsImpl
[180] [active] com.roo.addon.mysimple.MysimpleCommands
```

In the preceding output, numbers 180 and 181 denote the component IDs assigned by the OSGi container to the MysimpleCommands and MysimpleOperations types respectively.

▶ osgi scr info: shows detailed information about a component or service registered with the OSGi container. This command accepts a mandatory argument, componentId. You can use this command to find unresolvable dependencies of a component. If you have successfully installed the mysimple add-on, then executing osgi scr info --componentId 180 (substitute the component ID of MysimpleCommands as displayed by executing the osgi scr list command) should show if the dependencies of MysimpleCommands were satisfied or not, as shown here:

```
ID: 180
Name: com.roo.addon.mysimple.MysimpleCommands
State: active
Services: org.springframework.roo.shell.CommandMarker
...
Reference: staticFieldConverter
Satisfied: satisfied
Service Name: org.springframework.roo.shell.converters.
StaticFieldConverter
...
Reference: operations
Satisfied: satisfied
Service Name: com.roo.addon.mysimple.MysimpleOperations
```

The output shows that the StaticFieldConverter and MysimpleOperations dependencies of MysimpleCommands were resolved successfully.

See also

▶ Refer to the *Developing an advanced add-on* recipe to see how to develop an add-on, which creates new Java classes, interfaces, and AspectJ ITD files

Developing an advanced add-on

If you want to generate Java code (classes and interfaces) and AspectJ ITDs in response to the execution of one or more Roo commands, then you should create an *advanced* Roo add-on.

Spring Roo treats both simple and advanced add-ons the same way. The distinction between simple and advanced add-ons exists so that you can choose an appropriate add-on template based on your custom add-on requirement. The add-on template created by the `addon create simple` command is useful if you want to create a custom add-on meant for adding project dependencies to the `pom.xml` file and for adding configuration artifacts to the project. In this recipe we'll look at the `addon create advanced` command, which is useful if you want to create a custom add-on to generate Java code and AspectJ ITD.

Getting ready

Create a new directory `C:\roo-cookbook\ch07-advanced-add-on` in your system and start the Roo shell from the `ch07-advanced-add-on` directory.

How to do it...

The following steps will demonstrate how to create an advanced add-on:

1. Execute the `addon create advanced` command, as shown here, to create a `com.roo.addon.myadvanced` add-on project:

```
..roo> addon create advanced --topLevelPackage com.roo.addon.
myadvanced

...

Created SRC_MAIN_JAVA\...\MyadvancedCommands.java

Created SRC_MAIN_JAVA\...\MyadvancedOperations.java

Created SRC_MAIN_JAVA\...\MyadvancedOperationsImpl.java

Created SRC_MAIN_JAVA\...\MyadvancedMetadata.java

Created SRC_MAIN_JAVA\...\MyadvancedMetadataProvider.java

Created SRC_MAIN_JAVA\...\RooMyadvanced.java

Created SRC_MAIN_RESOURCES\...\configuration.xml
```

   The output only shows some of the important files generated by the Roo command that we'll discuss them in this recipe.

2. Execute the `perform eclipse` command to create Eclipse-IDE specific configuration files:

```
roo> perform eclipse
```

   Now, import the `com.roo.addon.myadvanced` Eclipse project into Eclipse IDE.

How it works...

The `addon create advanced` command creates a Roo add-on template which you can use as the starting point to create a custom Roo add-on which generates Java classes, interfaces and AspectJ ITDs. The following classes and interfaces are generated by the `addon create advanced` command. The `<last-part-of-top-level-package>` refers to the text after the last index of '.' in the value of the `topLevelPackage` argument. In case of our example, the `topLevelPackage` argument value is `com.roo.addon.myadvanced`, which makes value of `<last-part-of-top-level-package>` as 'myadvanced'.

  ▶ `<last-part-of-top-level-package>Commands.java` class: defines methods that are contributed to the Roo shell by the add-on.

  ▶ `<last-part-of-top-level-package>Operations.java` interface: defines methods that contain the processing logic for commands defined in the `*Commands.java` class.

  ▶ `<last-part-of-top-level-package>OperationsImpl.java` class: implements the `*Operations.java` interface.

  ▶ `<last-part-of-top-level-package>Metadata.java` class: represents the metadata associated with this add-on. In this class you write the code for creating Java classes, interfaces, and AspectJ ITDs.

  ▶ `<last-part-of-top-level-package>MetadataProvider.java` class: creates the metadata associated with this add-on.

  ▶ `Roo<last-part-of-top-level-package>.java` class: represents the Roo annotation (similar to other Roo annotations like `@RooEntity`, `@RooJavaBean`, `@RooSolrSearchable`, and so on) which triggers this add-on to generate Java classes, interfaces, and AspectJ ITDs.

You may have noticed that a `configuration.xml` file is also generated in the `SRC_MAIN_RESOURCES\com\roo\addon\myadvanced` directory. The `configuration.xml` file defines dependencies that are added by the add-on to the `pom.xml` file of the Roo project.

The MyadvancedCommands class

The following code shows the methods of the `MyAdvancedCommands` class that defines Roo commands exposed by the myadvanced add-on:

```
@Component
@Service
public class MyadvancedCommands implements CommandMarker {

  @Reference private MyadvancedOperations operations;

  @CliAvailabilityIndicator({ "myadvanced setup",
    "myadvanced add", "myadvanced all" })
```

```
public boolean isCommandAvailable() {
  return operations.isCommandAvailable();
}

@CliCommand(value = "myadvanced add",
   help = "Some helpful description")
public void add(@CliOption(key = "type",
  mandatory = true,
  help = "The java type to apply this annotation to")
 JavaType target) {
    operations.annotateType(target);
}

@CliCommand(value = "myadvanced all",
   help = "Some helpful description")
public void all() {
 operations.annotateAll();
}

@CliCommand(value = "myadvanced setup",
  help = "Setup Myadvanced addon")
public void setup() {
 operations.setup();
 }
}
```

As the code shows, the myadvanced add-on registers the following commands with the Roo shell:

- myadvanced setup: performs the initial setup that is required for using the add-on. When this command is executed, the myadvanced add-on updates project dependencies in the pom.xml file.

- myadvanced add: annotates the Java class (specified via the type argument of the myadvanced add command) with the @RooMyadvanced annotation. In the preceding code, you'll notice that the Java class passed to the add method is of type JavaType. The JavaType represents a Roo-specific class that simplifies accessing simple and package names of a Java type. Annotating a Java type with the @RooMyAdvanced annotation kicks off code generation by the myadvanced add-on.

- myadvanced all: finds all the Java types in the project that are annotated with the @RooJavaBean annotation (soon we'll see how the myadvanced add-on does this), and annotates them with the @RooMyAdvanced annotation. Annotating a Java type with the @RooMyAdvanced annotation kicks off code generation by the myadvanced add-on.

The `MyAdvancedCommands` class also defines a `@CliAvailabilityIndicator` annotated method, which decides the availability of the `myadvanced setup`, `myadvanced add`, and `myadvanced all` commands.

Let's now look at the `MyadvancedOperationsImpl` class, which provides implementations for the commands exposed by the myadvanced add-on.

The MyadvancedOperationsImpl class

The following code shows the `MyadvancedOperationsImpl` class. The code doesn't show the implementation of the `annotateType` and `annotateAll` methods, which will be discussed in detail later in this section.

```
import ...roo.classpath.PhysicalTypeMetadataProvider;
import ...roo.classpath.TypeLocationService;
import ...roo.metadata.MetadataService;
import ...roo.model.JavaType;
import ...roo.project.ProjectOperations;
import ...roo.project.Dependency;
import ...roo.project.DependencyScope;
import ...roo.project.DependencyType;
import ...roo.project.Repository;
import ...roo.support.util.XmlUtils;
import org.w3c.dom.Element;

@Component
@Service
public class MyadvancedOperationsImpl implements
    MyadvancedOperations {

 @Reference private MetadataService metadataService;
 @Reference private PhysicalTypeMetadataProvider
    physicalTypeMetadataProvider;
 @Reference private ProjectOperations projectOperations;
 @Reference private TypeLocationService typeLocationService;
 ...

 public boolean isCommandAvailable() {
  return projectOperations.isProjectAvailable();
 }

 public void annotateType(JavaType javaType) { ... }

 public void annotateAll() { ... }
 public void setup() {
```

```
projectOperations.addRepository(
  new Repository("Myadvanced Roo add-on repository",
  "Myadvanced Roo add-on repository",
   "https://com-roo-addon-
      myadvanced.googlecode.com/svn/repo"));

List<Dependency> dependencies = new ArrayList<Dependency>();
dependencies.add(
 new Dependency("com.roo.addon.myadvanced",
   "com.roo.addon.myadvanced", "0.1.0.BUILD-SNAPSHOT",
   DependencyType.JAR, DependencyScope.PROVIDED));

for (Element dependencyElement :
  XmlUtils. findElements("/configuration/batch/" +
   "dependencies/dependency",
  XmlUtils.getConfiguration(getClass()))) {
    dependencies.add(new Dependency(dependencyElement));
 }

projectOperations.addDependencies(dependencies);
 }
}
```

The MyadvancedOperationsImpl class references the following services offered by Roo:

- ▸ MetadataService: service provided by Roo for retrieving metadata information for the Roo project, Java types, fields, methods, and so on. Refer to the *Developing a simple add-on* recipe for more details.

- ▸ PhysicalTypeMetadataProvider: a metadata provider that provides metadata for a class, interface, enum, or annotation type. As we'll see later in this section, this metadata provider is used by the MyadvancedOperationsImpl class to obtain the metadata information about the Java type that needs to be annotated with the @ RooMyadvanced annotation.

- `ProjectOperations`: this is used by the myadvanced add-on in the `isCommandAvailable` and `setup` methods to check if a Roo project exists and to modify the `pom.xml` file of the Roo project, as shown in the given code. The `isCommandAvailable` method in the given code makes use of the `isProjectAvailable` method of `ProjectOperations` to determine if a Roo project has been created. The `isCommandAvailable` method is invoked by the `@CliAvailabilityIndicator` annotated method of the `MyadvancedCommands` class. The `setup` method in this code makes use of the `addRepository` method of `ProjectOperations` to add repository information of the add-on to the Roo project's `pom.xml` file. By default, the repository refers to the `repo` directory of the Google Code project of the add-on (refer to the `pom.xml` file of the myadvanced add-on). The `setup` method adds Roo project's dependency on the myadvanced add-on and the dependencies defined in the `configuration.xml` (inside SRC_MAIN_RESOURCES/com/roo/addon/myadvanced) file by using the `addDependencies` method. The `setup` method makes use of the `getConfiguration` method of `XmlUtils` class to load the `configuration.xml` file.

- `TypeLocationService`: a Roo service that helps with locating Java types in the Roo project. For instance, you can find Java types annotated with a particular annotation using `TypeLocationService`.

- The `annotateType` method of the `MyadvancedOperationsImpl` class is invoked when the `myadvanced add` command is executed. The following code shows the implementation of the `annotateType` method:

```
import ...roo.classpath.PhysicalTypeDetails;
import ...roo.classpath.PhysicalTypeMetadata;
import ...roo.classpath.PhysicalTypeMetadataProvider;
import ...roo.classpath.TypeLocationService;
import ...roo.classpath.details.MemberFindingUtils;
import ...roo.classpath.details.MutableClassOrInterfaceTypeDetails;
import ...roo.classpath.details.annotations.
AnnotationMetadataBuilder;
...
@Reference private MetadataService metadataService;
@Reference private PhysicalTypeMetadataProvider
                    physicalTypeMetadataProvider;
...
public void annotateType(JavaType javaType) {
  String id =
    physicalTypeMetadataProvider.findIdentifier(javaType);

  PhysicalTypeMetadata physicalTypeMetadata =
    (PhysicalTypeMetadata) metadataService.get(id);

  PhysicalTypeDetails physicalTypeDetails =
```

```
   physicalTypeMetadata.getMemberHoldingTypeDetails();

MutableClassOrInterfaceTypeDetails mutableTypeDetails =
  (MutableClassOrInterfaceTypeDetails) physicalTypeDetails;

if (MemberFindingUtils.getAnnotationOfType(
     mutableTypeDetails.getAnnotations(),
   new JavaType(RooMyadvanced.class.getName())) == null) {

  JavaType rooRooMyadvanced =
    new JavaType(RooMyadvanced.class.getName());
  AnnotationMetadataBuilder annotationBuilder =
    new AnnotationMetadataBuilder(rooRooMyadvanced);

  mutableTypeDetails.addTypeAnnotation(
    annotationBuilder.build()
  );
 }
}
```

The `annotateType` method accepts a `JavaType` argument. The `JavaType` argument represents the Java type that you specified as the value of the `type` argument of the `myadvanced add` command. The `annotateType` method performs the following actions to annotate the `JavaType` argument with the @ RooMyadvanced annotation:

- Obtains metadata identification string for the `JavaType` on which the annotation needs to be applied. This is achieved by using the `findIdentifier` method of the `PhysicalTypeMetadataProvider` class of Roo.

  Let's say that the `myadvanced add` command is executed as shown here:

  ... roo> myadvanced add --type sample.roo.flightapp.domain.Flight

  In the `myadvanced add` command, the value of the `type` argument is `sample.roo.flightapp.domain.Flight`. This Java type is passed to the `annotateType` method of the `MyadvancedOperationsImpl` class by Roo. The metadata identification string returned by the `findIdentifier` method of `PhysicalTypeMetadataProvider` is as follows:

  `MID:org.springframework.roo.classpath.PhysicalTypeIdentifier#SRC_ MAIN_JAVA?sample.roo.flightapp.domain.Flight`

- Uses the metadata identification string of the Java type to obtain the `PhysicalTypeMetadata` object, which represents the metadata information about the Java type.

▶ Makes use of the `getMemberHoldingTypeDetails` method of `PhysicalTypeMetadata` to retrieve `PhysicalTypeDetails`. The `PhysicalTypeDetails` provides details of the Java type represented by `PhysicalTypeMetadata`.

▶ Casts the `PhysicalTypeDetails` into `MutableClassOrInterfaceTypeDetails`. The `MutableClassOrInterfaceTypeDetails` is used to modify the Java type represented by it, which is the `JavaType` argument passed to the `annotateType` method of `MyadvancedOperationsImpl` class. Amongst other things, you can use the `MutableClassOrInterfaceTypeDetails` object to add or remove fields, methods, and annotations from the Java type.

 It is important to note that starting with Spring Roo 1.2.x, modifications to a Java type are performed using Roo's `TypeManagementService` instead of Roo's `MutableClassOrInterfaceTypeDetails`.

▶ Uses `MemberFindingUtils` utility class to check if the Java type is already annotated with the `@RooMyadvanced` annotation.

▶ Uses `AnnotationMetadataBuilder` to create the `@RooMyAdvanced` annotation, and adds it to the Java type using the `MutableClassOrInterfaceTypeDetails` object.

▶ The following code shows the `annotateAll` method of the `MyadvancedOperationsImpl` class, which adds the `@RooMyadvanced` annotation to all the Java types annotated with the `@RooJavaBean` annotation:

```
import ...roo.classpath.TypeLocationService;
import ...roo.model.JavaType;
...
public void annotateAll() {
  for (JavaType type:
     typeLocationService.findTypesWithAnnotation(
     new JavaType("org.springframework.roo.addon. " +
       "javabean.RooJavaBean"))) {
     annotateType(type);
  }
}
```

As shown in the preceding code, the `annotateAll` method makes use of `TypeLocationService` to find Java types that are annotated with the `@RooJavaBean` annotation, and then invokes the `annotateType` method to annotate Java types with the `@RooMyadvanced` annotation.

Let's now look at how the myadvanced add-on triggers code generation using the `MyadvancedMetadataProvider` class.

The MyadvancedMetadataProvider class

The `MyadvancedMetadataProvider` class represents an OSGi component which creates a `MyadvancedMetadata` instance when a Java type is annotated with the `@RooMyadvanced` annotation. The `MyadvancedMetadata` in turn creates an AspectJ ITD and adds a method and a field to it. In this section, we'll look at how Roo-generated `MyadvancedMetadataProvider` is implemented.

The following code shows some of the methods of the `MyadvancedMetadataProvider` class:

```
import org.apache.felix.scr.annotations.Component;
import org.apache.felix.scr.annotations.Service;
import org.osgi.service.component.ComponentContext;
import ...roo.classpath.PhysicalTypeIdentifier;
import ...roo.classpath.PhysicalTypeMetadata;
import ...roo.classpath.itd.AbstractItdMetadataProvider;
import ...roo.classpath.itd.ItdTypeDetailsProvidingMetadataItem;
import org.springframework.roo.model.JavaType;
import org.springframework.roo.project.Path;

@Component
@Service
public final class MyadvancedMetadataProvider extends
AbstractItdMetadataProvider {

  protected void activate(ComponentContext context) {
   metadataDependencyRegistry.
     registerDependency(PhysicalTypeIdentifier.
     getMetadataIdentiferType(), getProvidesType());

   addMetadataTrigger(
     new JavaType(RooMyadvanced.class.getName()));
  }

  protected void deactivate(ComponentContext context) {
   metadataDependencyRegistry.
     deregisterDependency(PhysicalTypeIdentifier.
     getMetadataIdentiferType(), getProvidesType());

   removeMetadataTrigger(
     new JavaType(RooMyadvanced.class.getName()));
  }
  ...
}
```

The preceding code shows that `MyadvancedMetadataProvider` extends Roo's `AbstractItdMetadataProvider` abstract class. The `AbstractItdMetadataProvider` class defines the common functionality required by add-ons that generate AspectJ ITDs. The `activate` method is invoked by the Apache Felix OSGi container when the myadvanced add-on is installed.

Dependency registration and unregistration

In *Chapter 4*, *Web Application Development with Spring Web MVC* you saw that if you redefine a method of the `*_Roo_Controller.aj` file in the `*Controller.java` class, then Roo automatically removes that method from the `*_Roo_Controller.aj` file. We also saw that when you modify a `@RooEntity` or `@RooWebScaffold` annotation, it results in modification of corresponding AspectJ ITDs. Roo maintains dependency between Java types (which could be a class, interface, or a `@Roo*` annotation) of the Roo project using metadata identification strings, making it possible for Roo to manage code contained in AspectJ ITD when changes are made to a Java type.

Let's now look closely at the following code snippet in the `activate` method of `MyadvancedMetadataProvider` class:

```
metadataDependencyRegistry.
    registerDependency(PhysicalTypeIdentifier.
    getMetadataIdentiferType(), getProvidesType());
```

The `metadataDependencyRegistry` is a `protected` attribute defined in Roo's `AbstractItdMetadataProvider` class and is of type `MetadataDependencyRegistry`. The `MetadataDependencyRegistry` instance keeps track of dependencies between metadata identification strings. The `registerDependency` method is used to specify dependency between metadata identification strings. `PhysicalTypeIdentifier` represents a Roo class that creates a metadata identification string for a Java type in Roo project.

In the previous code, the `PhysicalTypeIdentifier.getMetadataIdentiferType()` code returns `MID:org.springframework.roo.classpath.PhysicalTypeIdentifier`, and `MyadvancedMetadata.getMetadataIdentiferType()` returns `MID:com.roo.addon.myadvanced.MyadvancedMetadata`. As both the metadata identification strings don't contain the Java type to which they apply, they are class-level metadata identification strings. You can create dependencies between class level-or instance-level metadata identification strings.

The `MID:org.springframework.roo.classpath.PhysicalTypeIdentifier` represents the upstream dependency and `MID:com.roo.addon.myadvanced.MyadvancedMetadata` represents the downstream dependency. When changes are made to an upstream dependency, Roo takes care of notifying all the downstream dependencies, which results in recreating the downstream metadata. The `MetadataProviders` are responsible for handling the notification. So, in the case of the myadvanced add-on, when a Java type (represented by `MID:org.springframework.roo.classpath.PhysicalTypeIdentifier`) in the Roo project is changed, it notifies the `MyadvancedMetadataProvider` instance.

The metadata dependencies specified in the `activate` method should be unregistered in the `deactivate` method of the metadata provider. The metadata dependencies are unregistered using the `deregisterDependency` method of the `MetadataDependencyRegistry` instance, as shown here for `MyadvancedMetadataProvider`:

```
protected void deactivate(ComponentContext context) {
  metadataDependencyRegistry.
    deregisterDependency(PhysicalTypeIdentifier.
    getMetadataIdentiferType(), getProvidesType());


    ...
}
```

Registering and unregistering metadata creation trigger

Metadata dependency registration ensures that downstream dependencies of a metadata are notified when changes occur in the upstream dependencies. To specify what triggers creation of metadata, metadata provider makes use of the `addMetadataTrigger` method of the `AbstractItdMetadataProvider` class, as shown here for `MyadvancedMetadataProvider`:

```
protected void activate(ComponentContext context) {
  metadataDependencyRegistry.
    registerDependency(PhysicalTypeIdentifier.
    getMetadataIdentiferType(), getProvidesType());

  addMetadataTrigger(
    new JavaType(RooMyadvanced.class.getName()));
}
```

In the preceding code, the `addMetadataTrigger` method accepts `RooMyadvanced` Java type. It means that whenever a Java type is annotated with `@RooMyadvanced` annotation, `MyadvancedMetadataProvider` will create an instance of `MyadvancedMetadata`.

The metadata trigger is removed by the metadata provider in the `deactivate` method, as shown here for the `MyadvancedMetadataProvider` class:

```
protected void deactivate(ComponentContext context) {
  ...
  removeMetadataTrigger(
    new JavaType(RooMyadvanced.class.getName()));
}
```

Let's now look at how Spring Roo works behind the scenes to generate code when a Java type is annotated with the `@RooMyadvanced` annotation.

Code generation functionality of add-ons

The following sequence diagram shows how the myadvanced add-on processes the
`myadvanced add --type sample.roo.flightapp.domain.Flight` command, where
the `Flight` class represents a JPA entity in your Roo project to which you want to add the `@
RooMyadvanced` annotation.

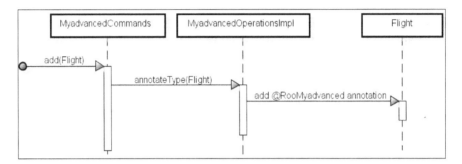

The figure shows that when the `myadvanced add` command is executed, the `add` method
of `MyadvancedCommands` instance is invoked and the `type` argument value is passed to
the `add` method. You may notice that the `add` method accepts an argument of `JavaType`
type, but we didn't register a custom converter with the Roo shell for it. This is because Roo
is responsible for converting the `type` argument value to `JavaType` type. The `JavaType`
contains the simple and package name information about the `type` argument value. In
our case, `JavaType` argument passed to the `add` method contains simple and package
name information about the `Flight` class that we specified as value of the `type` argument.
The `add` method of `MyadvancedCommands` invokes the `annotateType` method of the
`MyadvancedOperationsImpl` class and passes the `JavaType` instance containing
information about the `Flight` class. The `annotateType` method annotates the `Flight.
java` file with the `@RooMyadvanced` annotation.

Annotating `Flight.java` with the `@RooMyadvanced` annotation results in issuing a
notification to the file monitor service of Roo that the `Flight.java` file has been modified.
The following sequence diagram shows how file monitor service of Roo notifies change in
`Flight.java` file to `MetadataDependencyRegistry`:

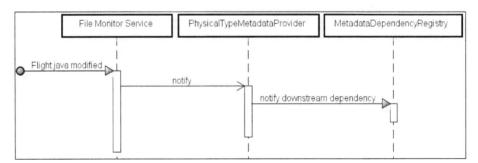

The preceding figure shows that the file monitor service notifies
`PhysicalTypeMetadaProvider` that the `Flight.java` file has been modified. As
discussed earlier, `PhysicalTypeMetadaProvider` provides metadata for a Java type
in the Roo project. `PhysicalTypeMetadaProvider` is notified when `Flight.java` is
modified because `PhysicalTypeMetadaProvider` is a registered listener for file change
events. After receiving the file change notification, `PhysicalTypeMetadaProvider`
asks `MetadataDependencyRegistry` instance to inform any registered downstream
dependencies. We saw earlier that `MyadvancedMetadataProvider`'s `activate`
method registers `MID:com.roo.addon.myadvanced.MyadvancedMetadata` as
the downstream dependency of `MID:org.springframework.roo.classpath.`
`PhysicalTypeIdentifier`. The `MID:org.springframework.roo.classpath.`
`PhysicalTypeIdentifier` represents a class-level metadata identification string created
by `PhysicalTypeMetadaProvider` and represents a Java type in the Roo project. So,
the change in `Flight.java` results in notifying the metadata provider that creates the
`MID:com.roo.addon.myadvanced.MyadvancedMetadata` metadata identification
string, which is `MyadvancedMetadataProvider`.

The following sequence diagram shows how `MetadataDependencyRegistry` notifies
`MyadvancedMetadataProvider` to create `MyadvancedMetadata`:

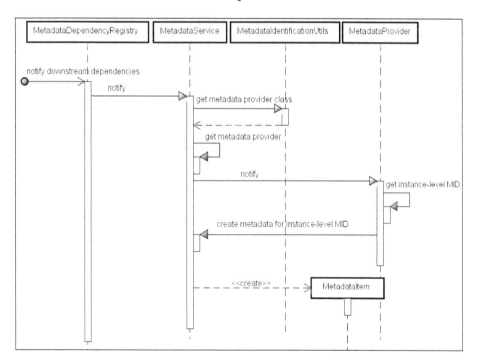

In the preceding figure, `MetadataProvider` represents an interface that is implemented by all the metadata providers in Roo, and `MetadataItem` represents the metadata that is created by `MetadataProvider` implementations. In the case of the myadvanced add-on, `MyadvancedMetadataProvider` implements the `MetadataProvider` interface and `MyadvancedMetadata` implements the `MetadataItem` interface.

The previous sequence diagram shows that `MetadataDependencyRegistry` notifies `MetadataService` to inform the `MetadataProvider` (which is `MyadvancedMetadataProvider` in the case of the myadvanced add-on) of the downstream dependency.

> `MetadataService` is a central service in Roo which knows about all the metadata providers in the system. You don't need to register your metadata providers with `MetadataService` because it can automatically detect an OSGi service as a metadata provider if it implements the `MetadataProvider` interface.

A `MetadataItem` (which is `MyadvancedMetadata` in the case of the myadvanced add-on) is created when `MetadataProvider` (which is `MyadvancedMetadataProvider` in the case of the myadvanced add-on) of the downstream dependency is notified, as we'll see shortly. `MetadataService` makes use of the `MetadataIdentificationUtils` utility class to obtain the `MetadataProvider` class corresponding to the metadata identification string of the downstream dependency. Once the `MetadataProvider` for the downstream dependency is obtained, `MetadataService` notifies the `MetadataProvider`.

The `MetadataProvider` needs to know the Java type for which the `MetadataItem` is to be created. For instance, in the case of the myadvanced add-on example, `MyadvancedMetadataProvider` needs to know that `MyadvancedMetadata` needs to be created corresponding to the `Flight.java` class. `MetadataProvider` converts class-level MID (`MID:com.roo.addon.myadvanced.MyadvancedMetadata`) of downstream dependency into instance-level MID (`MID:com.roo.addon.myadvanced.MyadvancedMetadata #SRC_MAIN_JAVA?sample.roo.flightapp.domain.Flight`) to identify the Java type for which the `MetadataItem` is to be created. When the `MetadataItem` instance is created, it results in code generation.

Now let's look at some of the methods of `MyadvancedMetadataProvider`, which play an important role in creating the `MyadvancedMetadata` instance:

```
import ...roo.classpath.itd.ItdTypeDetailsProvidingMetadataItem;
...
public final class MyadvancedMetadataProvider
   extends AbstractItdMetadataProvider {
  ...
 protected ItdTypeDetailsProvidingMetadataItem
  getMetadata(String metadataIdentificationString,
    JavaType aspectName,
    PhysicalTypeMetadata governorPhysicalTypeMetadata,
```

```
    String itdFilename) {

  return new MyadvancedMetadata(metadataIdentificationString,
    aspectName, governorPhysicalTypeMetadata);
}


public String getItdUniquenessFilenameSuffix() {
  return "Myadvanced";
}


protected String getGovernorPhysicalTypeIdentifier(
  String metadataIdentificationString) {

  JavaType javaType = MyadvancedMetadata.
    getJavaType(metadataIdentificationString);

  Path path = MyadvancedMetadata.
    getPath(metadataIdentificationString);

  return PhysicalTypeIdentifier.createIdentifier(javaType,
    path);
}


protected String createLocalIdentifier(JavaType javaType,
  Path path) {

  return MyadvancedMetadata.createIdentifier(javaType, path);
}


public String getProvidesType() {
  return MyadvancedMetadata.getMetadataIdentiferType();
 }
}
```

The `MyadvancedMetadataProvider` class extends the `AbstractItdMetadataProvider` abstract class and makes use of the template method design pattern. The methods shown in the preceding code are invoked by the concrete methods defined in the `AbstractItdMetadataProvider` class. The following table describes the purpose of each of these methods:

Method name	Description
getMetadata	This method is responsible for creating and returning the `MetadataItem` (which is `MyadvancedMetadata` in the case of the myadvanced add-on).
getItdUniquenessFilenameSuffix	This method returns the suffix that should be used for naming the AspectJ ITD file. As this method returns "Myadvanced", the name of the AspectJ ITD created by this add-on is `*_Roo_Myadvanced.aj`.
getGovernorPhysicalTypeIdentifier	Returns the instance-level MID of the Java type that receives the methods defined by the `*_Roo_Myadvanced.aj` AspectJ ITD file. In our example, `Flight` is the Java type that receives methods defined by `*_Roo_Myadvanced.aj`.
getProvidesType	This method returns a class-level MID that identifies the `MetadataItem` which this `MetadataProvider` implementation offers. This method delegates the responsibility of creating MID to the `MetadataItem` implementation class.
createLocalIdentifier	Creates a local instance-level MID for the specified Java type and path arguments. This method delegates the creation of MID to the MetadaItem implementation class.

The `getMetadata` method is responsible for creating the `MyadvancedMetadata` by passing information that `MyadvancedMetadata` is dependent upon. The following table describes the arguments passed to the `getMetadata` method:

Method argument	Description
`metadataIdentificationString`	This represents instance-level metadata for `MyadvancedMetadata`. As `Flight.java` file was annotated with `@RooMyadvanced` annotation, the value of this argument is: `MID:com.roo.addon.myadvanced. MyadvancedMetadata`
	`#SRC_MAIN_JAVA?sample.roo. flightapp.domain.F`
	`Light`. This value is created by the superclass of the metadata provider by invoking the `createLocalIdentifier` method and `getProvidesType` methods.
`aspectName`	This represents a `JavaType` corresponding to the AspectJ ITD file created by the add-on.
`governorPhysicalTypeMetadata`	Represents the `PhysicalTypeMetadata` instance that identifies the Java type corresponding to which the AspectJ ITD file is to be created. As the `Flight.java` file was annotated with `@RooMyadvanced` annotation, this argument represents the PhysicalTypeMetadata corresponding to `Flight.java` class.
`itdFilename`	This represents the name of the AspectJ ITD file that `MyadvancedMetadata` creates. The name of this file is derived by the superclass of the metadata provider by invoking the `getItdUniquenessFilenameSuffix` method. As the `Flight.java` file was annotated with the `@RooMyadvanced` annotation, the name of the file is `Flight_ Roo_Myadvanced.aj`.

Now, let's look at the `MyadvancedMetadata` class that is responsible for creating the AspectJ ITD file and adding methods and fields to it.

The following code shows the `MyadvancedMetadata` class:

```
public class MyadvancedMetadata
  extends AbstractItdTypeDetailsProvidingMetadataItem {

 private static final String PROVIDES_TYPE_STRING =
   MyadvancedMetadata.class.getName();

 private static final String PROVIDES_TYPE =
```

```
        MetadataIdentificationUtils.create(PROVIDES_TYPE_STRING);

    public MyadvancedMetadata(String identifier,
      JavaType aspectName,
      PhysicalTypeMetadata governorPhysicalTypeMetadata) {

      super(identifier, aspectName, governorPhysicalTypeMetadata);
      builder.addField(getSampleField());
      builder.addMethod(getSampleMethod());
      itdTypeDetails = builder.build();
    }

    private FieldMetadata getSampleField() {
      . . .
    }

    private MethodMetadata getSampleMethod() {
      . . .
    }

    . . .
    public static final String getMetadataIdentiferType() {
      return PROVIDES_TYPE;
    }
    . . .
  }
```

The preceding code shows that `MyadvancedMetadata` defines two constants and a couple of methods. The `PROVIDES_TYPE_STRING` constant refers to the fully-qualified name of the `MyadvancedMetadata` class and `PROVIDES_TYPE` refers to the metadata type provided by the `MyadvancedMetadata` class. The value of `PROVIDES_TYPE` is `MID:com.roo.addon.myadvanced.MyadvancedMetadata`.

`MyadvancedMetadata` extends the `AbstractItdTypeDetails ProvidingMetadataItem` abstract class, which provides the common functionality for add-ons that want to create an AspectJ ITD file corresponding to a Java type. The constructor of `MyadvancedMetatada` makes use of information passed by the `MyadvancedMetadataProvider` to create the AspectJ ITD file. To simplify creation of AspectJ ITD file, Roo's `ItdTypeDetailsBuilder` instance (represented by the `builder` variable in the constructor) is used. The `addField` and `addMethod` methods of `ItdTypeDetailsBuilder` are used to add information about fields and methods that form part of the AspectJ ITD. The `getSampleField` and `getSampleMethod` methods in the above code return `FieldMetadata` and `MethodMetadata`, which represent the field and method to be added to the AspectJ ITD.

The following code shows the `getSampleField` method of `MyadvancedMetadata` class:

```
private FieldMetadata getSampleField() {
  int modifier = 0;

  FieldMetadataBuilder fieldBuilder =
   new FieldMetadataBuilder(getId(),
    modifier,
    new ArrayList<AnnotationMetadataBuilder>(),
    new JavaSymbolName("sampleField"),
    JavaType.STRING_OBJECT);

  return fieldBuilder.build();
}
```

Roo's `FieldMetadataBuilder` is used to create a `FieldMetadata` instance. The following are the details of the arguments passed to the `FieldMetadataBuilder` constructor:

▸ `getId()`: identifies the Java type into which the field will be introduced by the AspectJ ITD

▸ `modifier`: represents the access modifier for the field

▸ `new ArrayList<AnnotationMetadataBuilder>()`: contains information about the annotations that must be added to the field

▸ `new JavaSymbolName("sampleField")`: name of the field

▸ `JavaType.STRING_OBJECT`: Java type of the field

Similarly, the `getSampleMethod` method of `MyadvancedMetadata` makes use of Roo's `MethodMetadataBuilder` to create an instance of `MethodMetadata`.

Now that you know how the myadvanced add-on works, you can use it in your Roo project the same way we used the mysimple add-on.

There's more...

Roo provides a `metadata for type` command to view metadata for a Java type. You can also use the `metadata trace` command to see how metadata event notifications happen.

See also

▸ Refer to the *Developing a simple add-on* recipe to see how to develop a simple add-on

Converting non-OSGi JDBC drivers into OSGi-compliant bundles

In *Chapter 3, Advanced JPA Support in Spring Roo* we discussed that the database reverse engineering process of Roo requires the JDBC driver for the database to be available as an OSGi bundle. In this recipe, we'll look at how to convert H2 database's JDBC driver into a OSGi bundle using the `addon create wrapper` command and use it in database reverse engineering.

Getting ready

Download the H2 database bundled as a ZIP file from , and unzip it to the `C:\roo-cookbook\` directory. Extracting the H2 database ZIP file will create a directory named `h2` inside the `C:\roo-cookbook` directory.

How to do it...

The following steps will demonstrate how to convert non-OSGi JDBC drivers into OSGi compliant bundles:

1. Go to the `C:\roo-cookbook\h2\bin` directory and double-click the `h2.bat` file. This will start the H2 database and also open H2 Console in your default web browser, as shown in the following screenshot:

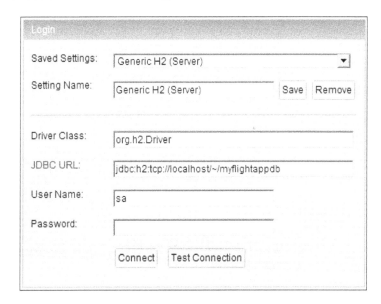

Make sure that you select **Generic H2 (Server)** as the value of the **Saved Settings** option and the value of the **JDBC URL** field is `jdbc:h2:tcp://localhost/~/myflightappdb`. Click the **Connect** button to log in to the H2 Console. This will automatically create the `myflightappdb` in H2 database.

2. After logging in to H2 Console, you will see the `myflightappdb` details, as shown here:

Now, paste the following SQL statement in the text area shown in the given screenshot and execute it by clicking the **Run (Ctrl+Enter)** button:

```
DROP TABLE IF EXISTS 'customer_tbl';
CREATE TABLE IF NOT EXISTS 'customer_tbl' (
  'cust_id' int(10) NOT NULL,
  'cust_dob' date NOT NULL,
  'cust_name' varchar(50) NOT NULL,
  PRIMARY KEY ('cust_id','cust_dob')
)
```

Executing the SQL statement will create the CUSTOMER_TBL table in the `myflightappdb` database.

3. Create the `C:\roo-cookbook\ch07-recipes\driver` directory and copy the h2*.jar file from the `C:\roo-cookbook\h2\bin` directory to the `driver` directory.

4. Open the command prompt and go to `C:\roo-cookbook\ch07-recipes\driver` and execute the `maven install` command:

```
C:\roo-cookbook\driver> mvn install:install-file
-Dfile=h2-1.3.160.jar -DgroupId=com.h2database -DartifactId=h2
-Dversion=1.3.60 -Dpackaging=jar
```

Here, it is assumed that H2 database driver JAR file is the `h2-1.3.160.jar` file.

5. Create the `C:\roo-cookbook\ch07-recipes\wrapper` directory and start the Roo shell from it.

6. Execute the `addon create wrapper` command to create a Roo add-on that wraps the `h2-1.3.160.jar` maven artifact:

```
... roo> addon create wrapper --topLevelPackage com.h2.roo.
jdbc --groupId com.h2database --artifactId h2 --version 1.3.60
--vendorName H2 --licenseUrl http://www.h2database.com
```

7. Modify the `pom.xml` file and add the following `<Import-Package>` element to the configuration of Maven Bundle Plugin:

```
<instructions>
  <Import-Package>javax.servlet.*;resolution:=optional,
    org.apache.lucene.*;resolution:=optional,
    org.slf4j;resolution:=optional,*
  </Import-Package>
  ...
</instructions>
```

8. Now, exit the Roo shell and execute the following maven goal to generate the OSGi version of the H2 database driver:

```
C:\roo-cookbook\ch07-recipes\wrapper> mvn bundle:bundle
```

This maven goal creates the OSGi-compliant H2 database driver in the `target` directory of the project with name `com.h2.roo.jdbc.h2-1.3.60.0001.jar`.

9. Create the `C:\roo-cookbook\ch07-recipes\flight-app` directory and start the Roo shell from it.

10. Create a new Roo project inside the `flight-app` directory:

```
... roo> project --topLevelPackage sample.roo.flightapp --java 6
--projectName flight-app
```

11. Set up Hibernate as the persistence provider for the `myflightappdb` H2 database:

```
... roo> persistence setup --provider HIBERNATE --database H2_IN_
MEMORY --databaseName myFlightAppDB
```

12. Set 'sa' as the username to use for connecting with the H2 database:

```
... roo> database properties set --key database.username --value
sa
```

13. Now, execute the `perform eclipse` command to create Eclipse IDE-specific configuration files:

```
... roo> perform eclipse
```

14. Import the `flight-app` project into Eclipse IDE and modify the `database.url` property in the `SRC_MAIN_RESOURCES/META-INF/spring/database.properties` file to point to the `myflightappdb` H2 database, as shown here:

```
database.password=
database.url=jdbc:h2:tcp://localhost/~/myflightappdb
```

```
database.username=sa
database.driverClassName=org.h2.Driver
```

15. Now, install the OSGi-compliant H2 database driver that we created earlier:

    **... roo> osgi start --url file:///C:/roo-cookbook/ch07-recipes /
    wrapper/target/com.h2.roo.jdbc.h2-1.3.60.0001.jar**

16. Execute `database reverse engineer` command to instruct Roo to create the JPA
    entity corresponding to the `CUSTOMER_TBL` in the H2 database:

    roo> database reverse engineer --schema PUBLIC

How it works...

The `addon create wrapper` command creates an add-on that wraps a Maven artifact. The
Apache Felix Maven Bundle Plugin's `bundle` goal creates an OSGi-compliant JAR for the
add-on project.

The `<Import-Package>` element specifies the packages that are required or optional for the
bundle.

See also

▶   Refer to the *Creating entities from database* recipe of *Chapter 3* to see how the
    database reverse engineer command works

Removing Roo with push-in refactoring

Spring Roo is responsible for managing the AspectJ ITDs in a Roo project. As AspectJ ITDs
are managed by Roo, you must not modify them. In some situations you may want to modify
the AspectJ ITD files to serve your application's requirements. For instance, you may want to
modify implementation of a method in an AspectJ ITD file.

In the *Sending emails using JavaMail API* recipe of *Chapter 6, Emailing, Messaging, Spring
Security, Solr, and GAE* we copied the `create(...)` method from `FlightController_
Roo_Controller.aj` file to `FlightController.java` file because we wanted to modify
the implementation of `create(...)` method. If Roo finds a method defined in the Java source
file, it removes the method with the same signature from the corresponding AspectJ ITD file.
So, when we copied the `create(...)` method to the `FlightController.java` file, Roo
removed the `create(...)` method from the `FlightController_Roo_Controller.aj`
file. The copy paste approach can be quite daunting if you need to do it at many places. In this
recipe, we'll look at how you can use Eclipse IDE to pushin specific methods and attributes to the
corresponding Java source file.

Getting ready

If you are using any IDE other than STS, then ensure that you install AJDT (AspectJ Development Tools).

Create directory `C:\roo-cookbook\ch07-recipes\push-in` and copy the `ch07_web_app.roo` script. Now, start the Roo shell from the `push-in` directory and execute the script using the `script` command. Executing the script will create a `flight-app` Spring Web MVC application.

How to do it...

The following steps will demonstrate how to remove Roo:

1. Import the `flight-app` Roo project into your Eclipse IDE.

2. Select the `Flight_Roo_ToString.aj` AspectJ ITD file from **Project Explorer**, as shown here:

3. When you open the `Flight_Roo_ToString.aj` file, in the Outline view of Eclipse IDE you'll see the details of methods and attributes defined in the `Flight_Roo_ToString.aj` file, as shown here:

4. Now, right-click the `Flight.toString() : String` element in the **Outline** view and select the **Refactor** option, as shown here:

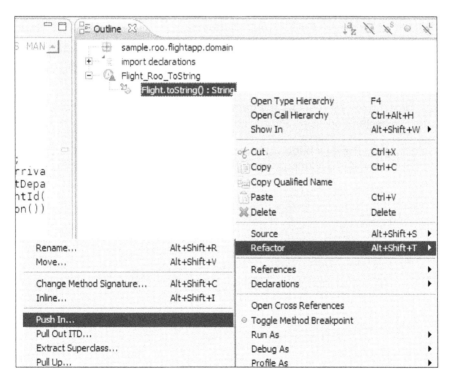

5. Selecting the **Refactor | Push In...** option shows the following dialog box:

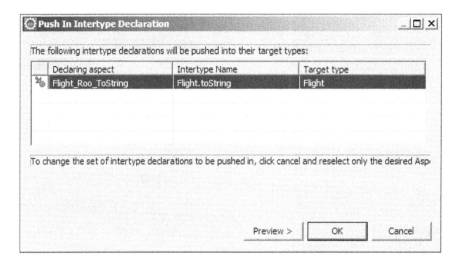

6. The dialog box shows the following information:

    ❑   `Declaring aspect`: this shows the name of the AspectJ ITD file

    ❑   `Intertype Name`: this shows the declaration in AspectJ ITD that we
        selected from the **Outline** view

    ❑   `Flight`: this shows the name of the Java class which is the target of the
        declaration

7. Selecting the **Preview** button shows the changes that will be made to the target
    `Flight` class if you continue with this refactoring, as shown here:

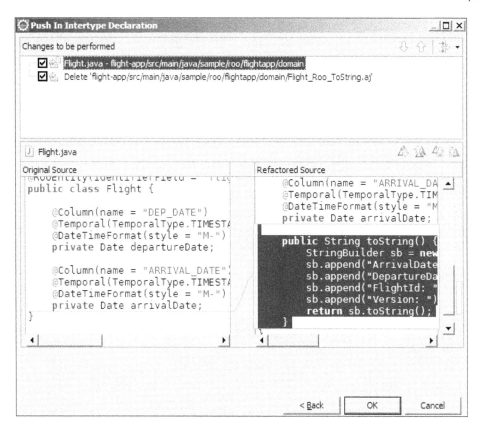

This screenshot shows that the toString method defined in Flight_To_String.aj file will be added to Flight.java file. Also, notice that if we continue with this refactoring it will result in deletion of Flight_Roo_ToString.aj file. If you want to keep the empty Flight_Roo_ToString.aj file, then uncheck Delete ...Flight_Roo_ToString.aj option.

8. Click **OK** button to complete the refactoring. You'll now see, that the toString method defined in Flight_Roo_ToString.aj AspectJ ITD has been moved to Flight.java file.

9. Optionally, if you want to revert back the refactoring, simply select the **Edit | Undo** option of Eclipse IDE.

How it works...

Push-in refactoring is like any other refactoring mechanism provided by IDEs. Based on the AspectJ ITD declaration, IDE figures out the target of the declaration, and moves the code from the ITD file to the target Java source file.

Note that if you are completely removing Roo from your project, then you also need to remove dependency on Roo from the `pom.xml` file of your project and remove all the `@Roo*` annotations (and corresponding `import` statements) from your project.

There's more...

Let's see how you can push all the declarations in a single AspectJ ITD file to the target Java source file, and how you can push all the declarations in all the AspectJ ITD files in the Roo project to their respective target Java source files.

Push-in refactoring—single AspectJ ITD file

To push all the declarations from a single AspectJ ITD file to the target Java source file, right-click the AspectJ ITD file from the **Project Explorer** or right-click the element in **Outline** view that represents the AspectJ ITD type, and select **Refactor | Push** In option.

The following screenshot shows the dialog box shown when you select `Flight_Roo_JavaBean.aj` ITD file of the `flight-app` project from **Project Explorer** and select the **Refactor | Push In** option.

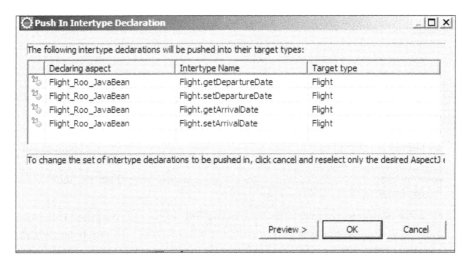

This screenshot shows that all the declarations in the `Flight_Roo_JavaBean.aj` file now form part of the refactoring process.

Push-in refactoring – across the whole project

To perform push-in refactoring across the whole project, select the project from Project Explorer and select the **Refactor | Push In** option.

- Refer to the *Adding Roo to a project using pull-out refactoring* recipe to see how you can pull out methods and attributes from Java class to an AspectJ ITD file

Adding Roo to a project using pull-out refactoring

The pull-out refactoring is the reverse of push-in refactoring. In push-out refactoring you extract methods and attributes from the Java source file and move it to an AspectJ ITD file. This feature is particularly useful in the following situations:

- If you had earlier performed push-in refactoring on your Roo project, and now you want to develop your project once again using Spring Roo

- If you have partially developed a project and now you want to use Spring Roo in its development

- In this recipe we'll look at how to pull-out the `toString` method from the `Flight.java` file to `Flight_To_String.aj` file.

Getting ready

Follow the instructions specified in the *Removing Roo with push-in refactoring* recipe to push the `toString` method defined in the `Flight_To_String.aj` file to `Flight.java` file.

How to do it...

Follow these steps to move the code from Java source file to an AspectJ ITD file:

1. Create a `Flight_To_String.aj` file in the `sample.roo.flightapp.domain` package, as shown here:

   ```
   package sample.roo.flightapp.domain;

   public aspect Flight_To_String { }
   ```

   This an empty aspect into which we want to pull-out fields, contructors, methods, and so on, from Java source file.

2. Open the `Flight.java` file in Eclipse IDE.

3. Right-click the toString method from the **Outline** view and select **Refactor | Pull Out ITD...**, as shown in the following screenshot:

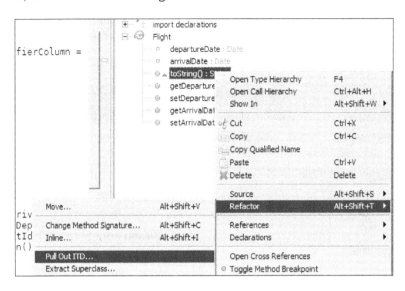

4. Selecting the **Pull Out ITD** option shows the following dialog box to let you specify the AspectJ ITD file into which the selected toString method should be added:

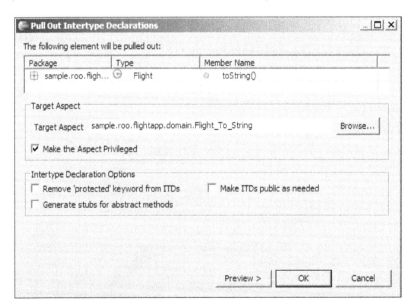

In the preceding screenshot enter sample.roo.flightapp.domain.Flight_ To_String as the name of the **Target Aspect** and make sure that you check the **Make the Aspect Privileged** option.

5. Click **OK** to pull-out the `toString` method to the `Flight_To_String.aj` file.

There's more...

IIf you want to use Spring Roo for an existing project, then you need to move the methods, attributes or constructors from Java source files to AspectJ ITD files. These ITD files are then managed by Spring Roo. You need to make sure that you only move those Java elements to AspectJ ITD files that can be managed by Roo. The naming convention followed by these AspectJ ITD files should follow the naming convention expected by Roo. You'll also have to add necessary Roo-related dependencies in your pom.xml file.

See also

▸ Refer to the *Removing Roo with push-in refactoring* recipe for removing Roo from your project

Upgrading to the latest version of Roo

Roo simplifies upgrading from a previous version of your project to the latest version. All you need to do is to start the Roo shell from the root directory of your Roo project. Roo makes the adjustments to AspectJ ITD files that are applicable to the version.

In this recipe, we'll look at a Roo project that was created on version 1.1.3 and now being upgraded to 1.1.5.

Getting ready

Unzip the `ch06-ldap-security.zip` file that accompanies this book. Extracting the ZIP file will create a directory `ch06-ldap-security`, which represents a Roo project developed using Spring Roo 1.1.3.

How to do it...

Follow these steps to upgrade your version of Roo:

1. Start the Roo shell from the `ch06-ldap-security` directory; you'll see the following output:

```
Updated ROOT\pom.xml [updated property 'roo.version' to
'1.1.5.RELEASE']

Updated SRC_MAIN_JAVA\...\domain\Booking_Roo_ToString.aj
... SRC_MAIN_JAVA\...web\FlightDescriptionController_Roo_
Controller_Finder.aj
...
```

The output shows that one of the files modified by Roo is `FlightDescriptionController_Roo_Controller_Finder.aj`. If you look at this file you'll find that Roo has added a method responsible for searching `Flight` entity instances. Now, take a look at this sentence from *Chapter 4, Web Application Development with Spring Web MVC*:

It is important to note that in Spring Roo 1.1.3, the method responsible for searching entity instances is not created in `FlightDescriptionController_Roo_Controller_Finder.aj`.

This bug is resolved in Spring Roo 1.1.4 and above.

You can see that upgrading Roo to 1.1.5 automatically fixed the bug that existed in Roo 1.1.5.

How it works...

We mentioned earlier that Roo is responsible for managing the AspectJ ITD files in your Roo project. So, when you upgrade to a later version of Roo, Roo takes care of modifying the code in the AspectJ ITD files of your project.

There's more...

Roo's upgradation process is destructive, that is, you can't undo the changes made by Roo during the upgrade process. So, make sure that you keep a backup copy of your project before starting the Roo shell from the base directory of your project.

Index

A

single AspectJ ITD file 424

R

S

Thank you for buying
Spring Roo 1.1 Cookbook

About Packt Publishing

Packt, pronounced 'packed', published its first book "*Mastering phpMyAdmin for Effective MySQL Management*" in April 2004 and subsequently continued to specialize in publishing highly focused books on specific technologies and solutions.

Our books and publications share the experiences of your fellow IT professionals in adapting and customizing today's systems, applications, and frameworks. Our solution based books give you the knowledge and power to customize the software and technologies you're using to get the job done. Packt books are more specific and less general than the IT books you have seen in the past. Our unique business model allows us to bring you more focused information, giving you more of what you need to know, and less of what you don't.

Packt is a modern, yet unique publishing company, which focuses on producing quality, cutting-edge books for communities of developers, administrators, and newbies alike. For more information, please visit our website: www.packtpub.com.

About Packt Open Source

In 2010, Packt launched two new brands, Packt Open Source and Packt Enterprise, in order to continue its focus on specialization. This book is part of the Packt Open Source brand, home to books published on software built around Open Source licences, and offering information to anybody from advanced developers to budding web designers. The Open Source brand also runs Packt's Open Source Royalty Scheme, by which Packt gives a royalty to each Open Source project about whose software a book is sold.

Writing for Packt

We welcome all inquiries from people who are interested in authoring. Book proposals should be sent to author@packtpub.com. If your book idea is still at an early stage and you would like to discuss it first before writing a formal book proposal, contact us; one of our commissioning editors will get in touch with you.

We're not just looking for published authors; if you have strong technical skills but no writing experience, our experienced editors can help you develop a writing career, or simply get some additional reward for your expertise.

Spring Persistence with Hibernate

ISBN: 978-1-849510-56-1   Paperback: 460 pages

Build robust and reliable persistence solutions for your enterprise Java application

1. Get to grips with Hibernate and its configuration manager, mappings, types, session APIs, queries, and much more

2. Integrate Hibernate and Spring as part of your enterprise Java stack development

3. Work with Spring IoC (Inversion of Control), Spring AOP, transaction management, web development, and unit testing considerations and features

4. Covers advanced and useful features of Hibernate in a practical way

Service Oriented Architecture with Java

ISBN: 978-1-847193-21-6   Paperback: 192 pages

Use SOA and web services to build powerful Java applications

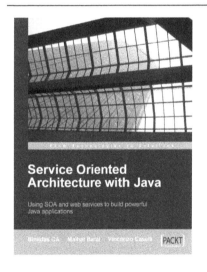

1. Build effective SOA applications with Java Web Services

2. Quick reference guide with best-practice design examples

3. Understand SOA concepts from core with examples

4. Design scalable inter-enterprise communication

Please check **www.PacktPub.com** for information on our titles

Spring Web Flow 2 Web Development

ISBN: 978-1-847195-42-5   Paperback: 200 pages

Master Spring's well-designed web frameworks to develop powerful web applications

1. Design, develop, and test your web applications using the Spring Web Flow 2 framework

2. Enhance your web applications with progressive AJAX, Spring security integration, and Spring Faces

3. Stay up-to-date with the latest version of Spring Web Flow

4. Walk through the creation of a bug tracker web application with clear explanations

Spring Security 3

ISBN: 978-1-847199-74-4   Paperback: 396 pages

Secure your web applications against malicious intruders with this easy to follow practical guide

1. Make your web applications impenetrable.

2. Implement authentication and authorization of users.

3. Integrate Spring Security 3 with common external security providers

4. Packed full with concrete, simple, and concise examples.

Please check **www.PacktPub.com** for information on our titles